Leadership in Supply Management

Lisa M. Ellram, Ph.D., C.P.M., CMA

Original Author:
Anna E. Flynn, Ph.D.

This publication is designed to provide accurate and authoritative information in regard to the subject matter covered. It is sold with the understanding that the publisher is not engaged in rendering legal, accounting or other professional service. If legal advice or other expert assistance is required, the services of a competent professional person should be sought.

Published by: Institute for Supply Management, Inc.®
Thomas Derry, Chief Executive Officer

©2014 Institute for Supply Management®, Inc.
2055 E. Centennial Circle, Tempe, AZ 85284
www.instituteforsupplymanagement.org

All rights reserved. No part of this publication may be reproduced, stored in a retrieval system or transmitted, in any form or by any means, electronic, mechanical, photocopying, recording, or otherwise, without prior written permission of the publisher.

ISBN: 978-0-9960434-3-4

ISM — Your Source for Supply Management Resources

Institute for Supply Management, Inc.® (ISM®) has served the supply management profession since 1915. As the first and largest supply management institute in the world, ISM works with affiliated associations to continually keep its members well informed and trained on the latest trends and developments in the field. ISM's membership base includes more than 45,000 individual supply management professionals. A not-for-profit institute, ISM provides opportunities for the promotion of the profession and the expansion of professional skills and knowledge.

The information available from ISM is extensive. One of the greatest resources is the ISM website, www.ism.ws. In addition to general information, this expansive site features a vast database of supply management information, including a list of general supply management references as well as an extensive article database, listings of available products and seminars, periodicals, contact information for ISM affiliate organizations worldwide and links to other related websites. The *members only* online Career Center is a valuable resource for both individuals seeking jobs and organizations recruiting prospective employees.

The monthly Manufacturing and Non-Manufacturing *Report On Business*®, including the PMI® for the manufacturing survey and the NMI® for the non-manufacturing survey, continues to be one of the key economic indicators available today. ISM members receive this valuable report in the pages of *Inside Supply Management*® magazine. *Inside Supply Management*®, a monthly magazine (available to members only), is the authoritative resource for supply management executives, focusing on leadership strategies and trends.

ISM also publishes the *Journal of Supply Chain Management*, a one-of-a-kind publication for supply management scholars. Authored exclusively by highly recognized scholars in supply chain management, this quarterly subscription publication offers up-to-date research and thought-provoking studies.

Members also enjoy discounts on a wide variety of educational products and services, along with reduced enrollment fees for educational seminars and conferences.

For supply management professionals interested in a professional qualification, ISM administers the Certified Professional in Supply Management® (CPSM®) program. ISM members receive discounts on test preparation materials, study books, and materials and examination fees.

To provide a forum for educational enhancement and networking, ISM sponsors the Annual International Supply Management Conference. The annual conference, which attracts thousands of participants from around the world, provides a unique opportunity for members and nonmembers alike to learn from each other and share success strategies.

To learn more about ISM and the many ways it can help you advance your career, or to join online, visit ISM at www.instituteforsupplymanagement.org. To apply for membership by telephone, call ISM customer service at 800.888.6276 (United States and Canada only) or +1 480.752.6276, option 8.

ISM PROFESSIONAL SERIES

Foundation of Supply Management
Janet Hartley, Ph.D.

Original Authors:
Joseph R. Carter, DBA, CPSM, C.P.M.
Thomas Y. Choi, Ph.D.

Effective Supply Management Performance
Linda L. Stanley, Ph.D.

Original Authors:
Darin L. Matthews, CPPO, C.P.M.
Linda L. Stanley, Ph.D.

Leadership in Supply Management
Lisa M. Ellram, Ph.D., C.P.M., CMA

Original Author:
Anna E. Flynn, Ph.D.

Series Overview

In the past several decades, the supply management profession has matured. No longer looked at as just "purchasing" or "procurement," supply management is viewed today as an integrative process that spans many disciplines and activities, providing both internal and external linkages across the supply chain. Today, ISM defines supply management as:

> *The identification, acquisition, access, positioning and management of resources and related capabilities that an organization needs or potentially needs in the attainment of its strategic objectives.*
>
> *Supply management includes the following components: disposition/investment recovery, distribution, inventory control, logistics, materials management, operations, packaging, procurement/purchasing, product/service development, quality, receiving, strategic sourcing, transportation/traffic/shipping and warehousing/stores.*

This definition cuts across industry sectors, global economies, private and public organizations, and types of purchases. It covers the day-to-day issues faced by supply management professionals, the strategic issues that shape supply management's structure, and its influence in the organization.

In keeping with the spirit of the new, broader definition of supply management, the Institute for Supply Management® broadened the scope of its qualification to fit the latest demands on supply management professionals. This three-book series was designed to specifically address the issues of concern to supply management professionals today. These books help professionals better understand the potential scope and concerns within supply management. These books also are designed to support the updated Certified Professional in Supply Management® (CPSM®) examination and professional credentials.

The three books are organized around the three examinations of the CPSM® as follows:

1. *Foundation of Supply Management*
2. *Effective Supply Management Performance*
3. *Leadership in Supply Management.*

These three books all support the strategic supply management concept across various industries, cultures and types of purchases. The strategic supply management concept is illustrated in Figure S-1, below.

On the far left of the figure is the vertical box, "Scope of Supply Management Strategy and Responsibility." This is the way the organization views the scope of supply management, and the way supply management views itself. It embodies the culture of the supply management organization as it works to support the objectives of the larger organization.

Figure S1: Strategic Supply Management Concept

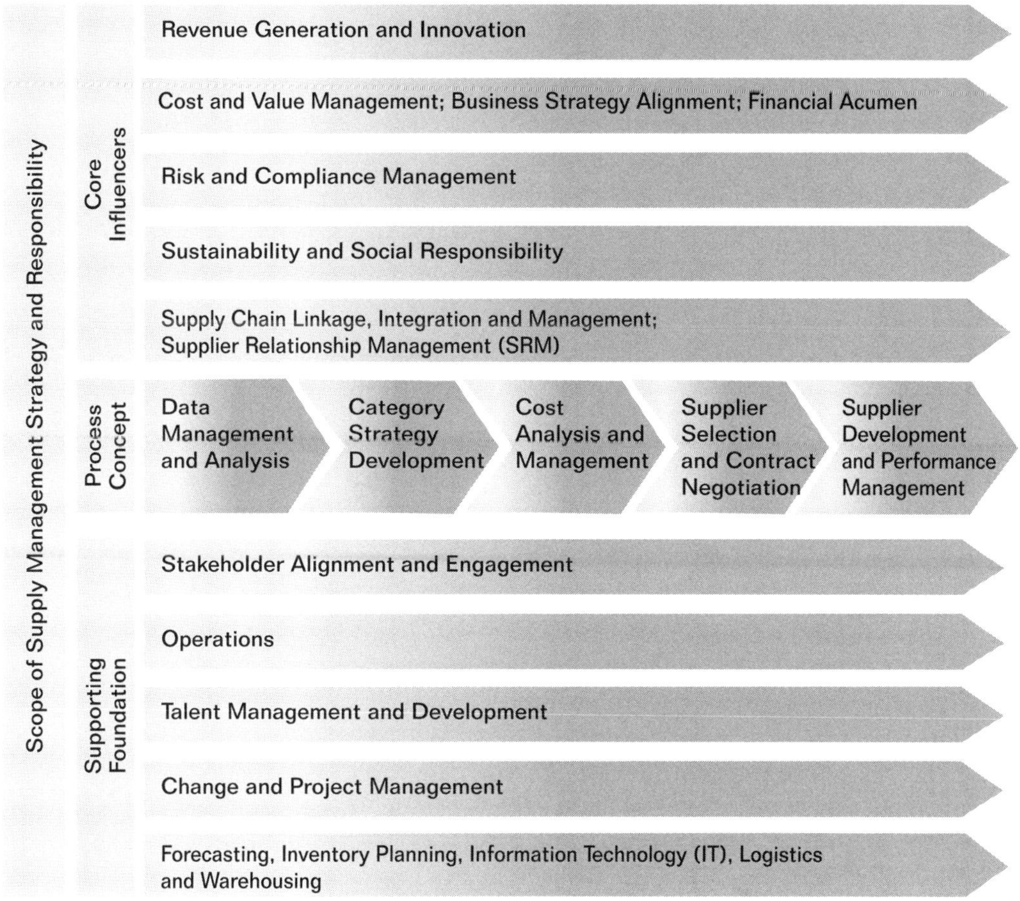

Scope of Supply Management Strategy and Responsibility

Core Influencers:
- Revenue Generation and Innovation
- Cost and Value Management; Business Strategy Alignment; Financial Acumen
- Risk and Compliance Management
- Sustainability and Social Responsibility
- Supply Chain Linkage, Integration and Management; Supplier Relationship Management (SRM)

Process Concept:
- Data Management and Analysis
- Category Strategy Development
- Cost Analysis and Management
- Supplier Selection and Contract Negotiation
- Supplier Development and Performance Management

Supporting Foundation:
- Stakeholder Alignment and Engagement
- Operations
- Talent Management and Development
- Change and Project Management
- Forecasting, Inventory Planning, Information Technology (IT), Logistics and Warehousing

Near the top of the figure, immediately inside the "Supply Management Strategy and Philosophy" box, is "Core Influencers," which covers five categories of major issues that supply management professionals face today:

- Revenue Generation and Innovation
- Cost and Value Management; Business Strategy Alignment; Financial Acumen
- Risk and Compliance Management
- Sustainability and Social Responsibility
- Supply Chain Linkage, Integration and Management; Supplier Relationship Management (SRM).

Supply management professionals must consider all five of these major issues in their strategic decision-making. While supplier relationship management and cost management have long been recognized as important by most progressive organizations, these have been expanded upon, and additional influencers added — which have taken on new importance in recent years. Because of their overarching nature, these influencers are touched on in each of the three books in a variety of ways. More specifically, supply management professionals must ask the following questions:

1. How can we in supply management contribute to the organization's revenue generation and innovation strategies, directly supporting the organization's financial success?

2. How can we contribute to the organization's cost savings goals while retaining or increasing the value that purchased goods and services deliver to the organization and its customers? This must be done in such a way that it demonstrates supply management's understanding of the financial implications of its actions and its alignment with business unit strategy.

3. What risks might the organization face, and how can we plan, prepare for and manage these risks?

4. How do the decisions we make and the actions we take fit with the organization's social responsibility and sustainability objectives? This includes environmental issues as well as social issues, and is grounded in ethical behaviors that are part of an organization's culture.

5. How closely should we work with others in the supply chain? How should we be linked in terms of physical, financial and information flows? Related to this, how do we manage our supplier relationships and segment our suppliers according to their importance, potential contribution to innovation and success, and the potential supply chain risk they present?

Within supply management, some basic process steps must occur, as illustrated in the middle of the figure and labeled "Process Concept." Virtually all organizations have a model for the execution of the supply management process that includes all these activities, although they may be segmented into a different number of steps depending on the needs of the organization. The process begins with a thorough analysis of internal and external data to better understand the threats and opportunities in the internal and external environment. Next, specific strategies are developed for the particular purchase category — including services — and tactics for implementing those strategies are identified. Closely related to this, the organization engages in a cost analysis, looking for ways to better manage and reduce costs, and increase value. It then narrows down the choice of suppliers through data analysis (and bidding if appropriate), negotiates if appropriate and develops the contract. Finally, ongoing supplier measurement and management occurs, and may include supplier development efforts to improve supplier performance.

Finally, there is a "Supporting Foundation," a structure that the business and supply management organization should have in place to facilitate success. As shown at the bottom of the figure, a supply management professional must engage in the following activities:

1. Identify key stakeholders, then align with and engage stakeholders so supply management understands and supports their success — and also works with them as partners. Stakeholders can include internal customers, research and development, finance, marketing, and other areas that affect and are affected by supply management activities.

2. Work closely with operations. Operations is core to supply management performance, as supply management supplies operations with materials to meet its objectives.

3. Have an exceptional talent management and development program in place to attract the best people in the organization and offer the opportunity for both growth and advancement, creating an excellent system for managing and developing the organization's most valuable resource — its people.

4. Be skilled in change management and project management, as both are essential elements in the success of supply management initiatives.

5. Work closely with the people or groups in charge of forecasting, inventory planning, information technology (IT), logistics and warehousing, and seek alignment of objectives. These areas form the foundation for supply management decision-making and successful execution. IT provides the systems to link information quickly and accurately so supply management can successfully execute the strategic sourcing process.

These elements, integrating the internal business needs with external forces, become the foundation on which supply management builds success.

Volume 1, *Foundation of Supply Management,* deals with several of the more traditional areas of concern for supply management, yet looks at these issues from a leading-edge perspective. This volume covers the various sources of data and its analysis, budgeting, cost management — including cost/price analysis and total cost of ownership analysis, and leasing arrangements. This book also provides an in-depth view of sourcing, negotiating and contracting with suppliers, and the management of those contracts. Taken as a whole, these chapters provide an excellent perspective on the process steps associated with strategic sourcing. The final third of the book focuses on three of the overarching concerns of supply management: supplier relationship management; social and legal responsibility emphasizing supply management's role in sustainability; and international issues, including global sourcing, logistics and exchange rates, and countertrade issues. Volume 1 is a critical read for those who might be relatively new to supply management, those who have not had a formal education in supply management, and anyone who wants to stay abreast of the latest practices in supply management.

Volume 2, *Effective Supply Management Performance*, focuses on many of the operational issues that are part of a successful supply management performance. The latest surveys show that supply management professionals are responsible for a majority of the components of supply management; many of these are detailed in the definition of supply management provided previously. These are new areas of interaction for many supply management professionals. Volume 2 provides coverage of many operational issues such as project management, new product and service development, forecasting, warehousing, materials handling, logistics and international transportation, asset and inventory management, and quality. These all provide supporting structures for supply management. The book closes with an in-depth discussion of supplier performance management and metrics, information systems, and how technology can support the supply management professional in the integration of knowledge within and across organizations. This book is a must-read for anyone newly assigned to operations-oriented issues or who supervises or manages transportation, logistics or inventory management personnel as part of his or her supply management responsibilities.

Volume 3, *Leadership in Supply Management*, focuses on many of the human resources issues that supply management professionals face. The first half of the book explores management issues within the supply organization, such as managing and leading, developing shared values, setting direction, creating alignment and creating commitment for the supply organization's shared vision. The chapters cover various leadership styles, and details on developing strategies, aligning with internal and external stakeholders, team building and managing conflict. These are critical supporting structures for supply management. The second half of the book focuses on risk management and mitigation, and developing business plans exploring supply's role in mergers and acquisitions. These are linked to the strategic sourcing process, including outsourcing, developing and staffing the supply management organization, providing rewards and professional development for supply management, and executing the strategic sourcing process. This section includes a look at issues related to the overarching concerns of supply management, the process steps of supply management and the supporting structures. Taken as a whole, this volume covers talent management and human resources as well as strategic issues of management that all supply management functions face. The implementation of supply management processes as they relate to legal issues, both domestically and internationally, are reviewed. This book should be read by anyone who manages the supply management function or who is involved in the supply management strategy setting and planning process.

It has been a challenge for all those involved to capture the vast amount of material represented in these three volumes. The extensive practical and theoretical knowledge and expertise of the original authors, along with those who participated in this revision for 2014, will provide the reader with both a broad and deep perspective of the topics covered here. ISM hopes you find these books both interesting and valuable as you study for the updated CPSM® examination or simply work on enhancing your own knowledge of supply management.

Institute for Supply Management®

Preface

This book is divided into two parts. The first section is a discussion on the differences and similarities between leadership and management and the three primary roles of a leader: setting direction, creating alignment and gaining commitment. The second part focuses on the managerial aspects of supply management. The aspects of leadership are fundamental to the overall scope of supply management strategy and responsibilities depicted in Figure P-1, and cut across the entire process.

Figure P1: Strategic Supply Management Concept

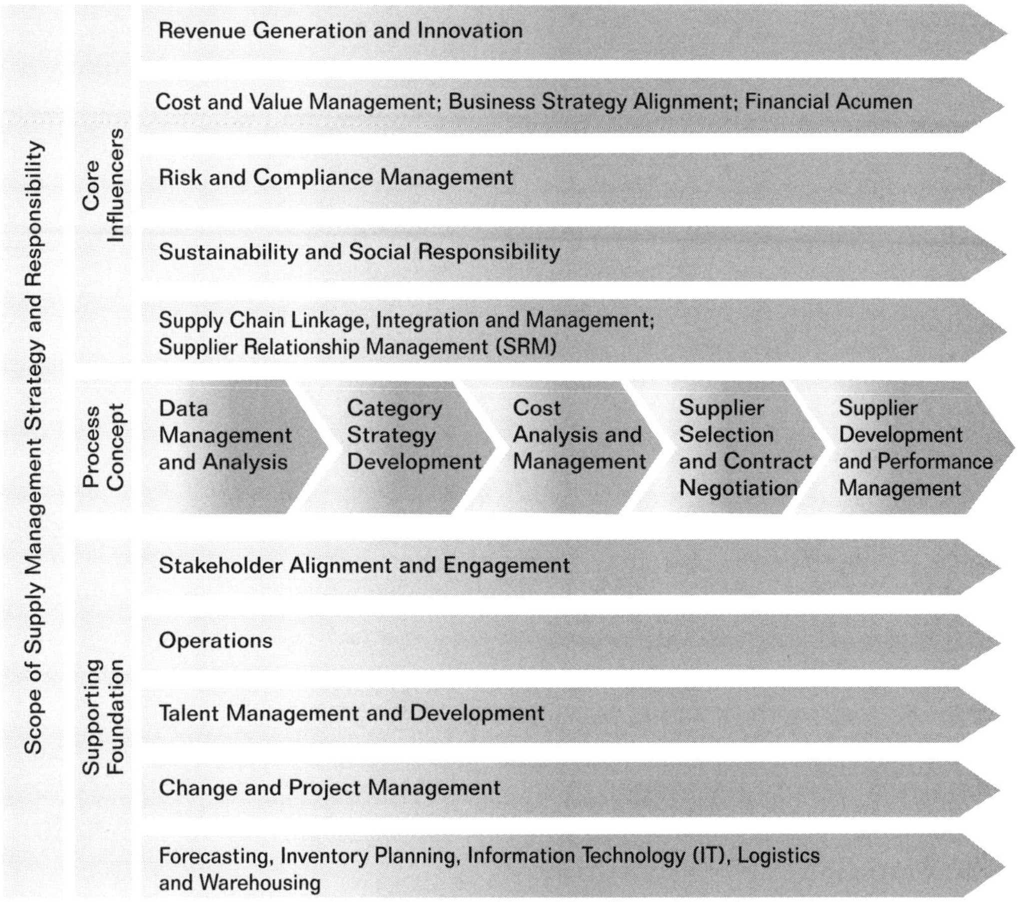

Scope of Supply Management Strategy and Responsibility

Core Influencers:
- Revenue Generation and Innovation
- Cost and Value Management; Business Strategy Alignment; Financial Acumen
- Risk and Compliance Management
- Sustainability and Social Responsibility
- Supply Chain Linkage, Integration and Management; Supplier Relationship Management (SRM)

Process Concept:
- Data Management and Analysis
- Category Strategy Development
- Cost Analysis and Management
- Supplier Selection and Contract Negotiation
- Supplier Development and Performance Management

Supporting Foundation:
- Stakeholder Alignment and Engagement
- Operations
- Talent Management and Development
- Change and Project Management
- Forecasting, Inventory Planning, Information Technology (IT), Logistics and Warehousing

"Vision is a key component of leadership; it is that mental journey from the known to the unknown, creating the future from the montage of current facts, hopes, dreams, risks and opportunities that effective leaders embrace in all walks of life."[1] A shared vision focuses, energizes and inspires commitment from everyone to attain it.

The first part of this book discusses the creation of that shared vision, and includes setting direction, creating alignment and gaining commitment. Chapter 1, "Leading and Managing," discusses the differences and similarities of leadership and management. Chapter 2, "Setting Direction," addresses three components: (1) creating a values-based organization, (2) assessing opportunities and risks, and (3) developing vision and strategies. Chapter 3, "Creating Alignment," focuses on developing internal and external business partnerships. Chapter 4, "Gaining Commitment: Motivating and Inspiring People," discusses the importance of internal partnerships, approaches to communicating vision and energizing people to attain that vision.

The second part of the book focuses on the managerial aspects of planning, organizing, staffing, controlling and problem-solving (budgeting is addressed in *Foundation of Supply Management*, Volume 1 of the ISM *Professional Series*). Planning is complementary to the leadership task of setting direction (along with budgeting), and is addressed in Chapter 5, "Assessing, Mitigating and Managing Supply-Based Risks," and Chapter 6, "Developing Business Plans." These chapters focus on the role of supply management professionals in assessing risks from a supply perspective, and developing sourcing and supply management plans that align with organizationwide plans. Organizing and staffing, complementary to the leadership task of creating alignment, are addressed in Chapter 7, "Organizing and Building Supply Management Infrastructure," and Chapter 8, "Developing a Strategic Sourcing Process and Adopting Enabling Technology." Chapter 7 addresses the issues around building an effective supply management structure, and Chapter 8 covers the development and implementation of an efficient and effective sourcing process with relevant policies and procedures along with performance-enabling systems and technology. Chapter 9, "Staffing the Supply Management Organization," focuses on attracting, retaining and empowering human capital, and Chapter 10, "Developing Supply Management Talent," addresses the ongoing professional development of that talent. Chapter 11, "Measuring the Supply Management Department Performance," addresses the tools and techniques available to measure and manage supply department performance relative to the vision, mission and strategies of the organization. Chapter 12, "Establishing Internal Controls and Ensuring Compliance," covers before-the-fact, during-the-fact and after-the-fact controls and compliance management as well as the implementation of supply management processes as they relate to legal issues, both domestically and internationally. Successful sustainability practices are reviewed as an important topic for today's supply management professionals.

The term *supply leader-manager* is used throughout this text. This does not imply that the same person always fulfills both roles. Rather, this reminds the reader that leadership and management are two different things and both are needed in an organization. Also, while reading this text, remember that organizations need many leaders at many levels, just as they typically employ many managers. Leadership potential can and should be recognized and developed to the fullest in each person.

About the Author

Lisa M. Ellram, Ph.D., C.P.M., CMA, Scor-S is the Rees Distinguished Professor of Supply Chain Management in the Department of Marketing at the Farmer School of Business, Miami University in Oxford, Ohio, where she teaches logistics and supply chain management at the undergraduate and graduate level. Prior to that, she was the John Bebbling Professor of Supply Management at Arizona State University's W.P. Carey School of Business, where she taught graduate classes in purchasing and supply chain management.

Her primary areas of research interest include sustainable purchasing, transportation and supply chain management, services purchasing and supply chain management, offshoring and outsourcing, and supply chain cost management. She has published in *Journal of Supply Chain Management, Academy of Management Journal, Journal of Operations Management, California Management Review, MIT Sloan Management Review, Industrial Marketing Management, Journal of Services Management, Journal of Business Logistics* and other managerial and academic outlets. She is the recipient of numerous research grants, including grants from the Council of Supply Chain Management Professionals (CSCMP), the Institute for Supply Management® (ISM®), CAPS Research and NSF. She currently serves as the Co-editor in Chief for the *Journal of Supply Chain Management*; is a member of the Editorial Advisory Boards of the *Journal of Business Logistics, International Journal of Physical Distribution & Logistics Management* and the *International Journal of Logistics Management*; and sits on the Editorial Review Board of *Journal of Purchasing and Supply Management*.

She has co-authored five books, the most recent about environmental purchasing. She has served as the Director for the A.T. Kearney Center for Strategic Supply Leadership (CSSL), and been a member of the CAPS Research Board of Directors. She has taught in over 20 countries across the globe.

Original Series Author

Anna E. Flynn, Ph.D. is an independent consultant and educator who provides supply management training and education for organizations all over the world. She is co-author of one of the top supply management textbooks, and was formerly a faculty member at Thunderbird, The American Graduate School of International Management and the W.P. Carey School of Business at Arizona State University.

Contents

Chapter 1: Leading and Managing
Chapter Objectives 3
What Is Leadership? 3
    What Do Leaders Do? 8
    Theories of Leadership 10
    Motivators of Behavior 10
    Six Leadership Styles 11
    Contingency Model of Leadership Effectiveness 12
    Competency Model of Leadership Effectiveness 13
    Leadership Is All About Results 14
    Transformational Leadership 16
    Pulling Together the Models 17
What Is Management? 18
    What Do Managers Do? 18
    Theories of Management 19
    Motivational Theories 19
    Management Styles 21
    Teams and Teamwork 24
    Emerging Leadership Trends 26
    Management of the Supply Process 27
Summary 28
    Key Points 29
Appendix: Time Line of Major Theories of Management 30

Chapter 2: Setting Direction
Chapter Objectives 34
Creating a Values-Based Organization 34
    What Are Values? 34
    What Can a Leader Do? 36
Opportunities and Risks 38
    Recognize and Assess Organization and Supply-Related
        Opportunities and Risks 39
    Assessing Risks 41
Developing Vision and Strategies 45
    Mission: Why Does This Organization Exist? 46
    Developing Strategies 48
    Aligning Supply Strategy With Organizational Strategy 49
Summary 51
    Key Points 52
Appendix: ISM *Principles of Sustainability and Social Responsibility* 53

Chapter 3: Creating Alignment

Chapter Objectives 56
Supply Alignment and the Leader's Role 56
    The Importance of Alignment 56
    The Leader's Role in Alignment 58
Communicating a Clear Understanding of Vision 59
    Who Are Stakeholders? 59
    Building Alignment Internally 61
Building Credibility 65
    Components of Credibility 66
    What Are the Current and Desired Perceptions of Supply Management? 68
    How Leaders Communicate Vision 69
    Developing a Communications Plan 69
    Leadership Styles 72
Empowering People 74
Summary 76
    Key Points 76

Chapter 4: Gaining Commitment: Motivating and Inspiring People

Chapter Objectives 78
Motivating and Inspiring 78
    Motivational Techniques 78
    Influence and Influencing Techniques 81
    Global Leadership Styles and Influence 85
Building Strong Internal Partnerships 87
    Vertical Relationships 87
    Horizontal Relationships 88
    Building Coalitions 88
    Lead or Participate in Teams 89
    Conflict and Conflict Resolution 94
Creating a Culture of Commitment 96
    Eight Steps to Transform Your Organization 97
    Maintaining Momentum 98
Summary 99
    Key Points 99

Chapter 5: Assessing, Mitigating and Managing Supply-Based Risks

Chapter Objectives 102
The Risk Management Process 102
    Step 1: Identify the Sources of Risks 103
    Step 2: Estimate the Probability of Occurrence 109
    Step 3: Estimate the Likely Impact 109
    Step 4: Develop a Risk Profile 110
    Step 5: Develop Risk-Management Strategies 111
    Step 6: Allocate Resources 114
    Step 7: Execute Strategy 115
    Step 8: Review Results 115
    Supply Management's Role in Assessing the Risks of Proposed Mergers,
        Acquisitions and Divestitures 116
    Contractual Issues 116
    Management of Redundancy and Complexity 117
    Liability Exposure 118
    Divestiture of Assets 118
    Global Economic Considerations 118
    Risks Associated With Outsourcing 119
Summary 124
    Key Points 124

Chapter 6: Developing Business Plans

Chapter Objectives 126
The Planning Process 126
    Why Plan? 127
    Types of Business Plans 127
Supply Management's Role in the Development of the Organization's
    Strategic Planning 128
    Strategic Tools 130
Supply Management's Role in Insource/Make or Outsource/Buy Decisions 130
    Step 1: Identify an Opportunity 130
    Step 2: Determine Feasibility 131
    Step 3: Collect and Analyze Cost Data 133
    Step 4: Assess the Results of a Feasibility Study and Make
        a Decision 134
    Step 5: Develop a Business Plan to Implement the Decision 134
    Step 6: Audit Results 134
    Step 7: Conduct a Post-audit Evaluation of the Decision 134

Supply Management's Role in Mergers, Acquisitions and Divestitures 135
The Development of Strategic and Operational Supply Management Plans 136
    Elements of a Strategic Supply Management Plan 137
    Goals 137
    Market Analysis 138
    Strategies 140
    Prioritized Implementation Schedule 141
    Develop a Supply Management Operating Plan 141
Strategies for Executing the Plan 142
    Communication Plan 142
    Rollout Plan 143
    Phased Time Line 143
Summary 143
    Key Points 144

Chapter 7: Organizing and Building Supply Management Infrastructure

Chapter Objectives 146
Organizational and Supply Management Structure 146
    Functional Structure 147
    Organizational Structure Types and Implications 147
    Creating a Globally Integrated Organization 151
    Centralized, Decentralized and Hybrid Supply Management Structures 152
    Impact of Supply Management Structure 158
    Organizing Human Resources 162
Systems and Processes 163
    Customer Segmentation 164
    Product and Service Pricing Strategy 164
    Sales Performance to Plan 165
    Product and Technology Roadmaps of Key Suppliers and Customers 165
    Financial and Information Flows Up and Down the Supply Chain 167
    Critical Customer Service Factors 167
    Customer and Supplier Collaboration Processes 167
Supply Management Technologies 168
Summary 168
    Key Points 169

Chapter 8: Developing a Strategic Sourcing Process and Adopting Enabling Technology

Chapter Objectives ... 172
An Overview of the Strategic Sourcing Process ... 172
    Step 1: Data Management and Analysis ... 173
    Step 2: Develop a Category Strategy ... 173
    Step 3: Cost Management ... 174
    Step 4: Supplier Selection and Contract Negotiation ... 175
    Step 5: Supplier Development: Build and Manage the Relationship ... 175
Developing Strategic Sourcing Plans ... 177
    Operational ... 177
    Financial ... 177
    Marketing ... 178
    Supply Management ... 178
    Technology ... 179
Leveraging Spend Through Sourcing Strategies ... 179
    Developing Category Sourcing Strategies ... 180
    Standardized Policies and Procedures ... 186
    Systems Assessment ... 187
Market Analysis ... 187
    E-Sourcing Tools ... 188
    Contract Management ... 192
Summary ... 192
    Key Points ... 193

Chapter 9: Staffing the Supply Management Organization

Chapter Objectives ... 196
Designing Roles and Assigning Responsibilities ... 196
    Determine Required Knowledge and Skills ... 198
    Assign Knowledge and Skills to Positions ... 202
Developing Global Employment and Talent Management Strategies ... 206
    Global Workforce Diversity ... 206
    Attracting Diverse Talent ... 208
    Recruiting Strategies by Level of Position ... 208
    References, Experience and Education/Training ... 209
    Employee Retention ... 210
    Employee Termination ... 215
    Succession Planning ... 216
Summary ... 217
    Key Points ... 218
Some Sample Labor Sites ... 218
Appendix: Sample Interview Questions ... 219

Chapter 10: Developing Supply Management Talent

Chapter Objectives 222
Professional Development Opportunities 222
    Skills Assessment.. 224
    Job Analysis/Diagnostic Evaluation 224
    Gap Analysis... 226
    Determining Training and Development Needs 226
    Team Building: Leadership, Decision-Making, Influencing, Compromising..... 227
    Strategic Planning Skills: Project-Scoping, Goal Setting and Execution 229
    Communication Skills: Presentation, Public Speaking, Listening and Writing....... 230
    Broader Financial Skills: Cost Accounting, Analytical, Cash Flow and Making the
        Business Case... 231
    Technical Skills: Web-Enabled Sourcing Analysis, Social Media and Market Intelligence............. 231
    Relationship Management Skills: Ethics, Facilitation, Conflict Resolution and Creative
        Problem-Solving.. 232
    Designing and Planning Training Programs 233
    Types of Training 234
Assessing the Effectiveness of the Professional Development Program 239
    Training, Cost Efficiency and Measurement of Outcomes 239
Summary...239
    Key Points 240

Chapter 11: Measuring the Supply Management Department Performance

Chapter Objectives 242
Aligning Department Performance Metrics With Organizational Objectives..................... 242
    Effectiveness in Meeting Organizational Needs 243
    Determine Effectiveness of Department Management...................................... 245
    Measure Improvement or Deterioration... 245
    Provide Incentives for Improvement 245
    Determine Resources Needed for Improvement 247
    Determine If Value Is Added 247
What to Measure: Linking Metrics to Goals... 247
    Measure Outsourced Supply Management Functions 250
How to Measure: Steps in Department-Level Evaluation 250
    Step 1: Identify Department Objectives.. 252
    Step 2: Identify Criteria for Success 252
    Step 3: Identify Appraisal Factors 253
    Step 4: Select and Execute Data Collection Methods 258
    Step 5: Exercise Management Control in Response to Results.......................... 260
Summary...263
    Key Points 264

Chapter 12: Establishing Internal Controls and Ensuring Compliance

Chapter Objectives 267
Establishing an Internal Control System 267
    Before-the-Fact Controls 269
    During-the-Fact Controls 270
    After-the-Fact Controls 271
Internal Operations Controls 272
    Internal Environmental Controls 274
    Supply Management's Role 276
Internal Records Management 284
Internal Financial Controls 289
    The U.S. Sarbanes-Oxley Act of 2002 289
Legal and Regulatory Controls 291
    Agency and Authority 292
    Role of Legal Counsel 293
    Types of Laws With Which Supply Management Should be Familiar 294
    Regulations Influencing the Development of Solicitations 307
Summary 309
    Key Points 310
Appendix: Laws and Regulations 311
Appendix: Resources for Types of Laws 314

Endnotes 317

References 339

Index 345

CHAPTER 1

The manager asks how and when; the leader asks what and why.
— WARREN BENNIS[1]

Great managers look inward; great leaders look outward.
— MARCUS BUCKINGHAM AND CURT COFFMAN[2]

You've got to think about big things while you're doing small things, so that all the small things go in the right direction.
— ALVIN TOFFLER

Leading and Managing

There are no answers to the how and when questions until the *what* and why questions have been answered. And once the leaders have looked outward to determine in what direction the organization should go and why it is going there, managers are needed to look inward to ensure that the processes, procedures, policies and systems are in place to execute strategies. There is no benefit to managerial-led efficiency if the organization is going in the wrong direction. Doing small things the right way is a waste of time if they do not align with the big things. Therefore, leaders need managers and managers need leaders. Organizations need both.

Warren Bennis drew 12 distinctions between leaders and managers in his 1989 book, *On Becoming a Leader*:

1. Managers administer; leaders innovate.
2. Managers ask how and when; leaders ask what and why.
3. Managers focus on systems; leaders focus on people.
4. Managers do things right; leaders do the right things.
5. Managers maintain; leaders develop.
6. Managers rely on control; leaders inspire trust.
7. Managers have a short-term perspective; leaders have a longer-term perspective.
8. Managers accept the status quo; leaders challenge the status quo.

9. Managers have an eye on the bottom line; leaders have an eye on the horizon.
10. Managers imitate; leaders originate.
11. Managers emulate the classic good soldier; leaders are their own person.
12. Managers copy; leaders show originality.[3]

The managerial and/or leadership behaviors a person will be called on to exercise will depend on the needs of the organization. These organizational needs are determined in large part by internal and external complexity and the pace of change. Effective leaders are in greater demand in times of rapid change. Effective managers are in greater demand in highly complex organizations. Both effective leaders and effective managers are in demand when a complex organization requires rapid, dramatic change. Most people would agree the world is experiencing both increasing complexity and rapid change.

If a complex organization needs dramatic and rapid change in how supply is managed, then the supply leader's ability to motivate and inspire people to embrace change may be the most important skill he or she possesses. Likewise, a supply management professional's ability to organize processes, structure, technology and people in alignment with the organization's vision may be his or her most important skill set. According to P. Fraser Johnson and Michiel R. Leenders, perhaps the greatest challenge facing CPOs is dealing with economic, political, social and technological external change compounded by internal change in structure, resources, responsibilities and roles. "The challenge of continuing change in the structure, responsibilities and role of the supply function requires a high degree of flexibility on the part of the CPO."[4] Lisa Martin, senior vice president and chief procurement officer for Teva Pharmaceuticals, has made job transitions due to changes in organizational structures. In her very first and second procurement positions, she was brought in to build a procurement organization from scratch. She did such a good job of suggesting ways to improve the procurement function at Sony that she re-engineered herself out of a job. However, leadership and change management skills are highly valued and important, and Ms. Martin was recently brought in by Teva in 2012 for the purpose of "…establishing processes, systems and tools to bring data visibility to this forward-thinking organization."[5]

Leading and *managing* are both action words. But the question is, do leaders and managers engage in the same activities or different ones? And can or should these actions be executed by the same person or different people, and how many people can play leadership and management roles in an organization? Additionally, how does the external environment drive the need for leaders and managers in an organization? Also, how does the internal environment shape the roles and responsibilities of its leaders and managers and either enable or disable them in successfully executing these roles? Lastly, how can leaders and managers work in harmony to ensure effective development and execution in the pursuit of an organizational vision?

The first step in answering these questions is to clarify the differences between a leader and a manager. This chapter explores these two concepts more fully and lays the foundation for the remaining chapters. Chapters 2 through 4 focus on the specific actions of leaders, and Chapters 5 through 12 address the corresponding actions of managers. All the chapters include organizational examples from different sectors, industries and countries. This chapter is divided into four sections: (1) what is leadership?; (2) theories of leadership; (3) what is management?; and (4) theories of management.

Chapter Objectives
- Discuss different theories and perspectives on leadership and management.
- Describe the different roles and tasks of leaders and managers.

What Is Leadership?

To lead people, walk behind them.

LAO-TZU
ANCIENT CHINESE PHILOSOPHER[6]

Leader. Leadership. These terms are weighted with expectations that all too often are met with disappointment by the leader and his or her followers. Is leadership an art or a science, or a little bit of both? Is it a skill that can be learned and developed, or is it an inherent trait or attribute of an individual? Can a person develop and exercise his or her leadership ability in any sphere of influence or only in formal positions of power? If an organization possesses leadership that is superior to that of its competitors, will this give it a competitive advantage? Or is leadership about relationships and what occurs between and among people? These are questions that researchers and practitioners have explored for decades with changing perspectives across time and culture.

Leadership has been defined in many ways. The roots to the English words *lead* and *leadership* are found in the Old English word *lithan*, which means "to go," and the ancient root *leith*, which means "to go forth and die," as in battle. Leaders, by this last definition, mobilize one group against another and fight to the death. Leaders were typically authority figures who had leader status by virtue of their position. Recently, the term *leadership* has been prefaced with a descriptor such as ethical, collaborative or transformational. According to the BusinessDictionary.com (2013), leadership means "The activity of leading a group of people or an organization, or the ability to do this."[7] This definition does not hint of conflict let alone death, but hints at being at the forefront and guiding people rather than commanding them.

The leadership approach reflected in the Chinese philosophical system of Taoism contrasts with this Western image of one person leading a group of followers. Philosopher Lao-tzu is credited with writing the *Tao-te Ching (Classic of the Way of Virtue)* more than 2,500 years ago. It contains 81 verses outlining a philosophy that stresses uniting with and yielding to the natural flow of the universe. Diane Dreher, Professor in the English Department at Santa Clara University in Santa Clara, California, and author of *The Tao of Personal Leadership*, points to one of the best known Tao verses as an example of its relevance to leadership: "With the best of leaders, when the work is done, the project completed, Tao people all say, 'We did it ourselves.'" According to Dreher, "The Tao leader is someone who can remain centered, be mindful, assess a situation, bring people together, build consensus and discover solutions by drawing on the talents of everyone involved."[8] Lao-tzu wrote that, "to become an excellent leader, you have to abandon addiction to praise from above and flattery from below. The excellent leader leads least. He studies the distinctive skills and natural inclinations of both those above and those below, and he directs their attention to accomplish what is required to benefit all. When this has been done, all declare they have been part of a worthwhile purpose."[9]

This Chinese leadership model places high value on managing relationships. According to Lien Siaou-Sze, former senior vice president of the Hewlett-Packard Technology Solutions Group in Asia-Pacific and Japan and now Senior Executive Coach at Mobley Group Pacific Ltd., "Before people will follow willingly and enthusiastically, they must truly believe in the leader. This is based on the leader's core values and the credibility that has been accumulated over time."[10]

The philosopher Confucius stressed the value of the thoughtful man, learning through mistakes while consciously respecting traditions and values. In Geert Hofstede's research on cultural influences in the workplace conducted from 1967-1973 in IBM in 70 countries, and subsequent studies up to the present in many countries, and occupations, China ranked the highest in terms of "long-term orientation" and lowest on "feelings of individualism."[11] This is reflected in the Chinese cultural tradition of *guan xi*, which stresses the relatedness and connections among individuals and the utmost importance of patience and perseverance. These differences require understanding and adaptation by all parties to work successfully in a multicultural business relationship or team.

In an interview in the *Harvard Business Review*, Zhang Ruimin, chief executive officer of the Haier Group, discussed his evolving leadership style. He believes that Haier employees "need to make decisions for themselves and not to feel they are following me in their work." In explanation, he quoted Lao-tzu, who said, "In the highest antiquity, the people did not know that there were rulers." Ruimin interpreted this to mean that "a leader whose existence is unknown to his subordinates is really the most brilliant one."[12]

Until fairly recently, many Western definitions of leadership focused on a single person and his or her personal qualities or attributes and skills. The goal in colleges, universities and organizations was to identify the qualities or abilities, traits and behaviors of effective leaders; and teach people how to exhibit these attributes to improve their leadership effectiveness as a result. According to Warren Bennis, "The most dangerous leadership myth is that leaders are born — that there is a genetic factor to leadership. This myth asserts that people simply either have certain charismatic qualities or not. That's nonsense; in fact, the opposite is true. Leaders are made rather than born."[13] Adherents to this thinking believe that organizations can seek out people with leadership potential and expose them to career experiences designed to develop that potential. With careful selection, nurturing and encouragement, dozens of people can play important leadership roles in a business organization.

The Western focus on the individual leader is changing in many settings. In their book, *The Leadership Challenge: How to Keep Getting Extraordinary Things Done in Organizations*, James M. Kouzes and Barry Z. Posner report, "What we've discovered, and rediscovered, is that leadership isn't the private reserve of a few charismatic men and women. It's a process ordinary people use when they're bringing forth the best from themselves and others. Liberate the leader in everyone, and extraordinary things happen."[14] According to *The McKinsey Quarterly*, organizations need a "cadre of leaders with the right capabilities at the right levels of the organization" to successfully execute strategy. "The leadership cadre typically includes the 3 to 5 percent of employees throughout the organization who can deliver breakthroughs in performance."[15] Other definitions of leadership have focused on the leader's sources of power or aspects of the situation to determine how to improve leader effectiveness. Recently, conversations about leadership have been about influencing others by one's actions as well as by one's words. According to mediation expert Mark Gerzon, effective leadership can then be viewed as "the ability to *involve others* in the process of *accomplishing a goal* within some larger system or environment. That is, a leader leads or influences a collaborator or group of coworkers toward achieving some end in the context of an organization, social community and environment. Leaders, therefore, have the ability to help people and organizations go from where they are to where they could or should be. Leadership is about change, growth and movement."[16]

Carlos Ghosn, for instance, the current chairman and chief executive officer of Nissan Motor Co., Ltd., assumed his post after Nissan reported its biggest loss ever. He is credited with returning Nissan to profitability in 12 months. This was especially impressive because Ghosn was chosen by Renault, a French automaker and Nissan's controlling shareholder, to run a Japanese company. In an interview with *The McKinsey Quarterly*, Ghosn said at the time that, "I had to make a decision, and a decision has to come from strong inner beliefs. And my strong inner belief was that it was time to totally break with the past ten years of Nissan. At the end, I made a decision to commit my own job if any one of the objectives was not met. It was very important for the credibility of the plan, both internally and externally, to make this kind of commitment so people knew that you are going to be 100 percent behind the Nissan revival plan. The ultimate sacrifice for the top manager is to say, 'I'm putting my job on the line if I don't achieve these targets.' You can't ask a manager for more than this, especially in my position, because I had nothing to do with this [company's problems]. I was not in any way responsible for the situation. On top of this, I was saying, 'I bet my job on this.' So it has a high level of credibility. In a certain way, this limited — not eliminated — the anxiety and the skepticism about the question, 'Are they really going to do this?'"[17]

Warren Bennis also explores the idea of leadership in groups — or "Great Groups" as he calls well-known, highly successful groups. Without exception, the leaders:
- Provide direction and meaning;
- Generate and sustain trust in the group and in the leadership;
- Display a bias toward action, risk taking and curiosity; and
- Are purveyors of hope.[18]

Joseph Rost, author of *Leadership for the Twenty-First Century*, defines leadership as an influence relationship among leaders and followers who intend to make real changes that reflect their mutual purposes. This definition of leadership is characterized by "collaboration, power sharing, facilitation and empowerment in a world that is more complex and diverse, mutually shaping and spontaneously changing."[19]

Contemporary definitions most often reject the idea that leadership revolves around the leader's abilities, behaviors, style or charisma. Today, scholars discuss the basic nature of leadership in terms of the "interaction" among the people involved in the process — both leaders and followers. Thus, leadership is not the work of a single person; rather, it can be explained and defined as a "collaborative endeavor" among group members. Therefore, the essence of leadership is not the leader, but the relationship.[20] This approach has relevance to the supply management leader who must collaborate internally with various stakeholder groups and externally with suppliers.

Other terms for leaders who focus on influencing and motivating disparate groups include "cross-boundary leaders" (John W. Gardner), "advocates for the whole" (Peter Senge), "bridging leaders" (Peggy Dulany and the Synergos Institute), "integral leaders" (Ken Wilber) and "third-side leadership" (William Ury). As the Welsh proverb says, "He that would be a leader must be a bridge." The command-and-control leadership style is believed may be less effective in today's fast changing, highly competitive markets. In its place is leadership that motivates people to want to take the leadership themselves to get from here to there.

While Western leadership experts generally have viewed leadership as an individual characteristic until fairly recently, in less individualistic cultures, more emphasis is on the collaborative, communal nature of leadership. "More traditional approaches to leadership often talk about *individual* leaders and their followers, usually within organizations," observes Jacinto Gavino, professor at the Asian Institute of Management in Manila. Like many of his colleagues in Asia, Latin America and Africa, Gavino believes there is an "inordinate emphasis on the self" in the European and North American leadership model. Indeed, in the several dozen in-depth case studies of "bridging leaders" gathered from seven countries, Gavino and his fellow members of the Global Leadership Task Force found that the subjects of their research did not think of themselves as separate individual "leaders" but as part of a leadership "web," "fabric" or "community."[21]

The use of cross-functional and cross-organization teams can be summed up in this quote of Peter Drucker who said, "The leaders who work most effectively, it seems to me, never say 'I.' And that's not because they have trained themselves not to say 'I.' They don't think 'I.' They think 'we'; they think 'team.' They understand their job to be to make the team function. They accept responsibility and don't sidestep it, but 'we' gets the credit. … This is what creates trust, what enables you to get the task done."[22]

The goals of leaders may also be influenced by culture. For example, University of Michigan Professor C.K. Pralahad says, "The quest is to develop a capitalism that 'puts the individual at the center of the universe,' placing employees and customers first so that they can benefit shareholders."[23] In an article titled, "Karma Capitalism," authors Pete Engardio and Jena McGregor discuss the trend of many senior managers and leaders to refer to and reflect on the teachings of the *Bhagavad Gita* to business.[24] One key message is that enlightened leaders should master any impulses or emotions that cloud sound judgment. Good leaders are selfless, take initiative, and focus on their duty rather than obsessing over outcomes or financial gain. "The key point," says Ram Charan, a coach to CEOs such as General Electric (GE) Co.'s Jeffrey R. Immelt, "is to put purpose before self. This is absolutely applicable to corporate leadership today."[25] While many Indian management and leadership theorists emphasize interconnectedness, India is so large and diverse economically and socially that many perspectives influence their work. "We are a fusion society," according to Harvard's Rakesh Khurana. As a result, many Indian management theorists "tend to look at organizations as complex social systems, where culture and reciprocity are important," he says. "You won't hear too many of us say the only legitimate stakeholders in a company are stockholders."[26] What's more, India's extreme poverty imposes a natural pressure on its companies to contribute more to the common good.

While hotly debated in academic circles, Geert Hofstede's "dimensions of culture scales" are one valuable resource for gaining perspective on the cultural influencers on leadership around the world. Through his research he developed five scales: power distance index, individualism, masculinity, uncertainty avoidance and long-term orientation. The power distance index focuses on the degree of equality, or inequality, between people in the country's society. A high score reflects greater inequality and less allowance for upward mobility. Individualism focuses on the degree the society reinforces individual, or collective, achievement and interpersonal relationships. A high score indicates that individuality and individual rights are paramount within the society. Masculinity focuses on the degree the society reinforces, or does not reinforce, the traditional masculine work role model of male achievement, control and power. A high score indicates the country experiences a high degree of gender differentiation. In these cultures, males dominate a significant portion of the society and power structure, with females being controlled by male domination. The uncertainty avoidance index focuses on the level of tolerance for uncertainty and ambiguity within the society. A high score indicates the country has a low tolerance for uncertainty and ambiguity. This creates a rule-oriented society that institutes laws, rules, regulations and controls to reduce the amount of uncertainty. Long-term orientation indicates a society's time perspective and an attitude of persevering; that is, overcoming obstacles with time, if not with will and strength. Values associated with long-term orientation are thrift and perseverance; values associated with short-term orientation are respect for tradition, fulfilling social obligations and protecting one's "face." A long-term orientation is thought to support a strong work ethic where long-term rewards are expected as a result of today's hard work. However, business may take longer to develop in this society, particularly for an "outsider."[27] Supply management leaders who are developing globally integrated supply networks must be able to lead people from many cultural backgrounds and orientations.

What Do Leaders Do?

No matter what style or approach a leader adopts, he or she takes action and performs tasks. What are the tasks or actions of leaders? According to Tom Peters, management consultant, "Leaders focus on the soft stuff. People. Values. Character. Commitment. A cause. All of the stuff that was supposed to be too goo-goo to count in business. Yet, it's the stuff that real leaders take care of first. And forever. That's why leadership is an art, not a science."[28] John Wooden, Hall of Fame basketball coach, echoes this sentiment. "Knowledge alone is not enough to get desired results. You must have the more elusive ability to teach and to motivate. This defines a leader; if you can't teach and you can't motivate, you can't lead."[29]

No matter which definition or theory of leadership, all of them assume that leaders do something different than managers do. The belief that leadership is about action fits well with those who believe that leadership is all about results. In *The Extraordinary Leader*, John Zenger and Joseph Folkman define leadership as a combination of attributes x results. The attributes of a great leader are those that drive results such as unit profitability, retention statistics, customer satisfaction and employee commitment metrics, as well as those attributes that mean the most to those being led.[30]

In the *Harvard Business Review on Leadership*, Charles M. Farkas and Suzy Wetlaufer describe five approaches to leadership, each with a singular focus: strategy, people, expertise, controls or change. The approach taken depends on the leader's philosophy about how he or she can best add value. Strategy-focused leaders devote the majority of their time to external matters such as customers, competitors, technological advancements and market trends, and delegate internal operational activities. People-focused leaders devote their time to managing and developing the organization's talent and to imparting the values, behaviors and attitudes they believe will lead to success. These leaders delegate strategy development to those close to the markets. Expertise-focused leaders devote their time to the area of expertise that is the source of competitive advantage. Controls-focused leaders devote time to creating, communicating and monitoring internal controls. This is evident in highly regulated industries such as banking. Change-focused leaders devote their time to creating an environment of continual reinvention through communication activities designed to motivate people to embrace change. Each of these five approaches was found to give structure and meaning to the CEO's leadership role and to enable the CEO to deliver "clarity, consistency and commitment."[31]

Each of these approaches might be applied to leadership of a supply management organization depending on the nature and complexity of the business, the degree of change needed in the supply organization and the specific strengths of the supply leader. For example, TI's CPO took a people-focused approach. At Thomson Multimedia (TMM), Charles Dehelly, senior executive vice president of Strategic Business Units, IT and sourcing from 1998-2002, focused on introducing supply management expertise from the high-tech sector that would make a difference to TMM competitively.[32] He introduced supply practices such as the Product Model Cost Follow-Up Process to track all costs for a particular product to take actions to improve margins and build joint responsibility for product success. He also focused everyone in supply management on measuring their return on capital employed, and was also personally involved in all major supplier initiatives.

Ram Charan identified eight things essential for leadership success:
1. Positioning and repositioning your business by focusing on the central idea that meets customers' needs and makes money;
2. Pinpointing patterns of external change ahead of others;
3. Leading the social system of your business by shaping the way people work together;
4. Judging people by getting to the truth of a person and unleashing his or her natural talents;
5. Molding a working team of leaders from a group of high-energy, high-powered, high-ego people;
6. Developing goals that balance what the business can become with what it can realistically achieve;
7. Setting laser-sharp priorities that become the roadmap for meeting your goals; and
8. Dealing creatively and positively with societal pressures that go beyond the economic value creation activities of your business.[33]

More recent studies, such as one by the Conference Board, confirm that these qualities still hold true, and emphasize the need for adaptability and connectivity above all else. Collaboration is essential to future success.[34]

Further citing case studies from his consulting practice, Charan identified personal traits of leaders that help or interfere with becoming a true leader:
1. *Ambition*. The drive to accomplish something but not win at all costs;
2. *Tenacity*. The drive to search, persist and follow through, but not too long;
3. *Self-confidence*. The drive to overcome the fear of failure and response, or the need to be liked and use power judiciously but not become arrogant and narcissistic;
4. *Psychological openness*. The ability to be receptive to new and different ideas but not shut down other people;
5. *Realism*. The ability to see what can be accomplished and not gloss over problems or assume the worst; and

6. *Appetite for learning.* The ability to grow and improve the eight "know-hows" and not repeat the same mistakes.[35]

The Center for Creative Leadership described the following leader behaviors that help create effective change:
- *Setting a direction.* The supply leader must develop a vision of the future and then define strategies for producing the changes needed to accomplish that vision. Key questions include: Where are we going? What are we going to do? Why are we doing it?
- *Aligning people.* Alignment involves communicating and building teams or coalitions with key stakeholders and making sure everyone understands where the organization is going and is acting cohesively to realize the vision. Key questions include: How can we stay together? How can we work better as a group? How can we improve cooperation?
- *Motivating and inspiring.* The leader generates commitment through the use of encouraging and supportive behaviors that keep people energized in the face of resistance to change. As John Quincy Adams said, "If your actions inspire others to dream more, learn more, do more, and become more, you are a leader." It is the relentless focus on the future and the movement toward that future that sets apart the leader from the follower. Key questions are: How can we develop a shared understanding of our situation? How can our actions be better coordinated?[36]

A number of theories of leadership have been developed to explain leadership effectiveness. These include motivational theories, contingency theories and competency models. These theories are addressed in the following section.

Theories of Leadership

Prior to the 1980s, leadership development in organizations primarily focused on identifying different leadership styles and matching the style to a specific situation. Effective leadership was a function of adjusting one's style and actions to a particular situation to get someone to efficiently accomplish a specific task.

Motivators of Behavior

David McClelland, the late Harvard psychologist, was a pioneer in research on the motives of leaders and how motives affect leadership behavior. He identified three "social motives" or internal drivers that explain behavior: achievement, affiliation and power.

McClelland's research showed that motives generate needs that generate aspirations that drive behavior. By identifying his or her primary internal driver, a person can assess his or her leadership style and make adjustments to improve leadership performance.[37]

Achievement-Oriented Leaders. A leader whose primary motivation is achievement will aspire to improve personal performance and meet or exceed standards of excellence, accomplish something new or plan for his or her long-term career advancement. As a result, the leader may micromanage subordinates, do things himself or herself, or set the pace for others to ensure achievement. These leaders may give little positive feedback and few directions or instructions. In high-stress situations, high achievement-oriented leaders may cut corners and focus on goals and outcomes rather than on people.

Affiliation-Oriented Leaders. A leader whose primary motivation is affiliation will aspire to establish, maintain or restore close friendly relationships in an effort to be liked and accepted. This person may participate in group activities primarily for social reasons. As a result, the leader may avoid confrontation and avoid giving negative feedback, worry more about people than performance and look for ways to create harmony.

Power-Oriented Leaders. A leader whose primary motivation is power will aspire to be strong and to influence others. Power comes in two forms: personalized, where the leader gets his or her strength from controlling others and making them feel weak, or socialized, where the leader gets his or her strength from helping people feel stronger and more capable.

PERSONALIZED POWER. Leaders with a high need for personalized power want to control, persuade or influence people. They take actions to impress people inside and outside the organization and to maintain their reputations, positions or strength. These leaders generate strong emotions, positive or negative, in other people. As a result, the leader may be coercive and ruthless, control or manipulate others, look out for his or her own reputation and interests, and focus more on impressing higher-ups (managing up) than on managing subordinates.

SOCIALIZED POWER. Leaders with a high need for socialized power want to help people feel stronger and more capable. They seek to persuade people and empower them. Leaders with a high need for socialized power, like those with personalized power needs, also take actions to impress people inside and outside their organization and to maintain their reputations, positions or strengths. However, their impact on others is more positive. These leaders give help, advice or support and generate strong positive emotions in others. As a result, the leader coaches and teaches, is highly supportive and more democratic, and involves others in decision-making. These leaders focus on the team or group rather than on themselves, and work through others. They enable others to do the work rather than doing it themselves.

Six Leadership Styles

Numerous researchers have identified six distinct leadership styles, each of which is appropriate in certain situations: directive/commanding, visionary, affiliative, participative/democratic, pacesetting and coaching.[38] Each style is appropriate in specific situations and with stakeholders who are motivated by different drivers. They are discussed in Chapter 3.

Emotional Intelligence. The Hay Group and Daniel Goleman have identified competencies that identify individuals with emotional intelligence. Emotional intelligence is defined as "the capacity for recognizing our own feelings and those of others, for motivating ourselves, for managing emotions well in ourselves and in our relationships." The competencies fall into four clusters: self-awareness and self-management (which relate to the individual's capacity for understanding one's own emotions and self-regulating behavior); social awareness (which relates to understanding the what and why of others' feelings and actions); and relationship management (which relates to the individual's ability to get desired results from others and reach personal goals).[39]

Contingency Model of Leadership Effectiveness

The contingency model focuses on changing the situation, not the leader. Based on research that dates back to the 1950s, the contingency model of leadership effectiveness influenced leadership training programs into the 1980s. This model suggests that leadership effectiveness is contingent on the degree of control the leader has over a situation, and the individual's style or typical way that the person interacts with members of the group. This model posits that the leader can improve effectiveness by focusing on changing critical aspects of the situation to enable the leader to better manage the situation, rather than focusing on changing his or her leadership style. The degree to which the leader has control over the tasks, the group and the outcome is referred to as situational control. When a person has the "right" amount of situational control, he or she tends to feel more secure, relaxed and at ease. The right level of situational control affects the leader's behavior and ability to function. A person must first establish the "right" level of situational control for optimal performance and then determine how to engineer or manage the situation to meet that right level.

Task Motivated or Relationship Motivated. The contingency model uses an assessment known as the least preferred coworker (LPC) to determine if a person is task motivated or relationship motivated. From this assessment, the leader is then able to determine how he or she is likely to behave if his or her level of situational control is low, moderate or high. A person's LPC score indicates the needs, goals and motivations that a leader will see as most important in various leadership situations. Behavior varies as the situation changes.

Leadership Situation. In the contingency theory, a leadership situation is classified by the degree to which it provides the leader with control and influence; the degree to which the leader can predict and determine what his or her group is going to do, and what the outcomes of his or her actions and decisions are going to be; and the degree to which the leader can predict with a high degree of certainty and assurance what will happen when he or she wants something accomplished. Control and influence are determined by (1) leader-member relations, (2) task structure, and (3) position power. A high-control situation is one in which the group is loyal, dependable and supportive; the task is clearly spelled out, goals are known and there is a clear and accepted procedure for performing the task. The leader also has formal organizational power with the power to recognize and reward good work or punish poorly performed work. Of the three factors, leader-member relations is the most important, followed by task structure and, lastly, by position power.

Competency Model of Leadership Effectiveness

The competency model of leadership effectiveness focuses on the attributes of effective leaders. According to *Merriam-Webster's Dictionary*, "an attribute is an abstraction belonging to or characteristic of an entity." An abstraction is a construct by which objects or individuals can be distinguished. Leadership attributes are often referred to as habits, traits, competencies, behaviors, styles, motives, values, skills and character. This movement has identified the knowledge, skills and behaviors that leaders possess.

According to a 2010 Conference Board report, *Go Where There Be Dragons: Leadership Essentials for 2020*, the most important leadership skills for twenty-first century leaders are listed below:

- *Building trust.* A leader will need to be viewed as ethical, inspiring and trustworthy. "In an open-source, network-based environment, success will depend on this," they predict.
- *Reflection.* Twenty-first century leaders will need to figure out what really matters and, based on these reflections, be willing to step backward to move forward if necessary.
- *Influencing.* This "power" will not be about command and control, they say; it will be based on a leader's ability to set subtle direction that unlocks the organization's creativity.
- *Thinking in the shape of a "T."* Future leaders must have deep subject expertise in one or more areas, as well as be knowledgeable about functions and issues that are important to the organization, the business and the social environment; for example, practice T-shaped thinking. "Single-subject expertise will be less relevant," they explain.
- *Facilitating the possible.* Being able to connect the dots within their own organizations ("knowing corridors where knowledge is created, and then forging links within the organization so the knowledge spreads") will be critical for twenty-first century leaders.
- *Embracing ambiguity.* Even under pressing time constraints, the next wave of leaders must be willing to make and drive decisions with limited (even unreliable) information, they say.
- *Telling a compelling story.* While information alone is not knowledge, they also point out that knowledge that's not communicated is wasted. "Future leaders must be able to communicate a visionary story that inspires and engages the workforce," they explain.
- *Inspiring innovation, creativity and open source thinking.* In the future, it must be understood that true innovation extends beyond technology or product development, they assert. To this end, leaders must create cultures that reward innovation and allow failure.
- *Going where there be dragons.* The next wave of leaders must face their fears of the unknown and "go where there be dragons." This will require them to stretch their horizons, leave the familiar and take the risks that lead to new ideas.
- *Embracing a "did-it-ourselves" attitude — but also preparing for and allowing failure.* In coming years, the most effective leaders will let their staff members be creative, help find solutions and contribute, but also allow for failure, according to the report constituents.

"Fail fast, fail often and fail early — but don't fail to say it's OK to fail," they advise. "Be ruthless in learning from failure. Without failure, there can be no innovation."

- *Knowing thyself.* Empathy, social and emotional intelligence — as well as an understanding of their and others' limitations — will be essential for future leaders.
- *Modeling adaptability,* they add, can be demonstrated by leaders putting into practice the behaviors and character traits they hope to see in others.
- *Harnessing the energy.* The next generation of leaders must not only know how to capture the energy of natural systems and of their organizations, but also to feed this energy back in. "Most revolutions happen with networks of people coming together, yet most companies ignore the energy crowds can create," they warn.

The report further notes that adaptability is essential — and connectivity to information and the C-suite is essential to leadership success.[40]

Leadership Is All About Results

In their book, *Results-Based Leadership*, Dave Ulrich, Jack Zenger and Norman Smallwood posit that it is organizational capabilities (such as agility or adaptability) and leadership competencies (such as trust, vision and character) that lead to and are connected to results. The formula is: *effective leadership = attributes x results*. Leaders must demonstrate the appropriate attributes and they must deliver the desired results. Results come in four major areas: employee results (human capital), organization results (learning and innovation), customer results (delight target customers) and investor results (cash flow). The focus is on identifying and developing effective measures of leadership results, because what gets measured gets attention and should improve over time. The attributes side of the equation frames the behavior of leaders so that they do not focus on results at all costs or on the "I don't care what you have to do, hit the numbers!" mentality and practice.[41] What is accomplished is important, and how it is accomplished is equally important. For example, according to Whirlpool Corp., Whirlpool Corporation's management team believes in the company's values-based strategy. As noted in their 2012 annual report, "For our people, it is our core value of integrity — doing what we say we will do. It is that simple."[42]

The Center for Creative Leadership developed a "Model of Leader Competencies" to help leaders see the broad repertoire of knowledge, skills and abilities that are needed to be effective. According to this model, it makes sense that different types of activities and assignments develop different competencies. The leader's task is to seek out experiences to gain the practice that is needed.[43] Cynthia McCauley, author of *Developmental Assignments: Creating Learning Experiences Without Changing Jobs*, offers guidelines for competency development (see Figure 1-1). This was updated in 2011, and the five most critical characteristics noted in that study are bolded in the table below.

Figure 1-1: Developing Leadership Competencies

BEHAVIOR	ACTIONS
Adaptability	Choose experiences that force you out of your routine or make you consider perspectives different from your own.
Self-awareness	Seek experiences in which people more readily give you feedback because you are new to the work or are trying to change or improve a situation.
Managing yourself	Find chances to set priorities, manage stress and keep balanced amid the pursuit of difficult goals.
Capacity to learn	Take on experiences that add diversity or require you to work in a completely different setting.
Leadership stature	Seek out experiences that you are attracted to and excited about taking on.
Drive and purpose	Find a way to play a key role in seeing that the organization achieves important outcomes.
Ethics and integrity	Commit to an experience in which having high-trust relationships is essential.
Managing effective teams	Practice managing a wide variety of teams in a wide variety of contexts.
Building and maintaining relationships	Choose experiences in which you are working with others to create change.
Valuing diversity and differences	Seek out opportunities that expose you to the value of diversity and difference.
Developing others	Find situations in which you must motivate and develop employees to be successful.
Communicating effectively	Practice your communication skills with different audiences.
Managing change	Choose experiences in which you are creating new directions or fixing problems.
Solving problems and making decisions	Find situations that require addressing ill-defined or recurring problems, or making decisions that require broad input from across the organization.
Managing politics and influencing others	Take chances to work across organizational boundaries, exert influence without hierarchical power or engage in high-visibility work.
Taking risks and innovating	Search for experiences in which you and others are bringing fresh perspective to a situation or need to find new solutions to problems.
Boundary Spanning	Effectively reach out to other disciplines within the organization.
Collaboration	Find win-win solutions by working internally and with others in the supply chain.
Network Thinking	Understand the broader implications of decisions on businesses, the organization and key trading partners.

Sources: Cynthia McCauley, *Developmental Assignments: Creating Learning Experiences Without Changing Jobs*, Center for Creative Leadership, 2006; and Nick Petrie, *Future Trends in Leadership Development*, December 2011, accessed September 10, 2013, http://www.ccl.org/leadership/pdf/research/futureTrends.pdf.

Transformational Leadership

The mid-1980s saw a shift in focus from "transactional" to "transformational" leadership. Transformational leaders promoted the expression of each individual's potential and helped the individual perform "beyond" the expected outcomes. Transformational leadership focused on vision, change management, motivation to continuous improvement and the key role of trust in promoting true team spirit.

The past two decades have seen an extension of transformational leadership through the skills of visionary leadership and meta-leadership (leading and developing other leaders). This has led to the emergence of other leadership abilities in relationship to promoting change, realizing core values, recognizing the potential of each individual, and developing and empowering people to collaborate and innovate.

In the emerging views of leadership, leaders do not have influence simply because they have positions of power. Rather, leaders are people who are committed to "creating a world to which people want to belong." This commitment demands a special set of models and abilities to effectively and ecologically manifest the visions that guide those committed to change. It involves communicating, interacting and managing relationships within an organization, network or social system to move toward one's highest aspirations. The transformational leader's tasks are outlined in Figure 1-2.

Figure 1-2: Tasks of the Transformational Leader

Task	Activities
Set vision and strategy	Work in situations that allow you to think about possible future scenarios and craft strategies for aligning people and systems to achieve long-term objectives.
Manage work	Choose experiences that draw on managerial knowledge and expertise.
Enhance business skills and knowledge	Find opportunities to be exposed to parts of the business or organization with which you are less familiar.
Understand and navigate the organization	Seek out ways to operate within broader strategic initiatives, competing priorities and a network of relationships.

Pulling Together the Models

According to the contingency model, basically, with the right level of situational control, a leader can be effective in any given situation. The competency model essentially says that if the leader has the right set of attributes, he or she can be effective. Jack Zenger and Joseph Folkman take this a step further and describe the leadership sweet spot where the passions of the leader, the competencies of the leader and the needs of the organization intersect.[44]

The challenge is, of course, to match up people and organizations where a person's mix of competencies and passion fills the needs of the organization. Leadership development initiatives can be directed toward this goal and focused on identifying and strengthening competencies, fueling the individual's passion for the work and matching individuals to the appropriate roles in the organization. This approach recognizes that leaders hold formal or informal leadership positions. The goal is to fully develop the leadership potential of each person within his or her sphere of influence.

Figure 1-3 illustrates the three major roles of the supply leader or leadership team. Each of these tasks is discussed in detail in this book.

Figure 1-3: Major Leadership Roles

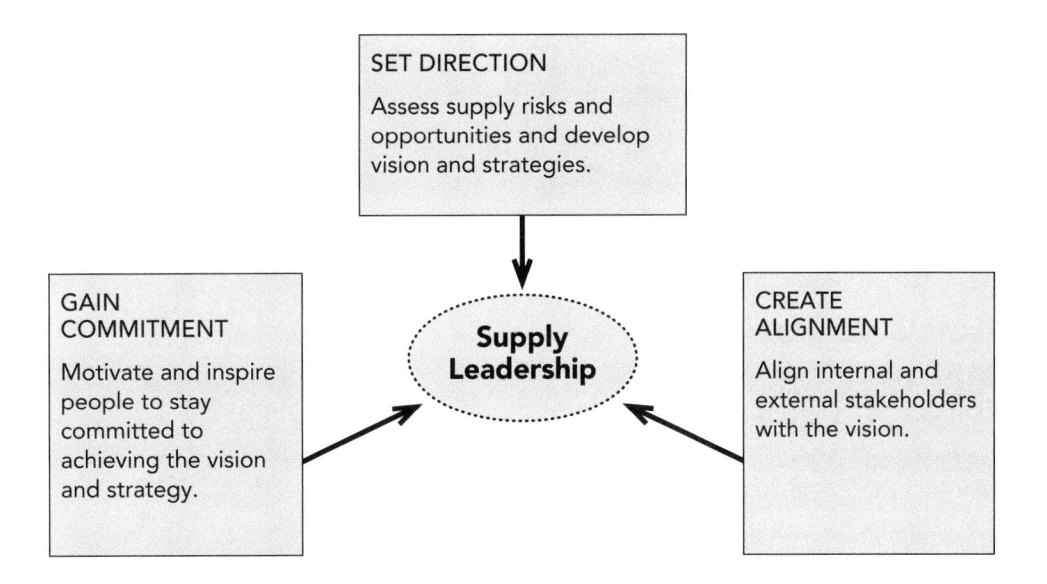

SET DIRECTION
Assess supply risks and opportunities and develop vision and strategies.

GAIN COMMITMENT
Motivate and inspire people to stay committed to achieving the vision and strategy.

Supply Leadership

CREATE ALIGNMENT
Align internal and external stakeholders with the vision.

What Is Management?

Management means, in the last analysis, the substitution of thought for brawn and muscle, of knowledge for folkways and superstition, and of cooperation for force. It means the substitution of responsibility for obedience to rank, and of authority of performance for the authority of rank.

PETER DRUCKER[45]

The root to the English word *management* is the Italian word *maneggiare*, the French word *manege* and the Latin *manus*, which all mean "to handle," in its original meaning to control a horse. In 1579, the English word was extended to other objects or businesses besides horses. The word *manager* came into use in 1588 and referred to one who manages, and in 1705 this term came to mean specifically "one who conducts a house of business or public institution." According to the 2013 edition of *Merriam-Webster's Dictionary*, management means "1) the act or art of managing: the conducting or supervising of something (as a business); 2) judicious use of means to accomplish an end; and 3) the collective body of those who manage or direct an enterprise." From the earliest of times, managing was associated with handling things. The things that managers "handle" and the tools they use to "handle" things change to fit the times.

Today, we live in an information age where knowledge, knowledge creation and knowledge management are key to competitive advantage. In his book, *Building Wealth: The New Rules for Individuals, Companies and Nations in a Knowledge-Based Economy*, Lester Thurow says that knowledge will replace natural resources as the asset most critical to economic success.[46] This modern concept is driven in large part by the easy accessibility to vast stores of knowledge brought to us by rapidly advancing technology. The challenges are (1) how to manage technology, (2) how to manage knowledge workers, and (3) how to manage the complexity of a global economy. For a manager, these tasks are ever-present.

What Do Managers Do?

According to Henry Mintzberg, academic and author, managerial work involves interpersonal roles, informational roles and decisional roles. These roles require skills — namely, developing peer relationships, carrying out negotiations, motivating subordinates, resolving conflicts, establishing networks and disseminating information, making decisions with little or ambiguous information, and allocating resources.[47]

Chris Chen described the following management behaviors that keep complex systems in order:

- *Planning and budgeting*. Planning and budgeting behaviors include setting time-phased performance measures, establishing targets and goals, defining detailed steps to accomplish these goals and allocating resources.
- *Organizing and staffing*. These behaviors ensure that the organization has the capacity

to carry out goals. They include creating the organizational structure: who reports to whom, who has decision-making authority and how information flows; defining job roles; interviewing and selecting organization members; and monitoring job performance.
- *Providing supervision and problem-solving.* These behaviors include monitoring results versus the plan, identifying deviations or exceptions, and solving problems or disputes.[48]

Theories of Management

The development of management thought and practices can be traced back to early human organizations. It was the Industrial Revolution of the 1800s (the first Industrial Revolution) that catalyzed the movement to find ways to increase efficiency and profits in the new factory environment enabled by power-driven machinery. The appendix at the end of this chapter provides a quick reference to major management theories. The major contribution of each theory provides the thread connecting current management thought and behavior with the origins of these ideas.

Western management thought ruled for many decades in most large, multinational organizations. Then the success of many Japanese companies based on quality and lean thinking infused Japanese management theories into many organizations around the world. The challenge with any culturally based theory is transplanting that theory successfully to a different culture. For example, early adopters of just-in-time or total quality practices in Western organizations often failed miserably because American workers and American management did not approach teams, quality and work in the same way the Japanese did. Likewise, Western ways of managing may not work in other cultures for similar reasons. The emerging Indian-inspired management theory of creating value and creating social justice may not take the same form in organizations around the world. However, the globalization of business and management thought indicates a move toward globalized management theory adapted to fit local cultures, customs and norms. "Think global, act local" applies. This is especially relevant to any discussion of motivation.

Motivational Theories[49]

The extent to which a manager is successful in motivating and developing employees depends largely on his or her own skill in creating an operating environment that elicits voluntary dedication and the desire to excel among departmental employees. An effective manager of human capital involves employees in the decision-making processes in an attempt to effect a harmonious blending of individual and departmental objectives.

As a basis for creating such an environment, it is important that a manager understand the basic factors that motivate individuals, as well as the relationship between motivation and ensuing behavioral patterns. Three major schools of thought emerged to explain motivation and its relationship to performance: (1) content theory focuses on the needs of the individual, (2) process theory focuses on the variables that influence and motivate behavior, and (3) reinforcement theory focuses on the influence of consequences on behavior.

Content Theory: Maslow's Hierarchy of Needs. One of the most well-known and widely accepted content theories was developed by Abraham Maslow. His theory, Maslow's Hierarchy of Needs, holds that the satisfaction of basic human needs, in varying degrees, produces certain somewhat predictable behavior patterns. In Maslow's hierarchy, physiological and security needs are more basic and concrete than other needs. On the other hand, social, esteem and growth needs are abstract and more difficult to recognize. He suggests that each lower-order need must be at least partially fulfilled before the next higher-level need becomes dominant in terms of an individual's motivation.

In practice, assuming that concrete needs are reasonably well fulfilled, supply managers should attempt sequentially to provide satisfaction first for each employee's social needs, then for his or her esteem needs, and finally for his or her growth needs. Progressive satisfaction of each of these types of needs tends to produce a higher and more positive level of motivation.

Herzberg's Motivation-Hygiene Theory. A related and somewhat more application-oriented theory of motivation was developed by Frederick Herzberg and his associates during the 1950s. Herzberg's Motivation-Hygiene theory (sometimes called the "two-factor" theory) separates motivational factors into two categories: (1) those intrinsic to the job, and (2) those extrinsic to the job.

According to this theory, for most people the major causes of job satisfaction — and, thus, motivation — stem largely from the work itself in the form of intrinsic job-related rewards. These rewards include achievement, recognition, responsibility, personal growth and advancement. An individual gains these rewards (typically in a developmental sequence) by good job performance.

Extrinsic factors that lie outside the job itself are not considered motivators in a positive sense. Factors such as working conditions, pay, relations with coworkers, supervisory style and organizational policies tend to be "dissatisfiers" if they do not exist at an acceptable level. It seems that most people expect some minimum level of satisfaction with respect to these peripheral elements of the work environment. Beyond this threshold level, however, enhancement of these extrinsic factors does not turn them into "satisfiers" that produce a stronger positive motivation to any significant extent. Thus, Herzberg terms them "hygiene" factors.

McClelland's Achievement Motivation Theory. As discussed in the section on leadership, McClelland identified three needs that motivate human behavior: the need for (1) power, (2) affiliation, and (3) achievement. From a managerial perspective, an assessment of employees along these lines may help a manager determine the types of activities in which individual employees might perform best, the work environments that might be most conducive for success and the rewards that might motivate.

Expectancy Theory. Another approach to understanding employee motivation more recently suggested by Victor Vroom, Lyman Porter and Edward Lawler is called the Expectancy theory.[50] According to this process theory, an individual's course of action will be guided heavily by two factors:

1. The importance or value attached to a successful outcome of the action, and
2. The individual's assessment of his or her ability to achieve a successful outcome of the action.

This rather common sense concept holds that people will select alternatives that they believe to be both attainable and highly rewarding.

Equity Theory. Another process theory of motivation is Equity theory. Equity theorists argue that the motivation level of employees is determined by how fairly or equitably they believe their work is judged in comparison to others' work. Each employee will make this assessment, and the outcome (positive or negative) will impact job motivation and performance. The original concept focused on pay, but other variables have been included in more recent research.

Reinforcement Approach. The Reinforcement approach to motivation is based on the work of B.F. Skinner on operant conditioning. The basic concept is that individuals will be motivated to continue behavior if the consequences are favorable, and they will be motivated to stop or alter behavior if the consequences are unfavorable.

Measurement and Reward/Incentive Programs. Incentive programs are designed to inspire appropriate behaviors by sharing the benefits of cost reduction and other financial improvements with those who help bring them about. For the procurement function, incentive programs may be designed to reward and motivate employees of the function and/or suppliers to the organization.

At a large consumer products company, for instance, the reward system has been changed to look at measures beyond profit, including total shareholder return — cash, profit and stock price, profit and loss, working capital and capital investment, forecast accuracy, and working capital in terms of operating cash flow. Procurement is rewarded for getting the best value, including price, supplier innovation, capital investment, and so on. Customer service logistics is rewarded for on-time delivery, perfect order and combining enough volume to ship efficiently. Engineering is rewarded for service to business units on corporate initiatives, broad application of its ideas, development of new ideas, and service. Total delivered cost is key to the product supply manager. The business unit is rewarded for delivering projects on time, within budget and for complexity reduction.[51]

Departmental performance measurement is discussed in greater detail in Chapter 11, and supplier performance measurement is more thoroughly explained in *Foundation of Supply Management* (ISM *Professional Series*).

Management Styles

The views managers hold about theories of motivation, and about people in general, heavily influence the management styles they develop and employ in practice. The application of certain theories of motivation produces a related management style. Frederick Taylor is generally accorded the distinction of being the "father of scientific management." In studying the elements of work and job design at the turn of the century, Taylor observed that the output of individual workers increased as a job was made more specialized. Removal of the elements of planning and control, as well as some peripheral operational elements, permitted the individual to become more proficient at the core job activities and become more productive. Subsequently, the concepts of functional job specialization and detailed job supervision became well accepted as a basic management technique. When carried beyond a certain point, however, functional specialization can produce repetitive, monotonous and, at times, demotivating jobs. In recent years, this traditional approach has been tempered or supplemented with a variety of human-centered (as opposed to job-centered) approaches. Among these are Deming's 14 Points for Management, McGregor's Theory X and Theory Y, Ouchi's Theory Z and the team concept.

> *Long-term commitment to new learning and new philosophy is required of any management that seeks transformation. The timid and the fainthearted, and the people that expect quick results, are doomed to disappointment.*
>
> W. EDWARDS DEMING[52]

Deming's 14 Points for Management. W. Edwards Deming was a consultant in statistical studies and a professor of statistics at New York University. He is best known for his work in applying statistical methods to the improvement of quality in manufacturing. His work was the basis for the Japanese quality movement in the 1950s and, finally, recognition and application in the United States in the 1980s. The Union of Japanese Scientists and Engineers, supported by Japanese industry, instituted the annual Deming Prizes, a sum of money awarded to a Japanese scholar for his or her contributions in statistical theory or its application, and a medal to a Japanese company for using statistical methods for the advancement of precision and the dependability of the product.

Deming's 14 points for management apply to all types of organizations, small ones as well as large ones, the service industry as well as manufacturing, and to a division within a company. According to the W. Edwards Deming Institute, listed below are the 14 points:

1. Create constancy of purpose toward improvement of product and service, with the aim to become competitive, stay in business and provide jobs.
2. Adopt the new philosophy. We are in a new economic age. Western management must awaken to the challenge, learn its responsibilities and take on leadership for change.
3. Cease dependence on inspection to achieve quality. Eliminate the need for inspection on a mass basis by building quality into the product in the first place.
4. End the practice of awarding business on the basis of price tag. Instead, minimize total cost. Move toward a single supplier for any one item, on a long-term relationship of loyalty and trust.
5. Improve constantly and forever the system of production and service, to improve

quality and productivity, and thus constantly decrease costs.
6. Institute training on the job.
7. Institute leadership. The aim of supervision should be to help people, machines and gadgets to do a better job. Supervision of management is in need of overhaul, as well as supervision of production workers.
8. Drive out fear, so that everyone may work effectively for the organization.
9. Break down barriers between departments. People in research, design, sales and production must work as a team, to foresee problems of production and in use that may be encountered with the product or service.
10. Eliminate slogans, exhortations and targets for the workforce asking for zero defects and new levels of productivity. These exhortations only create adversarial relationships, for the bulk of the causes of low quality and low productivity belong to the system and thus lie beyond the power of the workforce.
    - Eliminate work standards (quotas) on the factory floor. Substitute leadership.
    - Eliminate management by objective. Eliminate management by numbers or numerical goals. Substitute leadership.
11. Remove barriers that rob the hourly worker of his or her right to pride of workmanship. The responsibility of supervisors must be changed from sheer numbers to quality.
12. Remove barriers that rob people in management and in engineering of their right to pride of workmanship. This means, inter alia, abolishment of the annual or merit rating and of management by objective.
13. Institute a vigorous program of education and self-improvement.
14. Put everybody in the company to work to accomplish the transformation. The transformation of the organization is everybody's job.[53]

Theory X and Theory Y. In the 1960s, Douglas McGregor developed his widely known "Theory X - Theory Y" approach to management. McGregor found that many managers employing the traditional approach treated their subordinates as though they were lazy, uncreative, undisciplined and generally not interested in doing a good job. He called these characteristics Theory X assumptions about the nature of people. In the work environment, Theory X assumptions tend to lead to an autocratic, close supervision style of management.

In contrast to Theory X, McGregor proposed another set of assumptions —Theory Y— that he believed were more consistent with the underlying nature of most people. Theory Y assumptions presume the following:

1. Work is a natural activity, just like recreation and rest.
2. Under appropriate conditions, most people tend to accept and to seek responsibility.
3. Creativity and imagination are possessed to a reasonable extent by a large number of people, but are not fully utilized in most jobs.
4. Most people naturally take pride in what they do and, consequently, want to do a good job if they think the job is worthwhile.

McGregor holds that managers who genuinely believe Theory Y assumptions will employ a participative management style, designed to involve subordinates more actively in the total planning/operating/controlling process. According to McGregor, the end result should be greater development of individuals' capabilities and greater fulfillment of individuals' personal goals for self-actualization.[54]

Theory Z. In the early 1980s, William Ouchi conducted an intensive study of major Japanese organizations to identify the management characteristics that contribute significantly to their success. He found one common thread running throughout the total fabric of Japanese management. Virtually all Japanese firms employ a companywide managerial philosophy built around an overriding concern for the individual employees and managers alike. The extensive use of quality circles and other techniques of participative management appears to the Western observer to represent, in part, an extension of the Theory Y concept. Ouchi calls this Japanese approach Theory Z. In addition, Theory Z successfully integrates achievement of personal goals of employees with the collective goals of the organization. Four key elements that characterize this type of management are listed below:

1. Long-term employment;
2. Slow but steady advancement to higher-level positions;
3. Shared decision-making at all levels of the organization; and
4. Intense individual loyalty to the organization.[55]

As noted previously, one's management style can assume two broad orientations: (1) an employee (or human orientation), and (2) a job (or production orientation). Few managers use a style that focuses completely on one orientation, or the other. In daily operations most managers employ a mix of the two orientations, depending on their commitments concerning the nature and motivation of their subordinates. Additionally, as the type of job and situational environment change, a perceptive manager will vary the management mix to suit the circumstances at hand. One of the management styles that attempts to meld the human orientation with the job orientation is the use of the team concept.

Teams and Teamwork

The focus on teamwork has received such widespread attention in recent history that it may be hard for some to comprehend that as early as 1945 Elton Mayo (famous for the Hawthorne studies) wrote in *The Social Problems of an Industrial Civilization* about the importance of groups.[56] He was interested in methods of understanding the behavior of groups, whether formally organized and recognized by management or self-constituted, informal organizations.

Today, many organizations use teams to accomplish organizational objectives. The supply management function is no exception. New product design teams, process improvement teams, source selection teams and system implementation teams, to name a few, may include team members or team leaders from the supply function. Some procurement teams are comprised solely of procurement department staff, while some may include personnel from other functions in the organization (cross-functional teams) and/or suppliers. At Shell Oil, for example, a cross-functional team reduced the total cost of ownership of PCs by more than 25 percent by (1) consolidating purchases with two major suppliers, (2) decentralizing buying decisions to the department level, (3) implementing electronic ordering, and (4) establishing a dedicated PC support group.[57]

Regardless of its composition, a team is made up of a collection of people who work or function together in varying degrees to achieve a common goal. Many variations on the team concept exist, ranging from informal teams to highly structured to self-directed teams.

Informal Work Groups. Within every formal organization, experience demonstrates the existence of one or more informal groups. Typically, these groups are fairly small and structured informally around specific interests of their members. They may be social groups, special interest groups or sometimes pressure groups pushing for change. Whatever the case, these informal groups are an integral part of the organization, and their attitudes and actions can either assist or hinder the attainment of objectives.

A wise manager uses the potential influence of informal groups in a constructive manner. To do this, he or she must first recognize the existence of such a group and identify the informal group leader(s). Then, by practicing the concepts of open communication and group involvement in the decision-making process, the manager attempts to align the objectives of the informal group with the objectives of the department. This represents an extension of the participative management strategy employed in dealing with individuals and formal work groups within the department/organization. Specific approaches that can be used include the following:

1. Solicit appropriate input on decisions that affect individuals and the informal group through various individual, committee and brainstorming techniques. Use this input to arrive at genuinely group-oriented decisions whenever possible.
2. Create and develop a work climate and a reward system that encourage teamwork and cooperation.
3. Develop informal group cohesiveness that produces a positive influence on the activities of the formal work group.

The manager's goal in using this integrative approach is to promote cooperation of the various groups, formal and informal, in daily activities that contribute to attaining the department's overall objectives.

Formal Teams. Formal teams are made up of individuals who are designated members of a formal group. Cross-functional teams are assembled for many reasons in an organization, including product quality improvement; process improvements; sourcing, evaluating or selecting a supplier; or new product development.

For example, when Jill Bossi, C.P.M. took the role of the American Red Cross' first chief procurement officer, she restructured and created formal cross-functional teams to improve processes around the principles of "Simplicity, Synergy and Savings — S3." She restructured to create teams that could work closely with each of the business units. The teams included contracting, procurement, warehousing and real estate, saving US$31.4 million in the first 18 months, and winning the 2012 Institute for Supply Management® — Michigan State University Awards for Excellence in Supply Management award in the Organization/Structure category.[58]

Group or Team Management. Managing a team or group of any size requires the skills and attributes described by Chris Chen earlier in this chapter. Chen's description of leaders as individuals who set direction, align people, and motivate and inspire means that leaders empower others to work together to achieve the vision. Empowerment works to build people so they will develop and act, often without supervision, to jointly contribute to the organization and themselves.

Empowerment includes being empowered (creating power for oneself), giving empowerment (helping others grow toward a state of empowerment) and an empowering environment (giving power to other groups for organizational benefit). For empowerment to work there must be a vision of where the organization needs to go and a strategy for getting it there. Managers need to delegate more and employees must have more to say in daily and future work. Implementing empowerment requires serious background work; preparation of all people involved; careful training; and the development of interpersonal skills, incentives, resources and action plans.

Emerging Leadership Trends

Much of the current focus on leadership today revolves around flexibility, adaptability, collaboration and information sharing. Change is fast, and ubiquitous availability of a great deal of information creates opportunities as well as hazards. There are emerging issues of privacy, while at the same time organizations are being encouraged and even pushed into greater participation in social media.

The emerging workforce wants to feel empowered and involved. Individuals from diverse ethnicities, cultural backgrounds and belief systems expect — and have the right — to be included in decision-making. These different perspectives create the opportunity for synergistic workplace solutions as well as the opportunity to serve new markets. Some of the keys to success in this emerging model include flexibility, adaptability and acceptance. Balancing control and access to information with transparency is essential in today's competitive environment.

Management of the Supply Process

The many changes in the way business is conducted have had a huge impact on the way the supply management function is managed. Technology allows organizations to automate and streamline many of the activities that were historically considered the primary activities of purchasers. Even with the delays and problems that occur with the implementation of any new technology, the changes in the way that goods and services are bought and sold have allowed those in the procurement function to move from a transaction-oriented activity to a knowledge and relationship-oriented role. The alignment of supply strategy with organizational strategy, the focus on the value chain starting with the needs and wants of the end customer, and the drive to identify and focus on core competencies have all led to the realization that the supply process must be managed differently than it has been in the past.

If the supply function is to make a strategic and operational contribution to the organization, then how the function is organized, managed and evaluated matters. The objective of supply management is to capture the contribution of the supply base to the organization. Suppliers carry influence. Therefore, the management of suppliers is critical to the success of the organization. Also, because of the influence of suppliers on an organization's success, it is too important to leave to just one department. As the procurement side of the organization comes into the spotlight, managers and owners of the procurement process must drastically change their orientation to internal customers, suppliers and end consumers. Linking the contribution of the procurement function and the suppliers to the overall mission of the organization is critical if the procurement function is to truly make the greatest contribution to the organization. Working with, not against, internal customers is a necessity. As Dave Nelson, former Chief Procurement Officer at Delphi, Corporate Officer and Senior Vice President of Purchasing and Corporate Affairs at Honda of America Manufacturing and Vice President of Worldwide Supply Management at Deere & Company noted in addressing a group of students in fall 2011, "If there was one thing I could have done differently in my career, it would have been to be more service oriented to the internal customer."[59] Interdependence among functional areas requires the ability to cross functional boundaries and forge alliances within the organization as well as outside of it. Focusing on the results of supply management professionals and the supply management department rather than on activities is the difficult, but essential task of those leading, managing and assessing the supply function. For best results, the role of the supply function in the organization must first be understood.

Figure 1-4 illustrates the major roles of the supply manager or management team. These roles are discussed in detail in Chapters 5 through 11.

Figure 1-4: Major Management Roles

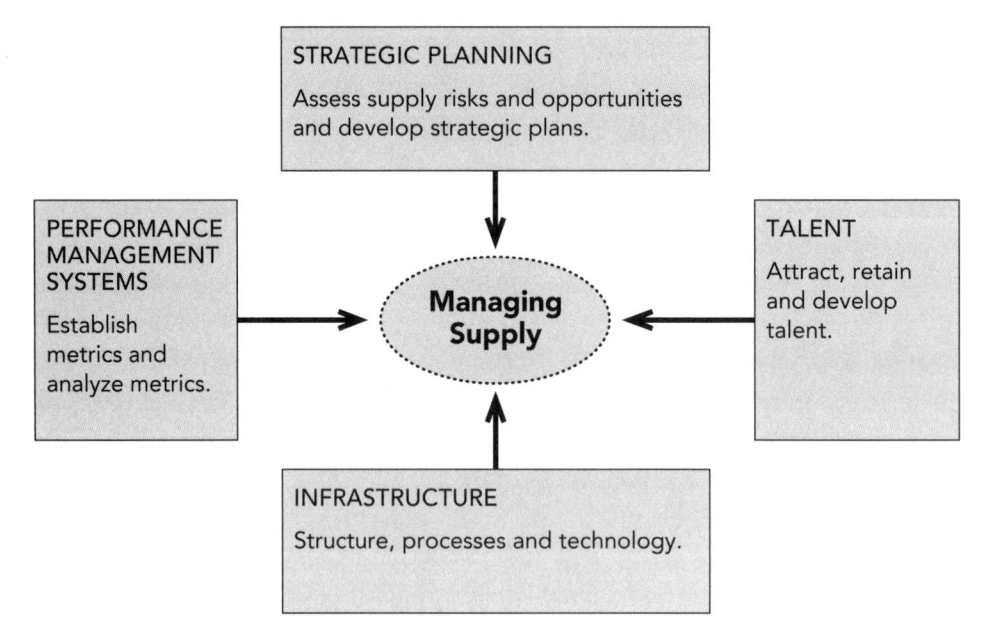

STRATEGIC PLANNING
Assess supply risks and opportunities and develop strategic plans.

PERFORMANCE MANAGEMENT SYSTEMS
Establish metrics and analyze metrics.

Managing Supply

TALENT
Attract, retain and develop talent.

INFRASTRUCTURE
Structure, processes and technology.

Source: PRACTIX, CAPS Research, Volume 8 (July 2005), 3.

Summary

Effective leaders and managers are in high demand; however, it is important to recognize the differences between leading and managing. Leaders' behaviors include setting direction for the supply management organization, making sure the right people are working in his or her supply group, and motivating and inspiring them. Leaders have emotional intelligence along with characteristics of self-awareness, self-management, social awareness and relationship management — and employ all of these traits to achieve organizational and department-level goals and results.

Managers, on the other hand, "handle" people and things, and focus on planning and budgeting, organizing and staffing, and providing supervision and problem-solving. There are many management theories and styles, including W. Edwards Deming's 14 Points for Management, that help guide managers in all types and sizes of organizations in handling daily tasks. Teamwork across the organization is becoming more and more critical to success, and managers implement and manage formal and informal teams and work groups to accomplish department goals.

Becoming both an effective leader and an effective manager may be the biggest challenge facing each person in an organization, whether he or she is in a formal or informal leadership or management role and whether he or she manages hundreds of people or just himself or herself. Increasingly complex environments coupled with the need for rapid, dramatic change add to the pressure to deliver results quickly. These situations reinforce the importance of both the what and why, and the how and when.

Key Points
1. Leaders and managers do different things in organizations.
2. Leaders have three primary responsibilities: set direction, create alignment and gain commitment.
3. Managers have corresponding tasks. While the leader sets direction, the manager assesses risks and develops plans; the leader creates alignment and the manager organizes and staffs; the leader gains commitment and the manager assesses performance and establishes internal controls.
4. Leadership today revolves around flexibility, adaptability, collaboration and information sharing.

Chapter 1
Appendix: Timeline of Major Theories of Management

Dates	School of Thought	Major Contributors	Major Contributions
1850s to 1860s	Systematic Management	Daniel McCallum Henry Poor	• Organization = division of labor • Communication = management reporting system • Information = analysis of reports to improve operations
From the 1880s on	Scientific Management and Operations Research	Frederick W. Taylor Henry L. Gantt Frank Gilbreth Lillian Moller Gilbreth Harrington Emerson	• Application of scientific study • Efficiency studies • Wage systems and motivation • Specialized management knowledge • Use of mathematical models in managerial decision-making
1880s through early 1900s	Administrative Theory or Universal Theory of Management	Henri Fayol	• Universality of management • Principles of managerial thinking • Elements of management: planning, organizing, command, coordination and control
1920s and 1930s	Behavioralists' Theory	Hugo Munsterberg Walter Dill Scott Mary Parker Follett Elton Mayo	• Focused on social needs of employees and motivation • Applied psychology to business • Link physical and mental qualifications with ideal psychological conditions and provide optimal motivational influences • Concept of working with, not under, someone
Early 1900s on	Organization Theory	Max Weber Chester Barnard Herbert Simon	• The central unit of analysis is the total organization • Weber's model of bureaucracy: organization must be effective and efficient to be successful • Function of management is to keep organization (decision-making structure) running • Limit decision-making scope through policies, procedures, hierarchy, and so on.

CHAPTER 1: Leading and Managing

Dates	School of Thought	Major Contributors	Major Contributions
1950s in Japan and 1980s in the United States	The Deming System of Profound Knowledge	W. Edwards Deming	• The four related parts of profound knowledge: 1. Appreciation for a system 2. Knowledge about variation 3. Theory of knowledge 4. Psychology • Also included 14 Points for Management
1960s and 1970s	Systems Theory	Ludwig von Bartalanffy	• Identify parallels among disciplines • Integrate into one theory
1970s on	Contingency Theory	Fred Luthans Todd I. Stewart	• Focuses on flexibility and adaptability • No universal management principles; circumstantial
1980s on	Excellent Companies or Best Practices	Thomas J. Peters Robert H. Waterman	• Attributes of excellent organizations: 1. Bias for action 2. Closeness to the customer 3. Autonomy/entrepreneurship 4. Productivity through people 5. Hands-on, value-driven 6. Stick to the knitting 7. Simple form; lean staff 8. Simultaneous loose and tight properties
1980s and early 1990s	Management by Objectives	Peter Drucker Douglas McGregor Edward Schleh George Ordiorne	• Integrates planning, participation, communication, managerial development, performance appraisal

Dates	School of Thought	Major Contributors	Major Contributions
1980s on	Continuous Improvement (Kaizen)	Japanese management theorists such as Shigeo Shingo and Taiithi Ohno	• Collaborative, collegiate, people-based management that extends beyond the borders of the organization and aims at long-term payoffs • Kaizen or continuous improvement: Anything and everything can be improved. If it can be, it must be; otherwise, you are creating muda, or waste. • Meikiki, or "foresight with discernment," is how the Japanese describe a process that, of course, they fully understand and apply. • Concept I: "Change the basis of competition continually" (as with small copiers) • Concept II: "Multiple sources of competitive advantage" • Concept III: "Organizing to achieve new levels of agility" • Concept IV: "Sophisticated collaboration" with suppliers and customers to new heights • Concept V: "Focusing on core capabilities to execute strategy successfully"
1980s on	Toyota Production System	Taiichi Ohno	• Production depends on people, not just machines.
1980s on	Lean Organization Theory	Shigeo Shingo James P. Womack Daniel T. Jones	• Precisely specify value by specific product. • Identify the value stream for each product. • Make value flow without interruption • Let the customer pull value from the producer. • Pursue perfection.

CHAPTER 2

A leader takes people where they want to go. A great leader takes people where they don't necessarily want to go but ought to be.

— ROSALYNN CARTER
FORMER FIRST LADY, UNITED STATES[1]

Setting Direction

Setting direction is the primary task of a leader or leadership team. It involves clarifying the core values of the organization; identifying future opportunities and risks; and devising a compelling vision, mission and strategies. According to John P. Kotter, Konosuke Matsushita Professor of Leadership Emeritus at Harvard Business School, "A leader gathers a broad range of data and looks for patterns, relationships and linkages that help explain things. He or she creates visions and strategies that describe what a business, technology or organizational culture should become over time and articulates a feasible way to get there."[2]

The chapter is organized into three sections: (1) creating a values-based organization, (2) opportunities and risks, and (3) developing vision and strategies. From a leadership perspective, how these actions unfold and what they entail depends in part on the style, role and attributes of the leader that were discussed in Chapter 1. The chapter concludes with an appendix that details the ISM *Principles of Sustainability and Social Responsibility*.

Chapter Objectives
- Describe how the leader creates a values-based organization.
- Explain how opportunities and risks might be identified and assessed by the leader or leadership team.
- Discuss how a vision is developed.
- Explore how strategies are developed to support the attainment of the vision.

Creating a Values-Based Organization

If you lead the people with correctness, who will dare not to be correct?

— CONFUCIUS

The supply management leader and the leadership team develop the core values of the supply organization in alignment with those of the organization and instill those values in the supply management organization through words and actions. The supply leader is the primary driver of both alignment and adherence to established core values throughout strategy execution. To understand this role, it is important to briefly discuss values and ethics (covered in greater detail in *Foundation of Supply Management* (ISM *Professional Series*). In this book, coverage focuses on the establishment of core values to guide the decisions and behavior of supply management employees, other internal stakeholders and suppliers.

What Are Values?

The English word *value* comes from the French verb *valoir*, meaning "to be worth." Our values describe how we intend to operate, on a day-to-day basis, as we pursue our vision. Some organizations develop a set of core values with and for stakeholders to define behavior within the group and behavior with external stakeholders such as customers, suppliers and the community. The vision statement tells where the organization wants to go, and the value statement describes the means (how) the organization will use to get there. Globalization increases the pressure on each person to fully understand and live the core values of the organization.

Ethical principles are the rules of conduct that derive from ethical values. For example, honesty is a value that governs behavior in the form of principles such as tell the truth, do not deceive, be candid, do not cheat. In this way, values give rise to principles in the form of specific dos and don'ts. Figure 2-1 illustrates the relationship between values and behavior.

Figure 2-1: The Relationship of Values and Behavior

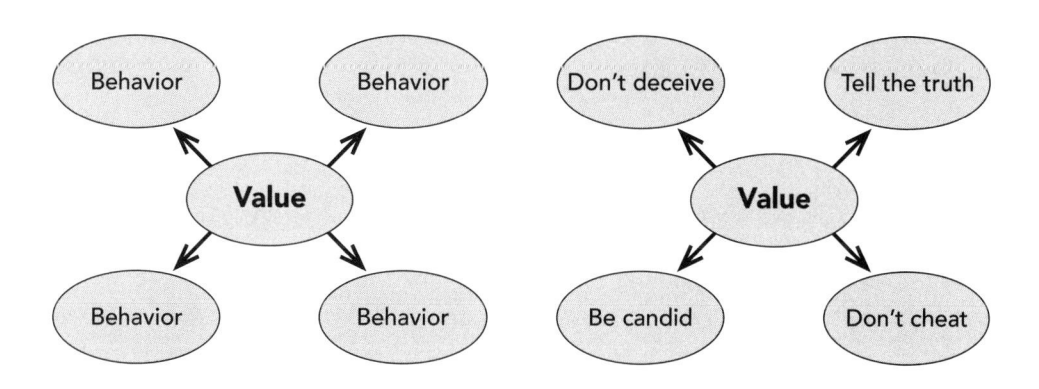

Ethics and Action. Ethics is about putting principles into action. Consistency between what we say we value and what our actions say we value is a matter of integrity. According to the Josephson Institute, "It is also about self-restraint. Not doing what you have the *power* to do. An act isn't proper simply because it is permissible or you can get away with it. Not doing what you have the *right* to do. There is a big difference between what you have the right to do and what is right to do. Not doing what you *want* to do. In the well-worn turn of phrase, an ethical person often chooses to do more than the law requires and less than the law allows."[3]

While the concern with ethical behavior in business is not new, the international business environment presents significant and unprecedented ethical challenges. A recent large scale research project confirms that successful leaders in developed economies lead differently than successful leaders in emerging economies. There are also differences among emerging and developed economies. As a result of this, the research found that expatriate programs are on the decline — companies can lead more effectively by using local talent when possible.[4] The challenge for any person operating in another culture is twofold: how to avoid moral imperialism, demanding that international organizations and colleagues act just like us; and against cultural relativism, conforming to whatever behavior is the local norm. This challenge exists for each of us whether we are Japanese sourcing in Vietnam, German sourcing in China or North American sourcing in Mexico.

What Can a Leader Do?

The best thing you can give as a leader is a reason to trust. People want to trust. They're hungry for it. But they're selective. They'll only give it to a motivator, a communicator, a teacher, a real person. Someone who in good times and bad always does the right thing.

— JEFFREY R. IMMELT
CEO OF GE, DARTMOUTH, 2004[5]

Armed with a better understanding of values and ethics, the question remains, how do leaders develop core values for an organization and embed them in the actions of each and every stakeholder, especially in a large global organization? Leaders can take several actions to focus everyone's attention on how results are obtained, to support the practice of ethical decision-making and to guide the behavior of others. These actions are exhibiting ethical behavior; creating a strong ethical culture; establishing a code of conduct, including ethical issues in employment decisions; formally including ethics in performance evaluations; and engaging in meaningful ethics training.

Exhibiting Ethical Behavior. Research findings suggest that the higher the achieved level of moral reasoning development, the more likely the person is to make an ethical decision. Leaders can support the development of moral reasoning through training and example. Transparency in the decision-making process demonstrates the thinking process used to resolve an ethical dilemma.

Creating a Strong Ethical Culture. Leaders make a critical contribution to ethics by creating a strong organizational culture that sets the tone at the top and establishes expectations about the use of values in guiding behavior and business outcomes.

Establishing a Code of Conduct for the Supply Organization. Most procurement organizations have written codes of conduct for supply management personnel as well as suppliers. *Foundation of Supply Management* (ISM *Professional Series*) discusses this issue in greater detail. ISM's *Principles and Standards of Ethical Supply Management Conduct* can be accessed at www.ism.ws. Ethical concerns extend beyond the walls of the organization, and greater focus is now on ethical supply chains.

Including Ethical Issues in Performance Evaluations and Employment Decisions. Leaders should openly include and weigh ethics when deciding who to hire, fire, retain or promote. They should express this thinking in terms of behaviors so that it is evident how organizational values are translated into actions. Recall the Nissan example in Chapter 1 in which the CEO announced that he would voluntarily resign if he did not achieve the required results in turning the company around.

Engaging in Meaningful Ethics Training. Leaders should avoid once-a-year mandatory reviews and individual sign-offs on the code of conduct if this is the only time employees hear the word *ethics*. Leaders should find ways to engage in frequent discussions about the ethics of supply situations and use real experiences as learning opportunities. They should support the development of moral reasoning through training.

Core values are the guiding principles behind the actions of everyone in the supply organization. Supply management leaders are well positioned to play an organizationwide leadership role in the policy and practices related to an organization's core values as well as the corresponding core values of the supply management group. For example, Deere & Company focuses on its longevity when it states, "For nearly 175 years, John Deere has benefitted by strong, decisive leaders at its helm, dedicated to the core principles of integrity, quality, commitment and innovation."[6] Figure 2-2 lists the core values of the procurement group of the Lenovo Group, Beijing, China.

Figure 2-2: Lenovo's Core Values — Global Procurement

Lenovo procurement embodies those core values of customer service, innovative and entrepreneurial spirit, accuracy and truth-seeking, trustworthiness and integrity that the company and all its divisions hold to the highest esteem.

Customer service	Vigorously seek a full understanding of the capabilities, wants and needs of the entire supply chain: Lenovo's customers, our internal clients, our suppliers and our suppliers' suppliers. Actively articulate both Lenovo's and our suppliers' viewpoints, and facilitate communication at all levels and functions.
Innovative and entrepreneurial spirit	Continually seek to improve and never be satisfied with anything less than a competitive advantage in technology, price, quality, delivery, responsiveness, speed and efficiency.
Accuracy and truth-seeking	Firmly believe in and insist on true cross-functional participation to ensure our business decisions are based on carefully understood facts.
Trustworthiness and integrity	Ensure both Lenovo and suppliers keep the letter and spirit of all agreements. Build long-term relationships with suppliers based on trust, honesty and candor. Never compromise Lenovo's overall best interests in the pursuit of local or divisional interests. Expect teamwork, integrity, respect and excellence from each other.

Source: Lenovo, accessed August 5, 2013, http://www.lenovo.com/global_procurement/us/en/core_values.html

As Figure 2-3 illustrates, Whirlpool Corp. focuses on the importance of its values and how it does business as the key to its success internationally.

Figure 2-3: Whirlpool Corporation's Core Values

Our values are constant and define the way that all Whirlpool Corporation employees are expected to behave and conduct business everywhere in the world.	
Respect	We must trust one another as individuals and value the capabilities and contributions of each person.
Integrity	We must conduct all aspects of business honorably — ever mindful of the longtime Whirlpool Corporation belief that there is no right way to do a wrong thing.
Diversity and Inclusion	We must maintain the broad diversity of Whirlpool people and ideas. Diversity honors differences, while inclusion allows everyone to contribute. Together, we create value.
Teamwork	We must recognize that pride results in working together to unleash everyone's potential, achieving exceptional results.
Spirit of Winning	We must promote a Whirlpool culture that enables individuals and teams to reach and take pride in extraordinary results and further inspire the "Spirit of Winning" in all of us.

Source: Whirlpool®, accessed August 5, 2013, http://www.whirlpoolcorp.com/about/overview.aspx.

The leader is on the way to success if he or she has successfully established core values; these values drive each person's decision-making process and actions. From this base, the supply management leader or leadership team is ready to assess supply opportunities and risks.

Opportunities and Risks

A major precursor to turning a leader's vision into a shared vision is assessing the present state of affairs. For the supply management leader this means taking a high-level view of the present state of the supply management organization to determine the external risks and opportunities, internal strengths and weaknesses, and the past and present vision. The leader or leadership team then thinks about the future and asks: What are the potential changes in markets and products, key stakeholders and constituencies, and the economic, social, technical and political environments? It is only through a thorough and rigorous assessment of the present and a deep exploration of future potential that a vision can be created.

One critical aspect of creating a shared vision is stakeholder analysis. This process includes identifying all the individuals and groups, internally and externally, who have a stake in the outcome; and understanding each stakeholder's underlying interests to invent options that tap into these interests. By doing this early in the visioning process, the leader stands a better chance of getting buy-in and gaining commitment.

This chapter started with the idea that the supply management leader sets direction first by creating a values-based organization. Along with creating and sustaining a values-based supply management organization, the supply leader must continually assess supply risks and opportunities. The following section explores what this means from a leadership perspective. Chapter 5 presents the managerial side of this leadership task and addresses the details of assessing risks and developing business plans.

Recognize and Assess Organization and Supply-Related Opportunities and Risks

The type and number of opportunities and risks that exist for the organization from a supply management perspective vary with the company, industry and economy as a whole, and are dynamic as situations change. Some of the areas where a leader might look for opportunities and risks include growth of markets, especially in low-cost countries or in markets concerned with sustainable products, strategic partnerships, mergers and acquisitions, financial markets and government-industry partnerships.

Growth of Markets. Where do market growth opportunities exist for your organization's products or services? To what extent is your supply base ready and able to support these market incursions? What are the sources of supply base vulnerability? What opportunities and risks might these new markets create from a supply perspective? Also, where are growth opportunities or risks for the supply base? Does the host government and its laws and regulations favor international businesses? Are there legal or regulatory hurdles to overcome? Is there political or social unrest?

Growth of Markets in Low-Cost Countries. Are there growth opportunities for selling or buying in low-cost countries? Has a decision(s) been made to stay out of low-cost countries, to go into cities and countries where operating internationally is well established or to explore second-tier cities that have not suffered from overexposure?

For example, many supply management teams are either considering or already sourcing from low-cost countries such as (rural) China, Vietnam, India and countries in Eastern and Central Europe. The opportunities typically come from abundant low-wage labor for items that offer high savings potential, stable quality and availability. Critical questions include: How stable and mature is the environment? To what extent is there market transparency? Are appropriate laws and intellectual property rights in place? If so, are they enforced? How wide is the regional disparity in economic development, infrastructure, traffic congestion, pollution levels, education levels, wage rates, and so on? How stable do labor costs and other conditions appear? How might these factors affect the supply decision and goals such as savings, cycle time and productivity? In addition, as workers in these countries begin to receive higher wages, they may become potential customers.

Offshoring, defined as "A relocation of business processes (this may include production/manufacturing) to a non-domestic location, usually to reduce costs" (ISM *Glossary* 2014) grew rapidly in the 1990s and 2000s. Increasingly, developed nations are answering the above questions and realizing that the total cost of pursuing low-cost country sourcing or manufacturing is actually equivalent to doing things domestically (homeshoring), or closer to their home country (nearshoring). Nearshoring is formally defined as "A form of outsourcing in which business processes are relocated to locations which are geographically nearer to the buying organization than alternate, more distant supply choices (farshoring), usually to reduce costs; also called "nearshore outsourcing" (ISM *Glossary* 2014). As a result, manufacturing and services are moving offshore at a slower rate. In some cases, they are even being brought back to more developed home countries. This idea of considering all realistic possibilities before making a decision on where to locate is referred to as "rightsourcing."[7]

Growth of Markets Concerned With Sustainable Products and Services. Is there an existing or emerging market for sustainable products and services? If not, is there an opportunity for the organization to capitalize on this trend or to respond to customer demands in this direction? Seventh Generation and Method are among the leading brands of nontoxic household products for a clean home, a healthy family and a safer world. Organic foods retailer Whole Foods Market is generally credited with rapidly and dramatically expanding the market for organic products.

Strategic Partnerships. Is there an opportunity to form a strategic partnership with a for-profit, not-for-profit, nongovernmental organization or governmental organization to understand emerging issues, create business opportunities, capitalize on innovation or avoid negative events or outcomes? The Environmental Defense Fund, the Rainforest Action Network, Carbonfund.org and the World Wildlife Fund are examples of organizations working with multinational companies on a variety of issues, including green product design, carbon offset programs and sustainable harvesting of forest and marine products. The Rocky Mountain Institute (RMI) and Wal-Mart have been working together since 2005 to help reduce Wal-Mart's fossil fuel consumption in retail stores and transportation.[8]

Mergers and Acquisitions. Assess supply-related opportunities from changing internal and external environments through acquisitions, mergers and/or divestitures. What is on the horizon and how well prepared is the supply management group for any eventuality? Are there opportunities that the supply leader sees and wants to bring to the attention of key decision-makers? If a merger or acquisition is under review, the supply management team can provide valuable data and insight into two critical pre-merger questions: (1) Is the proposed deal commercially attractive? (2) Can the organization capture the full potential value of the proposed deal? Post-merger, the supply management team looks for risks to supply continuity and opportunities to capture synergies in five primary areas: contracts, reducing redundancy and complexity, reducing liability exposure, divestiture of assets and global economic considerations.

Financial Markets. Financial markets increasingly recognize and reward organizations exhibiting sustainable business practices. The number of socially responsible investors and funds is growing; sustainability is a key component of socially responsible organizations. A reflection of the growth in socially responsible investing is the Dow Jones Sustainability

World Index created in 1999. The DJSI family is offered cooperatively by RobecoSAM Indices and S&P Dow Jones Indices. The family tracks the stock performance of the world's leading companies in terms of economic, environmental and social criteria.[9] Are there supply opportunities to enhance your organization's reputation and brand image? Is your company's reputation exposed because of any existing supply policies, processes, procedures, contracts or supplier relationships?

Government-Industry Partnership Initiatives. Government agencies have launched programs in partnership with organizations across many industries in areas related to sustainability. Western European countries are among the leaders in sustainability programs at the local, national and European Union level; EU regulations are, in fact, driving some corporate environmental policies for multinational companies. In the United States, the Environmental Protection Agency (EPA) runs numerous industry programs that can contribute to an organization's sustainability efforts, from improving transportation efficiency through SmartWay membership[10], pollution prevention and climate change to product stewardship and green product design. Supply management can play a role by scanning the external environment for opportunities such as suppliers of green products or new technology, and by assessing the needs of internal stakeholders to bring them together with innovations from the supply base.

Assessing Risks

Risk management is the process of "directing or conducting the activities necessary to reduce, eliminate or mitigate the impact of factors that could lead to injury, loss, damage or failure" (ISM *Glossary* 2014). In general, the strategies employed include transferring the risk to another party, avoiding the risk, reducing the negative effect of the risk, and accepting some or all of the consequences of a particular risk. Traditional risk management focuses on risks stemming from physical or legal causes (for example, natural disasters or fires, accidents, death and lawsuits). Financial risk management focuses on risks that can be managed using traded financial instruments. Supply and supplier risk management focuses on risks that are either caused by a supply chain issue or that can be managed through the execution of the appropriate supply strategy. Regardless of the type of risk management, all large organizations have risk management teams; small groups and organizations practice informal, if not formal, risk management.

The Matrix Approach to Risk Assessment. The matrix approach to risk assessment and risk management offers a higher-level focus and graphic display of risk. A matrix is formed with the organization's business units on one axis and a set of high-level risks on the other axis (see Figure 2-4). The number of risks is usually between 12 and 16, although viable models may have as few as four. A team assesses each business unit for each risk, and the results are displayed in the appropriate cell on the matrix: G for low risk, Y for moderate risk, R for high risk and W — or blank — for "not applicable."

Figure 2-4: Example of a Risk Matrix

Risk 5	W	Y	G	R	G
Risk 4	R	Y	R	Y	Y
Risk 3	Y	G	Y	R	G
Risk 2	G	W	G	W	R
Risk 1	G	R	W	W	Y
	BU 1	BU 2	BU 3	BU 4	BU 5

G = Low risk   Y = Moderate risk   R = High risk   W = Not applicable

Advantages of the matrix approach are that it is flexible and quick to implement, and it provides a three-dimensional look at risk by including the cell contents. Although assumptions are not so easily explained, the impact of the graphical representation of risk is enormous.

This approach requires that the assessment team possess a great deal of business knowledge to be credible. In addition, maintenance of the matrix can be challenging, because the assessment must be performed any time a significant change is noted. Tracking possible changes in the business units that would warrant a new assessment can be difficult, depending on the strength of management information systems and reporting. As a result, the matrix does not display the dynamics of the risk profile as easily as a database does. Alternatively, each business unit may create its own matrix using the same risks, but apply them against smaller work groups within the business unit. These assessments can then be combined to create the organization's total risk matrix.

This same approach could be used to focus on supply related risks by business unit. The types of risks that might be applicable are (1) financial risk; (2) operational risk (including end-of-life cycle); (3) brand/reputation risk from either ethical, social responsibility or sustainability issues or organizational culture; (4) legal and regulatory risk (risk of litigation, Sarbanes-Oxley [SOX] compliance, employment law and intellectual property issues); (5) environmental risk; and (6) technical risk. This assessment can be compiled to create a supply and/or supplier risk profile as illustrated in Figure 2-5.

Figure 2-5: Supply Risk Profile by Business Unit

Technical risk	W	Y	G	R	G
Environmental risk	R	Y	R	Y	Y
Legal and regulatory risks	Y	G	Y	R	G
Brand/reputation risk	G	W	G	W	R
Operational risk	G	G	Y	R	W
Financial risk	G	R	W	W	Y
	BU 1	BU 2	BU 3	BU 4	BU 5

G = Low risk   Y = Moderate risk   R = High risk   W = Not applicable

Each risk factor may also be subdivided into specific aspects of risk. Figure 2-6 illustrates the subdivision of the risk factor — availability — into five categories: incoming materials, sourcing process capability, volume capacity, technologically capable, and supplier lead time. In this example, each subcategory is assessed as a showstopper (the process or action comes to a standstill), a high risk, medium risk, low risk or qualified risk. An item rated a "showstopper" is characterized by open or unresolved critical issues that are serious enough to delay a product or service introduction. A high-risk item is characterized by a key problem that may become a "showstopper," such as a reduction in yield, known reliability or defects, variability that has not been qualified or a high level of uncertainty. High-risk items require an action plan for risk mitigation. A moderate-risk item is characterized by a low to moderate impact on product performance. A qualified rating means that all key issues have been resolved and, at most, only minor issues remain. A qualified rating means that all attributes are fully qualified.[11]

Figure 2-6: Example of Risk Assessment for Availability

RISK FACTOR: AVAILABILITY	SHOW-STOPPER	HIGH RISK	MODERATE RISK	LOW RISK	QUALIFIED
Incoming materials	No source identified	Raw material scarcity	Sole sourced with multiple production operations in close proximity	Sole sourced with multiple production operations separated by 50 miles	Multiple sources with no supply shortages
Source process capability	Unknown, new technology or supplier	Manufacturing capability only proved on pilot scale	Manufacturing or service capability demonstrated for a similar material	Data demonstrates process is in specification	Source process is stable and capable
Volume capacity	Availability requirements not supported with existing sources	Suppliers identified; plans to support volumes not in place	Capacity plans developed by supplier and implementation in process	Capacity mostly in place; no known issues	Capacity fully in place
Techno-logically capable	Industry moving toward different standards	Industry movement toward different standards known with no plans to address	Industry movement toward different standards understood with plans to address	Industry adopting multiple standards	Technology chosen is standard
Supplier lead time	No quick turn capability exists at supplier	Quick turn capable for new design is greater than lead time	Supplier lead time reduction plans on track	Quick turn capability for new design lead time or meets goals	Supplier and supplier tooling meet lead time goals

Source: George Zsidisin and Lisa Ellram, "Supply Risk Assessment Analysis," PRACTIX, CAPS Research (June 1999), 9.

A recent CAPS study also highlights the fact that organizations may perform risk assessment on a supplier-by-supplier basis, and modify their behavior and monitoring of the suppliers accordingly. For example, an automotive company has developed a supplier risk identification system that combines supplier financial data (financial statement and key ratio analysis), observed supplier performance data (delivery, quality) and on-site observation to watch trends in supplier risk and provide them with an early warning of potential supplier problems. Supplier risk is rated on a low-medium-high scale. Suppliers rated as high risk are given special attention by a team including procurement, legal and finance to work with them and get them back on track.[12]

The third phase of direction setting is the development of a vision of supply management and a corresponding set of broadly defined strategies to achieve the vision.

Developing Vision and Strategies

> *Perhaps the most distinguishing trait of visionary leaders is that they believe in a goal that benefits not only themselves, but others as well. It is such vision that attracts the psychic energy of other people, and makes them willing to work beyond the call of duty for the organization.*
>
> — JMIHALY CSIKSZENTMIHALYI
> CLAREMONT GRADUATE UNIVERSITY[13]

A vision is a picture of the future you seek to create, described in the present tense, as if it were happening now. A statement of "our vision" shows where we want to go, and what we will be like when we get there. The word comes from the Latin *videre*, which means "to see." This link to seeing is significant; the more richly detailed and visual the image is, the more compelling it will be. Because of its tangible and immediate quality, a vision gives shape and direction to the organization's future.

A clear and compelling vision also helps people set goals to take the organization closer to the vision. As the Roman philosopher Seneca "The Younger" said, "If a man does not know to what port he is steering, no wind is favourable."[14] The leader endeavors to create a sense of shared purpose and destiny. According to Tsun-Yan Hsieh and Sara Yik, both formerly from McKinsey & Co., stated leadership is the starting point of strategy, and top managers must assess the leadership gap in the short, medium and long run for the organization to realize the full potential of opportunities.[15]

A vision statement should be a broad statement that captures the overarching purpose of the organization. It describes what the organization wants to become; it is future-oriented. A concise statement that attracts attention and interests and appeals to the audience is far better than a lengthy statement. Whole Foods Market's motto is "Whole Foods, Whole People, Whole Planet."[16] The Swedish home furnishings company IKEA's vision statement is to "create a better everyday life for the many people."[17] Method Products, which was formed by two college friends to make nontoxic cleaning products that are clean, safe, green, attractive and smell good, has this vision statement: "We're here to make products that work, for you and for the planet."[18] Amazon.com's vision statement is "We seek to be Earth's most customer-centric company for four primary customer sets: consumers, sellers, enterprises and content creators."[19] The Boeing Co.'s vision is "People working together as a global enterprise for aerospace leadership."[20]

A vision statement embodies the future that has been visualized by the leader or leadership team. Whole Foods Market includes this statement in its philosophy: "Our vision statement reflects the hopes and intentions of many people. We do not believe it always accurately portrays the way things currently are at Whole Foods Market so much as the way we would like things to be. It is our dissatisfaction with the current reality, when compared with what is possible, that spurs us toward excellence and toward creating a better person, company and world. When Whole Foods Market fails to measure up to its stated vision, as it inevitably will at times, we should not despair. Rather, let us take up the challenge together to bring our reality closer to our vision. The future we will experience tomorrow is created one step at a time today."[21]

The vision of Deere & Company is "Thriving by helping customers deliver vital resources now, and for generations to come."[22] At Whirlpool, the vision is "Every Home … Everywhere. With Pride, Passion and Performance."[23] The vision of Lenovo is "Becoming the leading personal technology company in the world."[24] These short statements quickly and successfully convey where these organizations are going.

The management of many organizations also adopts a mission statement to express the organization's purpose. The following section provides various examples of mission statements.

Mission: Why Does This Organization Exist?

> *When people can see which direction the leaders are going in it becomes easier to motivate them.*
>
> — JLAKSHMI MITTAL
> PRESIDENT OF THE BOARD OF DIRECTORS AND CEO
> OF ARCELOR MITTAL STEEL COMPANY[25]

Mission comes from the Latin word *mittere*, meaning "to throw, let go or send." Also derived from Latin, the word *purpose* (originally *proponere*) meant "to declare." Whether you call it a mission or purpose, it represents the fundamental reason for the organization's existence. What are we here to do together? For example, the Josephson Institute cited earlier in this chapter adopted the mission: "To improve the ethical quality of society by changing personal and organizational decision-making and behavior."[26]

The mission statement of an organization should flow from its vision. It should concisely answer fundamental questions such as those listed below:
- Who are we?
- Whose needs do we want to meet?
- What needs do we want to meet?
- How do we intend to meet these needs?
- What are our central values?

A supply management organization, for example, might state its mission as: "Establish supplier relationships that bring maximum value to the customers, owners and employees of the enterprise." ABB's statement is "Our mission is to support ABB's business strategy by developing and managing a preferred supply base that enhances ABB's competitiveness and success of our customers."[27]

The mission statement describes the important business capabilities, based on the customers' needs identified in the market research. Themes emerge from the vision statement to form the mission statements for the business. The mission statements provide the basis for measuring success and progress. At Deere, for instance, the strategy or mission is: "For those who cultivate and harvest the land. For those who transform and enrich the land. For those who build upon the land. John Deere is committed to your success."[28]

At Lenovo, the mission (objective) of procurement is "to:
- Drive quality improvements from our suppliers of goods and services;
- Deliver lowest overall cost and greatest competitive advantage; and
- Improve client perception of our values through increased influence and exemplary customer service and support."[29]

At Whirlpool, the mission is "Everyone … Passionately creating loyal customers for life."[30]

It is clear from these examples what the organizations are trying to achieve and how they define and measure success. A generic vision statement for a supply management organization might be: "A team and process that produces supplier contributions to the business and is seen as the world-class benchmark of performance." At IBM, the global procurement mission is "…to achieve the lowest overall cost for goods and services being procured, to ensure that the goods and services provided meet required quality standards and/or customer expectations, and to deliver correct quantities of goods or services at the right global location at the time specified."[31] Because of IBM's large global presence, as noted in Chapter 1, it specifically includes the global aspect of its procurement in its mission statement.

In the early 2000s, LG Electronics (LG) had a vision to be in the global top three by 2010. This vision was supported by a growth strategy, focus on core competencies and a supportive and enabling corporate culture. And, at its foundation, "Great company, Great people." This vision was supported and enabled by LG's global supply chain management (GSCM) organization. LG's GSCM system combines "design, parts supply, procurement, inventory, production and cost management into an integrated process to enable strategic flow of information and gathering of standardized production data. The system was expected to help strengthen LG's competitive edge with operation integration with overseas subsidiaries, to maximize operation efficiency with the introduction of advanced management system, and to save about US$45 billion won per business location for the next three years."[32] Further, LG's global purchasing system was expected to improve the purchasing process, facilitate the implementation of global standards to help strengthen LG's presence in e-business and to make possible real-time sharing of production cycle information."[33] Having achieved these goals, "LG is pursuing its vision of becoming the top global consumer electronics and appliance company with solutions that can change the landscape of the markets."[34] LG Electronics won the 2010 ISM R. Gene Richter Award for Leadership and Innovation in Supply Management for the Organization/Structure category for its procurement transformation initiative.[35]

Developing Strategies

Vision without action is a daydream. Action without vision is a nightmare.

— JAPANESE PROVERB

Given the direction and vision of the future, what are the strategies that will lead the supply management organization to achieve its vision? At this point, the leader wants to develop higher-level strategies that align supply vision and strategy with corporate vision, strategy, mission, and goals and objectives. This alignment might occur in specific areas such as sustainability and social responsibility or technology roadmaps. For example, in its *Corporate Sustainability Report*, Procter & Gamble states the alignment this way: "In 2010, we declared our long-term sustainability vision that inspires how we innovate our products. It includes powering our plants with 100 percent renewable energy, using 100 percent renewable materials or recyclable materials for all products and packaging, having zero waste go to landfills, and delighting consumers with products that meet their needs while enabling them to conserve resources. This vision is being brought to life through our innovation and productivity programs. We believe most of the sustainability challenges the world faces can be solved with innovation, and that this innovation can have a positive business impact."[36]

In Figure 2-8, I. Bulow, U. Schott-Wullenweber and F. Hedderich propose three implementation strategies based on the status of supply management in the organization and its developmental level.

CHAPTER 2: Setting Direction

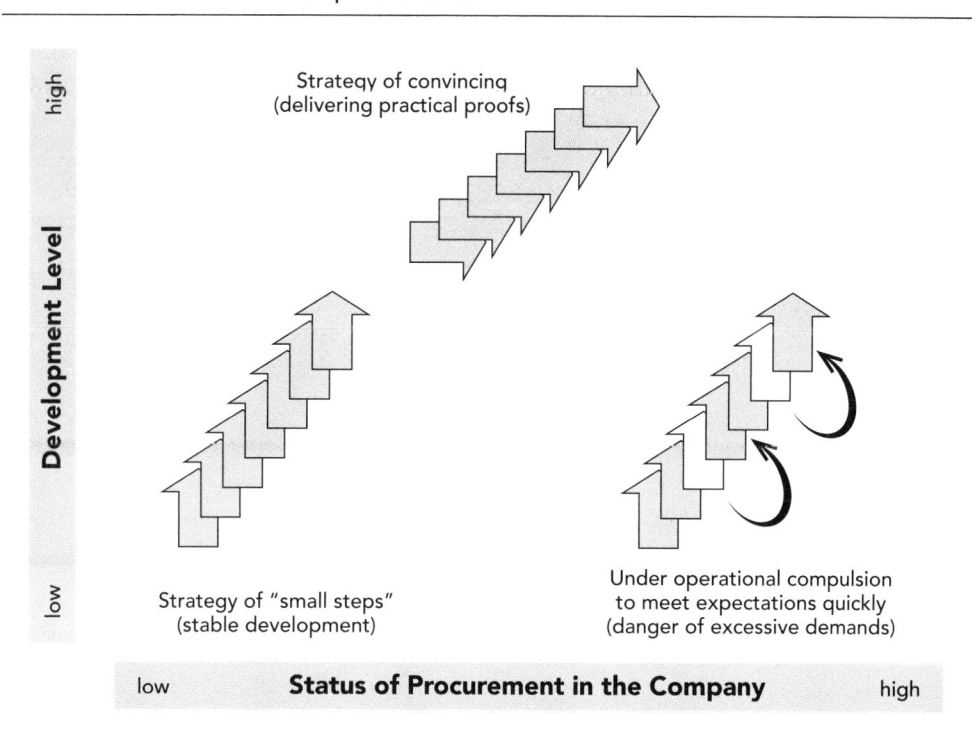

Figure 2-8: Implementation Strategies Based on Supply Management's Status and Development Level

Source: I. Bulow, U. Schott-Wullenweber and F. Hedderick, "Change Management in Purchasing: Best Practices from Germany's Number 1 Airline Deutsche Lufthansa AG," PRACTIX, CAPS Research 9 (July 2006).

Aligning Supply Strategy With Organizational Strategy

A key factor in the concept and development of a strategic supply management department is that this will lead to greater alignment of supply strategy with organizational strategy. As internal alignment improves, supply management will be better able to realize its full potential as a major contributor to sustainable success. Ultimately, the true test of the vision, and the leader behind it, is results. John Kotter offers a matrix approach (see Figure 2-9) to assess if the vision will drive to sustainable success for the organization.

Figure 2-9: Vision, Results and Sustainable Success

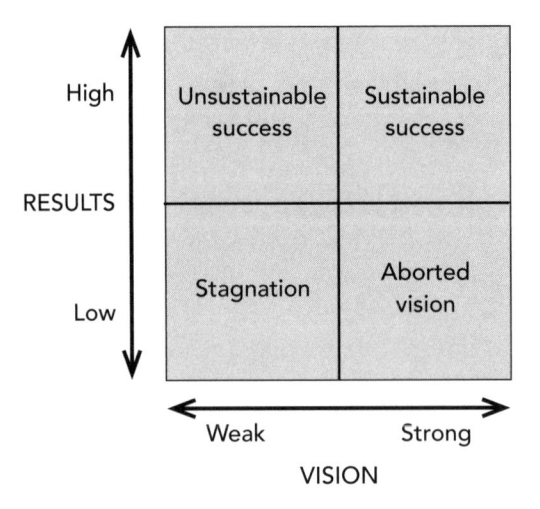

	Weak Vision	Strong Vision
High Results	Unsustainable success	Sustainable success
Low Results	Stagnation	Aborted vision

Source: John P. Kotter, "Winning at Change," *Leader to Leader* 10 (Fall 1998), 27-33.

At Nissan, Carlos Ghosn found that the company had no long-term vision. The organization was in the lower left-hand quadrant of Kotter's matrix. Targets were set at the regional level (Japan, United States and Europe) and there was no coordination across regions. Suppliers were approached multiple times for price reductions to offset the eroding performance of the organization. Once a strong vision was established and stakeholders bought into it, the organization was able to move to the right on the vision axis and to begin obtaining better results. Once suppliers believed that the targets were real and that Nissan procurement employees would not keep coming back with new targets throughout the year, they could begin to turn things around.[37] Its recent sales have been strong, hampered mainly by the lack of availability of the redesigned Altima.[38]

How the leader of supply management aligns supply strategies, goals and objectives to effectively and efficiently contribute to overall organizational goals and objectives is the key question. To accomplish this, he or she must have access to and understand the business unit plans and objectives, ideally through involvement in their development. Then, using that knowledge, a supply management strategy is developed that best supports the organizational strategy. The alignment of supply management strategy and objectives with organizational strategy and objectives requires two-way communication during the planning process at all three levels of planning (strategic, operational and tactical). Supply management receives input from the corporate and business unit strategy process that enables the development of supply management strategy. Equally important to the success of the organization is input from the supply leaders and managers about supply opportunities and risks that may influence the development and direction of corporate and business-unit-level strategy. Strategy development is discussed in detail in Chapters 5 and 6.

When former vice chair and CEO Yong Nam joined LG in 2007, he brought with him significant international experience and a powerful drive to charge up innovation and globalization for the company. The goal as a company was to become "Global Number One," and Nam firmly believed that LG could not reach this level of performance without a strategic sourcing organization. After all, procurement in the company accounts for a full 75 percent of LG's revenues. In the June 2009 CEO letter, Nam stated: "Recently, we formed a Global General Procurement organization ... It is important in our transformation to 'Global Number One' that we have a consolidated, centralized approach to procurement. This is a great opportunity to leverage our growing scale and capabilities."[39] As stated previously, in recognition of the success it achieved, LG received the 2010 R. Gene Richter Award for Leadership and Innovation in Supply Management by the Institute for Supply Management®.

The next chapter addresses the challenges and rewards for the supply management leader who can develop meaningful internal and external business partnerships.

Summary

Core values are developed by the supply management leader, creating a strong ethical culture and embedding this behavior into the supply management department. Many organizations ask employees, especially those in supply management who can spend significant resources for the organization, to sign an ethical code of conduct.

The supply management leader also identifies opportunities and risks that range from the current situation, to growth of markets in general — and growth of markets in low-cost countries as well as those developing sustainable products and services, to how mergers and acquisitions and changes in the financial markets might affect their organizations. They then develop risk assessment and mitigation strategies, perhaps by product/service and/or by business unit, to minimize risk.

Using these tools, leaders develop a vision for the supply organization, asking, Where are we going/what do we want to become? The mission statement follows, answering, Why do we exist? Strategies are then developed to support the vision and mission.

As the primary owner of the supply management process, the supply leader plays a crucial role in communicating the vision and strategies of supply to internal and external stakeholders including top management, users of the process, the supplier community and the surrounding community. The supply leader's most important task may be in successfully communicating supply opportunities beyond traditional price and volume considerations and creative ways to mitigate risks. It will be through these efforts that supply management takes its place at the strategic level in the organization.

Key Points

1. Direction setting is the primary task of a leader or leadership team. It involves clarifying the core values of the organization, identifying future opportunities and risks, and devising a compelling vision, mission and strategies.
2. Values drive the behavior of all members of the organization and contribute to the corporate culture of the organization. They describe how we intend to operate, on a day-to-day basis, as we pursue our vision.
3. Ethical principles are the rules of conduct that derive from ethical values. These principles guide behavior.
4. A vision statement tells where the organization wants to go, and the value statement describes how the organization will get there.
5. To focus attention on how results are obtained, to support the practice of ethical decision-making and to guide the behavior of others, leaders can exhibit ethical behavior, create a strong ethical culture, establish a code of conduct, include ethical issues in employment decisions, formally include ethics in performance evaluations and engage in meaningful ethics training.
6. Supply opportunities and risks may exist in any number of areas, including growth of markets, especially in low-cost countries or in markets concerned with sustainable products, strategic partnerships, mergers and acquisitions, financial markets and government-industry partnerships.

Chapter 2
Appendix: ISM *Principles of Sustainability and Social Responsibility*[40]

Introduction

ISM firmly believes the supply management profession is a strategic contributor in the development and implementation of sustainability and social responsibility programs and behavior. Supply professionals are in a unique, critical position to impact the global supply chain and therefore should supplement their organization's work in sustainability and social responsibility by promoting sustainability and social responsibility through leadership and participation on appropriate committees, boards and panels of governmental and nongovernmental organizations.

Creating principles across social, industry, public and private, profit and nonprofit, political and country boundaries is both a challenge and an opportunity. This diversity presents a particular challenge in the area of sustainability and social responsibility, which does not have a lengthy history resulting in the development of well-known and universally acceptable best practices.

Laws, regulations, trade agreements, customs and practices pertinent to sustainability and social responsibility must also be considered in the development and implementation of business strategies, policies and procedures. In addition, the advent of new technologies that enable a "virtual" world influence the evolution of sustainability and social responsibility in a supply chain context.

Principles

1. **Anti-Corruption**
   Corruption in all of its forms, including extortion and bribery, will not be tolerated.
2. **Diversity and Inclusiveness — Workforce and Supply Base**
   Workforce. Workforce diversity and inclusiveness is the attraction and retention of a workforce that reasonably represents the customer and communities in which the organization operates.
   Supply Base. Attraction and retention of a diverse supply base is the responsibility of each supply professional.
3. **Environment**
   Supply management promotes protection, preservation and vitality of the natural environment.
4. **Ethics and Business Conduct**
   Every supply management professional is responsible for behaving ethically and actively promoting ethical conduct throughout the supply chain.
5. **Financial Integrity and Transparency**
   Financially responsible supply management is characterized by integrity and transparency in all supply-related dealings and decisions.

6. **Global Citizenship**

    Global citizenship is the ethical and moral obligation to act for the benefit of society locally, globally and virtually.

7. **Health and Safety**

    Health and safety is the condition of being protected or free from the occurrence of risk of injury, danger, failure, error, accident, harm and loss of life.

8. **Human Rights**

    Human beings have universal and natural rights and status regardless of legal jurisdiction and local factors.

9. **Labor Rights**

    Supply management is committed to protecting and respecting labor rights globally.

10. **Sustainability**

    Sustainability is the ability to meet current needs without hindering the ability to meet the needs of future generations in terms of economic, environmental and social challenges.

CHAPTER 3

An environment where people have to think brings with it wisdom, and this wisdom brings with it continuous improvement.

— TERUYUKI MINOURA
SENIOR ADVISOR TO TOYOTA,
FORMER PRESIDENT OF DAIHATSU MOTOR COMPANY[1]

Creating Alignment

Creating alignment is the second stage of effective leadership. *Merriam-Webster's Dictionary* defines *alignment* as "an arrangement of groups or forces in relation to one another." When it comes to leadership, alignment is the process of arranging internal and external groups in the appropriate relationship to one another so that they are all moving in the direction set by the leader or leadership team. In this way, the leader or leadership team turns the vision into a shared vision among all key stakeholders. Communication is the key leadership task at this stage. To create a shared vision the leader must communicate in multiple ways with multiple internal and external stakeholders. During this ongoing communication process, the message must be compelling, the leader must be credible and the behaviors must be consistent.

This chapter addresses the role of the leader as the chief communicator who brings together internal and external stakeholders behind the vision. The complementary managerial concepts of organizing and staffing are addressed in Chapters 7 and 9, respectively. To attain the shared vision, the leader must then gain commitment from stakeholders to persevere throughout the change process and execute the necessary tasks. Motivating and inspiring, which are the key leadership tasks in stage three, are discussed in detail in the next chapter. This chapter is organized into four sections: (1) supply alignment and the leader's role, (2) communicating a clear understanding of vision to disparate stakeholders, (3) building credibility, and (4) empowering others to own the vision.

Chapter Objectives
- Define alignment and discuss alignment in the context of supply management.
- Identify key internal and external stakeholders.
- Discuss the communication tools and techniques leaders can use to impart a clear and compelling message about the vision of supply management.
- Discuss the ways the leader establishes and maintains credibility.
- Explore the opportunities and obstacles that might occur during the alignment process.
- Discuss the behaviors the leader must display consistently throughout the change process to capitalize on the opportunities of alignment and eliminate or reduce the obstacles.

Supply Alignment and the Leader's Role

In the context of supply management, alignment refers to the relationship of the supply leader to members of the supply management organization as well as the position of the supply management group relative to other major groups in the organization, such as finance, marketing and engineering; and to major groups outside the organization, such as suppliers, the community, professional associations and so on. Alignment is achieved by successfully communicating the vision of supply management to these stakeholders. Successful alignment is achieved when multiple stakeholders accept or buy in to the vision of supply management to the extent necessary to move toward attaining the vision.

The first stage of leadership — setting direction (discussed in Chapter 2) — addressed the importance of aligning the supply management vision and strategies with the organizational vision and strategies (see Figure 3-1). If this has been carried out successfully, the supply leader or leadership team will be well positioned to align internal stakeholders with the supply vision. If, however, conflicts exist between the organizational vision and strategies and those of supply management, then there will undoubtedly be problems. Likewise, if the supply vision and strategies conflict with that of individual internal stakeholders such as finance, marketing, engineering and so on, then the organization has even bigger challenges ahead. It is this lack of horizontal alignment that often creates problems between and among members of different functions and business process owners. The desire to avoid these types of conflicts affects the leaders and top managers of the various functions when they are setting direction and making plans at the organizational and functional levels.

The Importance of Alignment

The alignment role in supply management is especially critical and challenging because in many organizations the scope of supply management is expanding to include more components that are approached from a more strategic perspective. P. Fraser Johnson and Michiel R. Leenders reported that the overall trend in the aggregate was for increases

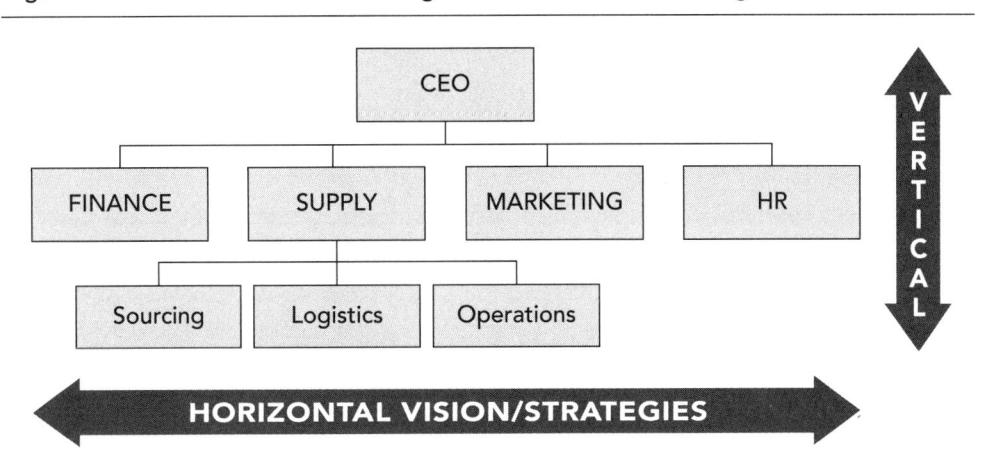

Figure 3-1: Vertical and Horizontal Alignment of Vision and Strategies

in supply chain responsibilities, although there were substantial gains and losses among those organizations that participated in their 1995, 2003 and 2011 study of roles and responsibilities. The most frequently identified responsibilities were supplier development, supplier cost management/value analysis, outsourcing and subcontracting, and material and purchasing research.[2]

According to the Institute for Supply Management® (ISM®), supply management includes the identification, acquisition, access, positioning and management of resources and related capabilities that an organization needs or potentially needs in the attainment of its strategic objectives. This includes the following components: disposition/investment recovery, distribution, inventory control, logistics, materials management, operations, packaging, procurement/purchasing, product/service development, quality, receiving, strategic sourcing, transportation/traffic/shipping and warehousing/stores. This expanded scope means the supply management process involves more and different stakeholders than the historical purchasing role and often entails major changes in processes, human capital, reporting relationships and responsibilities. Reliance on strong managers may not achieve the transformation that both supply and the organization as a whole require. Consequently, strong leadership in supply management is more important than ever to successfully market the value of strategic sourcing along with sourcing strategies and initiatives to management and internal customers.

Demands on CPOs have changed, as CPOs have moved from the role of cost reduction to value enhancement and commercial capabilities. The critical success factors for CPOs today include the following:

1. Interpersonal skills and organizational IQ internally. This requires building strong stakeholder relationships and early involvement in key decisions.
2. Leadership skills to shepherd transformational change. This includes influence with suppliers, internal stakeholders and the ability to elevate the function internally.

3. Broad perspective to deliver value beyond price reductions. This includes managing demand and value controls that may exploit the inherent and structural cost aspects of a product or service.
4. Market savvy and a keen eye for mitigating risk.[3]

These key skills were demonstrated by the CPO of Boston Scientific in a recent reorganization, when the CEO of Boston Scientific, a manufacturer of surgical devices, directed his staff to "optimize the company." For the CPO, this meant transitioning from a very decentralized indirect sourcing organization to a center-led, global approach. In the decentralized operation, procurement best practices were not communicated or leveraged on a broad basis, visibility into spend was fragmented and full value from suppliers was not being realized. The CPO noted that three innovative solutions were the keys to developing a leaner, more flexible and effective organization, while enabling a smooth transition:

1. A comprehensive resource activity allocation model. The team created a comprehensive resource activity allocation model to identify, assess and allocate resources by region, site and procurement/sourcing activities. Management of attrition was essential, as the attrition rate throughout the transformation was approximately 33 percent. A communication plan was put in place that included frequent updates from the executive level downward. This involved face-to-face meetings with site vice presidents, as well as monthly meetings with site material directors and weekly meetings with human resources to streamline the hiring process and facilitate the communication of organizational changes to all stakeholders.
2. Lean principles. Prior to the transformation, there was limited sharing of best practices across the organization, with many procurement areas focused on their own businesses and the avoidance of looking across to other sites for leveraged opportunities. Once the resource activity allocation model was in place, redundancies or gaps in the procurement activities at each site were eliminated and lean practices put into place.
3. A global resource optimization model. This model was developed to flex transactional resources within the Boston Scientific procurement network to optimize capacity. For example, at the start of the transition, the team found that it took 7.7 days to route a purchase request through approval and PO creation. Improvement was made to the PO process by implementing automated workflows and resource optimization, which improved efficiency by 30 percent.[4]

The Leader's Role in Alignment

To successfully align people behind a vision and future direction, the leader must execute three activities: (1) impart a clear understanding of the vision to a broad and disparate group of stakeholders; (2) build credibility with stakeholders by exhibiting consistent behaviors that support and promote the vision and strategies; and (3) empower people to take ownership of the vision and make it happen.

For example, the Supply Chain Management (SCM) division leadership at a leading financial institution had a vision of being recognized as world class in supply chain management throughout the financial services industry. This vision first had to be clearly understood within the ranks of supply chain professionals. Then, the SCM team worked with its leader(s) to impart an understanding of this vision throughout the organization and to external stakeholders as well. To gain credibility with stakeholders, the supply chain professionals had to understand the business, be able to implement innovative supply chain processes, and possess the capability to flawlessly execute those processes while working as a value-adding, high-performing part of the business. A consistent display of these behaviors built credibility and further support for the vision. By working in partnership with internal customers, the supply management group empowered other bank employees to execute parts of the supply vision.[5]

Communicating a Clear Understanding of the Vision

The first step in creating alignment is to impart a clear understanding of the vision to disparate audiences. A critical role for the supply management leader is that of chief advocate, chief communicator and chief salesperson of the transformation to the new vision and direction of supply management. The leader must answer three questions at this stage: (1) Who are the target audiences/stakeholders? (2) What are the underlying interests of each stakeholder or stakeholder group? (3) How can the leader link the supply vision and strategy to the stakeholders' interests?

Who Are Stakeholders?

A *stakeholder* is someone who has a legitimate interest in the outcome of a project or decision. A stakeholder's level of interest depends on the magnitude of the potential gain or loss from the success or failure of the project. Stakeholders may be members of the organization or members of external groups affiliated with the organization in some fashion. The supply leader(s) faces the twin tasks of aligning internal stakeholders and external stakeholders with the vision.

Internal Stakeholders. Target audiences or stakeholder groups may be people inside the supply organization itself; without buy-in from supply management professionals, the leader has little chance of success at achieving the vision. Supply personnel are the people who must "flawlessly execute" the vision. Target audiences may also be inside the organization, but outside of supply management — examples include marketing, engineering, design, and so on. Without alignment with these internal stakeholders, the supply leader may find it impossible to deliver on the vision. Alignment is required internally to efficiently and effectively transform the supply organization from a tactical operation to a strategic one according to the specific vision and direction set by the leader. Figure 3-2 lists some of the interests of internal stakeholder groups and examples of how the supply management team might link their goals to the stakeholders' interests.

Figure 3-2: Internal Stakeholders and Their Interests Linked to Supply Management

WHO (the audience)	WHAT (is being communicated)	EXAMPLES
Top leadership or management of the organization	Supplier performance	Price and cost trends, effect of lead times on firm performance, shortages, labor strife and cartel actions that may affect the firm, new technology, mergers affecting the supply chain.
	Performance to plan	Budgeted expenditures, savings plan, quality improvement, training.
	Supply market conditions	Impact of present and forecast raw material availability and cost, supplier capacities, mergers and acquisitions on the firm.
Employees	Special supplier terms for employee purchases	Hilton Hotels, for example, offers employee purchase discounts on mattresses.
	Terms of certain supplier agreements affecting employees	Travel, services, utilities, temporary help, printing and so on.
	Policies and procedures relative to supply management	Ethics policy (the organization's commitment to treat suppliers fairly and honestly, rules about accepting gifts and gratuities); sustainability goals, objectives.

Source: Adapted from Anna E. Flynn and Samuel Farney, *The Supply Management Leadership Process*, Volume 4 of the ISM *Knowledge Series* (National Association for Purchasing Management, 2004), 234.

External Stakeholders. Lastly, target audiences may be external groups, and may include suppliers, the community, professional associations and any other group that has a vested interest in the outcomes of the organization and supply's contribution to these outcomes. Alignment is required externally to extend supply's reach and influence up and down the supply chain. Stakeholder alignment requires continuous communication about the central message embedded in the future vision. Figure 3-3 lists some of the interests of external stakeholder groups and how the supply management team might link their goals to the interests of these stakeholders.

CHAPTER 3: Creating Alignment

Figure 3-3: Internal Stakeholders and Their Interests Linked to Supply Management

WHO (the audience)	WHAT (is being communicated)	EXAMPLES
Investors	Cost and customer value improvements	Quality, delivery, lead time, cost improvements, specifications
	Key supplier relationships	Strategic alliances that may (or do) significantly impact value
Community	Supplier diversity programs	Percentage of annual spending awarded to minority-owned or women-owned businesses or small businesses
	Local and regional content	Percentage of end product that is composed of material made, mined or assembled locally
	Sustainability	Environmentally friendly practices in manufacturing and locating facilities, community outreach and presence
Customers	Product or service improvements	Quality, delivery, lead time, cost improvements
	Innovations in process or delivered value	Specifications — new features, advantages or benefits
	Faster response time	Accurate and predictable delivery dates
	Corporate social responsibility	Environmentally and community-friendly practices, labor practices
Suppliers	Performance feedback	Quality, delivery, lead time, cost improvements
	Schedule needs	Forecast, quantity versus date, annual requirements
	New product plans	Specifications, quantities, production dates
	Key expectations of suppliers	Design innovation, continuous improvement, competitiveness, speed-to-market, sustainability

Source: Adapted from Anna E. Flynn and Samuel Farney, *The Supply Management Leadership Process*, Volume 4 of the ISM *Knowledge Series* (National Association for Purchasing Management, 2000), 237.

Building Alignment Internally

The approach taken by the leader to build alignment internally depends in large part on the drivers of change. Is the new vision the result of a crisis that threatens the survival of the organization? Or is it the result of external pressures that are negatively affecting key performance metrics, but not survival? Or is it internally driven because of a change in leadership or structure or technology? The supply leader's alignment approach will vary depending on the driver(s) and the audience.

For example, at Boston Scientific, the CEO looked internally and saw the opportunity to improve operations, thus charging his staff to "Optimize the company." This led to the very favorable changes in the way the organization managed and purchased its indirect spending.

External or internal drivers may stimulate the change management initiative. The leader or leadership team must carefully assess the drivers of change and build the alignment plan accordingly.

Create Alignment Within Supply Management. The first place that alignment must occur is within the supply organization itself. Target audiences may include supply personnel transitioning from the old paradigm to the new as well as those being incorporated under a new and expanded supply umbrella. The level of difficulty in aligning supply personnel behind the new vision of supply management depends, in part, on the level of change or transformation that will be experienced by these people during the change process. The CPO of Boston Scientific noted the importance of engaging people effectively in the transformation process. She stated, "We're blessed with a highly motivated team that knows the value of working in a team environment, and can play off the strengths of one another, spark open and honest dialogues throughout the organization, and challenge one another. By achieving bottom line savings and reducing risk, these efforts showcased the achievements of indirect procurement and sourcing to the C-suite."

Boston Scientific also noted the importance of continuously communicating with employees about attrition and other changes during its reorganization. Overall, the goal for the global indirect sourcing and procurement team is identical to the mission of Boston Scientific Corporation: to improve the quality of patient care and productivity of healthcare delivery. Employees worked to identify and reduce waste and develop standard processes, so that more money was available to reinvest in R&D to further improve patient care. [6]

To be successful, the leader must clarify and communicate to supply personnel the changes in roles, responsibilities and reporting relationships, including the reasons for the changes and the expected benefits from the changes. In situations where people were involved in the visioning process, a certain level of acceptance or buy-in may have already been achieved. In other cases, there may be little or no buy-in to a vision the leader is announcing. In the latter case the leader may have a tougher job during the alignment process because stakeholders were not part of the thought process and may need to walk through the leader's thinking to accept it. The buy-in process varies depending on the circumstances and the organizational structure, culture and current state. As noted by Boston Scientific's CPO, "Being competitive in the future requires objectivity as well as a way to uncover any talent gaps and mobilize to close those gaps in an efficient, timely manner." We must assess current capabilities rigorously and dispassionately; too frequently, we try to build the future around today's players and end up short. Including a process to discover "talent in the organizational hinterlands" is necessary.[7]

At United Technologies Corp. (UTC), the supply management process change was top-down. The CEO brought in Kent Brittan, named him vice president of supply management, made him responsible for pulling together the spending of UTC's diverse businesses, and set a cost reduction goal of US$750 million in four years. Brittan's challenge was rooted in the highly decentralized nature of UTC. Each UTC business at the time — Carrier, Hamilton Sundstrand, Otis, Pratt & Whitney, Sikorsky, UTC Fire & Security and UTC Power — operated autonomously and had its own supply management operation. Brittan had to align the disparate supply groups around the new vision of supply management without changing the basic decentralized structure and culture of the organization. By focusing on common areas with clear benefits from collaborating, Brittan was able to deliver results beyond savings.[8]

Alignment within supply management at UTC was facilitated by a council composed of vice presidents of supply management at each business who meet 11 times a year to share best practices and make decisions about supply management policy and procedure. The supply group was also able to develop corporate contracts with common terms and conditions to minimize the risk of doing business in a highly regulated environment and made it easier for suppliers to do business with UTC. Supply managers at businesses within UTC with little common spend categories, and therefore little opportunity to leverage spend, communicated frequently and shared supply initiatives with each other.[9]

Create Alignment Internally, But Outside of Supply Management. The supply leader must also develop alignment with internal stakeholders outside of the supply organization to generate buy-in and commitment to the leader's vision of supply management. To build the necessary level of connectivity between and among internal groups, the supply leader must determine who the key internal stakeholders are and what their interests are in the specific situation — and then how to help them meet their interests while also effecting the desired change in supply roles, processes and systems.

When it comes to these internal stakeholders, the starting point is often an assessment of the perception of supply and its role in the organization. How much credibility does the supply organization currently have in the organization? What are the sources of this credibility? Perhaps supply management has credibility when it comes to driving the lowest prices from suppliers, but no credibility when it comes to input in the design stage, assessing and delivering lowest total cost of ownership or balancing the needs of disparate stakeholders and arriving at the "best value" combination of quality, delivery, service and total cost. One result of the assessment needs to be a determination of the level of credibility relative to the vision and the changes that will be required to achieve the vision. The leader may also begin to put together a plan to build credibility where it is lacking.

This assessment might be accomplished through regular or special communication in the course of developing or maintaining "thick, informal internal networks" or it may be in a more formal manner such as with surveys of internal users of supply processes or interviews with key stakeholders. A level of trust must be developed between the parties if there is any hope of getting accurate feedback. Developing surveys that do not introduce bias and that respondents believe will be carefully considered is also important.

In some organizations, the change management process is highly structured. At American Red Cross, change began at the top when a new CEO came in to bring financial discipline to the organization. She hired a new CPO, who surveyed the business partners to understand how procurement was meeting their needs. Leaders were then identified to lead teams that would work closely with business units, yet be centrally organized to create synergy.[10]

Creating Alignment With External Stakeholders. The supply leader must also align external stakeholders behind the supply vision to the extent necessary to execute it. The supply leader represents the supply organization in meetings with corporations, government agencies, professional associations and other organizations and, of course, with suppliers.

Suppliers represent perhaps the most important external stakeholder group in the supply process. A change in the vision of supply typically entails changes in sources and the location of sources. A new vision may mean new and different demands on suppliers and very real differences in how business is executed. For example, UTC's vision of supply management at the time led to a transformation in the expectations of suppliers and supply managers. For instance, four purchasing professionals in UTC's aerospace businesses were dedicated to developing suppliers in the emerging markets of China, India, Eastern Europe, Turkey and Brazil. In other areas of UTC's aerospace business, the focus was on involving suppliers in design for manufacturing initiatives such as the development of its PW600 engine for very light jets to meet anticipated customer demand. On the commercial business side, lean tools were used to create a new supply chain to develop technology for Otis' Gen2 elevator.[11] These types of initiatives require consistent behaviors that are very different from those used by buyers and suppliers focused on prices and operating out of adversarial relationships.

External pressures from global competition and external opportunities from an international talent pool and an international supply base may also influence the change management process. For example, IBM's vision is of a "globally integrated company," and its strategy is to draw more efficiently on its global capabilities and capitalize on emerging market opportunities. To advance this vision, IBM chose (at the time) Shenzhen, China, for its global procurement headquarters. IBM had procurement and logistics professionals in the region, many of them at its China Procurement Center in Shenzhen, which (at that time) had been in operation for more than a decade. The center was one of IBM's largest procurement organizations outside the United States. Although IBM had been purchasing in Asia for more than 50 years, changes in global demand for services required the development of relationships with new partners and suppliers as well as working with existing ones to help them build skills, processes and management practices to compete globally in the services market.[12] In 2011, IBM's global procurement office moved to Budapest, Hungary, again working toward developing a more geographically distributed executive structure.[13] IBM has a very sophisticated global procurement website that explains its operations and access. As part of this, it has also opened a portal called "Procurement One Place" so that clients all over the world have a single point of contact to either resolve their issues, or to be efficiently directed to the right source.[14]

It is just as important to clarify the expectations of external stakeholders as it is to clarify those of internal stakeholders. Supplier representatives have been through every supply management fad that has come along so it may take some time and effort to convince them that this transformation is for real. For example, a commodity manager might refer to an online auction as an online negotiation and stress the importance of buyer-supplier relationships. However, if the supplier perceives a negotiation as involving give-and-take and the online auction as a one-way exchange mostly or solely benefiting the buyer, then the commodity manager may have little or no credibility with the supplier. The perception may not be changed until or unless the commodity manager understands the perspective of the supplier and adjusts his or her words and actions accordingly.

Understanding the interests of the other party is critical to the alignment process. For example, supply management may consider how long it takes to get innovative new products to market a key performance indicator of a successful supplier relationship. Suppliers may focus on expected revenue growth and the potential for increased business from buyers. Once both parties have a clear understanding of the key performance indicators for their respective stakeholders, this paves the way for creating options for mutual gain. Exhibiting understanding of the other parties' interests is a solid first step toward credibility. Other tools and techniques for building credibility are discussed in the following section.

Building Credibility

Experto credite. (Trust one who has proved it.)

— VIRGIL
2,000 YEARS AGO

According to *Merriam-Webster's Dictionary*, credibility is "(1) the quality or power of inspiring belief, and (2) capacity for belief." This is an interesting definition because it reflects action on the part of the messenger and the receiver of the message. The messenger must possess or develop the power to inspire belief, and the listener must have the capacity for belief. Even if the message is understood, how does the leader get people to believe it? The ability to build credibility requires the supply leader (messenger) to inspire belief through his or her character, words and actions. The leader must also seek to understand if he or she has credibility in the eyes of stakeholders — and why or why not. A truthful message alone will not inspire belief. Building credibility with stakeholders is a critical element of successful alignment and change management.

For example, the supply management vision of an organization in the transportation sector (referred to as Fleet) was to have a "lean, focused, world-class supply base providing a competitive advantage that could be readily accessed by its end users." Part of this vision involved "purposely choosing suppliers."[15] Jeffrey A. Ogden and Matthew W. McCarter report that under the old vision of purchasing, the organization collaborated very little with suppliers; relationships were marked by short-term, price-oriented contracts, multiple suppliers and frequent supplier switching, especially if difficulties were encountered. This resulted in highly variable pricing across suppliers and locations.

Under the new vision of supply management, suppliers were gradually brought into alignment as the size of the supply base was reduced and the remaining suppliers focused on improvements in price and delivery. The benefits envisioned under this supply direction went way beyond price improvements to lower total cost of ownership. To achieve this, Fleet and its suppliers had to collaborate through long-term, integrative partnerships and strategic alliances. Once Fleet was successful at building a supplier relationship according to this new model, other suppliers became interested in working toward a similar deal. Actual performance in accordance with supply's new vision established credibility with other suppliers as well as the partner-supplier. This example illustrates the importance of backing up words with actions. Because of past experiences with Fleet, suppliers were understandably cautious in believing that things would truly be different.[16]

Components of Credibility

Credibility is built through a number of actions and behaviors, including demonstrated performance; consistency; commitment; existing relationships; the reputation of the messenger; the message itself; the ethics, integrity and trustworthy behaviors of the messenger; and the perceived concern of the messenger for the listener's interests. Figure 3-4 captures the components of credibility.

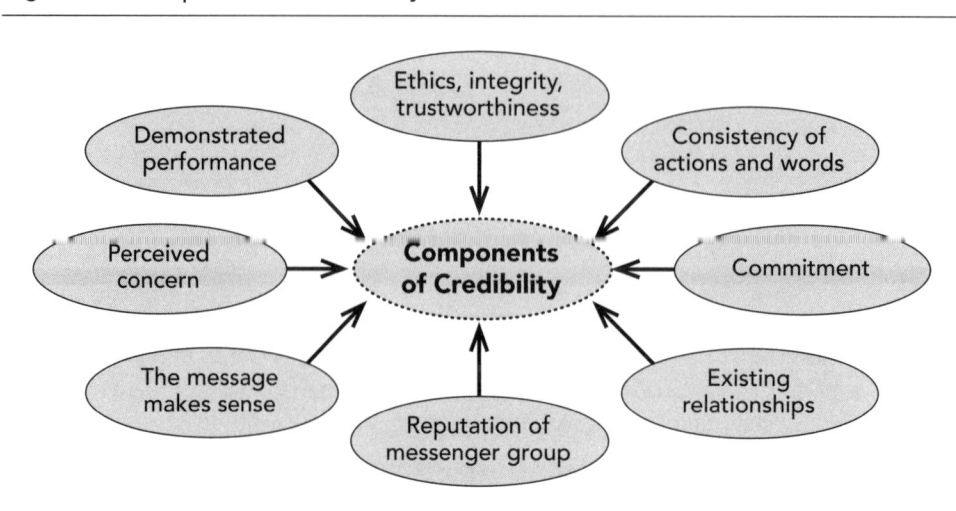

Figure 3-4: Components of Credibility

Ethics, Integrity, Trustworthiness and Reputation. Ethics, integrity and trustworthiness are at the heart of credibility. If the leader is perceived by stakeholders as unethical, lacking in personal integrity or untrustworthy, it may be very difficult to bring these stakeholders into alignment with the vision and direction of supply management. While it is possible to proceed in the absence of trust, it may take skills and abilities that are underdeveloped in many people to do this successfully.

Demonstrated Performance and Reputation. An established reputation for fairness paves the way for change. People will tend to think, "They were fair to me in the past; I believe they will be fair to me in the future, even if some things change." Without the reputation firmly in place, stakeholders may be wary of process changes and cautious in adopting new procedures until there is evidence to support the claims of supply management.

The messenger, in this case the supply management leader or leadership team, and the supply management organization will be more believable if, individually and collectively, they have a performance track record to back up the current vision. A reputation for getting the job done may lead people to believe that the leader or team can get the current job done as well.

Often, this is not the case. If the supply organization is undergoing transformational change from a tactical to a strategic organization, building credibility with stakeholders may be the first and foremost challenge if supply management's past performance has not measured up in the eyes of stakeholders. For example, if supply and suppliers are perceived as unreliable, if the organization lacks a rigorous sourcing process or the existing process is perceived as bureaucratic, and if there is any question at all about the individual and collective trustworthiness of supply personnel, then the supply leader should expect to have to stimulate a transformational change in the perceptions of supply management.

Fleet, the company in the transportation sector, earned greater respect among people working in organizations in its supply base as a result of the behavior of its supply personnel in a partnership with one supplier. Consistent behaviors involving shared resources, open communication, shared risks and rewards and joint accountability in the partnership relationship have made other suppliers eager to develop a similar relationship. Consistency is a major driver of credibility. If the supply management team talks about the value it can add, and the actions of supply personnel consistently support this claim, then credibility will be established. If results are below projections, then a serious review of why and how to do better next time may shore up or rebuild supply's credibility.

A Clear and Consistent Message. Stakeholders are more likely to believe the message if it is presented in a straightforward, logical manner supported by objective data, evidence and thorough analysis. Basically, the message needs to make sense. In communicating the improvements made in indirect procurement at Boston Scientific, the CPO noted that the metrics had to be clear, and had to measure what stakeholders were concerned about. The consistent, underlying theme was how to better serve the end customer.[17]

Commitment. The supply leadership team must remain committed to the changes and demonstrate this commitment in words and actions through good times and bad. Carlos Ghosn, CEO of Nissan, put his own job on the line to demonstrate his commitment to Nissan's change strategy.

The supply leader, and the entire supply management team, must build credibility and gain the trust of stakeholders. Toward this end, the supply leader or leadership team might conduct gap analysis to answer three questions: (1) What is each stakeholder group's current perception of the supply management group? (2) What is the desired perception? (3) What actions will it take to close the gap between the stakeholders' current perception of supply management and where they need to be to embrace the vision and new direction of supply management?

What Are the Current and Desired Perceptions of Supply Management?

A primary influencer when aligning stakeholders behind the vision of supply management is the existing role and perception of supply management in the organization. A new vision typically entails a major change in the role of supply management in organizational strategies and requires a change in the perception of supply internally and externally for the vision to be realized.

Gap analysis often helps to determine the changes needed in an organization. For example, as a starting point, the supply management leadership team should discuss with top management supply management's potential functions, operating range and role in the organization. In this way the team ensures that the vision and strategies developed for supply management are aligned with top management's expectations. Second, supply management employees should complete a questionnaire about everyday work procedures to determine the status quo and compare it to the requirements based on the new vision. The information gathered from these two activities can illustrate gaps to support the development of the change management plan. Figure 3-5 illustrates the checklist for the analysis of the takeoff point for change management in a supply management organization. It illustrates the process used to ensure vertical alignment with the company and horizontal alignment with employees in other functional areas.

Figure 3-5: Checklist for Supply Change Management Takeoff Point

CHECKLIST ANALYSIS OF TAKEOFF POINT (SELECTION)	
Company	
• Top management philosophy • Economic situation/pressure to act	• Change readiness and tradition • Status of procurement in the company
Procurement Organization	
• Development level (methods and so on) • Existing procurement information technology and collaboration tools	• Change management experience in purchasing • Tendency of outsourcing and offshoring
Employees	
• Qualification profiles (capabilities) • Mind-set (willingness)	• Personal traits • Fear of change • Succession planning

Source: Adapted from Ingo Bulow, Ulrich Schott-Wullenweber and Fabian Hedderich, "Change Management in Purchasing: Best Practices from Germany's No. 1 Airline Deutsche Lufthansa AG," *PRACTIX*, CAPS Research, Volume 9 (2006), 4.

How Leaders Communicate Vision

The leader must clearly and consistently communicate the vision. Jack Welch, former CEO of General Electric, said, "Without question, communicating the vision has been, and is continuing to be, by far the toughest job we face."[18] In a global organization this difficulty is compounded by numerous differences such as culture, norms, time zones and language.

Developing a Communications Plan

The supply leader needs a communication plan that fits the organizational culture and the targeted audience's preferred way of receiving and participating in communication. Carlos Ghosn spoke about the challenges of devising communication strategies in a global organization. He noted that communication strategies with the Japanese focused on the listeners gaining understanding of the concept. On the other extreme, communication strategies with Latin American or Anglo-Saxon audiences were all about execution. Ghosn said that because of the differences, delays on the front end should be anticipated in Japan until everyone understands the concept, and delays in Latin American and Anglo-Saxon countries should be anticipated during execution as people start to realize they have different perceptions of the concept. As has been stated before, understanding disparate audiences is a leadership imperative and a key driver in the successful development and execution of a communications plan.[19]

Once broad approaches have been established, the leadership team can devise specific communication strategies to facilitate the alignment process. These strategies might entail verbal and/or written elements depending on the preferences of the listeners. They may be delivered face-to-face or in a web-based meeting, through a video, via an mp3, in chat rooms, on social media, or using whatever communication media works with the intended audiences. To ensure true alignment, the leadership team must focus on developing trustworthy feedback mechanisms such as 360-degree surveys. They might also have their presentation skills assessed to determine the impact of presentation style on what listeners hear and how they react to what they hear. The last thing a leader wants to do is ruin an acceptable message with poor presentation.

Communication Techniques. Verbal communication obviously plays a huge role in building alignment. The supply leader or leadership team can use a number of verbal communication techniques to bring stakeholders into alignment with the vision of supply management. These range from communicating one-on-one to interacting in small groups of like-minded people to hosting large town hall–type meetings. Figure 3-6 lists different techniques, the purpose of using each one, and how the information might be disseminated.

Figure 3-6: Possible Components of a Verbal Communications Plan

TECHNIQUE	PURPOSE	METHOD(S)
One-on-one: Top leader meets one-on-one, face-to-face with key people internally and externally.	Sell the vision to each person by demonstrating an understanding of each person's interests and by making the connection between the vision and the stakeholder's interests.	Face-to-face; internal conference call with or without video
Flow down: Top-level leader meets with direct reports who then meet with their direct reports.	Formulate direction and strategies for each group aligned with the overall vision and flow it down the chain of command.	Face-to-face; internal conference call with or without video
Town-hall meetings: Top-level leader holds quarterly town hall-type meetings with large groups of stakeholders segmented by interests, reporting lines, roles, responsibilities and so on.	Recognize achievements that have been made since the last meeting. Launch next-step actions.	Face-to-face; videoconferencing at desk or in conference room with or without ability to give feedback; posted on company intranet for asynchronous review
"State of the department" meetings held by managers with their direct reports.	Talk about improvements and next steps. Ensure continued alignment with and commitment to overall organizational strategy.	Face-to-face; internal conference call at desk or in office with or without video
Weekly meetings with direct reports.	Keep momentum, stay on track, maintain focus.	Face-to-face; internal conference call with or without video
Monthly meetings with different employees from each department or group within supply management.	Give multiple people a chance to voice issues and concerns and give ideas and input.	Face-to-face; internal conference call at desk or in office with or without video

Figure 3-6: Possible Components of a Verbal Communications Plan *continued*

TECHNIQUE	PURPOSE	METHOD(S)
Monthly town hall type meetings with organizational stakeholders who work in other functional areas.	Open forum to discuss any issues related to supply management.	Face-to-face; videoconferencing at desk or in conference room with ability to give feedback; posted on company intranet for asynchronous review
Topical forums held by supply managers for non-supply personnel.	Focused discussions (two-way communication, not formal presentations) on specific topics relevant to a select group of stakeholders.	Face-to-face; videoconferencing at desk or in conference room with ability to give feedback; posted on company intranet for asynchronous review
Hold events to recognize and reward top performers.	Opportunity for top leaders to recognize and reward performance and to reinforce their commitment to the change process.	Face-to-face is best; for those who are off-site and cannot physically attend, videoconferencing at desk or in conference room with ability to give feedback; posted on company intranet for asynchronous review

Written communication also plays a role in building alignment. This communication might be delivered in hard copy, via email and/or posted on the supply intranet or the organization's internal social media platform. Understanding the preferred forms of communication of groups within the organization would drive the delivery decision. The author worked with a large multinational organization that was undergoing transformative change in its global supply chain management organization. The change management team focused considerable resources on developing new processes, policies and procedures, and acquiring technology to support the new organization. However, the team faced massive resistance from supply chain employees around the world in large part because of how they communicated the change. All information was posted on the then-newly designed intranet, and supply chain employees were expected to check this site frequently and do whatever was posted. Even when the message was good, it was often badly received and adoption was slow. Perhaps because the change was being introduced via written instead of verbal communications, regular town hall meetings should have been held to communicate updates, supplemented by the intranet for reference only. One danger of communicating important information only through a web posting is that it assumes people will remember to look at the website. Such postings are often "pushed" via email to remind those affected to check the website.

Common forms of written communication used to facilitate change are listed in Figure 3-7. These can be communicated using internal paper, email, internal web and/or social media platforms. Electronically based formats are becoming much preferred, especially for newer generations in the workforce.

Figure 3-7: Potential Components of a Written Communications Plan

TECHNIQUE	PURPOSE
Monthly newsletter posted on company intranet	Recognize and reward achievements; share information about next-stage activities; provide a means for those in the trenches to write about their experiences and demonstrate their ownership of the vision.
Dialogue option	Allow employees to anonymously submit questions about any aspect of the vision and change management process. This is generally done electronically.
Charts and executive dashboards	Capture data on key metrics in one place and track over time. Post in high traffic areas and on the company intranet with lots of visibility so everyone can see the results.
Symbols, pictures, short phrases, simple metaphors	Short, catchy messages that grab people's attention and stay in their minds. These can be used on PPT presentations, on the company intranet and at key meetings.

Never underestimate the power of symbols, metaphors, analogies and simple phrases. For example, former Deere CEO Bob Lane held up a big meat bone as he talked about putting more meat on the bone as the details of the strategy were finalized. It is easy to picture the meat bone, and the image may help people remember the message.[20]

Leadership Styles

According to the Center for Creative Leadership, versatility is a key element of leadership. Versatility relates to a leader's ability to use different ideas, tools, techniques and systems for executing leadership tasks. This is especially important for a leader trying to align stakeholders. Not all people will respond to the same leadership behavior so the leader must be versatile in his or her communication style.

Leadership styles come into play in this stage. Recall the six leadership styles presented in Chapter 1. Each style is favored by a particular type of leader and used in specific types of situations with rather predictable results. Figure 3-8 lists who tends to use each style, the behaviors of the style, when each is likely to be used, and the likely outcome.

Figure 3-8: Leadership Styles and Behaviors

LEADERSHIP STYLE	FAVORED BY	BEHAVIORS	APPROPRIATE APPLICATION	OUTCOMES
Directive/ commanding	Achievers under stress	Command-and-control; at times coercive; tell people what to do, when to do it, how to do it and what will happen if they do not	Crises; managing poor performers; when immediate improvement is needed in the short-term.	Stifles creativity and initiative in long run.
Visionary	People with a high personalized power drive under low stress and people with a high socialized power drive under high stress	Authoritative; gains employee support by clearly expressing their challenges and responsibilities in the context of the organization's overall direction and strategy	Environments of rapid change and high complexity where a new shared vision is required	Clear goals, energized team and increased employee commitment
Affiliative	Leaders who need to build trust and want to maintain close, friendly relationships	Emphasizes the employee and his or her emotional needs over the job; tends to avoid conflict	Dealing with employees to create harmony and increase morale, perhaps after a crisis or in high-stress situations	Ineffective unless coupled with visionary, coaching or participative styles
Participative/ Democratic	Leaders with high-affiliation needs in high-stress situations	Engage people in the decision-making process; collaborative and democratic	Team of highly competent individuals; the leader needs to tap the collective knowledge of the group	Builds trust and consensus; poor if fast decisions are needed
Pacesetting	High achievers in low-stress situations; leaders with high standards who make sure those standards are met even if they have to do the work themselves	Leads by example and personal heroics	Short-term crisis situations; high stakes; teams with highly competent and motivated people	Effective in the short term; demoralizing over the long term

Figure 3-8: Leadership Styles and Behaviors   *continued*

LEADERSHIP STYLE	FAVORED BY	BEHAVIORS	APPROPRIATE APPLICATION	OUTCOMES
Coaching	Leaders with a high socialized power motive who want to help develop individuals	Leader engages in long-term professional development and mentoring of employees	Stable environments	Develop broad and deep knowledge base throughout the organization; care must be taken to ensure it is not perceived as micromanaging

Source: Adapted from Daniel Goleman, Richard E. Boyatzis and Annie McKee, *Primal Leadership: Learning to Lead With Emotional Intelligence* (Boston, MA: Harvard Business School Press, 2004); and *Wall Street Journal*, "Developing a Leadership Style," n.d., accessed November 11, 2013, http://guides.wsj.com/management/developing-a-leadership-style/how-to-develop-a-leadership-style/.

Empowering People

Empowerment is a widely used term in business and other settings. To empower, according to *Merriam-Webster's Dictionary*, means to enable or to promote the self-actualization or influence of someone. As people embrace or buy in to the vision, the leadership team must empower people to take initiative and accept joint ownership and accountability for the successful implementation of the vision. Many leaders are challenged in the goal of an empowered workplace by entrenched mind-sets, policies, procedures and other aspects of organizational culture that inhibit rather than enable empowerment. Leaders must focus on removing organizational barriers and replacing them with useful tools to aid employees in taking action associated with ownership of the vision.

Sometimes the leader is a barrier to empowerment. Talking about empowerment while micromanaging every aspect of employees' daily work lives is likely to lead to frustration on everyone's part. Review the leadership styles in Figure 3-8 and think about the effect of each style on an individual's motivation and ability to be empowered. Visionary leaders may be capable of letting others take ownership of execution, but may fail to put into place the necessary tools for successful execution. Leaders with directive or pacesetting styles may not be able to let go of control to the extent required for multiple people to take ownership. While the visionary leader may not provide enough direction, these types of leaders may establish boundaries of behavior that are too narrow and constricting for the organization to fully benefit from the talents within its ranks. Affiliative leaders may be overly interested in being liked and therefore unable to allow conflict to emerge or, if it does emerge, lack the skills to manage it constructively.

Empowerment may also be hindered by the very people the leader wishes to empower. If the organization has a long history of bureaucratic processes and procedures, it also likely has a long history of employing people who are most comfortable working in a bureaucratic environment. This is not to say that transformative change is impossible, but the leadership team (if it is capable of transformative change itself) would have to recognize the level of effort required. Coaching and facilitative leadership skills would be needed to develop the existing human capital, attract new and different talent and transition to other places those who are unable or unwilling to change.

Figure 3-9 lists leader behaviors that are typically used to foster empowerment.

Figure 3-9: Behaviors That Empower

BEHAVIORS	EXAMPLES
Delegate	• Tasks and responsibilities that will help develop others • Decision-making authority
Encourage people to	• Take initiative • Improve their skills • Expand their interests and involvement • Actively seek ideas and promote ideas
Establish	• Clearly defined goals and metrics • Debrief and review sessions to discuss thought processes and link to and reinforce vision, mission and strategy • Tool sets that support the new behaviors • Guidelines and parameters for behaviors to limit fallout during the learning process
Coach	• Before changes to reduce stress and anxiety about change • During the change process to facilitate the transition to new behaviors • After changes are implemented to make changes permanent
Reinforce, recognize and reward, and	• Engage in informal recognition such as compliments • Engage in formal recognition • Provide incentives and rewards
Share	• Successes with a focus on best practices that can be replicated
Build trust and	• Be consistent in words and actions • Be committed to empowerment especially when things go wrong • Create a safe environment for trial and error
Provide support	• Formally through training, policies, procedures and work tools • Formally by removing organizational barriers • Informally through actions and words

Summary

Leaders set direction, as discussed in Chapter 2. To create alignment, leaders and the leadership team must effectively communicate this direction — both the vision and the mission. Leaders develop a comprehensive verbal and written communications plan, which includes concrete information on what and how to communicate with all stakeholders — internal, external, within supply management, and outside supply management — the clear and consistent message he or she wants to impart and implement.

If disparate stakeholder groups are aligned around a common vision, there is less likelihood of conflict; if conflict does occur, there is greater likelihood of a resolution. Recall Boston Scientific's CEO to "optimize the company" in support of the common vision to improve the quality of patient care. Leaders empower people when they provide them with the tools they need to consistently execute the new behaviors. Knowledge transfer refers to supply management personnel learning and adopting the relevant concepts of problem-oriented supply management. Learning by experience was an internal case-based simulation designed to allow supply management personnel to experience their new roles as problem-oriented critical partners and competition maximizers. Practical proofs are visible and tangible examples of the outcomes of supply management's new role derived from pilot projects. Daily support tools include various technologies that guide supply management through the new process and pattern, and a workflow management tool that guides the process while still allowing room for an entrepreneurial approach by the individual.

In the alignment process, the leader begins to build commitment if the message he or she delivers energizes the listener. Building alignment is a key step in transforming the supply management organization. The leader must take action to turn alignment into commitment, which is covered in Chapter 4 (stage three of the leadership process — gaining commitment).

Key Points

1. To align internal and external stakeholders, the supply management leader must impart a clear understanding of the vision.
2. The communication tools and techniques used to convey the vision depend on the drivers of change, the source of the change and the recipients of the message.
3. The leader must either already have credibility with the stakeholders or make a concerted effort to build credibility for the alignment effort to be successful.
4. The leader and the entire supply management team must exhibit consistent behaviors with stakeholders to solidify acceptance and buy-in of the vision and move stakeholders to a level of commitment necessary for success.

CHAPTER 4

Once you have a staff of prepared, intelligent and energetic people, the next step is to motivate them to be creative.

— AKIO MORITA
COFOUNDER OF SONY CORP.[1]

Gaining Commitment: Motivating and Inspiring People

To turn a shared vision into reality, the supply leader must gain commitment from internal and external stakeholders. This is the third and final stage in the leadership process. In this stage, the leader's primary role is motivating and inspiring people to take ownership of the vision and plan, persevere throughout the change process and execute the tasks necessary to implement the vision. This chapter focuses on energizing stakeholders to successfully execute the plans and strategies required to achieve the vision of supply management. The complementary managerial tasks of measuring department performance, establishing controls and ensuring compliance are covered in Chapters 11 and 12, respectively.

As discussed in Chapter 1, *management* relates to the execution of routine activities and *leadership* relates to nonroutine activities, especially change. Generating commitment to a new way of thinking about things and doing things necessarily involves change. The leader must do everything in his or her power to create the right atmosphere for change. According to management guru John P. Kotter, some of the keys to effectively leading organizational change include establishing a sense of urgency and a guiding vision, creating a committed team with the power to make changes, effectively communicating the vision for change, and empowering people to change.[2]

If successful, the alignment process will engage individuals at all levels of the organization. To gain commitment, the leader must focus on raising the expectations of employees and take actions that will permanently change behaviors. To this end, leaders perform three tasks: (1) motivate and inspire people, (2) build strong internal partnerships, and (3) create a culture of leadership. This chapter is organized around these three leadership tasks.

Chapter Objectives

- Discuss motivational techniques leaders use to energize stakeholders and generate commitment to the vision of supply management.
- Define informal internal partnerships and explain why they are so important in the leader's work of gaining commitment.
- Discuss techniques leaders use to build strong informal networks.
- Explain the concept of a culture of leadership.
- Discuss the supply leader's role in creating a culture of leadership within supply management.

Motivating and Inspiring

A leader leads by example, not by force.

— SUN TZU
AUTHOR OF *THE ART OF WAR*

According to *Dictionary.com*, to *motivate* means "to stimulate the active interest in a study through appeal to associated interests or by special devices; to provide with a motive or motives; incite; impel." The leader motivates people by stimulating their active interest in the vision of supply management and influencing them to take action.

Motivational Techniques

Fall down seven times, get up eight.

— JAPANESE PROVERB

In numerous ways a leader can motivate and inspire people to generate the necessary level of commitment to see people through tough situations and ensure the achievement of the vision (see Figure 4-1). Leaders motivate by appealing to other interests the stakeholders have that are related to supply. For example, the leader may appeal to the design group by linking the new supply vision to faster time to market for new products or services through longer-term relationships with fewer suppliers, leaner supply chains and better access to global distribution information. The leader may appeal to the marketing department by linking its objective of wider customer acceptance to early supply and supplier involvement in design.

Figure 4-1: Motivational Techniques

• Link the supply vision and strategies to the organizational and stakeholders' vision, strategies, goals and objectives.
• Stress the individual's values.
• Praise early, praise often and make it relevant.
• Involve the individual or group in decision-making to make them feel their views are important.
• Enhance the individual's sense of belonging.
• Enhance the individual's self-esteem.
• Increase the person's sense of ownership. Listen to the concerns people have about the changes.
• Model the behaviors you want people to adopt.

The leader also uses "special devices" to satisfy basic human needs. These "devices" typically stress the individual's values and feed their need to feel important; involve the individual in decision-making and contribute to their sense of control; enhance the individual's self-esteem and sense of professionalism; and recognize and reward accomplishments to feed into the individual's sense of accomplishment and belonging.

Commitment is about taking ownership of change. The leader looks for ways to incite or impel people to feel a sense of ownership and, as a result, to permanently change their behaviors. For example, at Safelite, the philosophy is to "Put People First." This initiative by Safelite has four clearly stated commitments to employees:

1. *You'll experience great leadership*. Employees will be treated with respect and will receive guidance to help reach their full potential.
2. *We focus on you first*. Tools, information and resources will be provided to position employees for success.
3. *We hire top talent ... that includes you*. By bringing ideas and applying skills, employees will have opportunities to grow both personally and professionally.
4. *You'll work in a caring culture*. Safelite strives for a culture that inspires its employees to achieve ... not just because they have to, but because they want to.[3]

According to the Center for Creative Leadership, team members are motivated to take ownership if they have opportunities to learn and develop, work on projects that build skills and experience without greatly exceeding their ability, make suggestions and give input and ideas, and have their concerns taken seriously by the leader.[4] It is important to understand the motivations of team members. According to a 2013 study from EY concerning Generation Y managers (beginning birthdates as early as the 1980s to the early 2000s), Gen Y managers are widely perceived as entitled, and score significantly lower as hard-working team players. "Entitled workers — those who feel they are owed things from their organization and that their excellence is a given — are less likely to lead teams effectively and advocate for subordinates."[5] This is presenting a new challenge in the workplace.

Acting as a role model is one motivational technique the leader may use to generate commitment. By modeling desired behaviors such as openness to criticism and active listening, the leader demonstrates the power of these behaviors and encourages others to adopt them. The leader might also identify role models within the organization. This might be individuals or teams who have achieved outstanding results by adopting the desired behaviors and committing to the vision. For example, after Boston Scientific completely reorganized and significantly improved the efficiency and effectiveness of its indirect procurement operations, it began to host an annual global face-to-face Indirect Summit to showcase best practices, report on prior-year achievements, and develop strategic goals and objectives for the coming year. Rewards and recognition were viewed as important to keep momentum going and encourage ongoing improvement, not only among Boston Scientific procurement team members but suppliers, as well. An annual Indirect Supplier Management Awards program was launched in 2011 as an opportunity to reward top performers.[6]

Another method is to assess where the supply organization is now compared to where the vision takes it, and create action items based on the assessment. This approach might work quite well with achievement-oriented employees who are motivated by a challenge. Safelite's employee engagement culture includes six core competencies, each of which presents challenges for continuous improvement. Employee engagement requires defining expected behaviors from associates; Safelite's six core competencies, listed below, define those expectations:

1. *Live our values.* Do what's right. In our supply management organization, for example, all supply managers must complete our ethics training program.
2. *Think people first.* Recognize that having great people is the ultimate competitive advantage.
3. *Have passion for creating customer delight.* Deliver an optimal experience internally and externally. Our supply management staff interacts most frequently with internal customers. One simple way we strive to provide top-notch service is to have a real person answer the phone within two rings and to respond to instant messages, texts and emails within the hour. When operating in a multi-location environment, the corporate office can get a bad customer service reputation. For supply management professionals this means that addressing the needs of the internal customer is one of our most important tasks.
4. *Understand the business (and your role in it).* Learn and apply position expertise and industry knowledge. At the supply chain level, that means implementing the latest warehouse management systems to streamline processes, staying abreast of recycling and energy efficient efforts within the industry, and constantly monitoring the efficiency of all our packaging and shipping options.

5. *Be innovative.* Think differently for better business results. Our warehouse team recently completed a pilot program to test the use of steel pallets as opposed to wood pallets. As a result, we are investing in this more durable, cost-saving, environmentally friendly format.
6. *Drive for extraordinary results.* Show personal desire, energy and focus to succeed against high standards. For example, the supply management organization quadrupled Safelite's warehouse space within a two-year period, opening two new distribution centers within 14 months of each other.[7]

"Learning by experience" and "practical proofs" can be especially useful in building commitment. One organization has found it very effective to use role playing to create meaningful experiences. Through a simulated environment with company salespeople acting as suppliers, supply management employees were able to practice the new problem-oriented behaviors required by the new vision. In the process, salespeople were able to see and believe what supply management could contribute. These initiatives helped to change the mind-set of the entire organization, and supply management's peers began to communicate the value-add potential of supply management to others in the organization. Generating "practical proofs" of supply management potential was accomplished through carefully selecting and executing pilot projects by handpicked members of the supply management group. By "practicing" the new behaviors in real settings, and capturing and communicating the results, supply management was able to build interest and momentum in its new vision.

Clearly, the leader must be versatile in terms of having the ability to switch from coaching to mentoring to acting as a role model to providing feedback. Not all leaders will be equally strong in each role. Therefore, the leader may want to ensure that the leadership team includes individuals with different strengths and multiple strengths.[8]

Influence and Influencing Techniques

Influence is defined by *Merriam-Webster's Dictionary* as "the act, process, or power of producing an effect without apparent exertion of tangible force or direct exercise of command." Often influence is not a deliberate effort nor intentional. Influence techniques may be positive (build strong relationships, understand stakeholders' interests, create options, motivate) or negative (manipulate, harass or trick people to get what you want). One's span of influence is not limited by one's position in the chain of command or by formal authority. According to John Kotter, "The better performers tend to mobilize more people to get more things done, and do so using a wider range of influence tactics."[9]

According to the Center for Creative Leadership, a leader may choose from three influence tactics. These are tactics that (1) depend on logic, (2) appeal to the emotions, and (3) support a cooperative effort.[10]

Logic. Logical appeals are targeted to the listener's rational and intellectual positions. Salespeople often employ this tactic when they plan a sales strategy around the features, advantages and benefits of the sale item. When they speak with a potential customer, they typically focus on the benefits from that customer's perspective.

Ravi Kant, vice chairman at Tata Motors, for instance, focused on selling new ideas to people rather than giving orders. In an interview with Gautam Kumra from *The McKinsey Quarterly*, Kant said, "The most effective way to sustain change is to make those involved internalize it rather than just getting someone to come and talk about it." The leadership team exposed people to the outside world so they would see what was happening, and they kept reasoning with people so they would come to their own conclusions about the changed context of the business. Customers were brought in to talk about problems and make product improvement suggestions. Competitors' products were taken apart so that Tata employees could compare them to Tata products to understand why customers chose a competitor's product over a Tata product. These logical appeals were used to sell new ideas internally.[11] When he was interviewed, Mr. Kant was a managing director; he has since been promoted to vice chair.

Emotion. Emotional tactics appeal to some affecting motivator such as the need to feel like one belongs, is providing a service or contributing an idea that supports his or her well-being. Safelite's stated core competencies, as listed above, are meant to challenge and inspire employees. For example, competency #6 states, "Drive for extraordinary results." It encourages employees to go above and beyond, and to show personal desire, energy and focus to succeed against high standards.[12]

Cooperation. Cooperation relies on building a connection between stakeholder groups and the leader. "We are all in this together" is the basic message that depends on all parties believing there is a connection and that people are jointly accountable for mutual goals. At Safelite, to create joint accountability and continuous improvement, an annual People Opinion Survey of the leadership and associates was created, and it is supported by monthly pulse checks (shorter surveys to a small percentage of employees, picked randomly) to measure what the employee base thinks about the business. Survey findings are used to drive internal improvements. In the supply management organization, the engagement scores become part of goals, objectives and personal development plans.[13]

Figure 4-2 lists these three types of influencing techniques and provides ideas for successfully making each appeal.

Figure 4-2: Influencing Techniques

TYPE OF APPEAL	TECHNIQUES
Logic	• Use facts, objective data and evidence to support your claim. • Present the idea clearly, logically and objectively. • Engage in a thorough explanation of the thought process used. • Compare advantages and disadvantages. • Focus attention on potential problems and proposed solutions. • Explain how the plan improves the person's job, how resources will be allocated, and what the feasible benefits and opportunities are for the person.
Emotional	• Focus on the listener's values and goals. • Link your vision and strategy to the listener's values and goals. • Use hypothetical statements and future-oriented scenarios. • Appeal to the listener's self image and need for accomplishment.
Cooperation	• Create the image of mutual goals and shared responsibility. • Focus on how you will help the listener make the vision happen. • Talk about the training, tools and other forms of support that will be available. • Discuss barriers and explain how you will work to remove them. • Reinforce your role as partners by listening carefully and thoughtfully to the person's concerns.

Robert Cialdini, a regents' professor emeritus of psychology and marketing at Arizona State University, founder and president of Influence at Work and author of *Influence: Science and Practice*, identified six business tools that can be used to influence people: (1) commitment and consistency, (2) reciprocation, (3) authority, (4) consensus, (5) liking, and (6) scarcity.[14] These tools are explained in Figure 4-3.

Figure 4-3: Tools of Influence

INFLUENCING TOOL	DEFINITION	EXAMPLE
Commitment and consistency	Find common ground and speak the same message continuously.	Identify a commitment that has been made by the organization (for example, to contain costs) and then show how the supply management strategy is consistent with the organizational commitment.
Reciprocity	Give-and-take; win-win.	Make a concession to motivate a reciprocal concession. Give time, energy and attention (legally and ethically) in return for a concession made by the listener.
Authority	Be seen as *an* authority, not *in* authority.	Ethically use authority. Supply managers need to demonstrate to suppliers and internal business partners that they are knowledgeable and credible. They must give people a reason to believe the message. Nothing sells like success. Pick pilot projects carefully, obtain measurable results and communicate them widely. Better yet, get your internal business partners to communicate your successes for you.
Consensus	Get people to realize that they are substantially in agreement.	Know the specific needs of each stakeholder and use this knowledge and understanding to link stakeholders to one another. In essence, build agreement and consensus where there was no perception of it among stakeholders. Build a consensus on some aspect of your vision, mission, plan or strategy. Use this as a takeoff point.
Liking	People tend to cooperate better with people they like, and who appear empathetic to their concerns.	Point out common interests and areas of understanding. Look for personal and professional similarities or goals. Avoid trying too hard to gain the approval of others by using too many compliments or trying to find common ground when there is none.
Scarcity	Being one of a privileged few may influence behavior.	Technique must be used carefully. It can involve offering information selectively (always legally and ethically). Supply managers may be able to use the fact that resources are scarce as a tool to influence internal stakeholders to work with them to ensure best value decisions.

Source: Adapted from Mary Siegfried, "The Power of Influence," *Inside Supply Management*®, (16:10), 2005; and Julie Melillo,"Powerful Persuasion," *Inside Supply Management*® (23:7), 2012, 34, accessed November 18, 2013, http://www.ism.ws/pubs/ISMMag/ismarticle.cfm?ItemNumber=23101.

CHAPTER 4: Gaining Commitment: Motivating and Inspiring People

These tools are used by many people in different settings. For example, Thomas Linton, who was executive vice president and chief procurement officer at LG Electronics at the time, led the global procurement organization at LG Electronics to change. Commitment and consistency was established through the development and execution of a clear plan and timetables for change. The CPO had also established a clear line of authority. All procurement teams reported to the CPO, and he in turn was part of the executive meetings between the business units and chief functional officers. Consensus support for the changes they made was also critical, using commodity councils and gaining executive support for the changes.[15]

Global Leadership Styles and Influence

Leadership styles and the effectiveness of influencing techniques vary across cultures and change with the times. Supply managers working in global situations must take the time to understand the leadership style of the person, organization and culture in a specific situation, and avoid stereotypes. For example, when one of the authors was teaching an MBA class made up primarily of Asian students in their late 20s, she asked whether or not the stereotypes of following leaders without questioning and putting the whole above the individual still held. The students laughed, and indicated that while these ideals may have been true for their parents, the current generation saw things very differently, much more individualistically, while still considering the whole. What is relevant here is that different cultures do have different leadership and team orientation styles. Perhaps it is because of this that many global organizations are leaning toward engagement of local managers rather than using expatriots, who may have difficulty understanding and working effectively with the local culture. The important issue is that effective leadership styles vary widely across cultures, and that they do change over time.[16]

Today, emerging market leaders such as China and India emphasize leaders who are operationally excellent, hands-on and heavily manage individual performance. Benelux and Nordic countries tend to focus more on managers who are "change leaders," providing planning, vision and communications to guide the organization.[17]

D. Quinn Mills, the Albert J. Weatherhead, Jr. professor of business administration emeritus at Harvard Business School, compared the prevalence of leadership styles in American and Asian businesses in a more general fashion. In "Asian and American Leadership Styles: How Are They Unique?," he notes that while the directive style is waning in America, it is still quite common in Asia, as confirmed in the above research. A participative or teamwork style is common in Europe, often to meet legal requirements, and in Japan because of cultural norms.[18] An empowering style where responsibility is delegated is common in divisional structures in America and is starting to be used by some young Asian leaders. Recall the story about Lenovo in Chapter 2, about very successful Chinese entrepreneurs with very different leadership styles.

The rise of professional managers in developing economies and companies brings similarities in leadership styles, but cultural and national differences influence how these styles are manifested. This is evident in statements made by Eastern leaders. For example, Ravi Kant, vice chairman of Tata Motors, said that the organization wants to grow and produce a healthy bottom line, be seen as an innovative organization and do it "the Tata way — transparently, ethically and meeting our corporate social responsibility. We want to make India proud."[19] Likewise, in a speech at an international conference in the early 2000s, Zhang Yue, chairman and founder of Broad Air Conditioning in Changsha, China, spoke futuristically of the world's most profitable and admired company in 2015. Although he was speaking about his own company, one that "quietly economizes on energy use around the world," he said, "It doesn't matter that people may not know the name of this company, but they should know it is a Chinese company."[20] This demonstrates Western charisma mixed with Eastern pride. With his company's success over the past several years, he has also modified his company's business to focus on environmental issues, such as reducing energy consumption and using cleaner energy that his products use, and more energy efficient building. He was recognized by the United Nations Environment Programme as a 2011 Laureate for his Entrepreneurial Vision.[21]

Individualist or Communitarian. In a global business environment it is also important to consider whether the individual's starting point is as an individualist or as a communitarian. An individualist values autonomy and initiative, and seeks achievement through setting goals and taking action to reach them. A communitarian values group harmony and cohesion, and makes decisions in consultation with other group members whose input is heavily weighted. A leader from a communitarian background seeking to generate commitment from a group of individualists may be perceived as indecisive. A leader from an individualist background may come across too strongly and autocratically for group members from a communitarian background. Recognizing these differences and respecting the preferences of parties the leader is trying to influence may increase the chances of gaining commitment.[22]

In developing economies such as that of China that have a communitarian tradition, an interesting mix of rising individualism — marked by successful entrepreneurs and a growing middle class — is emerging, while traditional collective approaches are still seen in employment, training and work practices in many successful Chinese ventures. This duality presents a challenge for a leader — especially a Western leader — who is working to turn an organization into a truly global company or trying to understand and conduct business with Chinese suppliers.

Former Singaporean Prime Minister Lee Kuan Yew and others refer to the Asian social bargain as "less individual latitude, more collective success." Chinese tycoon Zhang Yue, mentioned previously, is one of the richest men in China. He owns and runs Broad Air Conditioning. The company's business is nonelectric refrigeration, which is more energy efficient than compression coolers. Yue argues for worldwide systematic changes in energy, packaging and transportation. The company is guided by six Broad values: (1) not paying bribes, (2) paying taxes, (3) environmental protection, (4) respect for intellectual property rights, (5) no price gouging, and (6) no predatory competition. The company pays good wages by Chinese factory standards and trains employees at the Broad management training center. Yue believes that comfortable and happy employees will positively affect their work ethic and professionalism.[23]

He received recognition as a 2011 Laureate as a Champion of the Earth from the United Nations for his entrepreneurial vision. He notes, "When I set up my business, I challenged myself to create wealth. Now, I have completely shifted the focus of this business toward the direction of reducing emissions. I've taken on the challenge of climate change."[24]

Building Strong Internal Partnerships

The key to successful leadership today is influence, not authority.

— **KENNETH BLANCHARD**
MANAGEMENT WRITER AND LECTURER[25]

Motivational tools alone will not lead people to commit to change and to adopt new ways of doing things. The supply leader and his or her leadership team must also develop strong internal business partnerships throughout the organization. Management author John Kotter refers to these relationships as "thick informal networks."[26] As supply management leaders seek to transform the group, processes and functions, it becomes even more critical for them to develop a network of thick informal relationships and strong internal and external partnerships vertically and horizontally.

Vertical Relationships

Vertical relationships are those that involve people up and down the chain of command (see Figure 4-4). For example, the vice president of supply management might work to develop thick informal networks with people in positions above his or her level as well as with people in positions below the vice president level. The relationship that a direct report builds with his or her manager is an example of "managing up." An interesting question is, can a direct report also "lead up" the chain of command and exhibit leadership behaviors in the relationship with a superior? The relationship built with subordinates is partly based on the direct report having reporting responsibilities to the supervisor/manager. How successful a manager's relationship is with direct reports depends also on the leadership skills and behaviors exhibited by the manager.

Figure 4-4: Vertical and Horizontal Relationships

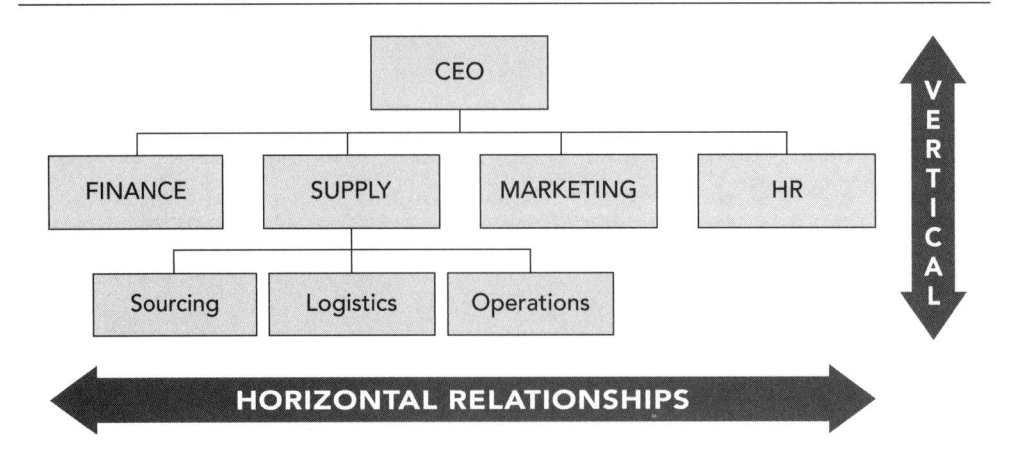

```
                        CEO
         ┌───────────┬───┴───┬───────────┐
      FINANCE      SUPPLY  MARKETING     HR
                ┌────┼────┐
            Sourcing Logistics Operations

         ◄────── HORIZONTAL RELATIONSHIPS ──────►
```

Horizontal Relationships

Horizontal relationships (see Figure 4-4) are those that involve peers (people at a similar level) across the organization in various functions representing different business processes. For example, the vice president of supply management would work to develop thick informal networks with the other vice presidents in the organization, managers with managers, and so on. Strong vertical and horizontal relationships lay the foundation for effective change management.

The interrelatedness of members of an organization is called *connectivity*.[27] The supply leader must recognize the degree of connectivity present at the start of the change management process and work to strengthen connectivity with the appropriate stakeholders in ways that make collaboration possible. The leader's versatility enables him or her to enhance positive connectivity and reduce or eliminate the negative impact of connectivity that is harmful to change.

The ability to perceive the patterns of connectivity within the organization and broader society is an important leadership quality.[28] Gro Brundtland, former director general of the World Health Organization and former chair of the World Commission on Environment and Development, is seen as such a leader. She inspired those around her into action, and succeeded in developing agreement on many major policy issues in Norway and globally, including the first global initiative to abolish tobacco usage.[29]

Building Coalitions

A coalition is a temporary alliance of distinct parties, persons or states for joint action. One of the main advantages of strong one-on-one internal business partnerships is the possibility of building coalitions. Because the changes in supply management affect many stakeholders in different ways, the supply leader must consciously build coalitions to stave off resistance, increase support and drive momentum. The leader can use his or her knowledge about the interests, options and alternatives of each party to identify common interests, create a sense of interdependence and overcome resistance to change. In today's heavily team-oriented business environment, the leader is often maneuvering among multiple teams with competing goals and objectives as well as multiple individuals within these teams who may also have competing goals and objectives. The leader needs strong negotiating skills and creative thinking abilities to reap the rewards of coalition building. Geographical dispersion and lack of active sponsors or advocates may hinder the leader's ability to build effective coalitions.

Lead or Participate in Teams

A team brings together interdependent people with varying knowledge, skills and expertise, often from different functional areas, to work on a common task or project. High performing teams are known to provide superior results compared to individual efforts as a result of the range of skills, knowledge and capabilities of team members. Teams also promote cross-functional cooperation, collaboration and communication, and may facilitate consensus building in the organization.

Some organizations use personality profiles to foster understanding of personal differences between and among team members. They then develop team contracts or charters that seek to accommodate personality differences. This helps in developing understanding and acceptance along with work rules that guide behavior, which then lessen the impact of differences. For example, in a supply chain organization in a major oil company, permanent supply chain teams were formed around key commodities. Team members completed the Myers-Briggs assessment; each team then spent time with an outside facilitator who explained the outcomes and worked with the teams to develop better working relationships.

In effective teams, team members have clear roles and responsibilities, share a vision and sense of purpose, and are collectively accountable for reaching the team's goal. Teams often have to collaborate with people or groups outside the team who may have competing or conflicting goals and processes. The team leader and the supply leader-manager must build relationships within and outside the team, negotiate and resolve conflicts, and communicate to build acceptance of team decisions.

Teams are used throughout organizations for many purposes, including improvements in quality, cost or delivery; product development; process engineering; and technology management. They can be project-oriented or ongoing. Project teams are brought together for a limited time to achieve a specific goal or outcome, such as completion of a capital project, implementation of a new technology platform or a new product development initiative. Ongoing teams continue indefinitely, such as a commodity sourcing team that manages the process and the supplier relationship. When building cross-cultural teams, the following should be kept in mind:
- Up front, determine and focus on the reason for the team's existence.
- Factor in the influence of personality differences.

- Don't underestimate the impact of culture on everything.
- Professional identities influence the way team members interact.
- Explore individual team members' emotional intelligence.
- Develop support systems for team members no matter where they are.
- Global team leaders need global competencies.[30]

Many corporate organizational structures are leaner, flatter, more adaptive and more flexible than in the past. Rigid functional structures have been replaced by a greater dependence on cross-functional teams that overlay the functional organization to push decisions lower in the organizational hierarchy. Senior management often tries to combine the flexibility of decentralized supply management and the buying power and information sharing of centralized supply through the use of teams. Cross-functional teams consist of personnel from multiple functions focused on a supply-related task. Generally, high-performing cross-functional teams will achieve better results on the task, with greater benefit to the organization as a whole, at lower costs, in less time, and with greater stakeholder buy-in. Effective cross-functional teams save time by allowing a simultaneous, rather than a sequential, approach. For example, if key stakeholder groups are involved in the development of a new process from concept through design, development and rollout, the process may be better from the outset, more widely accepted and adopted quickly.

Various types of supply management teams may be used, including cross-functional teams, teams with suppliers or customers — or both, supplier councils that include key suppliers, purchasing councils, commodity management teams, buying consortiums, sustainability and social responsibility teams, technology teams, and social media teams.

Role of Supply Management in Teams. Supply professionals are increasingly called on to lead or participate in cross-functional and cross-organizational teams, including project management, process improvement and international teams. Supply personnel may play a number of roles in a team including (1) providing support, service or information; (2) project management; (3) leadership; or (4) facilitation. Often supply personnel are on teams to provide support, service or information to the other team members. In these cases, supply personnel play an advisory role and may not have much say in the actual team decisions. The ability to influence without authority is an important skill in these situations. Other times, supply personnel play the role of the project manager and need skills in process, people and time management, along with a strong ability to see the big picture of the total project and keep track of the many project details. At still other times, a supply management professional is the team leader and must develop the skills to manage people, processes and time while taking primary responsibility for the outcome of the team effort. Another role is that of facilitator. A facilitator primarily manages the communication process of the team with the goal of fleshing out the thoughts and ideas of the participants rather than selling them on any one result. It is important to be clear about the role being played and to develop the appropriate knowledge, skills and expertise to fulfill the role requirements.

Phases of Team Building. Group dynamics play a critical role in team success. While group dynamics are driven by the interactions of the members of each team, certain dynamics may be observed in teams in general. Bruce Tuckman identified four phases of team formation (see Figure 4-5) — forming, storming, norming and performing. In stage one, forming, team members get acquainted with each other and learn three important things about each other: (1) what each person brings to the team, (2) what each person wants from the process, and (3) how team members will interact with one another. In stage two, storming, team members put forth their ideas, argue, and test to see whose ideas will dominate. In stage three, norming, team members have developed some trust in one another and are able to focus on the substance of the project, reaching agreement on task responsibility, workload and the decision-making process. In stage four, performing, the team functions effectively and decisions are reached.[31] The supply leader-manager plays a critical role in understanding these stages, recognizing which stage his or her teams are in, and coaching and mentoring team members to move through the phases and achieve the goals of the team.

Figure 4-5: Phases of Team Building

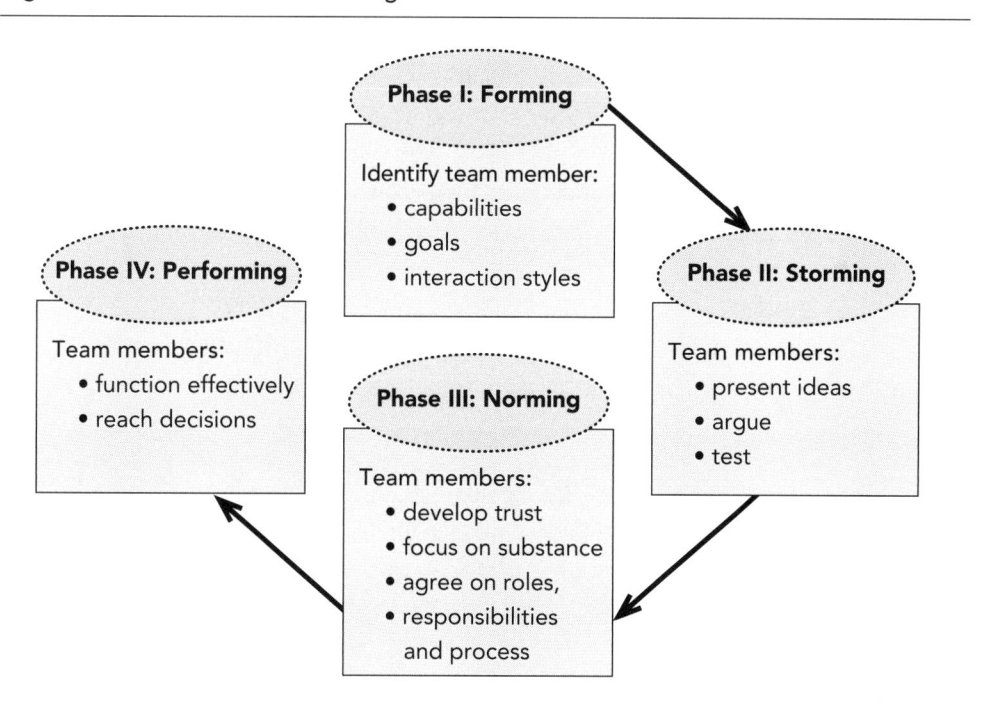

Phase I: Forming
Identify team member:
- capabilities
- goals
- interaction styles

Phase II: Storming
Team members:
- present ideas
- argue
- test

Phase III: Norming
Team members:
- develop trust
- focus on substance
- agree on roles,
- responsibilities
and process

Phase IV: Performing
Team members:
- function effectively
- reach decisions

Advantages and Disadvantages of Teams. There are a number of advantages and disadvantages to using teams. In many ways, whether something is an advantage or a disadvantage depends on the composition, structure and management of the team. Advantages and disadvantages may relate to the ability or inability to create synergy, reach a consensus, manage time to complete the task or project efficiently and effectively, introduce and manage change effectively, avoid groupthink, and resolve conflicts. The supply leader-manager must be quick to recognize obstacles and find ways to turn them into opportunities.

SYNERGY. *Merriam-Webster's Dictionary* defines *synergy* as a cooperative situation where two or more parts come together in a way that the result is more than the combined effect of what they could have achieved by acting alone — opposed to *antagonism*. In the business world, the "discrete agencies" may be individuals, groups or organizations that come together to achieve results greater than those that could be achieved independently. The possibility of synergy is a primary reason for forming teams, and the inability to achieve synergy is the root of many team failures.

CONSENSUS BUILDING. A consensus is when a group reaches a general agreement. Teams may facilitate consensus building because key stakeholders come together at the beginning of a decision-making process and work through all the issues jointly to reach a decision. The deal may be more widely accepted and adopted because of the level of buy-in secured during the team process. On the other hand, team discord may make it impossible to reach a consensus and ultimately derail the team process.

GROUPTHINK. *Groupthink* is a term used to describe a decision-making process in which group members do not critically evaluate each other's ideas and proposals. The result is a poor decision reached through a faulty consensus-building process. Irving Janis did extensive research on groupthink in several critical events in U.S. history — namely Pearl Harbor, Vietnam and the Bay of Pigs Invasion. He and other researchers have found certain conditions that foster groupthink, including the conditions listed below:

- High stress from external threats and low hope for a better solution than the one offered by the leader(s);
- Group homogeneity of backgrounds and ideology;
- The persuasive strength or directive style of the group's leader; and
- Insulation from outside ideas, perspectives and alternate opinions.

An organization faced with external threats such as global competition, rapidly rising commodity prices or increasing regulation mixed with a homogenous leadership team and inadequate research may easily fall prey to groupthink.

The leader and all team members must be sensitive to signs of groupthink and be ready to recommend alternate processes such as subgroups working independently of one another or bringing in outside experts. The leader must balance the desire for consensus against the dangers of groupthink and provide guidance and direction throughout the process.

TIME CONSIDERATIONS. The cycle time for a project may be less than the nonteam approach, but more of the work may be concentrated at the beginning of the process. Effective new product or service development processes can improve an organization's competitive position. Cross-functional teams can shorten development cycle times, improve quality and reduce development costs by operating concurrently rather than sequentially. Rather than each functional area performing its task and passing the project off to the next functional area, the key functional groups — usually design, engineering, manufacturing, quality assurance, supply management and marketing — work on the new product development simultaneously. Because a large percentage of a product's cost is purchased materials, early supplier involvement is often needed. When surveyed, many supply management professionals report greater involvement in new product/service design and development.

Harley-Davidson, the motorcycle manufacturer, has successfully used cross-functional teams for sourcing and product development. Teams are formed for a platform or line of Harley-Davidson motorcycles, and these teams are responsible for the life cycle of their line. Each platform team consists of a program manager who is generally from the design community, as well as a lead each from manufacturing, supply management and marketing. The platform team analyzes information from many sources and decides on the general design and style of the bike. Then the project is turned over to the company's engineering center of expertise, which is also a cross-functional team consisting of supply, engineers, suppliers and others who work together to integrate all design components in a cost-effective, high-quality manner. Once the design is complete, the platform team is responsible for getting the end product into the hands of customers, and accumulating and analyzing field reports, surveys of owner satisfaction levels and marketing information.[32] If supply is also included in teams with end customers, and there is a better opportunity to deliver the greatest value in the shortest cycle time.

OWNERSHIP ISSUES. Ownership of an idea, process, project or decision may be spread among the team members in such a way that buy-in across functions is achieved in less time. However, there is always the risk that no one in a team will take ownership and the lack of shared ownership and accountability causes the team process to flounder. There is less chance of this happening if team goals, roles and responsibility, authority, and measurement and rewards are clearly defined up front. Creating shared goals and rewards among team members encourages ownership.

MANAGING OR INTRODUCING CHANGE. Teams may be used either to introduce change or to manage the change process. If the team is successful at creating synergy, building consensus, avoiding groupthink and taking ownership of the change process, then the team may be a successful change agent.

Managing Multicultural Teams. Team members, team leaders and managers face special challenges when team members come from different countries, cultures and backgrounds. From their research on multicultural teams, Jeanne Brett, Kristin Behfar and Mary C. Kern identified four categories that can create barriers to team success and four strategies for dealing with these challenges: (1) direct versus indirect communication styles, (2) trouble with accents and fluency, (3) differing attitudes toward hierarchy and authority, and (4) conflicting norms for decision-making.[33]

DIRECT VERSUS INDIRECT COMMUNICATION STYLES. People from Western cultures tend to communicate directly and explicitly. In many other cultures, however, meaning is embedded in the way the message is presented, and the listener must know about the context of the message and the presenter. Direct confrontation and moving things up the chain of command may violate norms of behavior and lead to the direct communicator being isolated socially, and even physically, from the team. For example, in a culture where direct communication is the norm, a team member may be expected to identify a problem and explain the implications of the problem directly to the team and to the boss. In a culture where communication is more indirect, it may be more appropriate to ask the team "what if" questions to allow them to discuss the scenario and uncover the problem on their own.

TROUBLE WITH ACCENTS AND FLUENCY. English may be the language of global business, but fluency, accents, translations, interpretations and usage create challenges for multicultural teams. Some native English speakers are impatient with non-native speakers, and may allow the lack of fluency to influence their perceptions of the non-native speaker's competence or status. This behavior may mean that the team does not get the full benefit of the expertise in the team.

DIFFERING ATTITUDES TOWARD HIERARCHY AND AUTHORITY. People from hierarchical cultures may defer to higher-status team members even if the team itself has a flat structure. This behavior may damage the person's stature and credibility in the eyes of people from more egalitarian cultures. Those from more egalitarian cultures may communicate directly with people higher up the chain of command because this is commonly accepted in their culture, but their peers from a hierarchical culture would consider this disrespectful behavior.

CONFLICTING NORMS FOR DECISION-MAKING. In some cultures, decisions are made slowly after much analysis, while in others, such as in the United States, they are made quickly after little analysis.

The four strategies for dealing with these challenges are (1) adaptation, (2) structural intervention, (3) managerial intervention, and (4) exit. Adaptation occurs when team members recognize and adjust to each other's cultural differences or learn to work around them. When they are unable to adapt, people may be reassigned or the team reorganized (structural intervention), or the manager may intervene and make decisions for the team. An exit strategy is when one or more team members voluntarily leave the team or leave at the request of management. This strategy is used as a last resort, typically when permanent teams cannot function because of cultural challenges.[34]

Conflict and Conflict Resolution

Teams, partnerships and coalitions may be challenging to build and even more challenging to maintain. It is not only common but also inevitable, then, that leaders come into conflict. This conflict may be with recalcitrant "followers" who are not yet committed to change.

Or it may be with other leaders in the organization who have a competing vision to that of the supply leader. Because leaders lead in the interest of the group they represent, they will eventually encounter other leaders who are defending the interests of their group within the organization. These competing visions indicate that the organization as a whole has not committed to one clear vision or direction, perhaps because of a lack of direction from the very top of the organization or because of misalignment between and among business process owners and leaders. At this point, the organization needs a leader, or leaders, with the ability to avoid taking sides and work collaboratively to cross boundaries and bring visions into alignment.[35]

The benefits of thick informal networks may be less conflict generation in the first place and speedier resolution of conflict if and when it does occur. In situations where the driver for change comes from within the supply organization itself, rather than an edict from top management or from an external event that challenges the organization's survival, internal partnerships may facilitate the change process. A stakeholder may be more willing to at least listen to new ideas if the messenger is someone who is trusted and credible.

Conflict can be a powerful constructive force or a powerful destructive force in a team, partnership or coalition. If managed properly, disagreements, debate and different perspectives may be a source of creative thinking by pushing people out of their mental comfort zones. Ineffective conflict resolution may prevent the team from accomplishing its goal. Avoidance of conflict and a tendency to quickly reach consensus without debate may result in groupthink and a poor decision. Groupthink can be equally destructive because it prevents the group from capitalizing on the expertise of the team members. The challenge for team leaders is to minimize destructive conflict while encouraging constructive disagreement and open debate.

Conflict Resolution Skills. The ability to resolve conflicts is a valuable leader skill and important in gaining commitment. Conflict resolution is a model for resolving conflict that starts with the assumption that the parties involved in the conflict are stuck and need to get unstuck. It is a nonjudgmental model, as neither side is assumed to be inherently wrong, bad or evil. Supply management professionals need to develop a conflict resolution strategy for dealing with issues that arise out of process, policy or procedure changes, and internal or external performance appraisals or audits.

Nondefensive problem-solving is a process that focuses on finding and eliminating the root cause of a problem rather than trying to place blame on a person. An organizational culture that fosters blaming behaviors creates fear in employees. W. Edwards Deming noted that a major obstacle to process improvement is fear by the employee. Fear can be a debilitating emotion and one that often arises from the common practice of determining "who did it" when a mistake occurs.[36]

Deming also noted that even when human error is the apparent source of a problem, most often something in the system or process led to the person making the error. He said, "Put a good person in a bad system and the bad system wins, every time."[37] Therefore, it is necessary to seek the root cause behind the error, and develop and execute a plan of action to eliminate it. The plan would, of course, focus on improving the process or system. This approach is called *mistake-proofing* or *poka yoke* (pronounced POH-Ka YOH-Kay), a Japanese quality-control method developed by Shigeo Shingo, an industrial engineer at Toyota. It refers to the design of materials and assembly methods to prevent mistakes. For example, parts might be designed in such a way that it is impossible to assemble them in an incorrect configuration. Color-coding plugs and outlets helps ensure proper hookup; making each plug and outlet a different size or shape from each other prevents incorrect hookup.

Fostering a defensive problem-solving mentality and mistake-proofing during the design stage as part of organizational culture may help avoid the creation of some conflict and speed up the resolution of conflicts when they do occur.

Other tools and techniques available to resolve conflict include rational problem-solving methods such as the Kepner-Tregoe rational process analysis, Six Sigma processes and project management. These are discussed in detail in *Effective Supply Management Performance* (ISM *Professional Series*).

Creating a Culture of Commitment

> *You do not lead by hitting people over the head — that's assault, not leadership.*
>
> — DWIGHT D. EISENHOWER

The change management process requires multiple leaders throughout the organization and the hierarchy. Therefore, leaders must motivate other people to provide leadership within their sphere of influence. This is especially challenging if people perceive leadership as the equivalent of a formal position in the organization. For example, the author spent eight weeks with a company that was instituting a supply chain management initiative. When supply chain team members were interviewed about the change process, they typically stated that they could not move forward with the changes required by new supply processes because top management had not provided enough of the right kind of support. This perception persisted across the supply chain organization despite the fact that top management had taken the initiative to launch a formal supply chain management program, budgeted absolutely and relatively large sums of money to the initiative over multiple years, committed customized training resources, dedicated IT support and facilities — and even regularly communicated a consistent verbal message about the supply chain initiative. When asked what else top management was supposed to do, most people responded, "mandate the change."

A weakness in the change management process was that top management considered the leadership tasks of creating alignment and gaining commitment to be the responsibility of the supply chain management teams. Team members perceived their roles as largely managerial — plan, budget, organize, staff and control. When compliance was not forthcoming in all the operating areas, supply chain team members were ill-equipped to cope with the lack of commitment. Individuals had the skills, qualification, education and experience to manage routine processes and procedures, but lacked the leadership capability to energize people to commit to change.

Senior executives who were interviewed stated that mandates did not work in the company's organizational culture; they expected the supply chain team to sell the vision and concept to stakeholders and influence them to support the supply chain initiative.

The lack of buy-in was also influenced by managerial factors such as a lack of joint goals and joint accountability across business units and functions. The presence of competing and conflicting goals raised the requirement for strong leadership, but the organization had not developed leadership skills in multiple employees so there were not enough leaders who were ready, willing and able to fill the void.

This story is told to illustrate that organizations need more than one leader. They need many leaders at many levels, all of whom are aligned around a common vision. As these leaders develop a vision for their particular area, such as supply management, finance, marketing or engineering, the internal partnerships or thick informal networks they build enable them to align individual functional visions around the common organizationwide vision. By developing the leadership capability of the organization, current leaders are also laying the foundation for the availability of leaders in the future in both formal and informal roles.

Eight Steps to Transform Your Organization

The previous sections of this chapter have focused on tools, techniques and actions that can be used to motivate and inspire people to adopt a vision and, more important, change their behaviors to make that vision a reality. As anyone who has ever tried to change a behavior knows, making a permanent change is very difficult. The leader must be aware of the human tendency to backslide and take actions to institutionalize the changes without creating a new, rigid, suboptimal bureaucracy. John P. Kotter, the Konosuke Matsushita Professor of Leadership Emeritus of the Harvard Business School, suggests eight steps for a leader to take to transform an organization (see Figure 4-6).

Figure 4-6: Eight Steps to Organizational Transformation

STEP	ACTIVITIES
1. Establish a sense of urgency	• Examine market and competitive realities. • Identify and discuss crises, potential crises or major opportunities.
2. Form a powerful guiding coalition	• Assemble a group with enough power to lead the change effort. • Encourage the group to work as a team.
3. Create a vision	• Create a vision to help direct the change effort. • Develop strategies for achieving that vision.
4. Communicate the vision	• Use every vehicle possible to communicate the new vision and strategies. • Teach new behaviors by the example of the guiding coalition.
5. Empower others to act on the vision	• Get rid of obstacles to change. • Change systems or structures that seriously undermine the vision. • Encourage risk-taking and nontraditional ideas, activities and actions.
6. Plan for and create short-term wins	• Plan for visible performance improvements. • Create those improvements. • Recognize and reward employees involved in the improvements.
7. Consolidate improvements and produce still more change	• Use increased credibility to change systems, structures and policies that do not fit the vision. • Hire, promote and develop employees who can implement the vision. • Reinvigorate the process with new projects, themes and change agents.
8. Institutionalize new approaches	• Articulate the connections between the new behaviors and organizational success. • Develop the means to ensure leadership development and succession.

Source: John P. Kotter, "Winning at Change," *Leader to Leader*, Volume 10 (Fall 1998), 27–33.

Maintaining Momentum

While initiating change in an organization is typically difficult, maintaining the momentum over a long period of time is often even more difficult. Thomas Linton, who was executive vice president and chief procurement officer LG Electronics Inc. at the time of its procurement transformation, built a sense of urgency for change, with a time line, milestones, tracking and regular updates. He noted, "The speed, work ethic and culture to achieve this transformation are found in LG Electronics' consensus-driven culture. This culture has a strong 'teardown-rebuild' mentality whereby people get behind an initiative very quickly once a decision has been made."[38]

Summary

To implement the vision and mission requires the leader to gain commitment by building strong internal relationships, both vertically and horizontally. Leaders often need assistance from other leaders in the organization, and not only from those who are under the leader's direct control. He or she can use various influencing techniques and tools to use to influence others; these techniques may differ based on the culture of the organization, taking into account various global styles.

Leading and participating in teams is one way to inspire and motivate people and create a culture of commitment.

Making big transformational change is necessary to convert the vision and mission into reality. Eight steps (Kotter) a leader can take to transform an organization include the following:

1. Establish a sense of urgency.
2. Form a powerful guiding coalition.
3. Create a vision.
4. Communicate the vision.
5. Empower others to act on the vision.
6. Plan for and create short-term wins.
7. Consolidate improvements and produce still more change.
8. Institutionalize new approaches.

Key Points

1. Leaders use various motivational techniques such as appealing to people's sense of belonging, need for accomplishment and sense of control to energize stakeholders, and generate commitment to the vision of supply management.
2. Informal internal partnerships or "thick informal networks" are critical to successful change management.
3. Leaders build thick informal partnerships by using motivational techniques and knowledge of stakeholders' interests to build coalitions that provide enough benefit to each stakeholder group to maintain commitment.
4. A culture of leadership is created when multiple leaders exist in an organization and they are actively using their leadership skills while also developing these skills in others.

CHAPTER 5

Killing the project minimizes risks but also eliminates reward.

— JAMES McGRODDY
FORMER SENIOR VICE PRESIDENT, RESEARCH OF IBM[1]

Assessing, Mitigating and Managing Supply-Based Risks

Every organization faces a multitude of risks that must be identified, assessed, prioritized and managed either by avoiding the risk, mitigating the impact of the risk, accepting some or all of the risk, or transferring the risk to another entity. The direction-setting role of leaders is complemented by the risk assessment/risk profiling and business-planning roles of managers. *Risk* is the possibility of loss or injury. *Risk exposure* is the probability of a loss or injury occurring and the likely impact. High-risk events are those with greater probability of occurring and higher expected impact or loss.

Supply management professionals contribute to the organizational risk profile through their assessment of supply-related risks. During the planning process they are then better equipped to develop business plans that, if executed effectively, will maximize opportunities at acceptable levels of risk. The supply leader-manager is responsible for instituting processes and procedures to identify supply-based risks from all potential sources, assess the risk exposure, work internally to determine the acceptable level of risk given the expectations from a project or event, and then develop and execute the selected risk management strategies. Therefore, the analysis of risks and risk exposure, and the development of plans to manage risks, are critical activities of supply management professionals.

Chapter 2 addressed the supply leader's role in setting direction for the supply organization. The managerial counterparts to direction setting are risk assessment (discussed in this chapter), planning (discussed in the following chapter) and budgeting (addressed in *Foundation of Supply Management* [ISM *Professional Series*]). This chapter is divided into two sections: (1) the risk management process including risk assessment and profiling, and (2) supply's role in assessing risks related to two key business decisions — insourcing/outsourcing; and mergers, acquisitions and divestitures.

Chapter Objectives
- Outline the steps in the risk management process and discuss each one.
- Discuss the supply management professional's role in assessing risks related to the decision to insource/make or outsource/buy a good or service (supply chain design), supply interruption, and competition such as geopolitical risk.
- Discuss the supply management professional's role in assessing risks in proposed mergers, acquisitions and divestitures.

The Risk Management Process

The steps in risk management are (1) identify the sources of risks, (2) estimate the probability of occurrence, (3) estimate the likely impact, (4) develop a risk profile, (5) develop risk management strategies, (6) allocate resources, (7) execute strategy, and (8) review results. Figure 5-1 illustrates the risk management process. Each step is discussed in the following sections.

Figure 5-1: The Risk Management Process

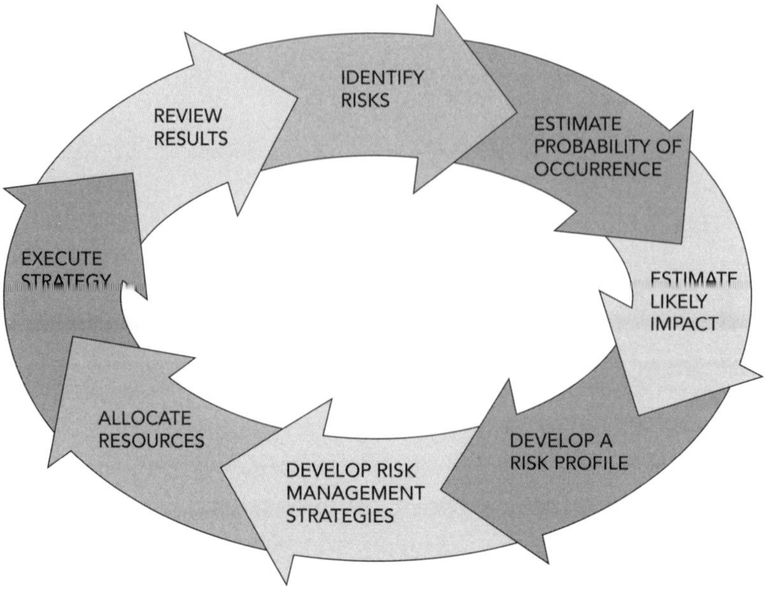

Step 1: Identify the Sources of Risks

The first step in risk management is to identify the sources of risk for each project. For example, the management of a German company in the telecommunications industry defined its risk as "the danger that events or decisions will obstruct the company's achievement of its objectives." This definition of risk was incorporated into the planning process of each functional area.[2] A team might determine typical sources of risk for specific projects or types of projects and use this information as a starting point in planning. In *Waltzing with Bears*, Tom DeMarco and Timothy Lister identify these most common software project risks:

- *An inherent schedule flaw*. Some flaw in the schedule-setting practice will result in an agreement to work to an unreachable goal.
- *Feature creep* (or scope creep as supply management professionals would call it). Changes and additions to the requirements will push the project over budget and schedule.
- *Employee turnover*. Key staff leaving the organization during the project will push up the budget and project duration.
- *An ambiguous specification*. A breakdown in communication at the specification stage leads to an ambiguous and unsuitable contract.
- *Poor productivity*. A failure to accurately estimate a team's performance will lead to project overrun.[3]

A software development team or a sourcing team that is procuring the services of a software development company might start with this list, estimate the likelihood of each event occurring, and estimate the impact. This assessment would drive the acquisition process in terms of acquisition strategy, negotiation goals, type of contract, and terms and conditions.

Because of the increasing recognition of risk in the world today, the Sarbanes-Oxley Act of 2002 requires that all publicly held companies in the U.S. report their major risks in their annual report to shareholders.[4] In addition, GRI — the Global Reporting Initiative, which is aimed at transparency and comparability in reporting across nations and companies, requires disclosure of key risks.[5]

Many sources of risks exist for every type of organization. The supply team members should continually scan the horizon to anticipate anything or anyone who creates or suggests a hazard or raises the possibility of loss or injury. A well-structured and well-staffed supply management organization should have multiple mechanisms in place, including systems, processes, policies, procedures and people, to support this internal and external environmental scan.

One approach to risk identification is to identify major categories of risk and then identify specific risks within each category. For example, a supply risk management team might focus on identifying supply-related risks in six major categories: (1) brand or reputation risks; (2) business continuity risks, including supply interruption such as that associated with geopolitical risks in international sourcing and operations; (3) financial risks; (4) operational risks; (5) legal risks; and (6) technical risks. Each risk category and possible mitigation strategies are discussed in the following sections.

Brand or Reputation Risks. The primary risk for an organization is that its reputation or brand will be harmed by some force that either goes undetected or that is detected but not mitigated. A worse case would be that this risk interrupts business continuity. In a sense, all roads in an organization lead to brand and reputation. For example, the brand and reputation risks to Federal Express Corp. are outlined and discussed in its 2013 Annual Report: "Our businesses depend on our strong reputation and the value of the FedEx brand." It goes on to note that adverse publicity could greatly damage its brand, and that social media spreads adverse publicity very quickly which makes it very difficult for the organization to repudiate let alone absorb the various costs involved to do so.[6]

The Code of Ethics at Deere & Company states, "Employees and directors will meet the highest standards of honesty, truthfulness and integrity in all communications, not just because it is good business, but because it is right. This applies in all our dealings, both as a Company and in our relationships with each other. We will abide by the laws that govern the states and countries where the Company operates. The Company will provide a working environment in which adherence to these high standards is clearly expected of all employees, and integrity is never compromised by pressures for immediate success."[7]

Business Continuity Risks. These are risks that imperil operations. The supply management team contributes to business continuity planning by anticipating supply disruptions and having emergency response plans and business recovery plans in place. Supply continuity risk is a major business concern that should be included in business continuity planning. *Business continuity planning* is defined as "an ongoing and comprehensive process for ensuring the continuity or uninterrupted provision of operations and service, including risk or contingency planning, disaster planning, disaster recovery, business recovery, business resumption and contingency plans" (ISM *Glossary* 2014).

One organization at a CAPS Research sponsored event shared two series of business continuity risks and related questions, one to ask internally (see Figure 5-2) and one to ask suppliers (see Figure 5-3). As indicated in the CAPS Research study on risk management, the questions will vary based on the industry and region in which an organization operates.[8]

Figure 5-2: Business Continuity Planning Assessment Questions to Ask Internally

Do we understand our core business vulnerabilities or potential failure points during a major, extended crisis? These would include:
• How do we redirect production and/or distribution capacity? • What capacity is available and how quickly can we redirect? • Do we have emergency management structures and defined roles and responsibilities in place to respond to a crisis? • How do we procure direct and indirect materials? How are supply chain disruptions accounted for?

CHAPTER 5: Assessing, Mitigating and Managing Supply-Based Risks

Figure 5-2: Business Continuity Planning Assessment Questions to Ask Internally

- Who is responsible for business continuity and crisis management at each site?
- What immediate action must we take to minimize loss and liability?
- Do you know your key support groups and their business continuity plans? Are your plans in alignment so that you would be able to continue operations?
- Do we need to prioritize customer demand? If so, which customers will be prioritized?
- What is the worst-case financial loss and legal exposure? Do you have a key contact list for individuals required to respond to the crisis?
- What is our global currency exposure, and where?
- How do we protect our data from loss, public release or theft?
- How long will it take to resume operations?

Source: Adapted from George Zsidisin, "Business and Supply Chain Continuity," *CAPS Research Critical Issues Report 2* (January 2007).

Figure 5-3: Business Continuity Planning Assessment Questions to Ask Suppliers

- What kinds of business functions are considered critical and have business continuity plans associated with them?
- What kinds of impacts are considered by your risk mitigation and recovery planning activities?
- How does senior management support the business continuity program? What management review and corporate governance mechanisms exist?
- Does your business continuity program ensure that all business processes and functions "critical" to your company are identified and documented?
- Does the business continuity documentation cover the components that make/support critical processes to an appropriate level of detail to ensure that single points of failure can be identified?
- Does your business continuity program ensure that business interruption risks are understood and prioritized, and their impacts comprehended?
- Do you have locations in an area subject to geopolitical disruptions, currency instability and/or natural disasters? How do you manage those risks?
- Have your business groups taken steps to reduce risks?
- How frequently is the risk and impact assessment refreshed so that changes to your business are reflected in the business-continuity program?
- Does your business continuity program ensure that the plans in place are well documented and current?
- Do these plans provide an effective crisis response and ensure that critical operations continue during a crisis?
- Is the business continuity plan documentation readily available to the people who need it and maintain it?
- What kinds of exercises and drills are performed to ensure the completeness of the plans? Is the organization prepared to perform effectively during a crisis?
- How do you protect your data from loss, public release or theft?
- Do you require your suppliers to sign a code of conduct related to sustainability, including corruption, social sustainability and environmental sustainability?
- Can your senior management confidently answer "Yes" when asked if everything reasonable and prudent has been done to be able to respond to and recover from an emergency?

Source: Adapted from George Zsidisin, "Business and Supply Chain Continuity," *CAPS Research Critical Issues Report 2* (January 2007).

Financial Risks. The supply management organization is a critical partner with the financial organization in managing financial risks and averting problems. For the supply management team, the main areas of responsibility relate to financial transactions, the organization's commitments to third parties, and the financial health of suppliers. The financial health of suppliers may pose an operational risk of supply interruption, as presented in the next section. Supply management must verify the existence, accuracy and completeness of relevant items. This is accomplished in three ways: (1) by being fully knowledgeable about and compliant with organizational financial reporting policies; (2) by being fully knowledgeable about and compliant with domestic and international regulatory requirements such as the U.S. Sarbanes-Oxley (SOX) Act, the Foreign Corrupt Practices Act and the UK Bribery Act[9]; and (3) by working with finance to avoid getting into situations that lead to financial settlements. This responsibility means supply management professionals must link decisions and actions related to intellectual property laws, employment laws, product liability, environmental issues and end-of-life-cycle issues to the financial risks as well as the brand and reputation risks.

For example, the Code of Ethics at Deere states, "To maintain the integrity of our system of accounting and internal control, the Company's accounting and financial records must be valid, accurate and complete. All transactions should be accurately and promptly recorded in the Company's books. The Chief Executive Officer, the Chief Financial Officer and other senior financial officers of the Company shall foster practices and procedures which ensure compliance with all applicable laws and regulations, including the United States securities laws, regarding full, fair, accurate, timely and understandable disclosures of Company information, and insider trading."[10] Financial processes and controls are discussed in greater detail in Chapter 12.

Operational Risks. Operational risks are the risks of loss from inadequate or failed internal processes, systems and staff, or from external events. Supply management plays a primary role in keeping the operation running smoothly through supply continuity. CAPS Research has identified five elements that define operational risk management: (1) event scenario planning, (2) event contingency planning, (3) risk monitoring, (4) risk event management, and (5) knowledge capture and feedback.[11] There are many sources of operational risks, including supply availability, intellectual property issues, data management, regulatory compliance, organizational policies, environmental issues and technology. These risks are key drivers in the development of overall supply strategy and specific category sourcing strategies.

For instance, Sonoco especially considers financial stability of its suppliers, and the financial risks associated with supplier insolvency. This became a critical issue during the great recession of 2008-2009.[12] To meet legal requirements of Germany's KonTraG amendment, a German telecommunications company initiated an intensive supplier risk management system, treating risk management information similarly to financial information, to achieve greater control of inbound supply, and to proactively reduce the occurrence of those supply risks. The supply risk process coordinator meets annually with each commodity and supply line manager to initiate the process. Each commodity is evaluated for its impact on earnings before interest and taxes (EBIT) and reported quarterly to the risk manager to evaluate risk.[13] CAPS Research has identified 13 major categories of risk:

1. Availability
2. Data Security and Protection
3. Financial
4. Intellectual Property
5. Legal/Regulatory
6. Natural Disasters
7. Political/Governmental
8. Quality
9. Reputational
10. Suppliers
11. Sustainability
12. Value Chain Security
13. Price Volatility.[14]

Legal Risks. While the supply leader-manager may not necessarily be fully knowledgeable about the various domestic and international laws and regulations that affect the supply organization, he or she must be certain that the risks and opportunities associated with the legal and regulatory environment are considered. Legal exposure arises from a number of internal issues related to supply management processes and procedures, and from external issues related to intellectual property, the environment and various laws and regulations.

As the owner of the supply management process, one of the first orders of business is to clearly establish who does and does not have the authority to commit the organization's funds. This basic issue communicates to employees the seriousness with which senior management views spend management and fiduciary duties. It also communicates to suppliers the degree of rigor and discipline that the buying organization brings to the marketplace. Risk exposure was defined earlier as *risk exposure = the probability of a loss × the expected impact*.

In the case of agency and authority, the probability of a loss is high if an organization is not properly managing both the actual and apparent authority of employees. Likewise, the less agency and authority are controlled, the greater the impact or loss. For example, it is more difficult to track spend, improve spend visibility and manage spend when agency status is diffused. It is also easier for suppliers to gather information, possibly proprietary or damaging, when employees lacking supply management training engage in contact with suppliers. Loss may also occur in terms of paying higher prices, agreeing to unfavorable terms and conditions, and compromising the buying organization's leverage in future deals. The link between process rigor and law is therefore a critical one.

The supply leader-manager must rely on his or her strong internal partnerships with chief legal counsel, peers at the executive level, and influence over process integrity. This ensures that the law of agency and limits to authority are calculated and understood as legal risk exposure that is endogenous in nature, meaning it is a risk that is completely within the bounds of internal actions to eliminate.

LEGAL RISKS: EMPLOYMENT. Supply management professionals may also contribute to risk assessment by recognizing legal risks related to employment in the supply management organization. In their capacity as hiring managers, they can assess the risks associated with hiring practices in the supply management organization relative to protected classes including race, color, religion, sex, national origin, disability or age. Supply professionals also bear responsibility for assessing behavior within the supply management group to prevent discrimination and harassment. This includes abiding by organizational policies and procedures, and ensuring they are aligned with current laws and regulations. When dealing with contract manufacturers in particular, the supply management professional may also need to be familiar with equivalent laws and regulations in other countries. With growing international commitments, supply professionals must be vigilant in ensuring adherence to applicable rules and regulations on an international scale.

LEGAL RISKS: INTELLECTUAL PROPERTY. *Intellectual property* (IP) includes "various types of intangible personal property that have an inherent commercial value and are protected by the government in different ways, including patents, trademarks, service marks and copyrights" (ISM *Glossary* 2014). Protection of intellectual property is a concern to management in many industries, as different cultures and nations view IP differently and may not enforce IP violations such as counterfeiting products.[15] While IP laws exist in many organizations, these laws vary greatly. Therefore, this is a high risk area for many organizations. Because the supply team is often heavily involved in acquiring intellectual property, the team bears a primary responsibility to recognize and eliminate or mitigate such risks. This includes educating internal stakeholders about the risks to which they may be exposing the organization.

LEGAL RISKS: ENVIRONMENTAL. Environmental laws and regulations affect many industries in many countries, and they vary considerably depending on the country. The supply management team plays an important role in acquiring current information on domestic and nondomestic environmental laws and regulations, and ensuring that the organization takes the necessary steps to be in compliance. Supply management professionals can assess environmental risks at three stages: (1) design, (2) acquisition and transformation, and (3) end-of-life cycle.

Technical Risks. Depending on the nature of the business, technical risks might include infrastructure security, risks to systems, process disruptions and data access disruptions. Risks to data include theft, alteration, destruction and loss of availability. Supply management professionals, working with IT, can assess the potential technical disruptions and the likely impact on the supply organization's ability to provide uninterrupted supply if the risk events occur.

Prioritizing risks is complicated when looking at a mix of risks where some have a high probability of occurring but a low impact, and others have a low probability of occurring but a high impact. An assessment of risk exposure provides the information necessary to prioritize risks and put together an action plan that addresses risks based on exposure. It is important to have a methodical process of examining supply risk and factoring that information into the overall assessment of organizational risk.

Step 2: Estimate the Probability of Occurrence

In mathematics, probabilities always lie between zero (an impossible event) and one (a certain event). Sometimes it is fairly easy to measure the two attributes, probability of occurrence and likely impact. Other times it is impossible to know the value of these attributes with any certainty if the necessary statistics are unavailable. In these cases, the best educated guess or a range of educated guesses is used to facilitate the process of prioritizing the actions in the risk management plan. For example, risk managers in one organization defined the probability of occurrence as A = very high, B = high, C = occasional, D = low, E = very low, and F = almost impossible. Calculating or estimating the likely impact or loss is the next critical step in risk assessment. This calculation may also be very difficult to quantify. The risk managers rated the likely impact if the risk event occurred as I = catastrophic, II = critical, III = significant and IV = marginal. In the software development project described at the beginning of the chapter, for instance, the loss or impact to the project might come in the form of diminished quality of the end product, increased costs, delayed completion or failure. Delayed completion or increased costs might be rated as a marginal impact, diminished quality as a significant impact, and project failure as a critical impact.

With the German telecommunications company, each of the 13 supply risk categories is assessed by the commodity manager using an 11-step process that is based on past experience and anticipated supply trends. The assessment process results in estimates of the expected impact on earnings before interest and taxes (EBIT) and the probabilities of those events occurring. Estimates are made for commodities both before and after risk handling measures are proposed, and for the current and next fiscal years.[16]

Step 3: Estimate the Likely Impact

Risk tolerance is the key comparison point for use as the basis of risk management strategies. *Risk tolerance*, often referred to as risk appetite by enterprisewide risk management experts, is the level of aggregate risk an organization can bear and still manage successfully over an extended period of time — that is, how much risk is the organization willing to accept? Different people and groups of people — management, shareholders and so on — may have different appetites for risk. The risk tolerance of an organization is determined by its capacity for undertaking risk.

Various questions can be asked when assessing the likely impact of major threats, vulnerabilities and key risks. The questions might include some or all of the following: What are the financial and asset impacts? What are the supply chain and stakeholder impacts? How can the network absorb these impacts and respond to them?

Step 4: Develop a Risk Profile

A risk profile captures all the risk exposure and casts it in light of the organization's risk aversion level (see Figure 5-4). Decisions about how to manage different levels of risks will emerge from or be based on this profile. To compile Figure 5-4, the team had to (1) determine the organization's tolerance for risk, which is shown as the risk tolerance boundary; (2) identify potential risks; and (3) assess each risk along two dimensions — likelihood and impact.

Figure 5-4: Total Risk Profile Before Changes

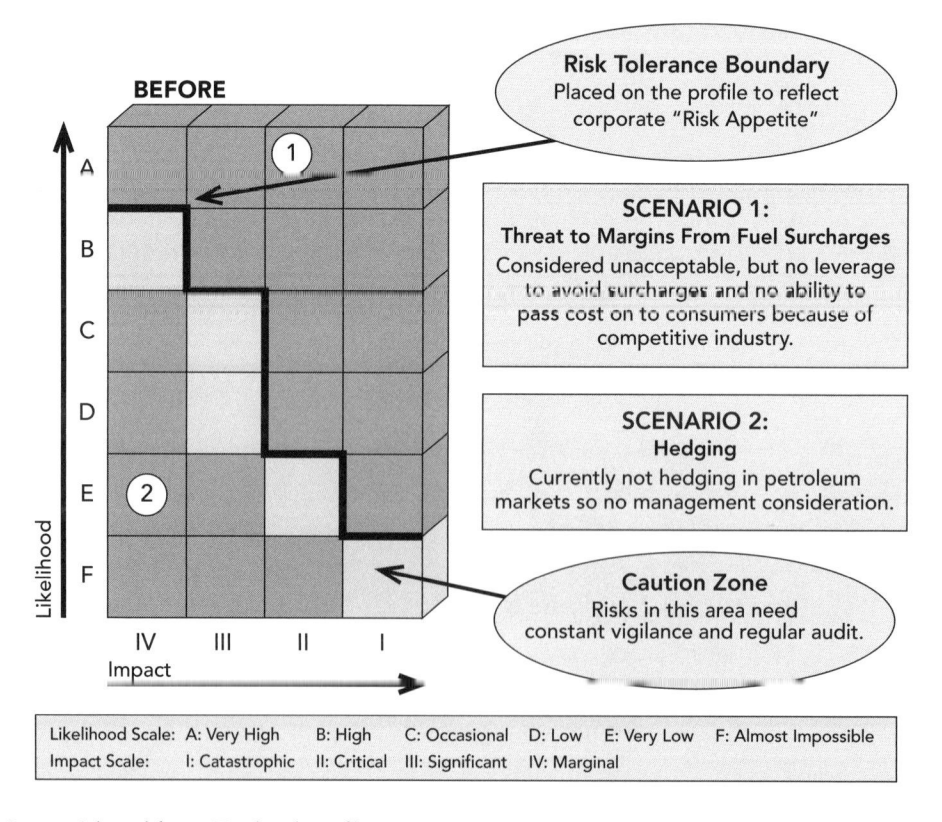

BEFORE

Risk Tolerance Boundary
Placed on the profile to reflect corporate "Risk Appetite"

SCENARIO 1:
Threat to Margins From Fuel Surcharges
Considered unacceptable, but no leverage to avoid surcharges and no ability to pass cost on to consumers because of competitive industry.

SCENARIO 2:
Hedging
Currently not hedging in petroleum markets so no management consideration.

Caution Zone
Risks in this area need constant vigilance and regular audit.

Likelihood Scale: A: Very High   B: High   C: Occasional   D: Low   E: Very Low   F: Almost Impossible
Impact Scale: I: Catastrophic   II: Critical   III: Significant   IV: Marginal

Source: Adapted from "Total Risk Profiling: Process Overview," Zurich Strategic Risk; and Matt A. Schlosser and George A. Zsidisin, "Hedging Fuel Surcharges," CAPS Research, *PRACTIX*, Vol. 7, May 2004.

Risk management strategies are then developed. These include action plans and required resources to change the risk profile. The example in Figure 5-5 considers both scenarios and their relation to one another. The risk management strategy actually moves scenario 2 into the cautionary zone to reallocate resources to move scenario 1 out of the danger zone.

Figure 5-5: Total Risk Profile After Changes

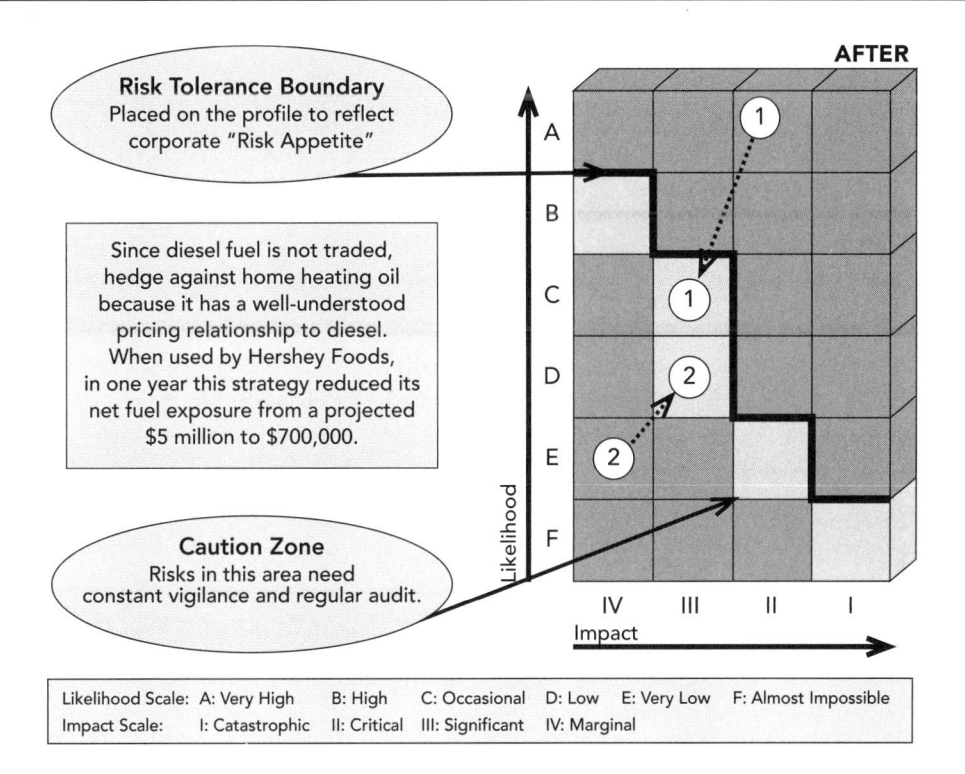

Risk Tolerance Boundary
Placed on the profile to reflect corporate "Risk Appetite"

Since diesel fuel is not traded, hedge against home heating oil because it has a well-understood pricing relationship to diesel. When used by Hershey Foods, in one year this strategy reduced its net fuel exposure from a projected $5 million to $700,000.

Caution Zone
Risks in this area need constant vigilance and regular audit.

Likelihood Scale: A: Very High B: High C: Occasional D: Low E: Very Low F: Almost Impossible
Impact Scale: I: Catastrophic II: Critical III: Significant IV: Marginal

Source: Adapted from "Total Risk Profiling: Process Overview," Zurich Strategic Risk; and Matt A. Schlosser and George A. Zsidisin, "Hedging Fuel Surcharges," CAPS Research, *PRACTIX*, Vol. 7, May 2004.

One technique for developing a risk profile is to classify risk stakeholders. For example, contractors might be classified as prime, sub or general, and the risks associated with each tier identified in accordance with existing contracts, applicable laws, regulations and organizational policy.

Step 5: Develop Risk Management Strategies

Once risks are identified, assessed and prioritized, risk management strategies can be developed. Typically, supply management professionals develop strategies to reduce risks and enhance value. Opportunities cannot be fully exploited, however, without taking risks. The challenge is balancing the risks against the opportunities presented by a given situation. For example, the value of an item that is customized may be increased if that item is further refined to provide unique features valued by customers (meaning they are willing to pay for it). This action would move the item to the strategic category. It might also increase risk or leave risk unchanged. If the opportunity from the standpoint of probability of increased revenue, market share or customer satisfaction is great enough, it may make it worth taking the risks.

Managers develop business plans based on their assessment of risks and opportunities relative to the overall risk appetite (where the thick line is drawn to establish the stair-step in Figure 5-4) of the organization. These strategies typically fall into one of four categories: (1) acceptance, (2) mitigation, (3) transference, and (4) avoidance.

Acceptance. In some cases, risk is identified and accepted, and no action is taken. The team should consider contingency plans for it knows it is allowing the risk to occur.

Mitigation. To mitigate means "to cause something to become less harsh or hostile; to make less severe or painful; or to moderate a quality or condition in force or intensity." Risk mitigation strategies are "specific steps undertaken by managers to reduce the impact of factors that might lead to injury, loss, damage or failure, and thus reduce the liability of the organization in its relations with various stakeholder groups, including employees and customers" (ISM *Glossary* 2014). They typically focus on core drivers of loss and are designed to prevent losses or reduce the cost of losses that do occur.

Transference. Some or all of the risk may be transferred to another party. For example, if a request for proposal is issued along with engineering drawings and a request to build to the specification, then the buying organization has decided (consciously or not) to assume all the design risk. If, however, the request is performance-based, then the buying organization has decided (again, consciously or unconsciously) to transfer the risk of design to the supplier. If a supplier is invited into the early stages of the design process with no guarantee of the business, then the supplier is assuming a high level of risk that the ideas of the selling organization's representatives will be included in the design and someone else may receive the business. The willingness to engage in this behavior reflects the supplier's appetite for risk and the expectation for reward. Supply managers should approach projects from a risk management perspective to ensure that the appropriate division of risk and corresponding reward is made.

Avoidance. Two situations may lead to a risk avoidance strategy. With the first one, the risk profile leads the manager to conclude that the risks are too high based on the likelihood of occurrence and the expected impact. With the second one, the organization has a very low tolerance for risk and thus risk intolerance is built into the organizational culture so that individuals throughout the organization avoid taking risks. The costs associated with not taking advantage of an opportunity in an effort to avoid the expected impact of risk taking may never be recognized or fully captured by management. Overly risk averse decision-makers can have a very costly impact on an organization.

In a German telecommunications company, managerial activities focused on either reducing the probability of the event occurring or on reducing the impact on EBIT (earnings before interest and taxes). Typically, efforts were made to reduce the probability of occurrence. Managerial actions included more intensive relationships with suppliers, increased supplier capacity levels, the creation of improved planning processes, derivation of alternative transportation routes, development of suppliers with quality issues, and adjusting forecasts to better reflect market demand.[17]

Risks are often interrelated, and managers must decide where to accept more risk in one case and to reduce risks in another. The example in Figure 5-5 illustrates this action. Scenario 1, the threat to production capacity, was assessed as highly likely to occur and the impact was predicted to be critical. In scenario 2, the likelihood of occurrence of the risk to the currency hedge was assessed as very low, and in the event of occurrence the impact was predicted to be marginal. Although scenario 2, the currency hedge, was considered well managed, the decision was made to take on more risks by adjusting the level of currency hedging to release resources to reduce the threat to production capacity (scenario 1). Figure 5-5 also shows that the end result is that both scenarios are now within the organization's risk tolerance boundary. These kinds of compromises across functions, disciplines and stakeholders make risk management both critical and challenging.

Risk assessment and risk profiling are critical inputs in the planning process (discussed in Chapter 6). The organization's appetite for risk drives strategy development as well as the behaviors of those responsible for strategy execution. A strategy that is more aggressive (bearing more risk) than management is comfortable with may never have the necessary resources allocated to it, and a less aggressive strategy may fail to maximize available opportunities.

Degree of Control. To establish risk management strategies, the risk analyst must determine the degree of control that members of the organization have over the risks. Risks may be exogenous or endogenous. Earthquakes and hurricanes are *exogenous* risks because they are not affected by our actions; we have no control over them. Building codes and architectural design are *endogenous* risks because they are affected by our actions. The probability of a risk event occurring is driven by the degree to which it is affected by our actions or endogenous risks. You may not be able to prevent a hurricane, but if you build in a hurricane-prone region, you can design and build your structure to decrease the probability that it will be demolished or severely damaged if a hurricane occurs.

For example, the risk to acquire an item in the marketplace is affected by exogenous risks (ones we cannot affect) and endogenous ones (risks we can affect by our actions). The exogenous risks might be overall supply and demand (assuming your organization is not McDonald's buying beef). The endogenous risks might relate largely to the specification that is clearly affected by the actions of people — people in the organization, people in the customer base and people in the supply base. For instance, if a requirement is external customer-driven, then this action is a key driver in the risks to acquire. If the unique specification is internally driven by a design team and supply is not represented on that team, then information about the impact of the unique design on the acquisition risk may be missing from the design team's decisions. In this case, the sourcing team leader may work internally to influence the design team without having any formal authority or membership on the team. The risk mitigation strategy might be threefold:

1. The sourcing manager works to directly influence the design team in this specific instance.
2. The sourcing manager works with the supplier to develop a supplier relationship that ensures supply availability in the short term such as bundling this business with a more attractive piece of business and eliciting assistance from the supplier to develop ideas about how to reduce the risks by reviewing the specification.
3. The supply leader works up the chain of command to influence the perception of supply and improve its role in new product or service design.

Step 6: Allocate Resources

Allocating resources to manage risk is also a challenge. The goal is to expend the least amount of resources possible to mitigate or lessen the impact of the risk. Assessing the impact of a risk to compare the cost of the impact to the cost of mitigation is also difficult. For example, an organization may be trying to decide whether to dual source an item that has a very high initial capital investment that each supplier must recover. They assess the potential risk associated with supply continuity to be quite high based on the fact that their current source is located in an area that has had much political and labor force unrest. The length of supply interruption is unknown; the cost is currently high and projected to last several weeks if it does occur, so they project a high impact if the risk event occurs. However, the opportunity costs of the mitigation strategy are difficult to calculate. They calculate the amount they will spend to get a new supplier up and running, and the increased costs of recovering the investment on two sets of production assets. Yet, there may be no interruption. On the other hand, having a second source might give them more leverage with the first supplier, or might cause them to be viewed as a less important customer, and actually lose leverage. They then need to calculate the impact of applying that estimated additional cost to other options to assess opportunity costs (the costs of a missed opportunity).

Supply management professionals and their internal partners must make these types of assessments regularly in the planning stage. The overlap between and among risk and the finite nature of resources further complicates matters. Managers need to be able to look at all the risks and how they intersect with each other to make optimal decisions about priorities and resource allocation. To aid this process, risk management teams often develop a risk profile to compare risk exposure to the organization's appetite for risk. Determining the tolerance for risk is, of course, an equally challenging task.

Step 7: Execute Strategy

Once risk management strategies have been developed, they must be executed. Successful execution depends on adequate human, technical and capital resources to ensure proper support for strategy execution.

The past mergers among global banks and the growth of regional banks through acquisitions, for example, leave the newly created entities at high risks from redundant operations. These risks have been mitigated in many cases through an outsourcing strategy. Demand is aggregated for all combined bank divisions into one enterprisewide procurement function to gain leverage through volume discounts, synergies and scale economies. A centralized process and new policies and procedures are then imposed, often faster, by the third party than they would be by an internal group. Outsourcing, with all its inherent risks, is chosen because the risks of a drawn-out integration with limited strategic, operational and financial results is projected to have a greater negative impact on stock performance, market reputation and customer service (losing customers is one of a bank's biggest risks). By outsourcing IT, regional banks access leading-edge technology and other best practices at lower risk levels and without the intensive capital investments required.

Step 8: Review Results

As with all plans, the assessment of results is critical to the improvement of risk management strategy development and execution. Performance is typically measured against projected outcomes for key metrics.

Clearly, supply leaders and managers can play a valuable role in the development of an organization's risk profile. There are two strategic decisions where supply management's role may be especially critical:

1. The decision to merge with or acquire another business, or to divest in a business; and
2. The decision to insource/make or outsource/buy (the supply chain design) specific tasks within a function (for example, payroll) or a whole function (for example, human resources).

The previously mentioned 2012 study on risk from CAPS Research outlines the following major challenges in developing future risk management plans:

- A formal risk management process that went beyond the first-tier suppliers was not regularly achieved. Almost all study participants viewed this lack of visibility as a major obstacle to their risk management strategies.
- The ability to capture risk-related data on technology, sustainability, conflict materials, legal/regulatory compliance and so forth on a timely basis was a challenge.
- Timely and informed decision-making must be employed.
- Achieving cross-functional collaboration and obtaining risk-related input from the appropriate individuals within the organization is challenging.
-

- Limited resources limit what can be focused on. Investment in risk-related tools and human resources is limited.
- Organizations are challenged to come up with new ideas and new approaches to risk management. Most changes are incremental improvements.[18]

Supply Management's Role in Assessing the Risks of Proposed Mergers, Acquisitions and Divestitures

Supply management professionals can make an important contribution to the organization's assessment of risks related to mergers, acquisitions and divestitures both pre-decision and post-decision. Supply's responsibilities extend to five primary risk areas: (1) contractual issues, (2) management of redundancy and complexity, (3) liability exposure, (4) divestiture of assets, and (5) global economic considerations.

Contractual Issues

The pertinent contractual risks in potential mergers and acquisitions/divestitures are related to (1) assignment consent, (2) confidentiality, (3) due diligence, (4) current contractual obligations, and (5) financial assessments.

Assignment Consent. *Assignment* is "the transfer by one contracting party (assignor) of his/her rights or obligations under a contract to another person (assignee). Sometimes also referred to as delegation of duties" (ISM *Glossary* 2014). *Assignment consent* is the "contractual provision giving the parties the right to approve or disapprove any requested assignment" (ISM *Glossary* 2014). An assignment is usually limited to the transfer of intangible rights rather than the property itself. For example, one organization buys another and the liability insurance coverage is part of the deal — the rights are assigned. An assignment may be qualified in some way, such as a partial assignment of trademark rights rather than global rights. Also, some contracts restrict the right of assignment. This might, for instance, leave the acquiring firm without liability insurance. The supply management professional may be involved in reviewing contracts to determine if there are restrictions and the extent of the associated risk level.

Confidentiality. Confidentiality is especially important when assessing the opportunities and risks of a merger or acquisition. A formal confidentiality agreement (or nondisclosure agreement) is a "freestanding agreement or contract provision restricting the disclosure of certain information, generally proprietary information, given by one party to the other in the course of contract performance, and imposing liability for unauthorized disclosure" (ISM *Glossary* 2014). Drafting the appropriate contract requires consideration of some key issues. One important consideration is to specifically identify the information that is confidential. There may be limitations on what information is deemed confidential, such as information already known to the signing party, or information made public, through government agency order, and so on. Another issue is whether the party is receiving or disclosing such information. A further issue concerns the duration for keeping the information confidential. Finally, consider whether the confidential information also qualifies as a trade secret. Also important is an explanation of the purpose for disclosure, such as when confidential information is only revealed to another party for a specific purpose. The agreement should set forth what that purpose is.

Due Diligence. *Due diligence* is the process of analyzing information concerning the status of a target organization (for example, its intellectual property portfolio or trademarks) and assessing the risks, exposure and potential benefits associated with the proposed transaction in relation to the strategic short-term and long-term business goals of the acquiring organization. Supply management may be represented on the due diligence team along with legal counsel and other executives and advisers. What is important in a particular deal will drive the approach to due diligence. For instance, the focus may be on intellectual property due diligence, notably trademarks and patents, trade secrets, copyright, and software, in particular. Due diligence may also be focused on assessing any limitations to brands that are being acquired such as trademarks licensed to a third party, key agreements that are nontransferable, or the seller's intention to retain some or all of the trademarks.

Current Contractual Obligations. Supply management professionals may also contribute to the assessment of risks by reviewing current contractual obligations of the targeted organization. They may find risks as well as opportunities that will result post-merger in terms of process, supply base, employee and technology synergies, and project costs and savings opportunities that will occur during post-merger integration.

The process should include more than a contract-to-contract comparison. Conducting a spend analysis will reap more benefits "when normalized data can be broken out for side-by-side comparison across the companies being merged. This makes it easier to identify situations where the combined new company would be engaged in one or more of the following:

- Paying different prices for the same items;
- Using the same suppliers for some goods and services and different ones for others;
- Giving business to nonpreferred suppliers; and/or
- Using far too many suppliers to effectively leverage purchasing power."[19]

Financial Assessments. Auditors are typically on the lookout for undervalued or overvalued and unrecorded assets such as software, marketable equity securities, intangibles and inventories. The supply management professional can assist in scrutinizing obsolete inventories and assets under construction to identify liabilities such as potential penalties for noncompliance and contract obligations.

Management of Redundancy and Complexity

Mergers and acquisitions are typically expected to bring synergies that lead to a reduction in redundancy and complexity. Pre-merger, supply management professionals can identify areas of redundancy and complexity, and conduct a preliminary assessment of the risk associated with these areas. There may be redundancies in the supply base, contracts, supply management processes, technology staff, job descriptions and roles. For example, one of the most difficult aspects of post-merger integration for U.S.-based airlines US Airways and America West Airlines was merging the pilots and flight attendants of the two airlines. In the process of creating a unified workforce, some employees lost seniority in the new system. This is being repeated with the merger of US Airways and American Airlines. Historically customer service and satisfaction levels suffer as the transition to a single operating unit occurs.[20]

The risk may come from service disruptions to internal or external customers during the integration period, and loss of institutional knowledge in supply management because of staffing changes. A pre-merger assessment will feed into the development of plans to quickly reduce these redundancies without experiencing costs that negate the expected synergies.

Liability Exposure

A supply management professional may also contribute to the assessment of liability exposure in the event the proposed merger/acquisition is successful. The supply professional may be able to provide valuable information and insight into potential liability. For example, ask what the target organization's potential exposure for liability might be because of the issues listed below:

- The use of its relevant assets;
- Environmental management systems, source or hazardous materials;
- Lack of compliance with laws or regulations; and
- Any other supply-related areas.

Divestiture of Assets

Supply management professionals assist in pre-merger assessments of the risks and opportunities associated with divesting assets in the event of the merger. Pertinent questions include the following:

- What relevant assets does the target organization own, and what is its ability to control those assets?
- What is the asset's strategic value to the target organization's business, and what is the extent of exclusivity in the marketplace that those assets provide?
- What is the target organization's potential exposure for liability resulting from the use of these assets?

Global Economic Considerations

Supply management professionals may also provide valuable information and insights into the supply-related risks from a global economic perspective. Will the proposed merger create global market power or operational efficiencies from a supply perspective? How will the proposed merger affect the organization's global supply base and its ability to create or maintain a competitive advantage as a result of its supply base? Supply professionals might assess the risks associated with language and culture; geographical barriers and boundaries that might lead to high logistics costs; political situations that affect trade barriers, tariffs and duties; domestic laws and regulations; and intellectual property rights.

A strong supply management organization can clearly be an asset in pre-merger risk and opportunity assessment. Supply's role in strategic and operational planning as it relates to mergers, acquisitions and divestitures is discussed in Chapter 6.

Whether to insource or outsource is the second strategic decision in which supply leaders and managers may make a valuable contribution during risk assessment and planning.

Risks Associated With Outsourcing

One of the most fundamental strategic decisions made by management is determining whether the organization should make a good or service internally, or should buy the good or service (specific tasks or an entire function) from an external supplier. Insource/make or outsource/buy analysis is driven by management's perspective on ownership and control. The analysis focuses on the question of which value stream activities can be performed internally and which should be handled externally to ultimately contribute to competitive advantage. Part of this analysis involves the assessment of the risks associated with outsourcing internationally.

To assess the risks and develop appropriate risk management strategies, it is important to define the terms and discuss the logic behind insourcing, outsourcing, nearshoring, offshoring and even reshoring. Figure 5-6 lists the definitions of these terms from the ISM *Glossary of Key Supply Management Terms*. These definitions are used throughout this book. Some people may define these terms in slightly different ways. It is important for a practitioner to know and use these terms as they are defined by their organization. More important, the analysis and decision-making process is likely to be essentially the same even if the terms are not defined exactly as they are in the ISM *Glossary*.

Figure 5-6: Definition of Terms

TERM	DEFINITION
Make or buy	A determination of what products or services an organization should manufacture or provide in-house, as opposed to purchasing them from outside sources.
Outsourcing	A version of the make-or-buy decision in which an organization elects to purchase a good or service that previously was made or performed in-house. Outsourcing may involve sourcing and using a supplier that provides the completed item or service rather than buying the components and manufacturing them in-house.
Insourcing	The act of bringing inside an organization a function that has been performed outside the organization (outsourced).

Figure 5-6: Definition of Terms   continued

TERM	DEFINITION
Nearshoring	A form of outsourcing in which business processes are relocated to locations which are geographically nearer to the buying organization than alternate, more distant supply choices (farshoring), usually to reduce costs; also called "nearshore outsourcing."
Offshore	Located or operating outside a country's boundaries.
Reshoring	The bringing of work and jobs back to the country in which the work/jobs initially existed.
Onshoring	Keeping work or jobs or work in the home country but moving jobs or work to a more economically favorable location in the country.

Source: Cavinato, J.L., A.E. Flynn, M.L. Harding, C.S. Lallatin, M.L. Peck, H.M. Pohlig, S.R. Sturzl and V. Tucker (Eds.). ISM *Glossary of Key Supply Management Terms*, 6th edition, Institute for Supply Management®, Tempe, AZ, 2014.

Vertical Integration. In a vertically integrated organization, some or all of the upstream suppliers and downstream supply groups are owned and controlled by one organization. The decision to vertically integrate reflects management's perspective that risks are lessened by controlling all the input streams. In a horizontally integrated organization, subsidiaries may be formed for marketing or production purposes. For example, companies in the oil industry are highly vertically integrated. Typically, an oil company such as BP or Petronas locates crude oil deposits, then drills and extracts, transports, refines and distributes fuel — often to company-owned stations to sell to consumers.

Variations of vertical integration occur all over the world. In Japan, a similar business group arrangement is called a *keiretsu* (pronounced kay-ret-sue), meaning series or "related sequence," which is a set of organizations with interlocking business relationships and shareholders rather than family ties. These relationships reflect decisions about the allocation of risks and rewards among member organizations. Toyota is often cited in literature as a traditional horizontal keiretsu, as are Mitsubishi and Sumitomo.[21] A vertical keiretsu is an organization of buyers and suppliers. A horizontal keiretsu (financial keiretsu) is a diversified grouping with a bank or trading company at the center and includes a range of large manufacturing firms.

In South Korea, *chaebol* (pronounced jay-BOL) are large conglomerates that are owned, controlled and managed by one family group with strong ties to government. Some are one large corporation and others are loosely connected groups of separate companies. Top five chaebol include Samsung, Hyundai Motor Co., LG Group, SK Group and Lotte. Chaebol are known to pay attractive salaries and are considered by Koreans to be progressive and desirable employers.[22]

Disintegration. The decision to outsource is a decision to disintegrate. In this case, management has decided that the risks associated with vertical integration are greater than the advantages. By disintegrating, the opportunities for competitive advantage can outweigh the risks of procuring goods, services or functions from a third party. The driver determining whether to make or buy should be based on the greater source of competitive advantage. The outsourcing decision should be based on a strengths, weaknesses, opportunities and threats (SWOT) assessment of internal strengths and weaknesses and external threats and opportunities, along with a thorough cost analysis. Supply management plays a vital role by performing the due diligence required to select an external provider and ensuring successful implementation of the outsourcing business plan. Supply management's role in supplier relationship management is especially important when outsourcing. Strategic alliances with suppliers are one means of gaining the advantages of vertical integration without the costs. As owners of the supply management process, developing and managing these alliances is another way that supply contributes to the organization's competitive advantage.

Management may revisit an initial make-or-buy decision and reverse course depending on the strategic direction of the organization and shifts in core competencies given the dynamics of the internal and external environment. *Outsourcing* is the term used to reflect a reversal of a "make" decision so that the organization now procures something that was previously performed in-house. *Insourcing* is the decision to perform an activity internally that was previously procured from an external source.

The fundamental force behind a decision to make or buy, or to bring back in-house something that had been outsourced, is the concept of comparative advantage that holds that countries and organizations are best off when they focus on sectors in which they have the lowest opportunity costs of production. The challenge for the management team is determining when and where the organization has a comparative advantage. This requires the knowledge, skills and ability to assess opportunity costs to determine if a task or function should be performed internally or externally.

The same decision is made in the public sector where the term *privatization* is used to refer to the decision to transfer responsibility to perform specified activities, functions or ownership of property from the public sector to the private sector. For example, the United Kingdom's government in 2013 decided to sell a majority stake in the state-owned postal service, Royal Mail Group Ltd. It was one of the biggest privatizations the country has seen in decades.[23] Privatization is occurring worldwide. The privatization of Britain's postal service follows similar moves by some European neighbors — for example Austria, Germany and the Netherlands have all privatized their postal services in part or fully.[24]

Privatization is the opposite of nationalization, which is similar to an organization deciding to vertically integrate. For example, in recent years Venezuela has nationalized the country's energy sector.

Risks of Outsourcing Onshore and Internationally. Outsourcing tasks or functions exposes the organization to risks. These risks typically fall into the categories of capabilities, management, ethics and markets. Figure 5-7 lists the typical areas of concern within each category.

Figure 5-7: Outsourcing Risks

CAPABILITY RISKS	MANAGEMENT RISKS	ETHICS RISKS	MARKET RISKS
Quality	Goal alignment	Business practices	Create a competitor
Technology	Long-term strategies	Social responsibility	Knowledge transfer
Capacity	Managerial philosophies	Proprietary information	Technology transfer
Cycle time	Business practices	Conflicts of interest	Impact on brand
Financial	No succession plan	Improper reciprocity	Political backlash
Expertise	Control and compliance performance	Gifts and gratuities	Customer perceptions
Intellectual property compromise	Important sources of competitive advantage are compromised	Supplier or partner's IP may also be compromised	Cheap imitations may hurt reputation; good imitations may steal market share

The decision to move a task, activity or function to an outside supplier naturally includes making a decision about the most desirable location for the supplier. It is fairly common for some organizations in most countries to outsource activities internationally. For example, Japanese automakers have had U.S.-based operations since the late 1970s, thus outsourcing manufacturing jobs from Japan to the United States. China and Japan outsource food production to other countries, and organizations in Japan, the United States and Europe outsource IT and back-office operations to India and Malaysia.

In the face of competitive pressures, financial institutions are outsourcing more business process work internationally. In a 2005 business process transformation study conducted by EDS and the Economist Intelligence Unit, a rapid increase in financial services outsourcing was revealed. A 2012 study by Elix-RR found that the value of services outsourcing is around US$153 billion globally, driven by banking, financial institutions and the federal and central governments. While India is the major location for business processes internationally, to reduce risks, banks also send work to secondary locations such as China, South Africa, Malaysia, Sri Lanka, Singapore and the Philippines.[25]

A critical piece of the assessment is determining why an organization might go international. Typically, the goal is to move tasks or functions to a lower-cost country (reduce cost). Low cost is most often driven by prevailing wage rates. The outsourcing team must either develop or acquire the ability to perform a thorough country analysis to assess the risk of doing business in a specific country compared to the opportunities, as well as the risk of cost increase. For example, poor working conditions and low wages in China have received much attention in the 2010s; as a result, wages in China have risen significantly, more than doubling in many cases. Yet, they are still low compared to more developed economies.[26]

For example, if the organization wants to expand its global footprint, then the discussion and alternatives may include outsourcing a task or function internationally. The starting point is vision and mission, and is not based on questions such as, "Should we outsource such and such a function? Should we go to China or India, Central Europe or Mexico?" Outsourcing is a strategic tool, but it is not a strategy unto itself. Unfortunately, in many cases the starting point is: "Savings of x amount must be generated. Labor rates are relatively cheaper in India, China, and Central and Eastern Europe, so go there." Or, "Everyone else in our industry is sourcing this from China, Vietnam or x, so why aren't we?"

Increasingly, there has been a growing understanding that organizations must look beyond savings in labor and manufacturing costs, and consider the length of supply chain, the amount of inventory needed, intellectual property, and other risks to gain a more holistic cost perspective, or total cost of ownership. With the shrinking cost differences and growing recognition of risk, companies are engaging in more nearshoring — where U.S. companies move to Mexico instead of China, and Western European countries choose Eastern Europe rather than Asia. There is also some reshoring or homeshoring, whereby companies in countries like the U.S. or UK relocate manufacturing to their own shores.

A critical and challenging role for the supply leader may be using the "thick informal networks" (see Chapter 4) and internal partnerships he or she has developed to influence his or her peers to perform the necessary analysis and understand the long-term implications and risks, and not rush to a decision based on partial, weak or faulty information, incorporating the possibility of homeshoring or nearshoring.[27]

As discussed earlier, decision-makers should determine the country with the lowest opportunity costs, which may even include their own country. This already difficult process is complicated by the number of variables that are hard to quantify. These include the risks and related costs of differences in language, time zones, country culture and business norms, along with the uncertainties related to customs regulations, long transit times, weather, political climate, social unrest and geopolitical concerns.

Chapter 6 covers the development of business plans, including (1) the planning process, (2) supply management's role in the development of the organization's strategic plan, (3) supply's role in mergers and acquisitions, (4) the development of strategic and operational supply management plans, and (5) strategies for executing the plan.

Summary

Supply management professionals are in a unique position to assess risk in many areas, including general supply management activities; insource/make or outsource/buy decisions; and mergers, acquisitions and divestitures. The risk management process includes the following steps: (1) identify risks; (2) estimate probability of occurrence; (3) estimate likely impact; (4) develop a risk profile; (5) develop risk management strategies; (6) allocate resources; (7) execute the strategy; and (8) review results. Risks range from brand and reputation risk to business continuity risk, and financial, operational, legal and technical risks.

This chapter covered the role of supply management professionals as managers in the risk assessment process at the organizational level, and how supply and sourcing risks feed into the organizational risk profile. With a clear understanding and assessment of the risks the organization faces, the leadership and management teams are ready to develop business plans to guide the behavior and performance of everyone in the organization. If supply management plans are executed properly, there is a greater probability of supply management making the maximum contribution possible to organizational goals for areas such as customer service, corporate profit and return on equity, while reducing the organization's risk exposure.

Key Points

1. Risk is the possibility of loss or injury. Risk exposure = the probability of a loss or injury occurring × the likely impact.
2. Organizational risks must be identified, assessed and prioritized, and managed either by avoiding the risk, mitigating the impact of the risk, accepting some or all of the risk, or transferring the risk to another entity.
3. Supply-related risks might be placed in six major categories: (1) brand or reputation risks; (2) business continuity risks, including supply interruption such as that associated with geopolitical risks in global sourcing and operations; (3) financial risks; (4) operational risks, including the geopolitical risks associated with international sourcing and operations; (5) legal risks; and (6) technical risks.
4. Supply management professionals contribute to two pre-merger/acquisition risk-related questions: (1) What are the risks associated with the proposed deal, and does the commercial attractiveness of the proposed deal outweigh these risks? (2) What are the risks associated with post-merger supply continuity and with capturing the full potential of the synergies of the two organizations, and what is the probability of occurrence?
5. The supply management team can contribute to the analysis of the risks associated with outsourcing (domestically or internationally) targeted areas of expertise.

CHAPTER 6

*If birds travel without coordination,
they beat each other's wings*

— SWAHILI/
EAST AFRICA

Developing Business Plans

In 1984, a man named Liu started a company named Legend Group to sell Sun Microsystems and HP computers at retail in China. In 1990, Legend began selling its own computers in China, but faced stiff competition when the market was opened to direct imports by international PC makers. As a publicly held company, Legend was ineligible for state support the way state-owned businesses were. In 1994, Liu created a separate PC division and put Yang Yuanqing in charge. By 1997, Yuanqing had turned the business into the number one PC player in China. He was named CEO and later Chairman, and the company name was changed to Lenovo. The success of the organization was built on innovation — innovation in sales and distribution by expanding from a direct sales force to a vast network of retailers, and innovation in design by focusing on low-cost, super-easy-to-use PCs based on current chip technology rather than on generation-old technology.

In 2001, globalization became the organization's strategic focus. Yuanqing's vision of Legend becoming "a global leader in technology" was advanced through three primary strategic initiatives: (1) boost sales and market share in China, (2) expand to other emerging markets, and (3) move into the West. The tools the organization used included design innovation to develop a new line of PCs offered through retailers in the West (as in China and other emerging markets) and the 2005 acquisition of IBM's PC division that brought technology, an existing manufacturing supply chain, linkage to large corporate customers, and brand and reputation spillover — and renamed the company Lenovo. *BusinessWeek* magazine called Yuanqing "the Bill Gates of China" in 2006.[1] It grew rapidly and was the world's largest PC manufacturer in 2010, forming a mobile internet digital home business to capitalize on consumer smart electronics. From its humble beginnings, it was named one of the world's "100 most reputable companies" by *Forbes* in 2011. In 2012 it expanded into storage solutions and acquired a major Brazilian consumer electronics company.[2] The vision Yuanqing has for Lenovo has come to fruition through planning and execution, and continues to grow.

Chapter 2 addressed the supply leader's role in setting direction for the supply organization. The managerial counterparts to direction setting are risk assessment (discussed in the previous chapter), planning (discussed in this chapter) and budgeting (addressed in *Foundation of Supply Management* [ISM *Professional Series*]). The planning process at the organizational level results in business plans that guide the behavior and performance of the entire complement of people in the organization. The planning process at the supply management level mirrors this process and results in business plans that, if executed properly, meet organizational goals for such areas as customer service, corporate profit and return on equity.

This chapter contains five sections: (1) the planning process, (2) supply management's role in the development of the organization's strategic plan, (3) supply's role in mergers and acquisitions, (4) the development of strategic and operational supply management plans, and (5) strategies for executing the plan.

Chapter Objectives
- Explain why planning is important, what types of plans are needed and what might be achieved by investing in an ongoing planning process.
- Discuss supply management's role and contribution to organizational strategic planning, including its role in mergers and acquisitions and make-or-buy decisions.
- Explore the process of developing a strategic supply management plan, including conducting insource/make or outsource/buy decisions as part of the strategic framework.
- Explore the process of developing an operating supply management plan.
- Discuss analytical tools that enable the planning process.

The Planning Process

Planning is defined by the WordReference.com dictionary as "a detailed scheme, method, and so on for attaining an objective; a proposed — usually tentative — idea for doing something." Planning is forward-looking and anticipatory. It requires thinking and action. As Peter Drucker said, "Plans are only good intentions unless they immediately degenerate into hard work."[3]

Why Plan?

The first hurdle a leader faces is establishing a clear vision of the future. Without this, the efforts of individuals and groups within the organization are disjointed and may be counterproductive. Once a vision is established as a shared vision, not the vision of a single leader, multiple stakeholders in the organization need to understand the path to get there and what course of action to take in the event of barriers or obstacles. A good analogy is a group setting out on a trip. First, they must agree on the destination. Second, they must agree on the route to take to get to the destination. Each possible route will likely have advantages and disadvantages, stemming from the group's individual and collective internal strengths (for example, several group members know some back roads and shortcuts) and weaknesses (no one in the group has a sense of direction so if they get off the familiar roadways the trip may go awry). The advantages and disadvantages will also be influenced by external opportunities (a new highway just opened) and external threats (the group will be on the new highway at exactly the peak of rush hour). The roadmap or route that is selected represents the best possible route given the internal strengths and weaknesses and the external threats and opportunities at the time of the analysis. Considering trends in all four factors enables the group to anticipate and develop contingency plans to lessen the impact of risk, which is the dynamic internal and external environment in which organizations operate.

When planning for organizations, desired routes and alternates are mapped. With effective planning, the organization has a greater probability of success in reaching its destination or vision. Effective planning is based on having a structured and disciplined planning process at multiple levels in the organization. Effective execution depends on assembling the right mix of talented people (covered in Chapter 9), structuring the organization for efficiency and effectiveness, and enabling execution by applying appropriate supporting technologies based on rigorous processes (covered in Chapter 8).

Types of Business Plans

There are two primary types of plans: strategic and operational. Strategic plans answer the question, Where do we want to go? Operational plans answer the question, How do we get there?

The word *strategy* is derived from the Greek word *strategos*, which means "art of the general." Strategic planning is a critical task of senior managers whose jobs typically include responsibilities for planning and goal setting. Strategic planning is a process in which the long-range direction of an organization is determined, and the means of reaching that goal are established. This process can be applied to businesses, agencies and organizations, and to virtually any situation in which people are pursuing collective achievement.

An operational plan is the result of thinking and formulating an action plan in the context of a specific strategic plan. It answers the question, How do we get where we want to go?

Management of all types of organizations — public and private; for-profit and not-for-profit; small, medium and large — develop strategic and operational business plans to set the course and determine the actions necessary to meet goals related to areas such as customer service, organizational profit and return on equity. Within each of these entities, functional managers in supply management, marketing, finance and so on also develop strategic and operational business plans.

Supply Management's Role in the Development of the Organization's Strategic Planning

When risk assessment is considered in light of opportunities, it is a foundation of good planning. Without this analysis, plans may reflect wishful thinking more than executable strategies. The functional owners of the major business processes in an organization must each answer the question, How can we effectively contribute to the attainment of the organization's vision and strategy?

In the case of supply management, the focus is on strategic resource management. Supply's contribution comes from actively participating, guiding and leading the determination of how the money spent does, or does not, add value in some specific way, such as more services delivered or more income earned or contributed.

Today, supply management is perceived as a key player in strategy development. One of the indicators that supply management has become a more strategic player in an organization is that supply is represented on the organization's executive planning committee, and that supply risk assessments are incorporated into the overall organizational risk profile. Supply's placement within the organizational hierarchy and the reporting relationship indicate both the perception of supply by the senior leadership team and of supply's role in setting the direction of the organization.

The supply management leader's involvement in the development of the organization's strategic plan serves two major purposes. First, he or she brings to the strategic planning process valuable data and insight about the supply side of the organization, and how supply management can contribute to attaining objectives (see Figure 6-1).

CHAPTER 6: Developing Business Plans

Figure 6-1: Supply Strategy Integrated with Organizational Strategy

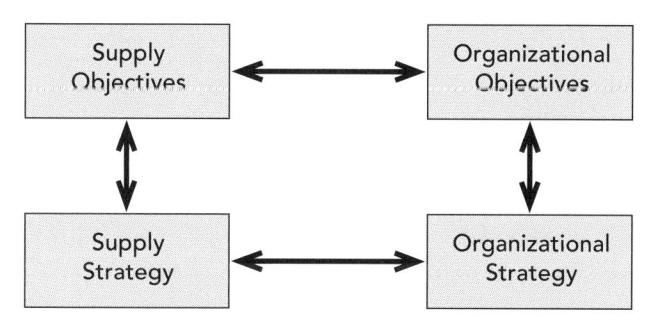

```
    Supply          <---->    Organizational
    Objectives                Objectives
       ↕                         ↕
    Supply          <---->    Organizational
    Strategy                  Strategy
```

Source: M. R. Leenders, P. F. Johnson and A. E. Flynn, *Purchasing and Supply Management*, 14th edition, McGraw-Hill Ryerson, New York, 2011, 28. Reproduced by permission of the McGraw-Hill Companies.

Secondly, the supply leader brings a thorough understanding of current and future markets and can relate this information to the current and future needs of the organization. The assessment of current and especially future markets from a risk and opportunity perspective provides much of the value of supply management's involvement in strategic planning. This is especially important for building alignment around supply's role in the organization and for generating better understanding of the supply opportunities and risks during the strategy development process (see Figure 6-2).

Figure 6-1: Supply Strategy Links Current and Future Markets and Current and Future Needs

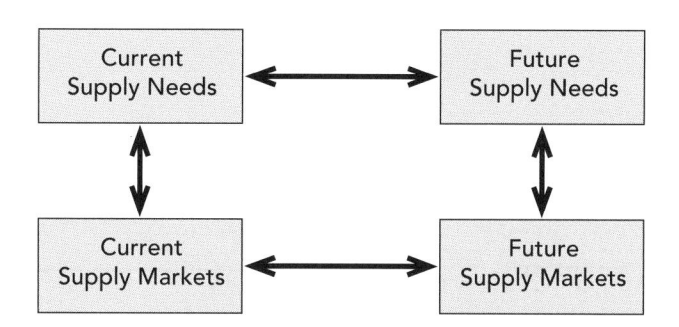

```
    Current         <---->    Future
    Supply Needs              Supply Needs
       ↕                         ↕
    Current         <---->    Future
    Supply Markets            Supply Markets
```

Source: M. R. Leenders, P. F. Johnson and A. E. Flynn, *Purchasing and Supply Management*, 14th edition, McGraw-Hill Ryerson, New York, 2011, 28. Reproduced by permission of the McGraw-Hill Companies.

The involvement of the supply management leader in organizational planning ensures that the supply perspective is brought to bear on key strategic decisions and key organizational metrics.

Strategic Tools

While a number of strategic tools are available to management, this chapter addresses two fundamental strategic decisions in which supply management can make a value-adding contribution:

1. Which areas of expertise should the organization develop and maintain as core competencies (insource) and which should it procure externally (outsource)?
2. If a growth strategy is pursued, should it be pursued organically or through mergers and acquisitions or some combination?

In both cases, the supply management team can play a vital role. As discussed in Chapter 5, in the initial strategy decision the supply management leader, as a member of the executive team, may provide valuable information about risks and opportunities from a supply management perspective. Once a strategy has been selected, the supply management team may be instrumental in the development of plans by assessing options and determining a specific course of action. Once a plan has been developed, supply managers then play a role in ensuring that full value is captured throughout strategy execution.

Supply Management's Role in Insource/Make or Outsource/Buy Decisions

One of the most fundamental strategic decisions made by management is whether or not the organization should make a good or service internally or buy the same good or service (specific tasks or an entire function) from an external supplier. Make or buy analysis is driven by management's perspective on ownership and control. The analysis focuses on the question of which value stream activities can be performed internally and which should be handled externally to ultimately contribute to competitive advantage.

Seven major steps are involved in this process: (1) identify an opportunity, (2) determine feasibility, (3) collect and analyze cost data, (4) assess the results of a feasibility study and make a decision, (5) develop a business plan to implement the decision, (6) audit results, and (7) conduct a post audit evaluation of the decision.

Step 1: Identify an Opportunity

The first step in an insource/make or outsource/buy decision is to identify an opportunity that is driven by the organization's vision and direction. Opportunity identification is the process of developing a clearly defined outline of one or more alternatives or scenarios relative to the central business issue. Early investigation and exploration of the business idea should prevent unnecessary investment in an in-depth feasibility study. At this point the key decision is, Does the idea have market and supply chain viability? If so, proceed with the feasibility study and include the initial market and supply chain analysis.

The starting questions should be, What business are we in? Where are we going with that business? How do we get there? From this perspective, specific outsourcing decisions hinge on whether or not the item or service is strategic, and what kind of capabilities the organization has or can develop. The decision to outsource some or all of the components of a product or service should flow from the vision and mission of the organization and align components with the core competencies that give the organization a competitive advantage. Products and services may be broken into their subsystems, subsystems into their components, and components into their parts to determine what is strategic and should remain in-house and what is not strategic and can be outsourced. Accurately determining this decoupling point has implications for the organization in the long term. In *Clockspeed*, Charles Fine stated that the ultimate core competency of an organization's supply chain design is defined by choosing what capabilities to invest in and develop internally, and which to allocate for development by suppliers. In a fast clockspeed world, this means designing and redesigning the firm's chain of capabilities for a series of competitive advantages in a rapidly evolving world.[4]

In the public sector, ideas are generated about how to perform activities more efficiently and cost-effectively. Advocates of privatization argue that the private sector can perform any task more efficiently than the public sector can. Opponents believe that certain tasks and activities should be performed by the public sector because these activities have a social support focus that is in opposition to the self-serving interests of market forces. In the public sector, much like the private sector, the initial discussion is often around the applicability of privatization. This discussion is quite similar to the private sector discussion about core competencies. Political considerations are also discussion points in both private and public sector outsourcing discussions. In the public sector, these discussions might center on the public entity's role in society; in the private sector, they might revolve around the organization's role in the community and the impact of an outsourcing decision on the local economy, especially if the decision involves outsourcing business internationally.

Step 2: Determine Feasibility

A feasibility study is an analysis of the viability of an idea, proposed project or program. The goal is to determine the likelihood of success before a full investment of money, time and other resources in developing a course of action. The feasibility study focuses on the analysis of alternatives. After thorough analysis, the overall best alternative is identified based on pre-established decision criteria — and a decision is made. A feasible idea is one that meets certain criteria such as withstanding the likely risks, long-term viability and contribution to organizational goals and objectives. A business plan is developed to execute the decision.

A feasibility study typically includes (1) an executive summary briefly stating the major findings and recommendations; (2) a section of background information; (3) a description of the proposed project or program including advantages and disadvantages; (4) impact on key areas such as staffing, service levels and assets such as facilities, equipment and technology; (5) a comparison of the current situation to the proposed one; (6) a project schedule; and (6) the final recommendation with supporting financial documentation.

The feasibility of an insource/make or outsource/buy decision depends on a number of influencing factors, including (1) strategic aspects, (2) the effect on assets, and (3) the degree of flexibility once the decision is implemented. Each of these factors requires careful analysis.

The strategic factors in an outsourcing decision relate to internal and external issues. Externally, these issues revolve around suppliers and the long-term implications of a buy decision such as supplier capability now and in the future, capacity now and in the future, supplier quality and technology, cycle time, and cost management. Internally, there may also be concerns about the socioeconomic goals and objectives for the supply base, especially if the buying organization has a supplier diversity program.

Other strategic considerations include the impact on the organization's core competencies and related strategies, such as loss of internal skills and especially labor; the supply risks that result from the degree of control required and the security of the process; the impact on total cost of ownership; and the overall effect of the decision on competitive issues. Any decision that involves intellectual property requires special consideration of the long-term impact.

The second area of impact to consider is the impact the decision has on the organization's assets, including capital investments in equipment and technology or investments in human capital assets. Will a decision to outsource lead to the inadvertent creation of a competitor or transfer of proprietary knowledge? For example, this was the case when Intel outsourced chip manufacturing to Advanced Micro Devices (AMD) in the early 1990s. Now, AMD is Intel's biggest competitor although Intel still holds about 80 percent of the market share for microprocessors.[5] If assets are eliminated or reduced, what are the projected costs in the near term and far term, and what if the decision is later reversed? These cost streams may be difficult to estimate.

The third consideration is the degree of flexibility to reverse course after the decision is made. If human capital and equipment are reduced or eliminated as part of an outsourcing decision, the cost and speed at which they could be reacquired may be prohibitive. On the other hand, for competitive reasons, the organization may deem that it really needs to do something internally, or bring back in-house an activity that has been done outside. This was the case for Wal-Mart, which brought a greater proportion of its transportation lanes in-house to help reach its CO_2 emissions reduction goals. In some cases, this will entail an investment in assets and human capital, and greater internal risk in downward business cycles. Wal-Mart took more control over transportation to improve its efficiency and reduce fuel consumption. From 2005 to 2011, it was able to improve the CO_2 emissions of its fleet by 69 percent, while delivering 65 million more cases and driving 28 million fewer miles than it would have prior to improvements.[6]

Step 3: Collect and Analyze Cost Data

Several analytical methods and processes are useful in a make-or-buy or insource/outsource analysis, including break-even analysis, cost estimation processes and incremental cost analysis.

Break-Even Analysis. Break-even analysis is the "method for identifying the output level at which revenues equal cost or that the costs of two systems are the same"(ISM *Glossary* 2014).

Cost Estimation Processes. Estimating the cost of making versus buying or insourcing versus outsourcing is one of the most critical and most difficult tasks in the decision-making process. The first challenge is identifying all the relevant cost components, and the second is estimating the associated costs. When considering outsourcing a service, the cost estimation may involve interviewing managers and line staff in addition to reviewing job descriptions to be sure that the RFP fully captures the activities and service levels performed in house. How activities are structured; what staff and material resources go into delivering a service; how professional time is consumed during a workday; economies of scale because of equipment, setup time, coordination and supervision requirements; and learning curves may all be factors in a cost estimation process. This method compares a baseline cost (for example, the cost of performing a function internally) with the total costs if the function were performed externally. This requires a thorough understanding of the underlying events or drivers that cause major costs to be incurred. Consideration must be given to the fixed costs that will remain in the organization as well as to the incremental costs of supervising the outsourced provider.

Incremental Cost Method. Incremental cost-analysis methods measure the economic consequence of decision alternatives by focusing on the relevant costs. The overall question is, How will the total costs for the organization change if we decide to do Y rather than continue to do X? For example, the executive committee of an organization has decided on a growth strategy. The next question is, How do we achieve the targets? Three alternatives are available: (1) continue to manufacture goods domestically and export to new international markets (status quo/baseline metric), (2) manufacture goods in local markets (countries or regions) and sell them in those markets, or (3) concentrate manufacturing in a country or countries with a comparative advantage in this type of manufacturing. The analyst identifies the set of relevant costs that are associated with this decision. This process recognizes that typically it is not possible to identify a single definitive cost per unit or total cost of the good or service. In addition, the costs continually fluctuate over time and must be monitored and analyzed to determine whether the location decision is still a good one.

Total Cost of Ownership (TCO). *Total cost of ownership* is defined as "the combination of the purchase or acquisition price of a good or service, and additional costs incurred before or after product or service delivery. Costs are often grouped into pre-transaction, transaction and post-transaction costs, or into acquisition price and in-house costs. To use cost of ownership analysis as a cost reduction tool, it is necessary to identify and analyze the cost drivers to look for any avoidable costs" (ISM *Glossary* 2014). TCO analysis is an essential approach to use to capture the true costs associated with the manufacturing location decision. The analysis needs to be revisited as internal and external conditions change. TCO analysis is discussed in detail in *Foundation of Supply Management* (ISM *Professional Series*).

Step 4: Assess the Results of a Feasibility Study and Make a Decision

The team must analyze the data and recommend a course of action. There is a danger at this stage that the decision had already been made (for example, we know we will outsource our call centers to India) and the data are forced to support the preconclusion. Or, it may be that the pressure is intense to take action and the team may want to achieve quick cost savings, so the data collection and analysis phase is weak.

Step 5: Develop a Business Plan to Implement the Decision

Once a decision has been made, the team develops a business plan to drive the execution. This is a detailed action plan complete with task assignments, deliverables and due dates, and performance metrics.

Step 6: Audit Results

The results should be measured and compared to projections in case adjustments need to be made. Clearly, financial auditing is in order. Equally important may be a relationship audit of the third party to whom tasks or functions have been outsourced and the relationship with manager(s) internally. If the decision was made to keep tasks or a function in-house or to bring tasks or a function back in-house, then a relationship audit might be performed to assess the quality of the relationships that employees performing the tasks and/or functions have with internal and external stakeholders against the projections if outsourcing had been chosen.

Step 7: Conduct a Post-audit Evaluation of the Decision

There are two primary benefits to conducting a post-audit of the decision. One, it may provide valuable insight into the next phase of management of a third-party provider or lead to a reversal of the original decision. Two, it is a feedback loop into the next outsourcing decision, and knowledge gained during the current process may lead to a better and/or faster decision in the future.

Supply Management's Role in Mergers, Acquisitions and Divestitures

Mergers, acquisitions and divestitures are also strategic tools that enable an organization to achieve its vision and mission. For example, if an organization has a vision to be a global leader in technology, it may decide that organic growth over time will not generate the growth necessary to achieve the organization's goals. The executive committee may decide to pursue a growth strategy through mergers and acquisitions, or concentrate on technology by divesting in nontechnology-related businesses. Many organizations pursue growth through acquisitions. China's Legend Group did this when it acquired IBM's PC division and became Lenovo.[7]

Supply management professionals can make a contribution to the organization's decisions and plans related to mergers, acquisitions and divestitures during both pre-merger analysis and post-merger integration. Historically, supply management has not been involved until after the "deal" is complete; however, supply management can play an important role in determining whether there may be supply base problems or irregularities present that can reduce the value of the deal. For example, if the acquired company has long-term purchase contracts that are over-priced or incorporate poor terms, that may lower the true value of the merger. The supply-related risks associated with mergers and acquisitions were discussed in detail in Chapter 5. Supply management professionals can provide the results of their risk analysis as inputs into the pre-merger planning process. Supply management expertise can be applied to two strategy-related questions: (1) Is the proposed deal commercially attractive? (2) Can the organization capture the full potential value of the proposed deal? From a supply management standpoint, issues to investigate in advance include the following:

- Strategic suppliers;
- Current contracts, terms, conditions and duration;
- Key supplier financial condition;
- Supplier management and measurement systems;
- Supplier relationship management;
- Supplier sustainability (both environmental and social); and
- Supply availability and volatility.[8]

Involvement of supply management professionals in reviewing these areas can significantly reduce the supply risk associated with the acquisition or merger, and help the organization to achieve its desired goals.[9]

Post-merger, supply management's primary role is to ensure continuity of supply and capture synergies from the merger or acquisition. Supply management's responsibilities post-merger extend to five primary areas: (1) contractual issues, (2) management of redundancy and complexity, (3) liability exposure, (4) divestiture of assets, and (5) global economic considerations. According to Booz Allen Hamilton, inadequacies in post-merger integration are the leading cause of failed mergers. Because procurement delivers the bulk of near-term savings in merger integration efforts, chief executives rely on procurement to deliver value from a deal.[10]

Booz Allen Hamilton recommends the following to ensure superior execution:
- Pre-merger planning between the CEO and the procurement chief;
- Anticipating changes and their influence on procurement, especially in the merged organization's vertical integration, product line and organizational structure; and
- Developing capabilities that will enable procurement to quickly capture the required savings.

A phased work plan is recommended. This focuses first on critical operational issues, then on capturing synergies, and finally on achieving the ultimate value of the merger. Savings come from three sources: (1) price harmonization, (2) economies of scale, and (3) adoption of sourcing best practices. "The first provides the 'low-hanging fruit,' while the second represents the value that was generally expected from the merger. The third, however, is often the greatest source of opportunity. The best way to achieve savings is to use a well-structured sourcing methodology that pursues the opportunities in waves, starting with the easiest first. If procurement is managed well, companies will capture much of the merger's potential."[11] When Pfizer acquired Wyeth in 2009, one of the immediate areas of focus was how to capture best prices and best practices of the old supply organizations into the new organization. The process should go beyond a contract to contract comparison and proceed to a comprehensive spend analysis. "The benefits of undertaking an in-depth spend analysis — as opposed to simply conducting a quick contract comparison between organizations — are enormous. In one situation, it resulted in cost savings exceeding 60 percent."[12]

Clearly, there are strong linkages between supply management and organizational strategy, strategic decisions and strategic tools. Supply leaders and managers will be better positioned for success if they align functional strategy with organizational strategy. The following section addresses the development of strategic and operational plans at the supply management level and strategic plans at the sourcing level.

The Development of Strategic and Operational Supply Management Plans

The strategic planning process may also be performed at the function level, resulting in a strategic supply management plan, a strategic marketing plan and so on. These plans should be aligned with the organizationwide strategic plan and should be congruent with one another.

Elements of a Strategic Supply Management Plan

A strategic supply management plan typically includes the following sections:
- The shared vision of supply management (future-oriented);
- The mission of the supply management organization: what supply does, why and for whom;
- The core values of supply management that will guide its activities; and
- Goals, strategies or specific courses of action to accomplish the goals and metrics for determining the degree of success.

The development of a supply management vision, mission and core values was discussed in Chapter 2. This section addresses the development of goals and strategies to attain those goals, and offers preliminary suggestions for metrics. Metrics for department performance are discussed in detail in Chapter 11, and metrics for supplier performance are discussed in *Foundation of Supply Management* (ISM *Professional Series*). The supply management vision statement describes what the supply organization wants to become; it is future-oriented. The mission statement(s) describes the important business capabilities of supply management based on the customers' needs identified in the market research. The core values are the guiding principles behind the actions of everyone in the supply organization.

The supply management leadership team must then focus on developing business plans that will meet customer service, corporate profit and return on equity goals as well as aligning with the corporate strategies and plans. Toward this end, supply managers must understand the organization's product price structure and how supply makes a contribution to profit.

Given the current price structure, how and where does supply contribute to that pricing strategy, and where are there opportunities to avoid, reduce or remove costs? Supply management professionals must identify precisely what effect their actions have on various costs in the supply chain to maximize the supply-driven contribution to profit. This knowledge is fundamental to the goal-setting phase of a strategic supply management plan.

Goals

Goals should be SMART:

Specific,

Measurable,

Attainable,

Results-oriented, and

Time-bound.

A visioning initiative needs not just a broad vision, but specific, realizable goals. Goals represent what people commit themselves to do, often within a few months, and are aligned with the overall organizational goals. The word *goal* may have come from the Old English *goelan*, which means to hinder; goals often address barriers and obstacles. Organizationwide planning typically includes a pricing strategy, as well as targets for profit and return on equity. Planning for supply management should include goals aligned with these targets, and metrics should be in place to determine the extent of supply's contribution.

At Whirlpool, strategy and goals are aligned globally. The company's vision is "Every Home … Everywhere. With Pride, Passion and Performance."[13] Its strategy is to expand its manufacturing and marketing presence around the world through a series of acquisitions to become the world's largest major home appliance manufacturer serving customers everywhere. The company website states, "Taking a 'global but local' approach, Global Consumer Design tests the relevance of its design vision and concepts to reflect local influences and market diversity. Projects are driven by innovation, yet they are also balanced by understanding emerging consumer trends, analyzing consumer experience and seeking out 'real-life' insights."[14] Goals at the functional level are aligned with the vision and strategy. Whirlpool notes that "Innovation comes from anyone and anywhere within our company. It recognizes every employee as an inventor who can contribute the next big idea that can change the company and transform the lives of our consumers."[15]

Market Analysis

Market analysis is the process of examining the external environment in conjunction with the internal one to develop strategies and business plans. Market analysis is a critical element in supply management, especially in light of supply management's broadening scope of influence and responsibility. A number of tools and techniques are available to analyze markets. This section addresses SWOT analysis, supplier marketing strategies, and risk and benefit analysis.

SWOT Analysis. SWOT is an acronym for strengths, weaknesses, opportunities and threats. SWOT analysis is a strategic planning tool that starts with the desired end state or objective. Strengths are internal attributes of the organization that may be helpful to achieve the desired objective. Weaknesses are internal attributes that may be harmful. Opportunities and threats are external conditions that are either helpful or harmful. Figure 6-3 illustrates the types of areas to consider in SWOT analysis.

Figure 6-3: SWOT Analysis

	HELPFUL	HARMFUL
Internal attribute	• Strengths 　Resources: financial, intellectual, location 　Customer service 　Efficiency 　Competitive advantages 　Infrastructure 　Quality 　Human capital 　Price/cost 　Delivery 　Service • Social responsibility • Green/environmental awareness • Innovation skills • Large number of retirees opens positions	• Weaknesses 　Resources: financial, intellectual, location 　Customer service 　Efficiency 　Competitive advantages 　Infrastructure 　Quality 　Human capital 　Price/cost 　Delivery 　Service • Supplier social responsibility • Supplier Green/environmental practices • Loss of internal R&D talent • Lack of strong external talent pool globally
External attribute	• Opportunities 　Governmental such as legislation 　Market forces 　Global 　Technology 　Emerging supply chain practices • NGO environmental and social partnerships • Government regulation • Climate change • Leveling of global energy availability	• Threats 　Governmental such as legislation 　Market forces 　Global 　Technology 　Emerging supply chain practices • NGO environmental and social pressure • Government regulation • Climate change and changing weather patterns • Resource shortages

Following the identification of all the strengths, weaknesses, opportunities and threats, it must be decided if the stated objective is attainable. If the objective seems attainable in light of the analysis, then the strengths, weaknesses, opportunities and threats are used to develop possible strategies that maximize strengths, mitigate weaknesses, exploit opportunities and defend against threats. It is important to compare strengths to weaknesses and opportunities to threats to avoid assuming that a weak strength will overcome a strong weakness or that a weak opportunity will overcome a strong threat. The expected results of strategies should be expressed as a range of alternative assumptions. Remember that SWOTs are descriptions of conditions, and possible strategies define actions.

Strategies

A *strategy* is defined as "a roadmap detailing the plan of action necessary to assemble and focus resources toward organizational goals" (ISM *Glossary* 2014). A strategy is how the work will get done and by whom. Strategies or action plans are developed and prioritized for each goal. For each strategy, the specific action plans or tasks required to implement each are defined. A strategy could be designing a new supplier relationship management program or streamlining the supply management process. For example, IBM states that its strategy is, "Delivering innovation using laser-like focus on the high-value spaces of our industry."[16] To support this, it develops a detailed roadmap each year that guides its actions. For example, the 2015 roadmap, published in March 2013, has nine major points, each supported by data or action points. Its first point in the 2015 document is "1. We continuously change our business mix toward higher-value, more profitable technologies and market opportunities. In support of that point, IBM shows that in 2000, 27 percent of its profit came from software. In 2012 it was 45 percent, and by 2015 it is expected to be 50 percent."[17] Supply management must adapt and change as IBM changes, to fully support its mission and strategy, and to help IBM achieve its objectives.

IBM Global Procurement's mission is to achieve the lowest overall cost for goods and services being procured, to ensure that the goods and services provided meet required quality standards and/or customer expectations, and to deliver correct quantities of goods or services at the right global location at the time specified.[18]

To support this, procurement has the following stated objectives:

"IBM Procurement aims to:

- Drive quality improvements from our suppliers of goods and services;
- Deliver lowest overall cost and greatest competitive advantage; and
- Improve client perception of our values through increased influence and exemplary customer service and support."[19]

One important strategy IBM Global Procurement uses to support its achievement of these objectives is the Procurement One Place Strategy, which is the first point of contact for suppliers and clients to use to get in touch with procurement.[20] In a large organization such as IBM, this is instrumental in finding the right source of information as readily as possible. Another strategy is the use of premier supplier relationships, which inherently recognize the important value-added contribution that suppliers can make to an organizations' success. Premier supplier relationships entail establishing relationships thatprovide the following to IBM:

- Access to the latest technologies;
- Supply continuity;
- Speed to market;
- Growth in e-procurement leadership; and
- Retention of the best talent within the profession.[21]

To achieve these objectives, IBM procurement developed their core values as shown in Figure 6-4. These core values mirror those of the IBM Corporation.

Figure 6-4: IBM Procurement Core Values

IBM Procurement Core Values portray the understanding, integrity, teamwork, initiative and urgency that the company and all its divisions hold in the highest esteem.	
Understanding	Vigorously seek a full understanding of the capabilities, wants and needs of the entire supply chain: IBM's customers, our IBM internal clients, our suppliers, and our suppliers' suppliers. Actively articulate both IBM's and our suppliers' viewpoints, and facilitate communication at all levels and functions.
Integrity and teamwork	Ensure both IBM and the supplier keep the letter and spirit of all agreements. Build long-term relationships with suppliers based on trust, honesty and candor. Never compromise IBM's overall best interests in the pursuit of local or divisional interests. Expect teamwork, integrity, respect and excellence from each other, our cross-functional partners and our suppliers. Firmly believe in, and insist upon, true cross-functional participation which results in better procurement decisions and smoother, faster implementation. Be driven by common sense both to lead and support IBM delivering winning products, services and solutions in the marketplace.
Initiative and urgency	Continually seek to improve and never be satisfied with anything less than a competitive advantage in technology, price, quality, delivery, responsiveness, speed and innovation. Add and protect shareholder value. Be driven by a sense of urgency and dedicated to the ever-increasing efficiency and effectiveness of IBM Procurement, maximizing the use of available e-procurement tools in so doing.

Source: IBM, Global Procurement, "Core Values," accessed November 22, 2013, http://www-03.ibm.com/procurement/proweb.nsf/ContentDocsByTitle/United+States~Core+values?OpenDocument&Parent=About+procurement.

In addition, IBM Global Procurement provides a very clear statement of its policies and procedures, the nature of its commodity councils, who to contact at IBM procurement, a detailed supplier guideline for working with IBM and more.

Prioritized Implementation Schedule

Goals and corresponding strategies are prioritized. A schedule, including start dates, milestone dates and anticipated completion dates for each strategy, must be documented. Resource allocations, adjustments and requirements can be developed from this schedule.

Develop a Supply Management Operating Plan

An operating plan is based on market conditions, business needs and available resources. At the organizational level, it starts with the sales forecast and flows down to a production (services or goods) plan and master schedule, with accompanying budgets for materials and services, labor, capital equipment, and MRO or supplies. The operating plan provides a more detailed picture of the resource allocation decisions that have been made in support of the organization's strategic plan.

A corresponding operating plan is developed at the business unit and function levels. The supply management operating plan includes all the component areas under the supply management organization.

Elements of an Operating Plan. A supply management operating plan typically includes forecasts, budgets, a staffing plan and metrics.

FORECASTS. The organizational forecast of the scope and magnitude of key operating activities is used as the starting point to forecast supply management activities. Forecasting is discussed in *Effective Supply Management Performance* (ISM *Professional Series*).

BUDGETS. The supply management operating plan includes budgets for the function. These budgets define the needed resources, such as personnel, equipment, furnishings and training, and estimate their dollar value. Once funding is approved, the supply management team uses the budgets to carry out the mission of supply management, and monitor and evaluate the resources consumed in the process. *Foundation of Supply Management* (ISM *Professional Series*) addresses budgets and the budgeting process in detail.

STAFFING. The staffing plan is another critical piece of the supply management operating plan. It outlines the talent requirements of the supply management function, including existing talent and succession plans, as well as identifying staffing needs to fulfill the vision and mission of supply. The proposed operating budget should reflect and align with the staffing plan. Chapter 9 addresses staffing issues in more detail.

METRICS. The operating plan should include the key performance indicators (KPIs). Metrics for the supply management department are discussed in Chapter 11, and metrics for suppliers are addressed in *Foundation of Supply Management* (ISM *Professional Series*).

Strategies for Executing the Plan

Planning is a waste of time if the people in the organization are unable to execute plans efficiently and effectively. It is beneficial to develop a communication plan, a rollout plan and a phased time line to enhance the probability of superior execution.

Communication Plan

A communication plan describes the different methods that will be used to communicate the strategic and operating supply management plans to everyone in the organization. For example, IBM includes its high-level roadmap on its website, for all stakeholders to access. More detailed information that might be considered more proprietary is behind firewalls on the IBM Intranet. This might involve holding town meetings face-to-face or electronically where the senior leadership team lays out the strategy, issuing newsletters, and fielding questions and concerns in an established format. The communication plan should use the types of communication tools that are preferred by employees so that the communication method itself does not hinder the delivery and receipt of the message.

At Deere & Company, former CEO Bob Lane credited giving a clear and consistent message to everybody — employees, dealers, suppliers — so that even though the details of the plan were still evolving, the direction was clear.

Rollout Plan

The rollout plan includes items such as a deployment schedule, required resources, personnel and training requirements, and a budget. Flawless execution depends, in part, on a carefully developed rollout plan that takes into consideration the risks and risk exposure.

Phased Time Line

The sequencing of the rollout is also a critical success factor. Former Deere & Company CEO Bob Lane reflected on the company's operational and cultural transformation: "Looking back, this desire to both grow and improve operational performance at the same time created an enormous amount of skepticism early on. And if I had it all to do over again, I would be clearer and crisper at the front end about the priorities. The lesson for me was that sequencing is very important in terms of establishing the right expectations with employees and investors, and when you don't get it right it causes a lot of skepticism — legitimate skepticism."[22]

Summary

Business plans can be strategic or operational; both types are important. Supply management plays a key role in strategy development, both from having insight into the supply side of the organization (valuable spend data) and the understanding of future markets — especially in the areas of risk (as discussed in the previous chapter).

Before developing strategic and operational plans, organizations should conduct market and SWOT analyses. The operating plan is much more detailed than the strategic plan, and is based on sales forecasts, then flows down to production for goods or services, budgets, labor, capital equipment and MRO/supplies.

This chapter covered supply management's contribution to the planning process at the organizational level, and how supply management and sourcing strategies are developed to align with organizational strategy. Business plans guide the behavior and performance of supply management personnel and, if executed properly, ensure supply management's contribution meets organizational goals for such areas as customer service, corporate profit and return on equity, while reducing the organization's risk exposure.

Key Points

1. Strategic plans answer the question: Where do we want to go?
2. Operational plans answer the question: How do we get there?
3. A strategic supply plan typically includes (1) the shared vision of supply management (future-oriented); (2) the mission of the supply management organization (what supply management does, why and for whom); (3) the core values of supply management that will guide its activities, goals, strategies or specific courses of action to accomplish the goals; and (4) metrics for determining the degree of success.
4. Supply managers contribute to two pre-merger/acquisition questions: (1) Is the proposed deal commercially attractive? (2) Can the organization capture the full potential value of the proposed deal? They contribute post-merger by ensuring continuity of supply and capturing synergies from the merger or acquisition.
5. The supply management team can contribute to strategic planning by involvement in decisions about which areas of expertise the organization should develop and maintain as core competencies, and which it should procure externally.

CHAPTER 7

An organization should, by definition, function organically; this means that its purposes should determine its structure, rather than the other way around, and that it should function as a community rather than a hierarchy, and offer autonomy to its members, along with tests, opportunities, and rewards, because ultimately an organization is merely the means, not the end.

— WARREN BENNIS[1]

Organizing and Building Supply Management Infrastructure

Chapter 3 addressed the leader's role in aligning people and resources around the direction he or she sets for the organization. From a managerial perspective, alignment relates to the infrastructure needed to support the people in their quest for the vision set forth by the leader or leadership team. In the case of supply management, this infrastructure consists of the structure of the supply management group, the human capital or talent that will carry out the strategies and plans, and the technology that will support and enable strategy execution. This chapter focuses on the options, issues and considerations around structuring the supply management group. Chapter 8 focuses specifically on processes and technology to enhance efficiency and effectiveness, while Chapter 9 addresses the organization of the people in the supply management organization.

According to Institute for Supply Management®, the definition of supply management is the identification, acquisition, access, positioning and management of resources and related capabilities that an organization needs or potentially needs in the attainment of its strategic objectives. This includes the following components: disposition/investment recovery, distribution, inventory control, logistics, materials management, operations, packaging, procurement/purchasing, product/service development, quality, receiving, strategic sourcing, transportation/traffic/shipping and warehousing. The structure around these processes and the systems and processes themselves should be aligned with the organization and contribute to the attainment of organizational goals and objectives. This chapter discusses various approaches to these issues and is organized in three major sections: (1) organizational and supply management structure, (2) systems and processes, and (3) technology.

Chapter Objectives
- Describe the different types of organizational structures: functional, divisional (based on project, product/brand, category/commodity or geography) and matrix.
- Discuss the implications of each type of organizational structure.
- Describe the approaches to organizing the supply management function: decentralized, hybrid and centralized.
- Discuss the advantages and disadvantages of centralized, hybrid and decentralized supply management organizations.

Organizational and Supply Management Structure

Organizational structure is the way interrelated people, processes and activities are arranged (see Figure 7-1). Organizational structure reflects decisions about who should do which tasks, who reports to whom, and how decisions are made. Structure addresses the complexity, formalization and centralization between and among the interrelated people, processes and activities.

Figure 7-1: Horizontal, Vertical and Spatial Aspects of Structure

ELEMENTS OF STRUCTURE	←	→
Horizontal complexity • Number of business units	Few	Many
Vertical complexity • Hierarchical levels • Span of control	Few Wide	Many Narrow
Spatial complexity • Geographical dispersion	Little	Much
Formalization of rules, job descriptions and procedures	Little standardization	Much standardization
Centralization of decision-making	Low	High

First, the degree of horizontal, vertical and spatial differentiation of organizational activities determines the complexity of the structure. The number of units across the organization represents its horizontal complexity. The depth of the organizational hierarchy is its vertical complexity. Flat structures have fewer hierarchical levels and each level has a wider span of control, meaning that more workers report to the same manager. Tall structures have many levels with narrower spans of control. The geographical dispersion of physical and human resources is the organization's spatial complexity. Second, the degree of standardization of rules, job descriptions, procedures and such represents the formalization of the structure. Third, the degree of concentration of decision-making reflects how centralized or decentralized the structure is.

Differentiation occurs through a division of labor and technical specialization. Integration occurs when specialists cooperate to achieve a common goal. Each organizational structure reflects trade-offs made between differentiation and specialization.

Functional Structure

The structure of each functional area in an organization flows from the organizational structure. The overall goal for each function (supply management, marketing, finance, and so on) is an efficient and effective process. When considering the structure of supply management, three primary questions should be answered:

1. To what extent does the structure enable efficient and effective management of the organization's annual spend?
2. To what extent does the structure enable efficient and effective aggregation of spend across departments, divisions and business units?
3. To what extent does the structure enable efficient and effective service levels to end users of the purchased goods and services?

The supply management professional has primary responsibility for ensuring these goals are achieved to the greatest extent possible given the organizationwide structure. Therefore, the leader-manager must fully comprehend the implications of organizational structure on supply management structure and processes.

Organizational Structure Types and Implications

Organizations may be structured in many ways. This chapter addresses three basic types of structure: functional, divisional (based on project, product/brand, category/commodity or geography) and matrix. Ideally, structure should maximize communication and coordination internally and externally, and optimize how products and services are delivered to customers. In a complex, global environment, it is especially challenging to reconcile top-down hierarchical management with matrix management at a project level along with the need or requirement for organizationwide information flows.

Structured by Function. If an organization is structured by function, it is arranged around knowledge areas such as sales, marketing, engineering, supply management, and so on (see Figure 7-2). This structure fits well with an organization that has a dominant product or service. Each area develops functional expertise, but there may be little integration, poor communication and conflicting objectives between and among functions. While functional ownership enables the development of expertise and establishment of standards, cross-functional projects may suffer from lack of flexibility and speed because of the hierarchical nature of workflows and decision-making. In this type of structure, supply management may be organized as one primary function with sub-functions such as procurement, logistics, operations, and so on.

Figure 7-2: Structured by Function

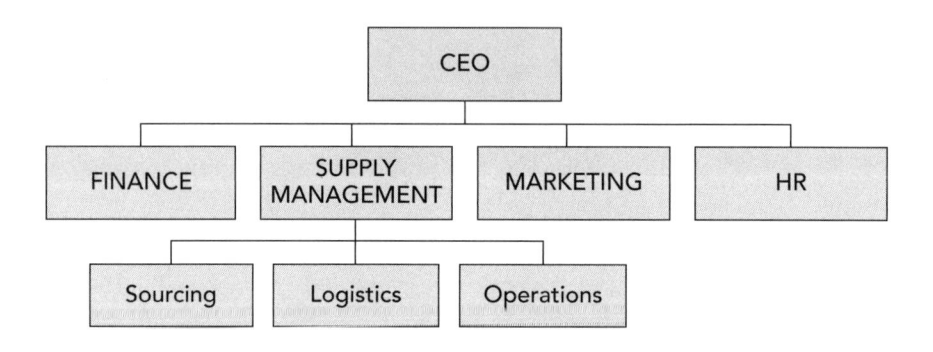

```
                    ┌─────┐
                    │ CEO │
                    └──┬──┘
        ┌──────────┬───┴──────────┬──────────┐
    ┌───────┐  ┌─────────┐  ┌──────────┐  ┌────┐
    │FINANCE│  │ SUPPLY  │  │MARKETING │  │ HR │
    │       │  │MANAGEMENT│ │          │  │    │
    └───────┘  └────┬────┘  └──────────┘  └────┘
            ┌───────┼────────┐
        ┌────────┐┌─────────┐┌──────────┐
        │Sourcing││Logistics││Operations│
        └────────┘└─────────┘└──────────┘
```

Structured by Division. Also referred to as structured by business unit, in this organizational structure, knowledge and expertise may be grouped by product or brand, category or commodity, or geography (see Figure 7-3). Product or brand management is an approach that centers organizational efforts on delivering a specific product to market or focuses on increasing the perceived value to the customer of a brand. Organizations that take a product or brand management approach may find that brand managers focus narrowly on their brand and the short-term financial objectives related to it rather than on organizationwide strategic objectives. Likewise, it may be difficult to link brand performance directly to key metrics such as shareholder equity. Different brands or products may also have conflicting objectives. For the supply management organization, the brand or product management approach may create conflicts over allocation of supply management resources, inability to consolidate spend, and difficulty in standardizing inputs to aggregate spend and increase purchasing power.

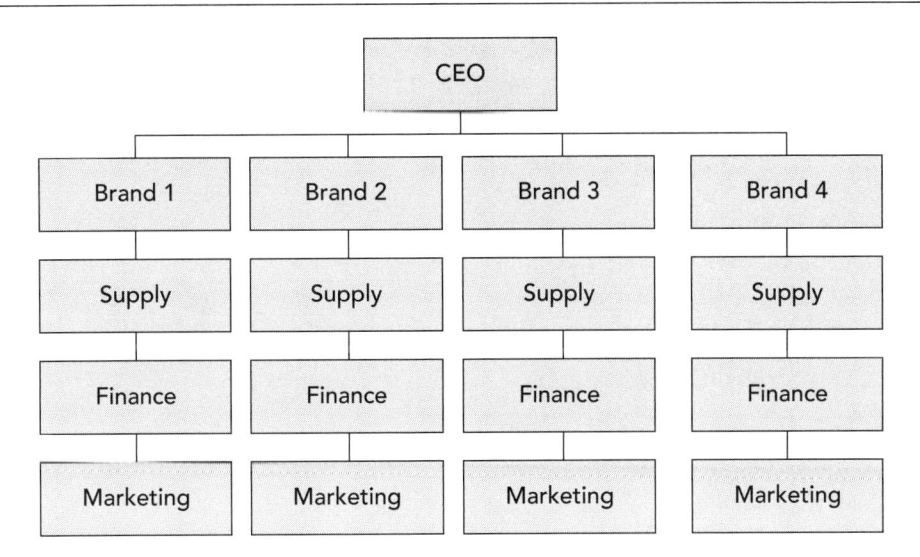

Figure 7-3: Product, Brand or Category Organizational Structure

```
                        CEO
         ┌───────────┬──────┴─────┬───────────┐
      Brand 1     Brand 2      Brand 3     Brand 4
         │           │            │           │
      Supply      Supply       Supply      Supply
         │           │            │           │
      Finance     Finance      Finance     Finance
         │           │            │           │
     Marketing   Marketing    Marketing   Marketing
```

Category management (within product management) is an offshoot of brand management. It developed in the retail sector where retail products are grouped into categories and managed as business units. The category manager oversees products and activities across the entire category to optimize producer and retailer profits. Categories contribute to store results and contribute to brand management. In this structure, the goal is to build customer loyalty through access to better and more timely information, faster response to consumers, and relationship management.

For example, when the German carmaker Volkswagen AG hired a new CEO, he changed the corporate structure to twelve brands under the name of the Volkswagen Group, further differentiating the brands, into a premium group and a volume group. The move was designed to better differentiate the cars within each brand in the minds of the consumers.[2]

Structured by Geography. Spatially complex organizations have wide geographical dispersion of physical and human resources. Given the difficulties created by differences in time, language, culture and business norms and practices, it may be determined that the organization is best structured around geography (see Figure 7-4). Conflicting and/or competing goals and objectives across countries or regions of activity on the sales and marketing side along with differences in location of sources increases the complexity of the business and may impede the ability to efficiently and effectively design, develop and deliver products or services to customers.

Figure 7-4: Structured by Geography

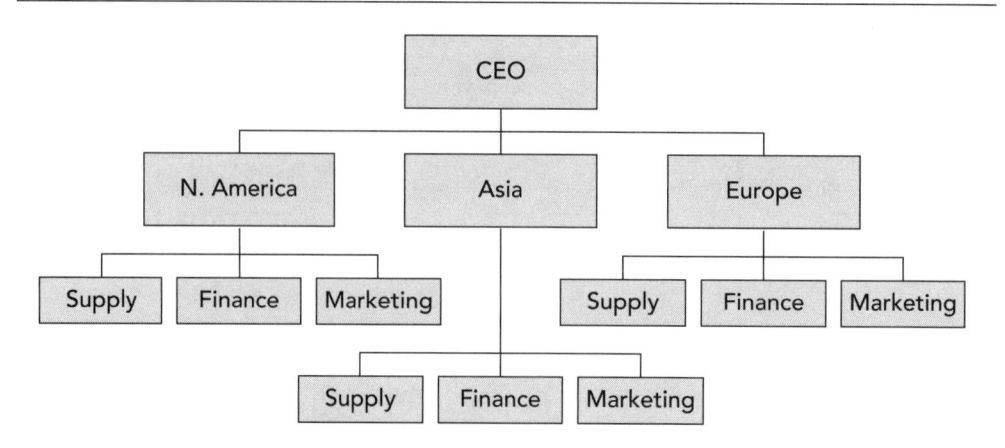

```
                        CEO
         ┌───────────────┼───────────────┐
    N. America         Asia            Europe
   ┌────┼────┐     ┌────┼────┐     ┌────┼────┐
Supply Finance Marketing Supply Finance Marketing Supply Finance Marketing
```

Structured by Function and Division: A Matrix Organization. A matrix organizational structure combines functional and divisional structures with cross-functional project teams responsible for the total project and its outcomes (see Figure 7-5). A project manager owns the project and takes responsibility for its successful and timely completion. Matrix organizations may be complex with high communication and coordination requirements between functional and divisional levels. A matrix structure offers speed and flexibility that may not be achieved in a purely functional organization. Overhead costs, however, are typically higher than in functional organizations because sufficient expertise is necessary in various functional areas for full-time assignment to multiple and simultaneous projects. In a project-based structure, supply management personnel are assigned to project teams and serve on these teams for their duration.

Figure 7-5: Matrix Organizational Structure

	Project 1	Project 2	Project 3	Project 4	Project 5	Project 6
Supply Management						→
HR						→
Finance						→
Marketing						→

Project team members report to a functional manager and to a project manager. For example, a supply management professional may be on a new product development team and report to a director of supply management as well as to the team project manager. There are three typical approaches to this model:

1. A project manager or administrator with limited authority oversees the project. The functional managers retain control over their resources and their aspects of the project. The project manager's role is primarily as the go-between to smooth communication flows between and among functional areas and track overall project progress.
2. A project manager oversees the project and shares power equally with the functional managers. The power-sharing aspect is the most difficult to manage, and this structure tends to be complex.
3. A project manager is primarily responsible for the project and functional managers provide area expertise and resources on an as-needed basis. Competition for resources becomes a difficult issue because functional managers with finite resources are asked to provide expertise to multiple projects.

Bank of America, for example, had a matrix structure with three main lines of business: Global Corporate and Investment Banking, Global Wealth and Investment Management, and Consumer and Small Business Banking. This structure was reflected in the organization of the Supply Chain Management (SCM) group. There were two teams that handled enterprisewide sourcing: (1) technology, services and fulfillment, and (2) the enterprise sourcing group. Both groups source traditional items specific to their areas and unique items specific to the line of business. Support groups within SCM also provided operational support for systems, processes, policies and procedures. and the supplier development group. Housed within the lines of business are business support functions and supplier relationship management teams. SCM reported to a global SCM executive who reported to the COO within the office of the CFO.[3]

Creating a Globally Integrated Organization

Size, geographical dispersion and cultural diversity complicate organizational structure at the enterprisewide level and at the supply management level. Management in many organizations is interested in reducing or removing the effects of organizational boundaries. These boundaries may result from differences in culture, conflicting goals or functional silos. *Barrier-free* approaches focus on removing internal boundaries to encourage teamwork and widespread sharing of information. *Virtual* and *modular* organizational forms are used to make external relations more permeable and create seamless knowledge systems across organizations. According to G. Dess, G.T. Lumpkin and A. Eisner, teams are an important part of barrier-free structures because they (1) substitute peer-based for hierarchical control, (2) often develop more creative solutions via brainstorming and other group problem-solving techniques, and (3) absorb administrative tasks previously handled by specialists.[4]

For instance, Carlos Ghosn, chairman of the board, president and CEO of Nissan since 2008, reorganized to create a more globally integrated organization. He made three major changes at the time:

1. He reduced the number of people based at the world headquarters in Tokyo, moved part of the headquarters to the United States and Europe, and made movement into and out of Tokyo more fluid based on a strong rationale for a presence there.
2. Experts were identified in a particular technology or process no matter where they were located.
3. The position of president in North America was eliminated at the time to reduce problems with communication and information flow between headquarters and the region. The executive vice president traveled every month to head the management committee of North America, and Ghosn himself headed the committee every three months.[5]

Structure affects processes, procedures, systems and relationships within and between functions. Whether the organization is structured by function, division or project, supply management professionals must develop and execute strategies that maximize the advantages of the structure and minimize the disadvantages.

The organizationwide structure impacts each function (for example, supply management, marketing and finance) within the organization. For example, if the organization tends to be highly decentralized (decision-making is spread throughout the organization), then supply management will also be highly decentralized. If the organization is highly centralized (decision-making is highly concentrated), then supply management will be highly centralized. It is the responsibility of the supply management professional to drive efficiency and effectiveness within a given structure and to use his or her influence to mold the supply management structure to achieve optimal performance. The supply management professional also uses his or her position on the senior leadership team to influence decisions about structure and to ensure that supply management processes are structured for efficiency and effectiveness.

Centralized, Decentralized and Hybrid Supply Management Structures

As discussed earlier in this chapter, centralization is one aspect of organizational complexity and refers to the centralization of decision-making. In supply management, the degree of centralization is reflected by the percentage of organizational spend managed or controlled by supply management. The three most common organizational models are the following:

1. *Centralized.* "The authority and responsibility for most supply management-related functions and decisions are assigned to a central organization. This term refers to the locus of decision-making, not necessarily that supply management staff is all physically located in one place. There are numerous advantages including the ease of standard-

izing products; reduction of administrative duplication; increased leverage from larger volumes; limited interdepartmental competition in times of short supply; more control over purchase commitments; greater administrative efficiency for suppliers; and the development of specialized expertise in purchasing activities" (ISM *Glossary* 2014).

2. *Hybrid.* "Authority and responsibility are shared between a central supply management organization and business units, divisions or operating plants. Hybrid structures may lean more heavily toward centralized or decentralized depending on how decision-making authority is divided" (ISM *Glossary* 2014). One type of hybrid supply management structure is a center-led organization in which strategic direction is centralized and execution is decentralized. In a more decentralized hybrid structure, management may use teams and lead buyers to achieve the advantages of spend aggregation while maintaining a highly decentralized structure.

3. *Decentralized.* The "decision-making authority is dispersed close to the point of service or action rather than being concentrated in a central group or location" (ISM *Glossary* 2014). There is no central locus for supply management decision-making and no specialized buying expertise.

In a survey of 249 organizations, P. Fraser Johnson and Michiel R. Leenders found that the hybrid structure (centralized hybrid, hybrid, decentralized hybrid) was the most popular organizational mode, accounting for 67 percent of survey respondents. However, 64 percent of respondents "leaned" toward centralization (centralized and centralized hybrid) and 26 percent "leaned" toward decentralization (decentralized and decentralized hybrid), while only 10 percent sat in the middle of the continuum.[6] Supply management organizational structure is one of the metrics in benchmarking studies conducted by CAPS Research (www.capsresearch.org). Respondents are typically asked to identify the supply management organization as either centralized, decentralized or a hybrid. A review of the industry-specific studies reveals a mix of structures both within and across industries.

These structures actually fall along a continuum from decentralized to centralized with numerous hybrid variations, such as center-led on the more centralized end of the spectrum and teams or lead buyers on the more decentralized end (see Figure 7-6).

Figure 7-6: Degree of Centralization in Supply Management

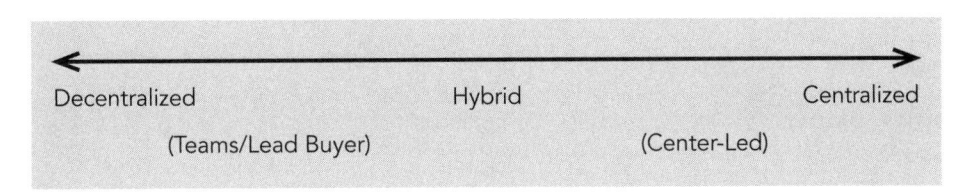

Decentralized	Hybrid	Centralized
(Teams/Lead Buyer)	(Center-Led)	

The supply management professional has three primary roles in terms of supply management structure:

1. Inform and influence internal partners about the advantages and disadvantages of structural types in terms of efficiently and effectively managing spend, aggregating spend and providing service to end users.
2. Develop the most efficient and effective supply management processes possible given structural constraints.
3. Enhance the ability of supply management professionals to collaborate efficiently and effectively, both internally and externally, by smoothing the path through structural barriers such as complicated structures, hierarchical silos and conflicting functional objectives.

To accomplish this role, the supply management professional must fully comprehend the opportunities and obstacles of various supply management structures. These are discussed in the following section in the context of degree of centralization of supply management decision-making.

Centralized Supply Management Structure. There are many advantages and disadvantages to a highly centralized supply management structure. Figure 7-7 summarizes the advantages and disadvantages of a centralized supply management structure.

Figure 7-7: Potential Advantages and Disadvantages of Centralization

ADVANTAGES	DISADVANTAGES
Strategic focus	Lack of business unit focus
Greater buying specialization	Narrow specialization and job boredom Cost of central unit highly visible
Ability to pay for talent	Corporate staff appears excessive
Consolidation of requirements — leverage	Tendency to minimize legitimate differences in requirements
Coordination and control of policies and procedures	Lack of recognition of unique business unit needs
Effective planning and research	Focus on corporate requirements, not on business unit strategic requirements Most knowledge sharing one-way
Common suppliers	Even common suppliers behave differently in geographic and market segments
Proximity to major organizational decision-makers	Distance from users

Figure 7-7: Potential Advantages and Disadvantages of Centralization *continued*

ADVANTAGES	DISADVANTAGES
Critical mass	Tendency to create organizational silos
Firm brand recognition and stature	Customer segments require adaptability to unique situations
Reporting line — *power*	Top management not able to spend time on suppliers
Cost of purchasing low	High visibility of purchasing operating costs

Source: P.F. Johnson, M. R. Leenders and A.E. Flynn, *Purchasing and Supply Management*, (McGraw-Hill/Irwin, 2011) 28. Reproduced by permission of the McGraw-Hill Companies.

Clearly, centralized decision-making creates an opportunity to transition supply management from a transactional to a strategic process and function by laying the foundation for spend aggregation and analysis that may lead to greater leverage in the marketplace. For example, when the American Red Cross faced a US$135 million deficit, it recognized that bringing discipline and efficiency through reorganizing procurement was going to be a key lever in improvement. It reorganized procurement around its business units, giving each business unit a primary contact. It also used commodity experts, which were not always exclusive to one business unit but would interface with the business unit's primary contact to serve the business. This fit with its three objectives: simple, synergistic and savings.[7]

The supply management professional must recognize that this transition may naturally lead to internal resistance from budget owners if they perceive a loss of decision-making control over spend decisions that affect their budgets. One of the greatest challenges may be the supply management professional's ability to create a shared vision of supply management's potential contribution and align stakeholders around this vision. A second challenge may be overcoming the difficulties in creating efficient processes when decisions are made from an organizationwide perspective rather than from a unit-level one. A third challenge may be attracting, retaining and developing the necessary talent to effectively manage resources from a centralized perspective.

Decentralized Supply Management Structure. Figure 7-8 summarizes the advantages and disadvantages of a decentralized supply management structure.

Figure 7-8: Potential Advantages and Disadvantages of Decentralization

ADVANTAGES	DISADVANTAGES
Easier coordination/communication with operating department	More difficult to communicate among business units
Speed of response	Encourages users not to plan ahead Operational versus strategic focus
Effective use of local sources	Too much focus on local sources; ignores better supplier opportunities No critical mass in organization for visibility/effectiveness — "whole person syndrome" Lacks clout
Business unit autonomy	Suboptimization Business unit preferences not congruent with corporate preferences Small differences get magnified
Reporting line simplicity	Reporting at low level in organization
Undivided authority and responsibility	Limits functional advancement opportunities
Suits purchasing personnel preference	Ignores larger organization considerations
Broad job definition	Limited expertise for requirements
Geographical, cultural, political, environmental, social, language, currency appropriateness	Lack of standardization
Hide the cost of supply management	Cost of supply management relatively high

Source: P.F. Johnson, M. R. Leenders and A.E. Flynn, *Purchasing and Supply Management*, (McGraw-Hill/Irwin, 2011) 28. Reproduced by permission of the McGraw-Hill Companies.

Clearly, decentralization offers some distinct advantages; the challenges for the supply management professional are to overcome the weaknesses by primarily designing processes, policies and procedures, overlays or temporary structures to enable the organization to aggregate and analyze spend and gain leverage in the marketplace when decision-making authority is dispersed throughout the organization. The ability to influence decision-makers and persuade them to collaborate across organizational barriers may be the leader's greatest asset. In addition, centralized procurement may not add significant value in highly diverse business units that are geographically dispersed.[8]

PURCHASING COUNCILS OR LEAD BUYING GROUPS. In a decentralized structure, a purchasing council or lead buying group might be created to aggregate volume and make spend decisions to maximize value. In lead buying situations, the site or group with commodity-specific expertise makes sourcing decisions for that commodity. For example, an IT commodity team might manage a structured, disciplined sourcing process in partnership with IT experts in the information technology department, and together they manage IT spend for all departments.

Hybrid Supply Management Structure. Many organizations attempt to capture the advantages of both centralized and decentralized structures by creating hybrid versions. One of the most common approaches is to create a small staff at the headquarters to manage common and high-impact requirements, with each individual site responsible for its own requirements for all other goods or services. In an organization with multiple business units, different divisions or business units often sell different products or services requiring a different mix of purchased items. Often the division or business unit is operated as a profit center where the division manager is given total responsibility for running the division, acts as president of an independent firm and is judged by profits made by the division. Because purchases are the largest single controllable cost of running the division and have a direct effect on its efficiency and competitive position, the profit center manager may insist on having direct authority over purchasing. This has led firms to adopt decentralized-centralized purchasing, or a hybrid organizational structure, in which the supply management function is partially centralized at the corporate or head office and partially decentralized to the business units.

Often the corporate supply management organization works with the business unit supply management departments on those tasks that are more effectively handled on a corporate basis — (1) establishing policies, procedures, controls and systems; (2) recruiting and training personnel; (3) coordinating the purchase of common use items in which more "clout" is needed; (4) auditing supply management performance; and (5) developing corporatewide supply management strategies. Therefore, hybrid organizational structures attempt to capture the benefits of both centralized and decentralized structures by creating an organizational structure that is neither completely centralized nor decentralized (see Figure 7-9). Both the product/brand management model and the geographic model can be used in a hybrid structure. Instead of pushing all decision-making to the product/brand level or to a specific geographic location, decision-making may be shared between the corporate supply management group and the supply management professional at the product/brand or geographic level.

Figure 7-6: Degree of Centralization in Supply Management

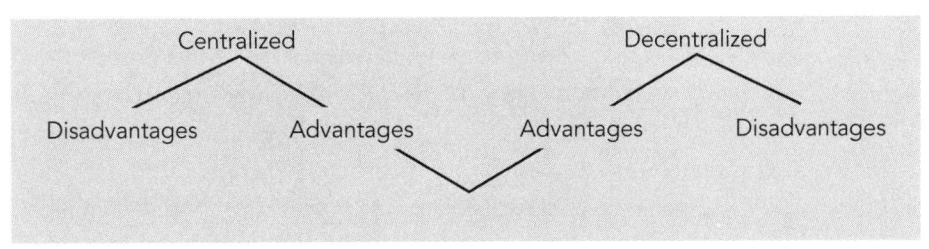

Source: M. R., P. F. Johnson and A. E. Flynn, *Purchasing and Supply Management*, 14th edition, McGraw-Hill Ryerson, New York, 2011, 54. Reproduced by permission of the McGraw-Hill Companies.

Organizations with a commitment to both a decentralized structure and spend aggregation find ways to leverage spend without changing the basic organizational structure. Center-led supply management tries to bridge that gap. As a growing global company, LG Electronics (LG) felt the need to improve its procurement organization, moving away from having procurement in each business unit. LG's CEO stated in his June 2009 CEO letter: "Recently, we formed a Global General Procurement organization ... It is important in our transformation to 'Global Number One' that we have a consolidated, centralized approach to procurement. This is a great opportunity to leverage our growing scale and capabilities." With this strong support, LG's Chief Procurement Officer took the initiative to create a commodity management structure for leveraging across business units. While providing this strategic, centralized leadership in key areas, yet still being respectful of the Korean culture, some business unit autonomy is retained. Commodity clusters across the companies and regions manage direct material sourcing and global operations teams; everything is under single leadership which helps reduce processing costs in back-end office functions. Some unique items are still purchased locally, creatig a hybrid approach that offers synergies while meeting local needs. This has allowed LG to reduce its direct material spend by US$5.9 billion on a US$24.8 billion spend.[9]

Impact of Supply Management Structure

Organizational structure affects individuals within the supply management organization and individuals in other functions and business processes, as well as external players such as suppliers. It is important for the supply management professional to fully comprehend the implications of the supply management structure and anticipate the responses and reactions of those affected by the structure to ensure optimal performance. The supply management structure affects workload distribution within the organization.

Workload Distribution. Work must be distributed to supply management personnel no matter which structure is in place. Depending on the size and capability of the supply management group, workload is typically distributed on the basis of (1) commodity or class, (2) department, (3) special project, (4) volume, (5) rotation, (6) type of contract, (7) staff expertise, or (8) supplier.[10] Each of these approaches is discussed in the following section.

COMMODITY OR CLASS. Assignments can be made to supply management professionals based on the various commodities the organization requires. This is especially common in large organizations with significant spending, where a high level of expertise can be developed. The term *commodity* means all goods and services purchased by an organization. Each supply management professional may specialize in a group of similar commodities or in a single commodity (generally in the case of large organizations), where it is a significant enough part of product cost to justify the position and where the supply management professional has a strong product orientation. There are a number of ways to categorize purchases, including monetary delineations, separating critical from standard commodities, or by individual units.

Pareto analysis (also known as ABC analysis or the 80/20 rule) can be used to categorize purchases according to dollar value. By conducting this analysis, managers can identify the 10 percent to 20 percent of purchased goods and services on which they spend 80 percent to 90 percent of the total annual expenditures. These "A" items, and the suppliers of these items, would be the commodities on which the greatest resources (time, people and attention) would be focused. For example, spend might be split into three major commodity groups using the ABC method with plateaus for dollar spend.

The high value "A" items (such as those above US$5 million) might be critical mass items. These might include raw materials such as grains, fuels and metals. "B" items (such as those between US$1 million and US$5 million) might include a specific packaging item. The "C" purchases (such as those under US$1 million) could include MRO items. In each commodity grouping, supply management professionals need different levels of knowledge and skills. Commodity teams with strategic skills would handle the items of US$5 million or more. The "B" items require less team emphasis, and the "C" items fall into the transactional category.

Portfolio analysis is another approach that assigns risk levels to value levels to further refine the categories. Figure 7-10 is one example of this approach. This analysis recognizes the importance of marketplace risk in acquiring a category when determining resource allocation for management of a specific commodity. Portfolio analysis results in four quadrants, often referred to as noncritical, leverage, bottleneck and strategic. This approach is discussed in more detail in Chapter 8.

Figure 7-10: Portfolio Analysis

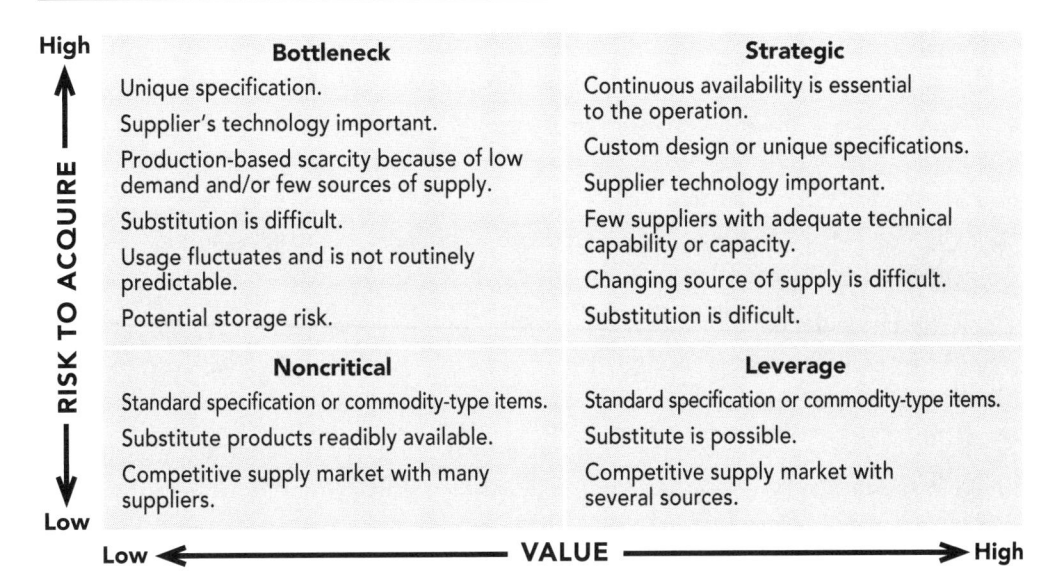

	Bottleneck	**Strategic**
High Risk	Unique specification. Supplier's technology important. Production-based scarcity because of low demand and/or few sources of supply. Substitution is difficult. Usage fluctuates and is not routinely predictable. Potential storage risk.	Continuous availability is essential to the operation. Custom design or unique specifications. Supplier technology important. Few suppliers with adequate technical capability or capacity. Changing source of supply is difficult. Substitution is dificult.
	Noncritical	**Leverage**
Low Risk	Standard specification or commodity-type items. Substitute products readily available. Competitive supply market with many suppliers.	Standard specification or commodity-type items. Substitute is possible. Competitive supply market with several sources.
	Low VALUE	High

(Y-axis: RISK TO ACQUIRE)

Source: Adapted from Peter Kraljic, "Purchasing Must Become Supply Management," *Harvard Business Review* (1983); available from www.harvard.edu.

DEPARTMENT. When purchase requisitions are assigned by department orientation, the supply management professional handles requests from certain departments assigned to the supply management professional. This type of supply management professional is more oriented toward serving the department and handling all its needs, as opposed to the commodity supply management professional whose focus is more on what is being purchased than for whom it is being purchased.

SPECIAL PROJECT. Requisitions may be assigned according to a special project or a new product line. The buyer may be assigned to provide materials and services to support the needs of a certain project. This is often applied in the case of a research laboratory or construction project. For example, after a competitive source selection process, supplier partnering may be used in construction contracts. The project team, consisting of the buyer's project representatives and the contractor's representatives, meet to identify shared objectives and establish a decision-making process that will be applied to every issue that comes up on the job. The contracts typically contain cost-incentive provisions that encourage contractors to propose innovations to reduce costs during the contract term; they also state that they will share the benefits of the reductions. This approach typically has led to sharply reduced claims, and projects are completed ahead of schedule and under budget.

Volume. So that the buyers in a department might have similar levels of responsibility, some departments make assignments based on dollar volume or number of requisitions handled annually. Care must be exercised in this case to ensure that the workload is reasonably distributed. Consider the difference in the nature and criticality of the tasks of an MRO buyer handling hundreds of low-value transactions compared with the capital equipment buyer who spends as much on a transaction for a single machine tool.

Rotation. Some organizations rotate supply professionals through different buying groups to develop expertise and tap as wide a range of skills as possible. The focus is less on the purchase activity itself and more on the individual's training. Rotational programs are often used to train new hires before placing them in a permanent position. This allows the new employee to understand the various jobs and functions within the supply management department, to forge relationships with coworkers, and to help the employee and the manager decide where the employee's skills can best be used.

The rotational method might also be used in a very routine situation such as replenishing crib items. The supply management professionals are rotated regularly to broaden their experience and to keep the work from becoming too routine.

Type of Contract. Assigning workloads according to the type of contract is especially useful if specific types of contracting involve a steep learning curve. One approach to delineating contracts is to apply portfolio analysis to develop a matrix of contract alternatives. For example, contracts that fall into the strategic segment in Figure 7-10 illustrating Portfolio Analysis represent the greatest risk, require increased resource commitments, and probably entail more complex terms and conditions. Better supplier segmentation and contract selection will result in reduced cycle time in contract negotiations, more informed understanding of risk, and increased optimization of the supply management professional's time to achieve cost savings.

Staff Expertise Assigned by Category. Distributing the workload according to the skills and capabilities of the persons in the group is also used. This approach can be employed in conjunction with any number of the other methods. For instance, a manager may conduct a portfolio analysis and identify critical suppliers for each quadrant: (1) acquisition, (2) critical, (3) leverage, and (4) strategic. Major categories of spend would be assigned to each quadrant based on an assessment of risk to acquire and value to the organization. For example, in a fast casual restaurant that specializes in ribs, strategic spend items might include beef ribs, signature sauces and customized seasonings. Bottleneck items might include agricultural products in short supply in the current season because of weather-related production problems or unavailability due to farmers transitioning to corn production for ethanol rather than for corn syrup or feed. Leverage items might include standardized restaurant supplies and food items, and noncritical items might include restaurant supplies procured on a unit rather than a corporate basis. The skills required of the supply management professional assigned to each category would be tailored to achieve the goal of each category. Figure 7-11 gives an example of possible categories, the key goal for each, and the associated skill sets required of personnel.

Figure 7-11: Goals and Skill Sets by Category

CATEGORY	KEY GOAL	REQUIRED SKILL SET
Noncritical	Minimize acquisition time and cost.	Efficient; able to establish and follow simple procedures and process; can recognize and eliminate non-value-adding process steps.
Bottleneck	Short term: Ensure supply availability. Long term: Eliminate.	Short term: Able to create options for mutual gain; creative thinker able to identify value for the supplier. Long term: Strong collaboration and negotiation skills to work internally on specification or statement of work to take out unnecessary customization.
Leverage	Minimize acquisition time and cost, and procure at lowest price/cost.	Efficient and good at price analysis; focused on total costs — especially nonprice-related process costs; strong ability to identify appropriate tools to drive lowest price per unit without adverse impact on process costs.
Strategic	Ensure continuous availability and work with suppliers to build competitive advantage.	Strong cost analysis and cost management skills; relationship builder; good negotiator; creative thinker; strong capability to work in teams with disparate stakeholders.

Source: Adapted from Peter Kraljic, "Purchasing Must Become Supply Management," *Harvard Business Review* (September/October 1983); available from www.harvard.edu.

Supplier. Finally, requisitions might be assigned by suppliers or groups of suppliers. This is often the genesis of the supplier relationship management concept discussed in *Foundation of Supply Management* (ISM *Professional Series*).

Organizing Human Resources

Implicit in decisions about organizational structure are decisions that affect human resources. These decisions address three main questions:
1. What is the chain of command in the organization?
2. What authority and responsibility should be delegated and to whom?
3. What is each person's span of influence?

Chain of Command. The chain of command refers to the line of authority and responsibility in the hierarchy of an organization. The chain reflects the organizational structure. In a functional organization, each function reports up to a higher level of supervision within that function. All functions ultimately report up to the head of the organization. In a divisional organization, where divisions are based on geography, each function in the division reports up to the president of the division who then reports to the CEO of the organization. In a matrix organization, people report to a functional superior as well as to a project superior. The supply management professional must be aware of the chain of command and work to develop his or her abilities to operate and influence within that chain. He or she must also coach subordinates about working within the chain of command while also extending their span of influence (discussed in Chapter 4).

Delegation of Authority and Responsibility. Delegation is a transfer of power from a superior to a subordinate. Organizational success depends in part on the ability of managers to delegate successfully. Decisions must be made about how and to whom authority and responsibility will be delegated. This relationship requires the superior to develop and empower subordinates to make certain decisions within the scope of the superior's position. The person performing the actions and the superior share accountability for the outcome. Successful delegation depends on superiors who are willing and are able to coach and develop subordinates, allow them to make decisions within established parameters, and let them learn from their mistakes. Employees must also be given appropriate authority to carry out the responsibilities that have been delegated. Successful delegation depends in large measure on the skills and abilities of the staff. The leader-manager therefore must pay careful attention to hiring, retention and the ongoing development of employees. These topics are addressed in Chapter 9.

In the supply management organization, decisions must be made about what should and should not be delegated. Some of the decisions about delegation are made in conjunction with decisions about organizational and supply management structure. The decision to adopt a highly decentralized supply management structure implies that responsibility and authority will be delegated to a broad range of employees throughout the organization. In a more centralized structure, transactional activities are delegated.

The tools adopted by the supply management group also have implications for delegation. For example, the adoption of an enterprise resource planning (ERP) system carries with it the implicit decision to delegate some level of buying authority to system users. The degree of authority granted depends on the decisions made about what can be purchased through the system, which suppliers are part of the system and how those suppliers will be paid. From a policy perspective, decisions must also be made about the delegation of spending authority and the levels of approval required for specific supply management decisions.

There are three steps to successful delegation within the supply management function:

1. The objectives of supply management must be laid out along with the specific tasks that constitute execution of the objective. Then decisions can be made about the appropriate level of execution — at corporate, in the field, in the user group, and so on, and the skill sets needed to execute the task.
2. Policies and procedures need to clearly articulate the plan of action for executing the tasks consistently no matter who is doing the activity. These might include desired results, guidelines, available resources, timelines and consequences.
3. The delegated tasks must be monitored for effectiveness and efficiency — and adjustments made to processes, policies, procedures or people — depending on the outcome.

Systems and Processes

Systems and processes are integral parts of the infrastructure of an organization. The supply management professional has primary responsibility for ensuring that supply management systems and processes are designed and/or redesigned to support the organization's strategy and goals, including sales goals. To ensure this alignment, the supply management professional must be knowledgeable about the link between customer requirements and supply management, and ensure that supply management contributes to customer satisfaction. To this end, supply management professionals must focus on developing strong internal business relationships (see Chapter 4) based on a greater understanding of, and linkage to, the following items:

- Customer segmentation;
- Product and service pricing strategy;
- Sales performance to plan;
- Product and technology roadmaps of key suppliers and customers;
- Financial and information flows up and down the supply chain;
- Critical customer service factors; and
- Customer and supplier collaboration processes.

Customer Segmentation

Customer segmentation is the process of grouping customers with similar characteristics to better manage customer relationships, meet existing customer needs, and identify unmet needs. Typically, segmentation focuses on identifying customer groups based on demographics and attributes such as attitude and psychological profiles. A different approach, value-based segmentation, groups customers in terms of the revenue they generate, and the costs of establishing and maintaining relationships with them. According to David Ross, another approach is based on lifetime customer value (LCV). LCV calculates customer profitability by taking the total sales revenue of a customer over the lifetime of the relationship, discounted by interest and inflation. Whatever the method, the goal of segmentation is to quantitatively determine exactly how each customer segment is contributing to or detracting from the profitability of each supply chain node and the supply network overall.[11] With the data from customer segments, managers can identify underserved segments and focus on outperforming the competition by quickly developing uniquely appealing products and services. Customer segmentation is most effective when an organization tailors offerings to segments that are the most profitable and serves them with distinct competitive advantages. This prioritization can help organizations develop marketing campaigns and pricing strategies to extract maximum value from both high profit and low profit customers. An organization can use customer segmentation as the principal basis for allocating resources to product development, marketing, pricing, service, sourcing, distribution and delivery programs.

Greater knowledge about customer segments coupled with equally comprehensive knowledge about strategic suppliers enables the supply management professional to enhance the abilities of the organization's supply management professionals to contribute to customer satisfaction and ultimately organizational profitability.

Product and Service Pricing Strategy

An understanding of the organization's pricing strategy and supply management's contribution to this strategy is one of the hallmarks of a more progressive supply management organization. Too often, supply management personnel are focused on cost-cutting without necessarily connecting cost-cutting goals to overall organizational strategy. This leaves open the possibility that the supply management strategies employed will conflict with or be detrimental to the organization's ability to maintain its pricing strategy in the marketplace.

For example, an organization's products or services might be experiencing downward pressure on prices because of competition. Supply management professionals need to know what is happening, and why, so they can proactively develop supply management strategies that enable the organization to remain competitive and attain projected margins. Target costing (discussed in *Foundation of Supply Management* [ISM *Professional Series*]) is one tool that links three critical elements: (1) pricing strategy, (2) operating profit goals, and (3) cost management by designing to cost.

Sales Performance to Plan

Knowledge of sales performance to plan is another valuable information stream that links supply management with organizational strategy. This is especially important if supply management professionals are to serve on cross-functional teams designed to determine the root cause of declining sales or slower-than-projected growth. The ability to accurately forecast and to accurately track sales performance to plan varies greatly within and across industries. For example, in the quick service restaurant business, limited time offers (LTOs) —such as a special salad during the summer season — are a commonly used method for testing menu items, increasing frequency of visits, bringing in new traffic, and increasing revenues and margins. In many small- to medium-sized chain restaurants with a large number of franchisees and no single IT platform, it is difficult to accurately forecast LTO sales; it is equally difficult to track actual sales and inventory in real time so that ingredients can quickly be moved to top selling locations. Food manufacturers are often asked to produce more in a shortened timeframe when sales exceed forecasts or to take back product when forecasts are too high. Implementing supply chain technology and developing appropriate relationships with supply chain members are two critical pieces of a successful program for managing sales performance to plan.

In addition, the sales to performance plan should monitor and adapt to issues of supply continuity. Supply management plays an integral role in supporting supply continuity through selecting excellent, reliable suppliers; managing them well; and communicating the organization's needs to the supplier on a timely basis. In addition, supply management assesses risk to supply continuity and develops contingency plans. Changing demographics also need to be incorporated into such plans, as the aging population, growth in ethnic groups, and families with children can have an impact on product demand. Supply management must work with sales to ensure that supply plans incorporate these perspectives.

Product and Technology Roadmaps of Key Suppliers and Customers

A roadmap is a plan that identifies the routes to a particular destination. A technology or product roadmap focuses on a single technology or product, describes the way it is expected to develop, and may include project plans to support that development. Figure 7-12 illustrates this process for the matchup of generations of technology to generations of a product. The roadmap focuses on forecasting development and commercialization of a new technology, the organization's competitive position relative to the technology, and how the technology and the organization's competitive position will develop. The roadmap may influence resource allocation, and it may be used to form subsections of complex product maps with development time frames, milestones, and ways to leverage R&D investments through coordinating research activities.

Figure 7-12: Product Planning Roadmap

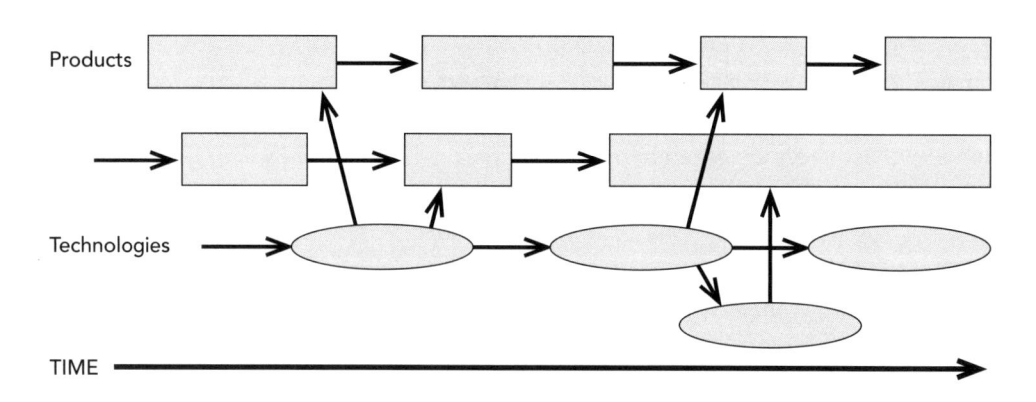

New or emerging technologies may be acquired, developed internally, or developed externally with a partner. Supply management may play several roles in product and technology roadmaps, including influencing which technology will be used before new product design begins, assessing the risk of switching to new technologies, determining the impact on the supply chain, working with engineering to evaluate and determine which suppliers will be included in new product development, and monitoring suppliers' investments in technologies needed in the future.

A 2013 CAPS Research study entitled *Collaboration Across the Extended Value Chain* found that upstream value collaborations — working with suppliers — can be essential to a project's success. For example, at Transco (company names disguised), top-level communication and commitments have played an important role in its 30-year-plus relationship with AGF, an important supplier of automation. Top executives from these companies meet two days each year sharing goals, strategies, plans and vision. Transco shares information on spending initiatives and upcoming projects strategy, while AGF shares in new product development plans, technology developments, and projects with noncompeting customers that may have application for Transco. The executives communicate several times a month to ensure that progress is being made and any roadblocks are being addressed.[12]

Organization sales and revenue objectives are typically good directional indicators for supply management professionals to use as guidelines for planning their organization's supply chain capabilities. Whether sales goals are high growth, low growth, flat, declining or highly variable due to seasonality and so on all have very different supply chain implications that impact how best to engage supply partners to ensure alignment with the sales strategy. Supply chain management can have a direct or indirect effect on the organization's top line revenue in a number of ways:

- Work with suppliers and internal operations to reduce product time to market, so revenue is realized earlier, with more time before competitors enter the market.
- Help bring new products and services to market on time and at the required capacity so that sales are not lost.

- Buy the required product and service inputs from a reliable, high quality source to prevent supply interruption.
- Buy at the lowest TCO so the organization can sell at the most competitive price possible to increase sales and market share.

These are just some examples. Increasingly, supply management is seen as an important source of revenue enhancement and top line growth. Leading edge supply organizations are measured on top line revenue growth that evolves from direct supply management initiatives.

Financial and Information Flows Up and Down the Supply Chain

Supply chain management is concerned with customers' customers' customers and suppliers' suppliers' suppliers. Financial and information flows up and down the supply chain enable better management of supply chains relative to competing supply chains. Managers and leaders of various supply management areas must partner internally with finance and information technology to ensure that financial and other information flows enable effective and efficient decision-making.

Critical Customer Service Factors

Along with knowledge and understanding of customer segmentation, supply management professionals need to stay current on critical customer service factors. The ability of the organization to meet customer service requirements in part depends on supply management performance. Stronger links between sales and marketing and supply management may lead to better overall organizational performance.

Customer and Supplier Collaboration Processes

According to CAPS Research, collaboration is defined as "two or more enterprises working closely together to achieve shared strategic goals that produce greater value for all parties than could be gained by acting alone."[13] Collaboration up and down the supply chain or network, from customers through tiers of suppliers, enables managers to better satisfy customer needs in a timelier manner. By aligning demand management with supply management, results can be achieved with lower levels of inventory and better asset use at a lower total cost of ownership. However, there must be greater integration of systems throughout the supplier network to capture and share this information.

Lack of systems integration internally and externally with major suppliers and major customers continues to plague many organizations, although it has improved considerably with the advent of cloud-based computing. Software tools such as Microsoft SharePoint, MS Lync, Google Circles, Dropbox, Yammer and others can facilitate document sharing and allow synchronous and asynchronous collaboration.

The CAPS Research study on collaboration supports the importance of collaborative software systems in facilitating sharing of information among supply chain partners. Such systems can facilitate the sharing of design information schedules and cost resources as well as goals and outcomes. These systems can create meaningful reform performance reports on individual aspects of projects as well as the overall collaboration effort.[14]

Supply Management Technologies

The supply management process is driven by customers; it is only with a thorough knowledge and understanding of the organization's customers, product and pricing strategies, and sales goals that the supply management professional can make appropriate decisions about supply technology. The technology choices come after strategy and process, and should enable attainment of organizational goals and objectives. The supply management professional plays a primary role in the identification, selection and implementation of technologies that support and enhance the efficiency and effectiveness of supply management processes.

Summary

There are a number of different ways an organization can be structured — from strict hierarchical, to functional (organized around general knowledge areas), to divisional (which may be aligned by brand, commodity or geography), to a matrix type. Naturally, there are pros and cons to each; however, the supply management professional can bring success to any type of organization if he or she is familiar with the various types and approaches to success.

Within each structure type, there may be distinct types of supply management approaches — centralized or decentralized. Sometimes, however, the best approach may be hybrid, where strategic direction is centralized but execution is decentralized. Workload distribution and volume is heavily dictated by organization type and structure. Human resources in the supply group identifies the chain of command, the authority and responsibility of each person, and each person's span of influence.

The supply management professional clearly plays a critical role in managerial decisions about the organization of supply management from its structure to its processes and technology. His or her ability to lead and manage effectively in these three areas may be one of the leader-manager's greatest contributions. Structure, processes and technology form the infrastructure of supply management, and either enhance or inhibit the ability of supply management professionals to contribute to the organization's success. The next chapter addresses the strategic sourcing process and enabling technologies. Chapter 9 covers the human capital side of the equation and discusses the role of the leader-manager in attracting, retaining and developing supply management professionals.

Key Points

1. The degree of horizontal, vertical and spatial differentiation of organizational activities determines the complexity of the structure. The structure of the supply management organization reflects decisions made at an organizational level.
2. In a centralized structure, the authority and responsibility for most supply management-related functions is assigned to a central organization.
3. In a hybrid structure, authority and responsibility is shared between a central supply management organization and business units, divisions or operating plants. Hybrid structures may lean more heavily toward centralized or decentralized depending on how decision-making authority is divided.
4. In a decentralized structure, authority and responsibility for supply management-related functions are dispersed throughout the organization.
5. The supply management structure affects workload distribution within supply management. Depending on the size and capability of the supply management group, the workload is typically distributed on the basis of (1) commodity or class, (2) department, (3) special project, (4) volume, (5) in rotation, (6) type of contract, (7) staff expertise, or (8) supplier.
6. Implicit in decisions about organizational structure are decisions that affect human resources in terms of the chain of command, how and to whom authority and responsibility is delegated, and each person's span of influence.
7. The supply management professional has primary responsibility for ensuring that supply management systems and processes are designed and/or redesigned to support the organization's strategy and goals. This requires greater understanding of and linkage to customer segmentation, product and service pricing strategy, sales performance to plan, product and technology roadmaps of key suppliers and customers, financial and information flows up and down the supply chain, critical customer service factors, and customer and supplier collaboration processes.

CHAPTER

8

If you can't describe what you are doing as a process, you don't know what you're doing.

— W. EDWARDS DEMING[1]

Developing a Strategic Sourcing Process and Adopting Enabling Technology

An organization is a collection of processes that are performed to attain the organization's goals. Managing these processes is basic to the success of the organization. However, many organizations are not organized around processes; they are organized around functions as was discussed in the previous chapter. Consequently, people are organized into functional departments such as manufacturing, supply management, sales and marketing, customer service and accounting. People in a function usually focus on performing the function rather than on managing a process. Consequently, sub-processes evolve within departments without consideration of the impact on other functional areas. The goals of the organization can easily get lost in the activities of the functions. Layers of communication and management are created to ensure desired outcomes, thus adding costs and lengthening cycle and customer response times. Inefficiency and waste become part of the system, robbing the organization of profits, productivity and competitive advantage.

Business processes must be designed to focus people's attention on what really matters — how each process and its relationship and integration with other key business processes drives toward organizational goal attainment. The objective is for the organization, or collection of business processes, to increase competitiveness by becoming more responsive in the marketplace while reducing total costs.

This chapter focuses on the strategic sourcing process and is organized in four sections: (1) an overview of the strategic sourcing process, (2) developing strategic sourcing plans, (3) leveraging spend through sourcing strategies, and (4) market analysis of e-solutions.

Chapter Objectives

- Define what a process is and discuss the strategic sourcing process.
- Explain how strategic sourcing plans might be developed and executed based on a category map.
- Explore different types of leveraging strategies, and when and where they are applicable.
- Discuss the role of policies and procedures in supporting a rigorous strategic sourcing process.
- Discuss the technologies that might be used to increase efficiency in various parts of the process.

An Overview of the Strategic Sourcing Process

A process is a set of activities that has a beginning and an end; these activities occur in a specific sequence, with inputs and outputs. The process design team answers a series of questions: Where does the process start? Where does it end? What are the steps in the process and how should they be sequenced? What are the inputs and outputs? Process design teams in different organizations may arrive at different answers based on the organization's vision, mission, structure, stakeholders' interests and external forces. People may have the same starting point and ending point, but may consider different inputs or outputs or do things in a different sequence leading to different processes. For example, a group of parents needs to establish a process to make 100 tacos for a children's event. One person lists the inputs as hard taco shells, pork, shredded lettuce, tomato and cheese. Another lists them as soft taco shells, chorizo and cheese. One person thinks the process begins with going to the market to buy masa to make taco shells and ends with each child assembling his or her own taco. Another person thinks the process begins with going to the market to buy taco shells and ends with the parents serving assembled tacos to their children. The strategic sourcing process across organizations is a lot like making tacos. The basic ingredients are similar, but there are many variations on the theme.

Institute for Supply Management® (ISM®) defines the supply management process as the identification, acquisition, access, positioning and management of resources and related capabilities that an organization needs or potentially needs in the attainment of its strategic objectives. This includes the following components: disposition/investment recovery, distribution, inventory control, logistics, materials management, operations, packaging, procurement/purchasing, product/service development, quality, receiving, strategic sourcing, transportation/traffic/shipping and warehousing/stores. Strategic sourcing is a sub-process within the supply management process.

ISM defines strategic sourcing as "the selection and management of suppliers with a focus on achieving the long-term goals of a business" (ISM *Glossary* 2014). Therefore, the strategic sourcing process in any organization is a clearly defined set of interrelated steps with starting and ending points in a specific sequence focused on selecting and managing suppliers to achieve the long-term goals of the business. This section provides one approach to developing a strategic sourcing process and then gives examples from several organizations. Strategic sourcing does not apply to all purchasing situations, but is generally applied when the purchase reaches a certain organization-specific dollar threshold or presents a certain level of risk or criticality to the organization. Typically, a strategic sourcing process includes the following steps or phases, as shown in Figure 8-1.

Figure 8-1: Strategic Sourcing Process Concept

Data Management and Analysis → Category Strategy Development → Cost Analysis and Management → Supplier Selection and Contract Negotiation → Supplier Development and Performance Management

These steps are the heart of the overall strategic supply management concept, as overviewed in the preface to this book.

Step 1: Data Management and Analysis

This step includes categorizing the spend and analyzing the market.

Categorize Spend. To categorize spend, the sourcing team must first be able to capture spend data and analyze how much is spent on what and from whom. Spend is classified into major spend categories. This step allows for a thorough internal analysis of requirements and the role of each requirement in the organization's products and services. This is a critical first step in aligning sourcing strategy with organizational strategic goals. This helps determine the level of time and resources that supply management should invest in the strategic sourcing process for a given purchase situation.

Analyze the Market. Determine the market structure (monopoly, oligopoly, and so on) and the number and nature of capable suppliers globally. *Effective Supply Management Performance* (ISM *Professional Series*) addresses this in detail.

Step 2: Develop a Category Strategy

Based on the internal and external scans in step 1, the sourcing team can now begin to develop a category strategy, including services. For example, discussions might focus on the desired number and size of the suppliers, the location and proximity, and the type of relationship to be developed. This allows the team to compare where they are currently in terms of managing a specific category and where they want and need to be in the future.

Conduct Market Intelligence. This is a crucial element at this point. *Market intelligence* is the process and the result of gathering and analyzing information about the aggregate forces (including economics) at work in trade and commerce in a specific service or commodity. Using the information gathered on internal requirements and the nature of the supplier market, the sourcing team can develop a short list of potential suppliers.

Step 3: Cost Management

Based on the organization's needs, past experience and industry data, the organization needs to develop an understanding of a reasonable expected price for the materials, services or capital it is acquiring. This may involve some combination of the following, all of which are discussed at length in *Foundation of Supply Management* (ISM *Professional Series*):

- *Cost analysis.* An "evaluation of actual or anticipated cost data (material, labor, overhead, general and administrative, and profit). The application of experience, knowledge and judgment to data to project reasonable estimated contract costs. Estimated costs serve as the basis for buyer-seller negotiation to arrive at mutually agreeable contract prices" (ISM *Glossary* 2014). This process is looking for better ways to manage and reduce costs as well as increase value.
- *Price analysis.* "The examination of a supplier's price proposal or bid by comparison with reasonable benchmarks, without examination and evaluation of the separate elements of cost and profit making up the price" (ISM *Glossary* 2014).
- *Total cost of ownership.* "The combination of the purchase or acquisition price of a good or service and additional costs incurred before or after product or service delivery. Costs are often grouped into pre-transaction, transaction and post-transaction costs, or into acquisition price and in-house costs. To use cost of ownership analysis as a cost-reduction tool, it is necessary to identify and analyze the cost drivers to look for any avoidable costs" (ISM *Glossary* 2014).

This will help as the organization further clarifies its specifications or statement of work. At this stage, the organization should also be ready to develop a bid package and send an RFx. The description of the requirement is a major cost driver. Therefore, the development of a clear and unambiguous description of the need is a primary focus of the sourcing team. This is also a main reason that supply management professionals must develop strong internal partnerships (see Chapter 4) to keep costs out from the earliest stages of the process. The RFx is issued to the short list of candidates (see *Foundation of Supply Management*, ISM *Professional Series* for more information on the solicitation process).

Step 4: Supplier Selection and Contract Negotiation

This entails the evaluation and selection of supplier(s). The sourcing team analyzes responses, possibly makes site visits, and narrows down the list of potential suppliers. As part of this step, the team may develop a negotiation plan (if appropriate). If negotiation is to be used, the team assesses the interests, options and walk-away alternatives of the stakeholders of both or all parties and develops a negotiation strategy. Negotiation, rather than an online or offline bidding event (which is typically used for complex items), high-dollar items and spend categories where buyer-supplier collaboration is desired, is presented in more depth in *Foundation of Supply Management* (ISM *Professional Series*).

This intensive step also involves putting an agreement/contract in place and managing it. A contract or purchase order is executed. The sourcing team as well as other stakeholders should see the contract as a means to an end. The real goal is performance. The team should work to ensure that the process to this point has been building commitment to perform on the parts of supply management and the supplier.

Step 5: Supplier Development: Build and Manage the Relationship

The sourcing team should determine the appropriate buyer-supplier relationship and develop an action plan for attaining the right relationship. Monitoring and feedback loops are especially important for longer term and more strategic relationships. If the supplier does not meet expectations initially (or as the relationship develops), and the buying organization still deems that this supplier is the best available choice, it may invest extensive assets or efforts in working with the supplier to develop its capabilities.

For example, a large petroleum company's global procurement organization's vision is to leverage the company's worldwide spending power: "Spending money smarter, without compromising quality and service." The goal of supply management was to elevate the company's global supply management business processes to achieve a sustained worldwide competitive advantage among its peers. At the company, strategic sourcing consists of four distinct stages (see Figure 8-2): (1) data analysis, (2) develop strategy and set targets, (3) supplier selection and negotiation, and (4) final contracting.[2]

Figure 8-2: Petroleum Company's Strategic Sourcing Process

| Advantage Through Data Analysis | Powerful Strategies | Supplier Selection and Negotiations | Contracting and Tracking |

[Flowchart:
- Scope Category and Identify Potential → Assess Supply Market, Collect Benchmarks and Best Practices, Conduct Internal Assessment
- These three → Develop Strategy and Set Targets
- Develop Strategy and Set Targets → Plan and Execute Negotiation, Plan Internal Change
- Competitive Supplier Selection and Supplier Development → Plan and Execute Negotiation
- Rationalize Specifications, Redesign Processes, Change Policies → Plan Internal Change
- Plan and Execute Negotiation, Plan Internal Change → Implement, Track and Continuously Improve]

Source: Joseph Carter, Thomas Y. Choi and Lisa Ellram

At a large financial institution, strategic sourcing is defined as follows:
- An organized, systematic, collaborative process for establishing and maintaining spend category relationships with suppliers;
- An ongoing process that applies joint expertise to new product and service designs creates genuine and unique supply management advantages and revenue opportunities and spurs innovation;
- Use of a strategy to define and rule sourcing decisions;
- Consideration of the global marketplace while uniting business intelligence with market intelligence;
- Understanding the line-of-business objectives and creating strategic relationships that meet these objectives;
- Developing and institutionalizing the application of an integrated suite of sourcing tools/techniques (for example, spend analysis, spend aggregation, demand management, supply base rationalization, e-sourcing, supplier risk management, industry analyses); and
- Creating competitive advantage.

Developing Strategic Sourcing Plans

If supply management is to play a more strategic role in the organization, it must anticipate and guide, rather than react to, internal user requests for goods and services. This analysis and involvement in the earliest stages of strategy development and product and service design and development should align with five strategy areas: (1) operational, (2) financial, (3) marketing, (4) supply management, and (5) technology. New Jersey-based pharmaceutical company Daiichi Sankyo Co., Ltd. did not have a strategic sourcing approach when it brought in a new CPO in 2011. As he created the vision for the company, he recognized the importance of having the support of his key functional peers to have strategic alignment and a successful new procurement organization. He thus created a Procurement Governance Board, which was championed by the executive committee. The governance board is composed of one senior colleague from each of the 11 departments, including marketing, sales, business development/new product planning, legal, finance, and others that report to the U.S. president and CEO. This board provided direction regarding policy, organization, opportunities and challenges. It still meets on an ad hoc basis to discuss strategic issues.[3] Supply management's boundary spanning role means that supply management professionals can directly influence and impact these strategic areas, as long as it understands their perspectives. As noted by this pharma company's CPO, "Procurement is most successful when we're part of the strategy at the onset of a project, not just a service provider at the end who works on pricing and contracts. We can help get the best result for our clients when we see and understand their objectives and goals."[4]

Operational

In any type of organization, an overriding concern is keeping operations running smoothly. The sourcing group plays a key role in the operational success of an organization. Coordination and cooperation between sourcing and operations is crucial. If sourcing is given insufficient time to obtain a needed item or service, the organization may sacrifice efficiency, competitive position or a negotiation edge. The end result of sourcing inefficiency is often higher total cost of ownership, special production runs or service delivery, or premium transportation or service provider costs — and ultimately lower customer satisfaction.

Financial

How and when an organization commits its funds depends on market trends, market and organizational forecasts, and risk assessment. At the need recognition and description stages, the sourcing team should analyze the buying plan to determine its appropriateness given economic factors and overall organizational goals. Deciding to buy in advance (forward buy) because of anticipated price increases or supply shortages despite increased carrying costs may be an excellent decision if cost analyses indicate lower total cost of ownership. Forward-buying fuel was a strong factor that contributed to Southwest Airlines' exceptional financial performance. Southwest had strong profits when all the other

U.S. airlines that did not forward buy their fuel were losing substantial sums of money.[5] In response to this long-term successful strategy, Delta Airlines recently acquired its own refinery to balance the risk for a portion of its fuel needs.[6] Reviewing the decision to buy and carry inventory against financial and economic circumstances and cash management strategies allows supply to make the best contribution to the organization. Financial forecasts and trends provide supply management with the information necessary to make the greatest bottom line contribution to the organization and assist in determining the appropriate exposure.

Marketing

Sourcing plans should also fit with marketing strategies. In recognition of this fact, procurement was invited to the marketing department's annual strategic planning sessions at Daiichi Sankyo Co., Ltd. to gain a deep understanding and have the opportunity to offer potential solutions.[7] Because sales forecasts often originate in marketing, the actual needs or purchase requirements of the organization flow down from sales forecasts. And because sales forecasts in most organizations are woefully inadequate, the sourcing group must track forecasts as accurately as possible and transmit this information to suppliers in a timely fashion so that suppliers will be able to plan and execute their fulfillment process effectively. In lieu of accurate forecasts, supply management may still contribute by sharing real time information with suppliers and by working to develop postponement strategies and supplier-managed inventory strategies that will lessen the effects of inaccurate forecasts. Buying organizations drive up costs unnecessarily when the forecast is inaccurate and suppliers must rush to meet demand.

Supply Management

Supply management strategies encompass all the various components of supply management. Sourcing strategies are one piece of this greater plan and must align with the plan of each of the other components. Part of the rationale for creating a supply management organization is that the structure will enable various functions and business processes to be integrated and aligned under the supply management umbrella. If this alignment does not occur, the supply management organization will find its own behavior, which results in undermining the business case for the supply management organization and its elevated level within the organization.

Technology

Technology strategies at an organizationwide level are often focused on acquiring and implementing enterprisewide solutions that enable each function to work from a common database and enhance customer interactions. As technology is used as an enabling strategy in supply management, sourcing strategies must be developed with consideration of the existing and future technological capabilities of the organization. This is especially true as an organization streamlines and automates the sourcing process and works to ensure the supply base is appropriately electronically enabled. (See *Effective Supply Management Performance*, ISM *Professional Series* for more information on ERP systems.)

Leveraging Spend Through Sourcing Strategies

Different spend categories require different levels of resources such as money, time and the attention of people at various levels in the organization. Misallocation of resources equals waste. To avoid generating waste and ensure that spend categories are optimally managed, decisions must be made about how to segment spend. A sourcing strategy should then be developed for each segment. There are several ways that supply management professionals segment spend, including type of spend — raw materials, packaging, services and so on; direct and indirect; and low-, medium- and high-dollar value through a Pareto analysis. A Pareto analysis is the process of determining the small minority of a population that accounts for the majority of a given effect. For example, in inventory management, 20 percent of the inventoried items account for 80 percent of the total dollars.

One approach that has been adapted and adopted by a wide variety of organizations is the portfolio analysis as discuss in Chapter 7. Originally introduced by Peter Kraljic, this analysis results in a two-by-two (2 x 2) matrix often referred to as the Kraljic Matrix. In this segmentation model, spend categories are assessed along two dimensions — the risk to acquire in the marketplace and the value or impact of the category on the organization.[8] Figure 8-3 describes the typical characteristics of the market and the item in each of the four quadrants. A spend and segmentation analysis may be conducted at an organizationwide level as part of an annual review of the organization's sourcing strategy. This analysis helps the supply management team identify potential risks and opportunities, and decide where it should focus attention over the coming year. Such an approach is followed by most Fortune 100 companies today. Remember that data management and analysis is the first step of the strategic sourcing process, whether considering one item or the organization's entire spend portfolio.

Figure 8-3: Characteristics of Quadrants

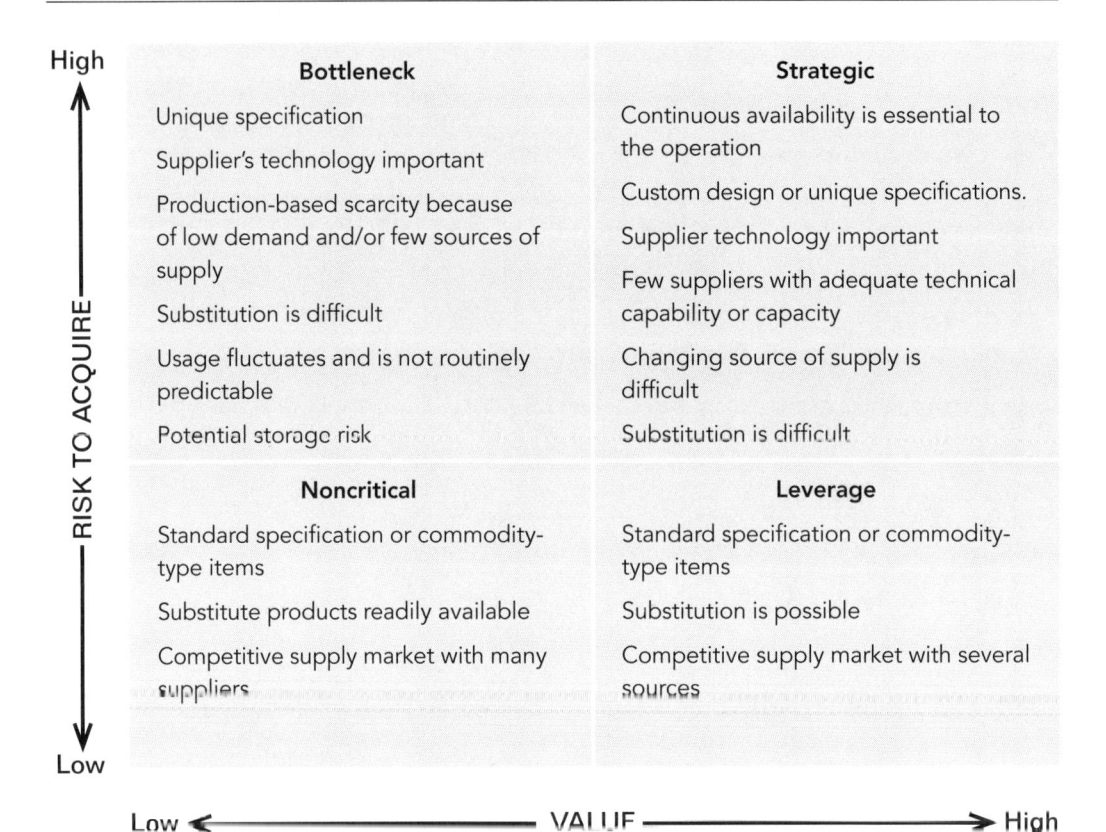

	Bottleneck	Strategic
High	Unique specification Supplier's technology important Production-based scarcity because of low demand and/or few sources of supply Substitution is difficult Usage fluctuates and is not routinely predictable Potential storage risk	Continuous availability is essential to the operation Custom design or unique specifications. Supplier technology important Few suppliers with adequate technical capability or capacity Changing source of supply is difficult Substitution is difficult
	Noncritical	**Leverage**
Low	Standard specification or commodity-type items Substitute products readily available Competitive supply market with many suppliers	Standard specification or commodity-type items Substitution is possible Competitive supply market with several sources

↑ RISK TO ACQUIRE ↓

Low ← VALUE → High

Source: Adapted from Peter Kraljic, "Purchasing Must Become Supply Management," *Harvard Business Review* (1983); available from http://hbr.org/1983/09/purchasing-must-become-supply-management/ar/1.

Developing Category Sourcing Strategies

As the second step of the strategic sourcing process, once an organization's spend has been mapped, sourcing strategies can be developed for each quadrant and refined for specific locations within a quadrant. General goals for each quadrant are listed in Figure 8-4.

The development of a strategic sourcing process enables the organization to leverage spend through the identification, prioritization, development and execution of strategies. The implications of organizational structure on the ability to execute leveraging strategies are discussed in Chapter 7. From the supply management perspective, the opportunities that exist for an organization are driven in large part by the value of the spend category to the organization and the risks of acquiring a category in the marketplace. Supply management professionals at all levels of the supply management organization bear some responsibility for the development and/or execution of leveraging strategies.

Figure 8-4: Basic Goals by Quadrant

Bottleneck	Strategic
Ensure supply availability in the short term and eliminate in the long term.	Diversify, balance or exploit. Ensure continuous availability at the lowest total cost of ownership.
Noncritical	**Leverage**
Process efficiently. Minimize acquisition cost and time.	Exploit purchasing power. Focus on price or cost per unit and minimize acquisition cost and time.

Spend segmentation enables the development of strategies that are best suited to the specific risk and value profile of the category. In general, process improvements are a primary goal when acquiring noncritical spend; spend aggregation is a useful strategy when trying to increase pricing leverage with suppliers; and capturing supplier innovation may be best suited to strategic inputs. The appropriate application of resources such as people, process, technology and money leads to greater supply management efficiency and effectiveness. For example, at Daiichi Sankyo Co., Ltd., they established a centralized procurement organization. In the process of analyzing the structure, they noted that the categories of research and development, IT, travel/meetings and supply chain were important enough to have their own designated procurement to facilitate category management.[9] Leveraging strategies may be short term, reflecting the current risk-value profile, and longer term, reflecting the targeted risk-value profile. For example, the short-term strategy for a high-risk/low-value item is to ensure availability through a long-term contract, reviewing production/delivery or service provision processes to shorten lead time, or bundling this item with something more attractive. Longer term, the category manager may want the supplier to work with the category team to conduct value analysis and find a lower cost way to deliver the required function. A value analysis is "a systematic and objective evaluation of the value of a good or service, focusing on an analysis of function relative to the cost of manufacturing or providing the item or service. Value analysis provides insight into the inherent worth of the final good or service, possibly altering specification and quality requirements that could reduce costs without impairing functional suitability" (ISM *Glossary* 2014).

Several types of analyses may be used to identify leveraging opportunities: spend, cost, risk, market and requirements. Spend analysis is one of the first steps in a structured, disciplined sourcing process. The ability to identify major spend categories and capture actual spend data is a critical first step in better managing spend. For example, armed with these data, the category management team can make better forecasts, provide information — especially changes — in real time and present a unified front to the supply base. Spend analysis and the savings potential are discussed in greater detail in *Foundation of Supply Management* (ISM *Professional Series*).

Cost analysis management is equally important in any concerted supply management process. Cost analysis moves beyond a price focus to consider the cost components relevant to a business decision. In the Kraljic Matrix, cost analysis is important in the management of noncritical and leverage spend categories, where the goal is process efficiency and the cost of the acquisition process is a key driver. In the leverage quadrant, cost analysis is also important from the standpoint of achieving the lowest total cost of ownership. In bottleneck and strategic spend categories, cost analysis is focused on acquiring knowledge about cost elements and cost drivers in a good or service to develop and execute strategies to take out or reduce costs. Figure 8-5 illustrates one approach to determining if price analysis or cost analysis is the most appropriate tool, which cost tools are best suited to determining a fair price, and which are best for reducing costs. The development of a strategic cost management program is discussed in *Foundation of Supply Management* (ISM *Professional Series*).

Figure 8-5: Applying Price or Cost Analysis

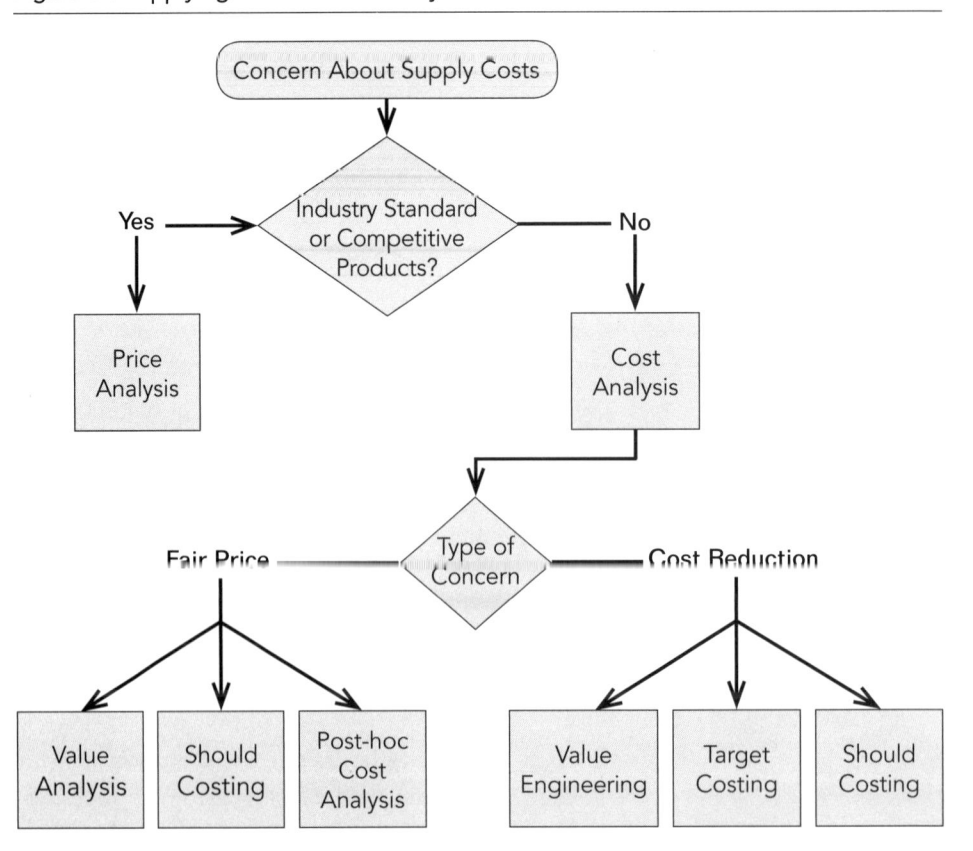

Source: Michael E. Smith, Lee Buddress and Alan Raedels, "The Strategic Use of Supplier Price and Cost Analysis," presented at ISM's 91st Annual International Supply Management Conference, Minneapolis, 2006.

As discussed in Chapter 5, risk analysis is an invaluable tool in determining and assessing the possibility and probability of injury. Equally important is the development of risk elimination and mitigation strategies. With the wide range of global disasters in the past decade, risk management and mitigation have become key concerns of CPOs. For example, Borg Warner, which manufactures power transmission, driveline systems and engine timing technologies for the automotive and light vehicle industry, received the 2013 Institute for Supply Management® — Michigan State University Award for Excellence in Supply Management in the Transformation of the Organization category for its pioneering work in commodity risk management. It developed a tool to track commodity risks, identify and reduce those risks, and accelerate decision-making.[10]

Market analysis is the basis of the determination of risk level in the Kraljic Matrix. This is also a critical element of the third step of the strategic sourcing process, and feeds in to supplier selection. This can be approached from two angles — first, what the current state of the market is for a specific spend category, and second, what impact the specifying and buying community has on market dynamics. For example, the drive toward national, regional and international contracts forces consolidation in an industry and changes the dynamics between supply management and supplier. Where there may have been many small- and medium-size suppliers, there are now fewer and much larger suppliers in total. Clearly, the sourcing and supplier management strategies change as the market changes. Market conditions and their impact on sourcing are discussed in *Foundation of Supply Management* and *Effective Supply Management Performance* (ISM *Professional Series*).

Requirements analysis also offers leveraging opportunities. Depending on the nature of the spend category, benefits may be derived from standardization, consolidation or bundling. For example, in an organization with disparate software packages, the decision to standardize across the organization may move the category to a higher value and a lower risk. In the case of software, standardization may also increase the risk to acquire by locking into a single supplier's software, but the benefits of greater data visibility and accessibility might be perceived as outweighing the risk. Then risk mitigation strategies would be a very important part of the sourcing strategy and execution. *Risk mitigation* is a set of "specific steps undertaken by managers to reduce the impact of factors that might lead to injury, loss, damage or failure and thus reduce the liability of the organization in its relations with various stakeholder groups, including employees and customers" (ISM *Glossary* 2014).

The sourcing analyst can also align tools and techniques (for example, price, cost and value analyses discussed in *Foundation of Supply Management* [ISM *Professional Series*]), knowledge and skills required of category managers, decision criteria for supplier selection, and the preferred type of supplier relationship (see Figure 8-6). The end result is a comprehensive sourcing plan.

Figure 8-6: Basic Strategic Tools by Quadrant

Bottleneck	Strategic
Value analysis	Collaboration for innovation
Cross-functional and cross-organizational teams	Strategic alliances
Cost driver analysis and cost management	Total cost of ownership
	Cross-functional and cross-organizational teams
	Multiple organizational levels of involvement
Noncritical	**Leverage**
Process efficiency	Spend aggregation
Standardization, bundling, consolidation to move category to the leverage quadrant	Price analysis
	Total cost (acquisition price and other related costs)
	Process efficiency
	Ease of doing business

Source: Adapted from Peter Kraljic, "Purchasing Must Become Supply Management," *Harvard Business Review* (September/October 1983).

The Kraljic Matrix may also be used to make future sourcing plans by assessing the likelihood of changes in the marketplace that are expected to affect the location on the risk axis and internal changes that may affect the impact of the spend category on the organization. This analysis is critical to step 4 of the strategic sourcing process, negotiate and contract. Both supply management and the supplier attempt to negotiate to minimize their risks and build protection for contingencies into the contract.

In general, the longer-term goal is to lower risk and increase value. This is critical in step 4 and step 5, supplier development, where the organization develops and manages the ongoing relationship with its suppliers. The analyst may identify strategies that will accomplish one or both of these goals. Risk is lowered by taking actions that make it easier to acquire an item in the marketplace, such as reducing or eliminating customization in the design specification. Clearly, this requires a cross-functional team to ensure that the uniqueness that is valued by the customer is not removed. Value may also be affected. If value has been equated to spend, the sourcing strategy may entail consolidation, bundling and standardization to move noncritical items to the leverage box. The move to commoditize everything from components to higher education shows up on the matrix as actions that will move categories to the leverage box. Then, tools that will exploit purchasing power, such as e-auctions, can be applied to the category. While this is inherently appealing to sourcing managers, it should not be entered into lightly given the possible negative impact on final customers. As Gary Hirshberg, co-founder of Stonyfield Farm Yogurt, said, "Quality, quality, quality: never waver from it, even when you don't see how you can afford to keep it up. When you compromise, you become a commodity and then you die."[11]

Outsourcing Supply Management Tasks or Functions. The outsourcing decision-making process is discussed in detail in Chapter 5. In a 2012 *Global Outsourcing and Insourcing Survey* conducted by Deloitte Consulting LLP, 60 percent of those surveyed classified outsourcing as a "normal practice" in their business and 19 percent said they were considering it. Outsourcing has matured as a business strategy. It is a tool supply management professionals can use to not only improve cost, but better use the talent and capabilities throughout the organization.[12] Any discussion about business processes outsourcing should include the option of outsourcing tasks within the process, or the entire process, to a third-party provider. Business process outsourcing has targeted a number of areas for consideration. For example, a major global pharmaceutical company had identified 26 human resources-related tasks that it planned to outsource. Supply management sub-processes have been and probably will continue to be targets for outsourcing assessment. Many organizations outsource some or all inventory management, transportation and other logistics-related tasks. Some organizations have developed in-house expertise for the acquisition of production materials and outsourced the acquisition of indirect materials and services to a third party.

The decision to outsource tasks within a component or sub-process of supply management is clearly a fundamental decision in the design of organizational structure. However, it is valid and legitimate to question whether or not an organization derives enough benefit from the development of expertise in specific supply management tasks to develop and maintain them as core competencies or if they should be outsourced.

In a study of fleet administration, M.R. Leenders, R. Kudar and A. Flynn found that specific tasks such as vehicle leasing or maintenance were successfully outsourced and, in some cases, the entire fleet administration was outsourced. In a pharmaceutical company, the tasks of leasing, licensing and maintaining the vehicles of pharmaceutical sales representatives was outsourced to a third party while the main contact person with the individual salespeople remained an employee of the pharmaceutical company. The rationale was that the salesperson's car was a motivator and a critical tool for job performance. Because the relationship the contact person had with each salesperson enhanced that person's performance, it was decided that this relationship could not be outsourced successfully. In another case involving a municipality, the maintenance of standard cars and trucks was outsourced while the expertise required to maintain specialized and customized city vehicles was retained by the city and performed by city employees at a city-run garage.[13]

Standardized Policies and Procedures

A strategic sourcing process gains structure and discipline through the development and consistent application of standardized policies and procedures. These are part of the foundation of a rigorous strategic sourcing process.

Regression Analysis. Regression analysis is one of the tools available to supply management professionals. In *regression analysis*, "measures of correlation are used to describe the degree of relationship between two variables (or data series). The correlation coefficient indicates whether the relationship is positive (both increase together) or negative (one increases while the other decreases). With the use of a regression equation, the scores of one variable can be predicted based on the other variable. Correlation and regression analysis is particularly useful in forecasting" (ISM *Glossary* 2014). It allows forecasters to determine the relationship among variables over time. It is useful in spotting trends in usage, pricing, linking price with volumes and a variety of other factors. Any statistics textbook will provide more information on regression analysis.

Best Practices. A practice is only a "best practice" if it works in a given situation. It is an "operation or process that is innovative and successfully implemented and thus provides a more efficient and effective means of conducting business, helping an organization to reduce its costs and improve quality and customer service" (ISM *Glossary* 2014). In general, best practices relate to an organization having control systems and processes in place before, during and after supply management decision-making (see Chapter 12). The details of these practices are context-specific. The hallmarks of policy and procedures best practices are listed below:

- They support the firm's vision, mission and strategies.
- They are accessible.
- People have been trained to use them.
- They are used consistently.

Processes to Disseminate and Communicate the Policy and Procedures. Policy and procedure changes must be communicated to stakeholders, especially those who are directly impacted either because they must execute the policies and procedures or because their work is affected by them in some way. Recall from earlier in the chapter the way that Daiichi Sankyo, Co. Ltd.'s new CPO engaged his functional peers in establishing the procurement policies and organization. Typical communication strategies include posting policies and procedures on the company intranet, and providing them either through online manuals or online training. Communication techniques to influence and persuade people as well as gain buy-in are discussed in Chapter 4. Failure to obtain buy-in at multiple levels may result in slower process adoption that may ultimately impact sourcing-related metrics.

Systems Assessment

What systems are currently installed, the functionality they provide and the total cost to maintain those is a critical step in establishing the baseline for comparing recommendations for future systems. Comparing current functionality to the future state identifies the gaps and drives identification of the various solutions available to create an improved supply management solution. Establishing functionality already in place can result in identifying capabilities the organization did not know existed as well as identifying additional options, such as upgrades to the current system, to obtain the future state. It is critical that the total cost to maintain the current operating environment be accurate and all-inclusive, as this will be the current cost which drives the calculation of the return on investment for the recommended solution. As with any information technology investment, a business case and budget should be developed. This will validate the need for the solution and ensure agreement on the estimated return on investment. Assessing the current systems will help build the business case by providing the following:

- Understanding of the ability to link systems and availability of data needed to facilitate the new solution;
- Perspective on what alternative solutions may already exist in-house; and
- Understanding of the resources required to implement the system and train resources.

Market Analysis

Process first; technology last. Rigorous business processes are the critical foundation of successful technology implementation. Therefore, the supply management professional must thoroughly understand business process design; provide the resources and support needed to improve supply management-related processes; and select and implement appropriate technology. He or she must also monitor the impact of supply management processes on other business processes to ensure efficiency and effectiveness.

Appropriate technology coupled with rigorous supply management processes sets the stage for a value-adding supply management organization. The supply management professional, in conjunction with internal IT and supply management specialists, must develop an overall technology strategy for supply management, determine the return on investment from IT solutions, and incorporate specific technology strategies at the category level. By understanding the opportunities (data accessibility, transparency, speed, shorter cycle times, operating efficiencies, greater internal compliance, and so on) and the obstacles (user, supplier and technology limitations), the supply management professional can manage the decision-making processes surrounding technology applications. Ultimately, the leader-manager must ensure that the operating efficiencies gained from workflow improvements free up people for strategic rather than transactional activities. He or she must also ensure that the appropriate human capital is available in supply management to use the readily available data to make better decisions. Technology may lead to greater efficiency and, when coupled with human brainpower, it may also lead to greater effectiveness.

E-Sourcing Tools

A number of e-sourcing tools are available either through ERP systems that are configured properly or through specialist e-sourcing tool system providers. The supply management professional will need to assess what set of tools are most appropriate for their organization based on individual operating environment, current (and expected) sourcing skill sets, and overall procure-to-pay systems.[14] The supply management professional must determine which tools are appropriate for the organization, given the capabilities of the people, the status of supply management processes, and the spend categories in the organization — along with the likely development of these. Key questions to ask include the following:

1. Which spend categories are appropriate for electronic tools?
2. What are the current and projected technical capabilities of supply management personnel?
3. Are rigorous processes in place for most supply management-related activities?

Spend categories may be assessed using portfolio analysis (the previously discussed Kraljic Matrix) in which major spend categories are assessed along dimensions such as value to the organization and risk to acquire in the marketplace. Electronic tools are readily available to routinize and systematize the acquisition of lower value-adding and lower risk-to-acquire items (standard, commodity-type items), often referred to as noncritical or routine and leverage items. Electronic tools that enable collaboration at earlier and earlier stages of the process, such as design collaboration, are more appropriate for higher value-adding and more risky items, often referred to as bottleneck and strategic items.

The supply management professional must link decisions about technology applications to the framework used to categorize and manage spend. This requires strong internal partnerships with other business process owners to ensure alignment with other processes and technology, and to allow the supply management professional to effectively manage change.

Supply management professionals may approach adoption of e-solutions with one or more complementary goals. Examples of these goals may be to (1) use e-procurement internally to improve tracking, compliance and other internal process efficiencies; (2) use e-solutions through its supply chain for all spend to get price reductions on commodity-type items and process efficiencies on all items; and (3) pick individual tools to achieve specific goals.

Collaborative optimization (CO) builds on the traditional e-sourcing approach. It is a best practice approach dealing with procurement in complex categories — such as logistics, packaging and MRO — and broader supply chain challenges such as managing the inherent complexity in product portfolios and components sourcing. CO sourcing incorporates "expressive bidding." Expressive bidding, trademarked by SciQuest in the U.S., enables supply management professionals and suppliers to conduct business in a flexible bidding environment, which allows suppliers to bid to their strengths and supply management professionals to analyze sourcing scenarios based on this expressive data.

On completion of the bidding process, an algorithm integrated into the expressive bidding analytic tool calculates the maximum possible savings.

When collaborative optimization with expressive bidding is used for sourcing decisions, a supply management professional will see the difference between a scenario with constraints that may limit cost savings and one without constraints that maximizes total savings. This ensures that the supply management professional understands the impact of self-imposed constraints such as establishing a limit on how much business the company can award to a new supplier.

The process maximizes cost-cutting potential as procurement can simply change the framework of conditions or specify certain suppliers to calculate the savings in various scenarios. For the supplier, the process offers flexibility and the opportunity for differentiation by submitting proposals that demonstrate and leverage their unique capabilities.[15]

Internal Process Efficiencies. Allergan, a healthcare company, recognized significant benefits from implementing an internal e-procurement system. "We realized we needed a system that would be more compliant when industry regulations changed," said Vicki Blankenship, manager, procurement services, e-procurement, Allergan. "Previously, we'd used a keycard or purchasing card system that wasn't sufficient to meet new industry standards and exposed the company to risk. With an e-procurement system, we were able to meet the compliance standards, and we sent a message to suppliers and partners that we were looking to take some of the risk out of procurement."[16]

End-to-End for All Spend. Allergan is on the path to implementing e-procurement solutions end-to end throughout its organization and its supply chain. It has been rolling out this process, first at its Irvine, California headquarters with its information systems (IS) staff. It then rolled through various groups at headquarters: corporate, commercial operations, R&D, and then manufacturing operations. Finally, the system was rolled out in four R&D labs, its 40 commercial locations, and six manufacturing sites.

Employees now have access to 40 online catalogs covering everything from IT to office supplies, lab supplies and more. The system seamlessly creates requisitions as authorized. Savings have come both from consolidating spend as well as increasing compliance and visibility. Visibility creates greater opportunity for negotiation and process improvement.[17]

In another example, at a Japanese company in the electric equipment industry, five steps were taken to transition to an automated end-to-end system. First, the existing information system was re-examined and EDI was implemented to automate supplier delivery processes (order sheets, change orders, receiving and so on). Second, the RFQ and bid process was automated. RFQs and specifications were sent via the Internet to all suppliers using a bid-support feature that displayed price, order and delivery date. Third, the Internet was used to source long-range inventory parts. Fourth, the team ensured that technology is XML-compatible and can be customized for various users. Fifth, an automated settlement feature was created to reduce the number of mistakes in the settlement process and to reduce transaction costs. The largest value came from reducing lead times.[18]

Pick and Choose. Through e-sourcing tools a supply management professional can source a number of commodity groups of substitutable and compressible items using an ERP system or a specialist e-sourcing tool. The organization has access to volumes of stock-keeping units (SKUs) (inventory items) through electronic catalogs maintained by suppliers. The supply management professional can then use the Internet to locate and qualify suppliers for future electronic auctions.

Reverse Auctions. The supply management professional must consider the appropriateness of reverse auctions (RAs) as a tool in the organization's supply management strategy. A CAPS Research study identified several issues that influence the success or failure of a reverse auction:

- The ability to clearly define specifications that are universally understood by the supply base, including international suppliers;
- Identifying a sufficient number of qualified competitors are willing to participate in the auction event;
- Potential impact on incumbent suppliers and plan to offset possible negative consequences (for example, supplier of a strategic item);
- Understanding the unique characteristics of the item's supply market structure, degree of competitiveness, key cost drivers and current open capacity (for example, if it is a buyers', suppliers' or neutral market); this information is essential for setting an appropriately aggressive reserve price;
- Degree of experience of both supply management and suppliers in participating in an e-RA event, including familiarity with the software being used;
- Event format — what will be revealed during the e-RA for this particular group of suppliers (price, rank, weighted price or rank, and so on); rules such as closing rule (for example, hard close, soft close, rules for soft close); participation rules (bird-watching, offline communications); and award rule (low price guaranteed the business, post-negotiations, no award guarantee); and
- Need to use a formal e-based RFx for this particular event.[19]

Spend Analysis. Organizations that have a complete view of their purchasing spend will reap many benefits, some of which were noted above. These include the following:

- Procurement oversight of large proportions of the total corporate spend, increasing compliance to corporate policies and reducing risk;
- Up-to-date views of spend activity, creating the ability to better forecast and anticipate needs;
- Automated data capture and analysis processes to improve timeliness and accuracy of data; and
- Improved visibility of spend to better leverage influence and assess areas for potential improvement.

These organizations have gone beyond simply capturing spend data from ERP or transactional electronic procurement systems. Instead of relying on periodic, backward-looking spend data reports, organizations with a wide view of their spend are able to generate ideas for appropriate organizational and policy structures; identify and close spend loopholes; classify, cleanse and aggregate spend data in real time; and integrate it with other data sets such as supplier demographics, supplier performance and different technology options.

Taking a cue from spend analytics techniques long used in the corporate world, the U.S. State of Georgia, Department of Administrative Services (DOAS) Spend Under Management (SUM) Initiative has been recognized as a winner in the Technology category in the 2011 Institute for Supply Management® Awards for Excellence in Supply Management. The complexities involved in local and state government (including educational spending), as well as the array of systems used by different agencies, can be prohibitive to developing a comprehensive and detailed view of state spend. While some U.S. states have undertaken one-time strategic sourcing projects, Georgia went well beyond this with its SUM Initiative. For Georgia, the SUM Initiative is an ongoing procurement process transformation that is designed to improve purchasing throughout the state for years to come.

The SUM Initiative's cornerstone is the use of a refreshable spend cube. This statistical tool helped gain a comprehensive view of purchasing in Georgia, and was developed after an initial spend cube was used to get details on spend data from all state agencies for fiscal year 2005. In 2009, a project was initiated with the main goal to create the spend cube to collect and analyze data from Georgia's more than 160 agencies, colleges and universities, and develop a spend management manual for educational use by other states.

The SUM Initiative tools have enabled the DOAS to actively monitor state buyer activity, from the beginning of the purchasing cycle through contract expiration, with access to everything from requisitions and purchase orders to contract administrative documentation.

"This virtual audit process produces speedy, extensive reviews that overshadow the intrusive and inconvenient on-site, paper audits of the past," says Kelly Loll, C.P.M., Knowledge Center Director for the State Purchasing Division. "We can now immediately address noncompliant or fraudulent activity, and management can track state entity performance levels and training needs related to conducting complex procurements, which is an important goal of our overall procurement transformation.

"Eight agencies make up 80 percent of the state spend, while the others are less than 1.5 percent apiece, so we involved them from the beginning," says Tim Gibney, C.P.M., the Assistant Director of the Purchasing division. "We also included some smaller agencies, so that when we laid out our business plans and requirements, we'd be sure that everything we implemented was feasible for everyone, not just the big agencies." As of 2011, approximately 90 agencies and/or universities are using the SUM Initiative tools. More than 100 contracted suppliers are conducting business directly through Team Georgia Marketplace, and 60 percent of total spending has been brought under management, with a goal of 80 percent by the end of 2011. Also, Georgia increased the percentage of purchases made from preferred, state contracts from 6 percent in 2008 to 80 percent as of January 2011.[20]

Contract Management

Contract management software can be used to manage a new contract request; capture data related to the contract; and document authoring, contract creation and negotiation. The software can then follow the contract as it goes through the review and approval process, providing documentation for digital signatures and execution of the contract, including post-execution tracking and commitments management. Such software not only provides the supply management professional with better visibility into the status of a specific contract but also within other functions of the organization. Additionally, the software facilitates reporting and compliance.[21] The software may be a module in the organization's ERP system or as a simple stand-alone web-based application. These software platforms can make contract terms accessible to every person within an organization who needs access, as well as to customers and suppliers if/as desired. The contract management function has two underlying goals: (1) ensure visibility of promises an organization is making and the obligations it is taking on, and (2) allow top management to see that what is being promised is acceptable. The fundamental purpose of contract management is to fully integrate the contract management process with the rest of the organization's operations.

Contract management software systems provide a central repository for all an organization's contracts. The goal is to manage business risks, cut expenses and increase revenues by reducing pricing errors, mistaken payments, operating and processing costs, and personnel.

Summary

Realizing success from setting strategic sourcing strategy means a robust strategic sourcing process, and associated strategic sourcing plans, need to be developed. ISM defines strategic sourcing as "the selection and management of suppliers with a focus on achieving the long-term goals of a business."

A typical strategic sourcing process includes the following steps: (1) data management and analysis; (2) category strategy development; (3) cost analysis and management; (4) supplier selection and contract negotiation; and (5) supplier development and performance management. Supply management develops strategic sourcing plans to anticipate the organization's needs, and aligns with five strategy areas: (1) operational, (2) financial, (3) marketing, (4) supply management, and (5) technology. Sourcing strategy is then developed for each segment of spend. Supply professionals usually use a two-by-two (2 x 2) quadrant analysis to categorize products and services as bottlenecks, strategic items, leverage items, or noncritical items; each is rated low to high by the risk to acquire as well as the value to the organization.

Many organizations employ very sophisticated systems and processes to manage their supply operations. The successful supply management professional will carefully evaluate what is available, and select and implement the systems that will enable them to be most successful.

Key Points

1. Strategic sourcing is a process that leads to "the selection and management of suppliers with a focus on achieving the long-term goals of a business" (ISM *Glossary* 2014).
2. The steps in the strategic sourcing process are data management and analysis, category strategy development, cost analysis and management, supplier selection and contract negotiation, and supplier development and performance management.
3. Category sourcing strategies help ensure that the appropriate type and level of resources such as money, time and attention are allocated to each spend category.
4. Outsourcing is viewed by most organizations as a "normal" practice to not only improve cost but to optimize the use of an organization's talent.
5. A strategic sourcing process gains structure and discipline through the application of standardized policies and procedures.
6. The supply management professional must determine the appropriate e-sourcing tools for their organization. Collaborative optimization builds on the traditional e-sourcing approach by enabling supply management professionals and suppliers to conduct business in a flexible environment.

CHAPTER 9

I believe the real difference between success and failure in a corporation can be very often traced to the question of how well the organization brings out the great energies and talents of its people.
— THOMAS J. WATSON, JR., CEO OF IBM (1956 1971)[1]

Staffing the Supply Management Organization

The supply management leader sets direction through the creation of a vision of what supply management can be and can do for the organization. He or she then aligns people around that vision, and inspires and motivates them to remain committed to achieving it. Human capital, therefore, is a critical factor in achieving the leader's vision. One of the primary roles of the supply management professional is to develop talent management strategies to ensure that human capital is available when and where needed with the right knowledge and skills necessary to make the vision a reality.

Because global organizations find it harder and harder to fill critical positions, talent management strategies are even more important. Supply management professionals keen to the situation struggle to land top recruits in emerging markets and know that preparing their own staff to step seamlessly into management slots becomes a critical strategy.

The supply management professional's talent management responsibility starts with the design or redesign of roles and responsibilities within the supply management group. The roles should not only center on what the requirements of the job are today but with the goal to hire someone who has potential for the job of tomorrow.[2] The effort continues with the development of strategies for attracting, hiring and retaining supply management personnel, then continually developing and supporting supply management personnel and ensuring that the organization has a succession of qualified leader-managers. The supply management professional should be the chief knowledge officer in supply management and the chief advocate for creating and sharing supply knowledge with internal business partners and across organizational boundaries with external partners such as suppliers of strategic and critical goods and services. The supply management professional also works with his or her peer in human resources to align supply management employee practices with organizational initiatives such as employee diversity initiatives, planning career paths in supply management and ensuring compliance with employment laws and regulations. The supply management professional must also take the lead in educating employees outside the supply management group about policies and procedures.

Chapter 3 focused on how to align people behind the vision of supply management. This chapter addresses staffing the supply management organization. It is organized around two of the supply management professional's primary managerial activities in this area: (1) designing roles and assignment responsibilities, and (2) developing global employment and talent management strategies.

Chapter Objectives
- Develop global talent management strategies in support of a globally integrated organization.
- Describe the process of determining position requirements and writing effective job descriptions to attract highly qualified individuals.
- Discuss the skills and attributes most desirable in candidates for supply management positions given the changing role of the function.

Designing Roles and Assigning Responsibilities

If an organization is only as good as the people who work for it, then a critical managerial task is to design roles and assign responsibilities in the form of job positions within supply management. These positions should be based on the knowledge and skills required to fulfill supply management's overall role that, according to Institute for Supply Management® (ISM®), is "the identification, acquisition, access, positioning, management of resources and related capabilities an organization needs or potentially needs in the attainment of its strategic objectives." The supply management professional must also determine the type of person who will fit into the corporate culture of the organization. Careful consideration must be given to the short-term and long-term goals and objectives of the organization when determining individual roles and responsibilities and creating the job responsibilities for each position.

The positions within the supply management group should align with organizational structure, business processes and enabling technologies to ensure that supply management professionals make an optimal contribution to the organization's success. Companies that develop an integrated approach to talent management can gain competitive advantage through improved support for key decisions related to talent management, improved processes and tracking, and freeing up Human Resources' time to focus on strategic issues. They are more likely to retain top-performing and mission-critical employees, and to be a high-performing organization.[3]

The roles played by supply management professionals — including levels of authority, actual job tasks, and reporting lines and relationships — are related to the structure of the organization and to the degree of centralization of supply management. For example, the skills and knowledge required to work successfully in a functional structure may be different from the skills and knowledge needed for a divisional or a matrix structure. Functional structures tend to be more top-down and bureaucratic. People who like structure, clear chains of command and well-defined roles and responsibilities may fare best. Matrix structures tend to result in dual reporting lines, more role ambiguity and potential for competing objectives. People who prefer less well-defined roles and responsibilities, who can deal well with ambiguity and who can maneuver between two bosses, may find a matrix structure to their liking.

The degree of centralization of supply management decision-making may also influence job design. In a highly decentralized structure, supply management personnel may play more of a consulting or advisory role, and their most important skill and ability may be the ability to build a strong business case and influence others. Depending on the internal user group, the position may require strong analytical skills, the ability to make the case quantitatively, and the skill to present the case convincingly in a spreadsheet format. For other internal users, a verbal presentation or a well-written document may be preferred. In a highly centralized organization, where policy and procedures are driven from a central decision-making process, positions may require more structure and compliance.

Supply management processes and enabling technologies also influence the knowledge and skills required for supply management positions. In a highly automated environment, individuals may need more facility with various information technology tools. In a highly decentralized environment with multiple processes spread across divisions or geographic locations, positions may require strong process orientation and the ability to design rigorous methods. Organizations shifting more of their services internationally or locating supply management requirements closer to their international suppliers may require individuals with already developed international experience. Role and job design, individual and collective performance assessment, and professional development can all be linked to and aligned with the knowledge and skills identified as critical success factors in supply management.

Job design decisions should also consider the organization and department stance on workplace issues such as flexible scheduling, compressed work schedules, telecommuting, job sharing, temporary assignments, consulting projects and part-time jobs. Changing domestic and global workforce demographics coupled with shifting sourcing locations also affect job design decisions. A CAPS Research study on roles and responsibilities reported that the number of supply management staff in U.S.-based organizations located outside the United States represented 30 percent of their total staff.[4]

Cultural intelligence is "the ability to adapt constantly to different people from diverse cultures and the ability to manage the interconnectedness of today's world."[5] Cultural intelligence involves three things: thinking about a new culture, being motivated and feeling confident to act, and creating the actions needed for the situation. Companies like IBM, Novartis AG, Nike, Inc., Lloyds TSB, Lufthansa and Barclays Bank PLC are organizations that use cultural intelligence as a source of competitive advantage.

Following its own consulting focus in this area, A.T. Kearney sums up talent management development with several keys to success. Its first suggested key to success means engaging leadership and an organization's commitment. A.T. Kearney also suggests developing a fact-based business case that creates the foundation for an ongoing talent management program. It advances frequent, open and honest communication with the organization that highlights a clear vision and objectives of the program, and communicates this to all levels within the organization. Finally, any talent management strategy designed by the supply management leader must align with the existing human resources programs — recruitment, performance management, professional development, succession planning and mentoring.[6]

Clearly, numerous issues must be considered when designing roles and assigning responsibilities within a talent management strategy in supply management. These include aligning roles with organizational goals and structure, the degree of centralization, business processes, enabling technologies, workforce composition and workplace issues. Once these influencing factors are recognized and considered, the supply management professional is in a better position to determine the knowledge and skills required for success in the organization's supply management group.

Determine Required Knowledge and Skills

The supply management professional might start the job design or redesign process by determining the knowledge and skills required for success in the supply management organization. *Knowledge* is defined by *Merriam-Webster's Dictionary* as "the fact or condition of knowing something with familiarity gained through experience or association; acquaintance with or understanding of a science, art or technique." A *skill* is defined by *Merriam-Webster's Dictionary* as "the ability to use one's knowledge effectively and readily in execution or performance, or a learned power of doing something competently." Knowledge then is knowing about something and skill is knowing how to use that knowledge to do something.

In a 2013 *Chief Procurement Officer Study* conducted by the IBM Institute for Business Value to identify what it takes to be a top performer, CPOs recognized that success depended on getting the skills and expertise needed to perform their job. Recruiting and talent development were key strengths for these top performers.[7]

Using the definitions of knowledge and skills, Figure 9-1 was constructed and may be used to guide hiring, retention, promotion and professional development strategies. Certainly, the knowledge and skills in a specific organizational setting might vary from these, but this approach provides a simple tool for the supply management professional to use as a starting point for developing talent management strategies.

Figure 9-1: Turning Knowledge Into Skills

KNOWLEDGE AREAS	SKILL SETS
Ethics	Access ethical situations.
	Make decisions, solve problems and resolve conflicts of an ethical nature.
Markets and industries, including prices, costs, suppliers and supply chains	Perform competitive market analysis.
	Analyze suppliers (and make decisions, solve problems or resolve conflicts).
	Conduct price analysis and target price analysis.
	Conduct cost analysis and total cost of ownership analysis, and make cost-related decisions.
	Develop and execute supply strategies and plans.
	Develop negotiation strategies.
	Develop appropriate relationships internally with stakeholders and externally with suppliers and other groups.
Financial and analytical acumen	Able to visualize, articulate, and solve both complex and uncomplicated problems and concepts, and to make decisions that make sense and are based on the analysis of available information.
	Respond to external market trends.
	Analyze and assess global issues and risks.
Communication and relationship building techniques	Communicate effectively, resolve conflicts, solve problems and make efficient and effective supply management decisions.
	Execute negotiation strategies, and effectively influence, persuade and compromise.
Flexibility and agility	Be inquisitive and flexible, maintain a desire for continuous learning and improvement.
	Look for opportunities to work on different projects.
	Maintain open-mindedness.
	Work with individuals with a range of viewpoints.
Sustainability and social responsibility	Manage costs and create "green" benefits.
	Ability to perform total life cycle assessment of goods and materials.
	Work with supplier community to support initiatives.

Global leaders require specific competencies and skills to enable them to work effectively with people from other cultures. The competencies and accompanying skills include the following:

- *Open-minded and flexible in thought and tactics.* The executive is able to live and work in a variety of settings, with different types of people, and is willing and able to listen to other people, approaches and ideas.
- *Cultural interest and sensitivity.* The executive respects other cultures, people and points of view; is not arrogant or judgmental; is curious about other people and how they live and work; is interested in differences; enjoys social competency; gets along well with others; and is empathetic.
- *Able to deal with complexity.* The executive considers many variables in solving a problem, is comfortable with ambiguity, is patient with evolving issues, can make decisions in the face of uncertainty, can see patterns and connections, and is willing to take risks.
- *Resilient, resourceful, optimistic and energetic.* The executive responds to a challenge, is not discouraged by adversity, is self-reliant and creative, sees the positive side of things, has a high level of physical and emotional energy, and is able to deal with stress.
- *Honesty and integrity.* The executive engenders trust and is authentic and consistent.
- *Stable personal life.* The executive has developed and maintains stress-resistant personal arrangements, usually family, that support commitment to work that may straddle time zones and countries around the world.
- *Value-added technical or business skills.* The executive has technical, managerial or other expertise that is sufficient to provide for his or her credibility.[8]

For global leadership skills, the Conference Board lists establishing credibility, giving/receiving feedback, obtaining information and evaluating people as required interpersonal skills. For global leadership, group skills such as building global teamwork, training and development, and selling and negotiating are core. Strategic planning, transferring knowledge, innovating and managing change fall into the organizational skill set a global leader needs.

These broad knowledge and skill areas can be further refined to reflect the specific duties and responsibilities of a particular position within supply management such as a position in logistics, inventory management, purchasing and so on. For example, for positions in services procurement at Bank of America, a service-based organization that relies heavily on teams, there was a strong preference for service-based supply chain experience, strong customer service capabilities, good cross-functional team skills and leadership ability to lead teams.[9]

Many supply management leaders developing an international staff identify change management and knowledge transfer skills as very important because of the fast-paced work environment in a global setting, especially for those global organizations dealing with dramatic growth in emerging markets. A 2013 survey of human resource executives indicates that tomorrow's leaders will be more diverse including race, gender and so on, but also diverse in work experiences. Tomorrow's leaders will also be diverse in terms of thought styles such as more analytical versus "by the gut."[10] One supply management professional highlights the example of working with dynamic young professionals who adapt well to changing environments; they are eager to transfer their experiences to a new class of supply management professionals who are raw recruits, yet who are earnest to learn.

The changing nature of the supply management process, the expanding role of supply management and the demands placed on supply management professionals have altered the knowledge and skill sets required for continued success. According to the 2011 CAPS Research study, *Supply Management Strategies for Success in the New Economy*, the new and evolving purchasing and supply/value chain strategies will require new and evolving skill development. These strategies are listed below:

- Value focused supply,
- Innovation,
- Extended global supply networks,
- "Green" supply,
- Talent management,
- Risk management,
- Supply chain analytics,
- Metrics and measurement systems, and
- Transformation and business strategy.

These new and evolving strategies may require the development of new, and growth in, various skill areas such as supplier collaboration and relationship building with strategic suppliers; development of and working with cross-functional/location strategic purchase category teams; risk identification and mitigation; green supply challenges; understanding global supply network costs; rigorous use and understanding of analytics to make effective decisions; development and application of metrics and measurement systems; and cross-cultural leadership and management skills.[11]

The leader-manager of a supply management organization must be continually alert to new requirements to keep the supply management organization in a competitive position. Determining future staffing needs in supply management will arise from factors such as sales forecasts, technology applications, changes in efficiency, productivity, and flexibility of labor as a result of other factors. These factors include training or structural change; changes in employment practices such as outsourcing — both domestic and international; new legislation or changes in existing regulations; policy changes that increase or decrease workload; and changes to workflow.

Assign Knowledge and Skills to Positions

While numerous job titles and positions are available in supply management, one approach to categorizing these positions is to establish a hierarchy of positions that includes levels such as vice president, directors, managers and analysts. At the vice president level, the roles and responsibilities are driven by the organization's long-term goals and strategy. At the director level, duties and responsibilities may be segmented according to the various components of supply management. There might be a director of purchasing, a director of logistics, a director of operations and so on. While the job description for each of these would reflect the specifics of purchasing, logistics or operations, in general the director levels would all reflect similar levels of responsibility. At the manager level, duties and responsibilities also may be segmented according to the various components of supply management. For example, there might be multiple managers of sourcing, each with specific areas of expertise such as raw materials, packaging, services and so on. There might be managers of logistics with specific responsibility for inbound transportation/ domestic, inbound/international, MRO inventory manager, and the like. While the job description for each of these would reflect the specifics of the component, such as sourcing or logistics, in general the manager levels would all reflect similar levels of responsibility. At the analyst level, the duties and responsibilities would again be very specific to a designated area, such as buying, and focus on execution and tactical or operational activities. Positions at this level might include inventory analyst, logistics analyst, buyer, and the like.

Each level in the hierarchy is based on the duties and responsibilities, the level of decision-making authority and the scope of the position in terms of supervisory or managerial oversight. These factors are reflected in the descriptions of duties and responsibilities in Figure 9-2.

Figure 9-2: Duties and Responsibilities by Role

ROLE	DUTIES AND RESPONSIBILITIES
Vice president	Set strategic supply management direction, lead the development of strategies and provide managerial support for tactical execution.
	Lead as the executive sponsor of supply management initiatives that align with organizational strategy and ensure supply management's value contribution as measured by key organizational metrics.
	Build effective internal partnerships and work within these to integrate people, processes and technology across organizational boundaries.
	Develop talent management strategies that ensure attracting, hiring, retaining and developing professional supply management personnel.
	Develop and maintain supplier resource management with strategic partners.
	Lead innovation and transformation initiatives.
Director	In conjunction with the vice president, set strategic direction (for example, for purchasing or logistics and so on).
	Lead the development of (for example, purchasing, logistics, and other) strategies and provide managerial support for tactical execution.
	Ensure that (procurement, logistics, and the like) initiatives align with overall supply management strategy and with organizational strategy.
	Develop and manage measurement systems to ensure (procurement, logistics, and so on) contribute to key supply management metrics and feed into key organizational metrics.
	Build effective internal partnerships horizontally (at the director level) and vertically (up the chain to the vice president and down the chain to direct reports) and work within these partnerships to integrate people, processes and technology across organizational boundaries.
	Deploy employment strategies to the manager and lower-level employees to attract, hire, retain and develop professional supply management personnel.
Manager	Efficiently and effectively manage processes relevant to a specific area of responsibility, (for example, commodity, services, MRO, and so on).
	Contribute to the development of the overall supply management strategy by providing specific area knowledge to the organization.
	Support employee self-development initiatives.
	Lead the development of area-specific strategies (for example, category strategy, raw material inventory strategy, and so on).
	Identify appropriate tools and techniques and incorporate into management of function.
	Provide managerial support for tactical execution.
	Ensure that (category, inventory, and other) strategies and initiatives align with overall supply management strategy as well as organizational strategy.
	Measure and manage performance (of the category, inventory, and others) and of direct reports.
	Build effective internal partnerships and work within these partnerships to flawlessly execute strategies.
	Attract, hire, retain and develop entry-level employees (for example, buyers, analysts, and so on).
Entry level	Effectively execute and follow through with work assignments and projects.
	Use appropriate tools and techniques on a daily basis to make decisions.
	Perform activities efficiently and effectively.

Source: Adapted from Institute for Supply Management®, Career Center, 2013.

Figure 9-3: Personnel Requirements

ROLE	DUTIES AND RESPONSIBILITIES
Vice president	Possess exceptionally strong global procurement and/or sourcing background.
	Be highly adept at influence and persuasion.
	Ability to embrace change and motivate others to change.
	Mentor and develop direct reports.
	Possess business acumen with an ability to anticipate impact of decisions and initiatives.
	Ability to connect with high-level stakeholders.
	Conceptual thinking capabilities that create innovative options.
	Ability to develop interpersonal relationships and deal with conflict management.
	Possess strong communication (written and verbal) and presentation skills.
	Have a willingness and ability to travel globally and to work long hours.
	May have credentials or degrees in the field or related field.
Director	Expert-level knowledge of (purchasing, logistics, and/or specific area of responsibility) processes, tools, techniques.
	Excellent interpersonal skills.
	Bachelor's degree in (supply management, logistics, and so on) required and master's degree preferred.
	Extensive experience in leading and managing a complex, diverse supply management, logistics, and/or other related organization.
Manager	Mentor and develop direct reports.
	High-level negotiation and cost reduction skills.
	Project management and change management proficiency.
	Business acumen with an ability to anticipate impact of decisions and initiatives.
	Analytical and financial modeling skills.
	Strategic planning and conceptual thinking that creates innovative options.
	Collaboration with (and ability to lead) cross-functional teams.
	Interpersonal relationships and conflict management.
	Customer-centric.
	Organization and time management proficiency; prioritize and manage multiple tasks simultaneously.
	Strong communication (written and verbal) and presentation skills.
	Problem-solving skills.
	Familiarity with e-procurement and e-sourcing tools.
	Credentials and/or degree in the field preferred or related field.

Figure 9-3: Personnel Requirements   *continued*

ROLE	DUTIES AND RESPONSIBILITIES
Entry level	Project management.
	Analytical/financial modeling skills.
	Basic research capabilities.
	Ability to collaborate with cross-functional teams.
	Interpersonal relationship skills.
	Customer-centric.
	Organization and time management skills.
	Able to prioritize and manage multiple tasks simultaneously.
	Strong written and verbal communication skills.
	Familiarity with e-procurement and e-sourcing tools.
	Associate's degree or equivalent experience in supply chain or business administration.

Source: Adapted from Institute for Supply Management®, Career Center, 2013.

These clearly defined roles and responsibilities set a positive course that the supply management organization's talent management strategies can adhere to. But global organizations are keen to anticipate what can be expected from future global leaders. Additional leadership roles and responsibilities key to global leaders of the future include the ability to:

- Build effective alliances with other organizations;
- Make decisions that reflect global considerations;
- Build effective partnerships across the organization;
- Be comfortable with ambiguity and be able to influence and collaborate; and
- Consistently treat people with respect and dignity.[12]

The supply management professional lays the groundwork for the successful execution of plans and strategies through the development of clearly defined roles and responsibilities at each level in the supply management organization. Once these roles have been defined or redefined, usually in conjunction with human resources, the leader-manager can develop employment strategies to attract and retain highly qualified candidates to the job opportunities.

Developing Global Employment and Talent Management Strategies

Most organizations establish employment policies that support the organization's mission and strategic plan, and provide parameters for employee behavior. A broadly defined policy gives the decision-maker greater latitude than a narrowly defined policy does. For example, if an organization has a hiring policy to diversify the workforce, then human resources managers and hiring managers will be expected to take actions that will lead to a larger pool of applicants from diverse populations — and thus a larger number of new hires from diverse backgrounds. If, on the other hand, the hiring policy restricts a hiring manager to promoting from within the organization, then the hiring manager has fewer options at his or her disposal. The supply management professional's role in employment strategies may range from ensuring compliance with human resources policies; to influencing these policies; to developing organizational plans that serve as a blueprint for recruiting, hiring, retaining and promoting supply management personnel. One of the biggest issues the supply management professional must consider when developing employment and talent management strategies is the extent and impact of workforce diversity.

Global Workforce Diversity

Diversity may be defined very broadly to include everyone as part of the diversity that should be valued or very narrowly according to an organization's specific need to rectify bias in employment. Workforce diversity is projected by many experts to become an increasingly important trend for the following reasons:

- More globalization of organizations, leading to a more global workforce, marketplace and economy;
- Diverse work teams becoming prevalent in organizations;
- Movement of diversity as more of a business concern than a social concern, closely linked to competitive strategies;
- Making and spending more money by diverse populations, empowering diversity;
- More involvement by senior managers in diversity issues as they realize that the diverse workforce needs to be better utilized to be competitive;
- More training professionals will face the challenge of dealing with adverse reactions backlash; and
- More integration of diversity training with other types of training.[13]

Workforce diversity, then, is a reality in most organizations either because of the presence of heterogeneous populations, migration patterns, marketing and sourcing locations, or laws and management initiatives that require managers to hire, retain and promote a wide mix of people. As the workforce composition changes throughout the world, multiethnic, multicultural and multilingual issues arise in the workplace. A global economy and shifts in economic centers with accompanying shifts in labor pools bring the question of managing a diverse workforce into focus for many managers no matter their location, nationality, race or ethnicity. For example, IBM has procurement professionals in more than 100 countries. Supply management professionals cannot afford to lose the competitive advantage that procurement provides. In the case of IBM, the organization, operating in over 170 countries, has a strategy to geographically distribute procurement professionals close to clients and suppliers around the world. Their goal was to build common processes and global IT solutions to guide the organization and its procurement professionals. This effort enabled procurement to achieve both savings and value within the organization. This type of strategy affects employment and professional development strategies.[14]

Recruitment and employee selection strategies must take into account shifts in workforce composition that come from an increasingly diverse mix of potential employees in terms of race, ethnicity, gender, age, sexual orientation and geographic location. For example, attention must be paid to the rapidly aging populations in the economically developed world, including in the United States, Japan, the EU, Russia, Canada, South Korea and China. These economies will all have more people leaving the workforce for retirement than joining it by 2020.[15]

According to PwC, a professional services firm, there were about 33.7 million university-educated people in the G7 countries in 2011, with a prediction of approximately 33.4 million in 2020. The population of G7 countries is rapidly aging. On the other hand, there will be approximately 68.1 million university-educated people in the BRIC (Brazil, Russia, India and China) nations, estimated to be 80.7 million by 2020.[16] This is more than twice the number in the economically developed world.[17] The rising number of college-educated people in the developing world opens up opportunities for employers and employees alike as labor pools continue to shift. Young, educated professionals may emigrate from the developing to the developed world on work visas. Most countries in the developed world have visas similar to the H1-B (employment-based nonimmigrant status) visa in the United States. Technology loosens the constraints of geography, thus enabling more of these college-educated young people to work from their native countries for organizations based anywhere in the world. Supply management professionals face many challenges when developing strategies for hiring, retaining, managing and developing a globally diverse and geographically distributed workforce. The supply management professional must lead the supply management group in recognizing and optimizing the opportunities presented by a diverse workforce and in developing an organizational sensitivity to the challenges employees face while learning to work with one another.

An employee base of different age groups may have the advantage of a steady inflow of current thought and practice melded with institutional knowledge and experience. Age diversity often brings its own set of challenges as well. A number of situations may arise, including (1) younger workers supervising older workers; (2) more formally educated younger workers being supervised by older, less formally educated managers; and (3) differences in ethics, work ethic, dress, behavior, and personal and career goals. These issues may take different forms depending on the culture in which they occur. For example, in a culture where elders are revered, a younger person may be very uncomfortable in a position of authority over an elder.

A commitment to diversity is also about bringing together people with very different viewpoints and creating an organizational culture based on a positive work environment. General Mills, Inc. supports nine employee and affinity networks based at its world headquarters, including the American Indian Council; the Asian Heritage Network; Betty's Family GLBT (gay, lesbian, bisexual and transgender) Network, the Black Champions Network; the Hispanic Network; the Middle East and North African Network; the South Asian Network; the Women in Leadership Network; and the Veterans Network. "These networks and councils are active, engaged components of our workforce."[18]

Manpower's 2013 Talent Shortage Survey indicates that 39 percent of U.S. employers and 35 percent of global employers indicate they are having difficulty filling jobs, meaning the challenge of matching needs with available talent. The reasons vary; however, about one-third of the time, the gap is attributed to lack of soft skills/workplace competencies. Nearly half the time, it is a lack of technical skills — usually an education gap — which creates the problem.[19]

These findings support the work of Henry Mayo, who studied the factors that paved the inside path to success in the last several decades. He found that a shift occurred — education is far more important today and a global perspective will be increasingly vital. Managing the level of complexity of a global organization requires a broader view — "one that is not restricted to a single gender, race or nationality. In fact, a diverse perspective at the top may be a key to unleashing talent and fresh opportunities throughout the firm."[20]

Attracting Diverse Talent

Lack of qualified applicants is the most common reason given for an inability for organizations to fill open supply management positions.[21] Thus, strategically developing the right hiring process is essential. The process an organization uses to attract talent can take several forms depending on the employment strategies in place and, more specifically, on the level of the position(s) to be filled, the required knowledge and skills, and the speed with which the position must be filled. Campus recruiting, search firms, the Internet and social media sites, and internal and external job postings can all be used to solicit resumes from potential hires.

Recruiting Strategies by Level of Position

Different strategies may be deployed depending on whether the job opening is an entry-level, middle-level or upper-level position.

Entry-Level Positions. For entry-level positions in supply management, many organizations require a bachelor's degree, often in supply management or some other area of business. Building a strong campus presence through on-campus recruiting, participation in career fairs, and involvement with faculty and student professional associations can result in a steady inflow of new, educated talent in entry-level positions. Developing a summer internship program or a six-month cooperative program for continuing students can give an organization the opportunity to check out potential hires, mutually verify their cultural fit with the firm, and employ hardworking, talented temporary help.

Middle-Level and Higher-Level Positions. Middle-level and higher-level positions may be filled by newly graduating MBA candidates who also have several years of work experience; through a search firm or on social media sites; or through alumni sites that can assist in finding a working professional interested in changing positions. Many hiring managers are finding that the demand for highly qualified supply management professionals is so high that it takes months of diligent searching and very competitive packages to attract the best candidates. To identify candidates who are best suited for the organization, the standard interview process is no longer enough. It is worthwhile to determine how the primary candidates perform in business situations, so hiring managers may ask the potential candidate to make a presentation on a supply management issue or to react to a planned scenario. Also, supply management leaders need to determine how candidates perform in teams, how they deal with workplace dynamics, how they handle cultural issues, and how they adjust to and interact with the virtual world. One way to "test" a candidate in some of these areas is to use a simulated environment replicating a real-world issue that a potential employee may face.[22]

Supply management professionals interested in hiring and must employ search organizations look for organizations that specialize in supply management and that have track records of successfully placing high quality supply management candidates. These organizations are also called on to help supply management leaders assess the market and attempt to take a measure of current conditions. The successful search organizations have some market research capabilities as well.

References, Experience and Education/Training

Reviewing the references, experience and training of job candidates is the first step in creating a short list of people for personal interviews. The resume is usually the first step in the process. The hiring manager should have a clear understanding of the roles and responsibilities of the position and the education, training and experiences that would indicate a high likelihood of success. The hiring manager, often in conjunction with a human resources professional, will develop a list of questions to ask all job candidates.

Questions in the Interview Process. A recruiter may take a number of different approaches when interviewing a job candidate. These include behavioral interviewing; case study responses and discussion; team interviews; and problem-solving exercises such as the simulated real-world issue mentioned previously. The type of questions asked and the way in which they are posed should be driven by a clear understanding on the part of the interviewer of the true purpose of the question. The interviewer must be aware of the questions or types of questions that are inappropriate and possibly illegal to ask a job candidate. For example, interviewers should never ask about marital status, number of children or plans to have children. A guiding rule should be that the questions have relevance to the job itself. If a job requires extensive travel, then this information should be made available to the job candidate in the initial job description. An interviewer should not assume or presume that a working mother would be unable to meet the travel demands of the job. It would be inappropriate to pursue a line of questioning regarding children and child-care arrangements. However, an interviewer could ask the interviewee about his or her interest in and willingness to travel, and about past jobs that involved traveling. Interviewers should check with the organization's human resources professionals regarding the legality of specific questions.

The appendix at the end of the chapter includes sample questions that might be asked to assess an interviewee's skill level for specific skill areas. These are merely samples and in no way are intended to be all-inclusive.

Employee Retention

Retaining high-performing employees requires as much thought and planning as attracting them in the first place. Authors Gary Berg, Mihaly Csikszentmihalyi and Jeanne Nakamura write that "good work is likely to happen when three conditions are met: (1) the work lives up to the best practices of the domain, (2) it responds to societal needs, and (3) it is experienced as meaningful and enjoyable by those who do it."[23] Retention plans focus on fostering, measuring and maintaining these conditions, and typically addresses how to do the following.

- Compensate employees in salary and benefits;
- Assess and recognize the value generated by each employee;
- Provide employees the opportunity to show their skills by involving them in important, timely projects and providing them with meaningful feedback;
- Provide structured coaching from top-level managers to help employees refine their skills;
- Offer a structured career path, even encouraging employees to move sideways as well as out of and back into supply management;
- Support and encourage professional development;[24]
- Measure and increase the employee's job satisfaction level;
- Create a supportive work environmen;t and
- Assist employees in balancing work and life.

Given the increasing level of difficulty and expense in finding and hiring qualified employees, retention is becoming an even more important focus.

Compensation. As the added value of supply management employees increases, so does the total compensation package. Total compensation includes benefits such as the ability to telecommute some or all of the time, flexible work hours, the ability to take time off for extended travel, and educational opportunities. Employees at different ages and life stages may place more value on time than on money. Organizations whose management allows flexibility in crafting the compensation package may be more attractive to some groups of job candidates.

Value Assessment. Assessing the value generated by each employee in a manner that is perceived as fair and equitable by employees is an ongoing challenge for human resources staff and managers throughout the organization. Recall the discussion about motivational theories from Chapter 1 and motivational tools and techniques in Chapter 4. Typically, individuals perform better, or at least try to, if they believe their efforts make a difference and that they will be valued.

Career Progression. In today's flatter organizations, often fewer opportunities for upward mobility and more for lateral moves or the expansion of responsibilities in an existing position exist. Selling employees on the value of lateral moves may be difficult in light of the individual's career aspirations and the value that society places on attaining higher levels of managerial responsibility. As noted by a pharmaceutical executive, "We can't hire them and we can't keep them." One of the advantages of a broad-based, strong supply management organization is that it offers diversity in jobs, duties and responsibilities. Supply management employees may be satisfied if they are able to learn and rotate through various components of supply management. Managers must also recognize that some people will use the opportunities to move to a higher-level position in another organization. By understanding what motivates a person, the manager may be able to tailor experiences and opportunities to the individual's motivational drivers.

Job Satisfaction. People are often motivated by what is measured and rewarded. Therefore, identifying and measuring the level of satisfaction with different aspects of a job is an important tool in improving overall job satisfaction. Often, the HR team administers an annual survey to measure satisfaction; this may be supplemented with anecdotal evidence as well as the perceptions and perspectives of people at various levels in the organization. Surveys might address salary, benefits, the work environment, the availability of proper tools to execute job responsibilities, educational opportunities, flexibility and so on.

Work Environment. The leadership and management team defines what constitutes a supportive work environment, and is then responsible for fostering it through policies, processes and procedures. For example, Google's workplace culture encourages innovation and a healthy disregard for the impossible. They offer an impressive array of benefits and conveniences to make employees' lives easier. Their benefits are designed to take care of the whole person to help keep their employees healthy — whether physically, emotionally, financially or socially. They want their employees to focus on productivity without sacrificing their personal lives. The Google work environment appeals to self-motivated, high-energy people.[25] Atento, headquartered in Madrid, Spain is one of the world's largest Customer Relationship Management (CRM) companies in the Business Process Outsourcing (BPO) sector. One of the reasons it has been named one of the world's 25 best multinationals to work for is their employees' high degree of commitment to the organization. This commitment is developed through various educational programs around the world that provide training and professional tools to employees. Atento also promotes job market inclusion and employee bonding programs, and raises funds for NGOs through its Voces que Ayudan volunteer program. They are recognized for their outstanding capacity for job creation and as a driver of change in communities — where young people are trained to enter the workplace — and through hiring of minorities and disadvantaged groups. Their talent management strategy has enabled them to employ capable and committed professionals.[26]

Balance of Work and Non-Work Lives. In an environment marked by complexity and rapid change, there is perhaps nothing as challenging, individually and collectively, as the balancing act between work life and non-work life. Stories abound of employees who are essentially on call 24/7 because of the international reach of their activities and/or the technology available today. The culture of some organizations is such that the focus is on results; how and when employees do their work is less important than the results. Other organizational cultures embody the belief that employees require constant hand-holding and supervision, and that presence on the job for long hours equates to productivity. The ability to retain high-performing individuals depends in part on the extent to which individual managers and the overall organizational culture fit with work-life requirements.

Employee Promotion. An organization's management team must have some means of identifying employees with promotion potential as well as a plan for grooming these individuals for greater levels of responsibility or for higher positions in the organization. In many organizations the number of layers of management has been reduced, and there are consequently fewer rungs on the ladder. This means there will be fewer slots available for employees with managerial capability, which creates a dilemma for an organization whose management wants to retain its best people. Developing lateral moves with increasing responsibilities, challenges and rewards is essential to retaining the best and the brightest. Management may also have to accept that certain individuals or categories of individuals may not be long-term employees. For example, hiring someone with an MBA degree may be desirable, but it may be realistic to expect that employee to stay for only four or five years before he or she will have peaked in the organization's hierarchy.

Developing solid promotion practices and communicating those practices to all employees can eliminate much of the confusion and anger that the promotion process can generate in an organization. For instance, an organization may require attaining a professional certification as a first step in career advancement. Linking the organization's training program and training requirements to specific jobs and job levels will make it clear to everyone what the basic body of knowledge is for different levels of authority in the organization. In some organizations, promotions always come from within the ranks of the organization, thus signifying to current employees that career advancement is a real possibility. Other organizations take the opposite approach and hire from the outside for management slots in an effort to cross-fertilize from other companies and industries. The behavior of employees will be driven by whichever approach an organization takes on a regular basis.

Career Advancement. The supply management professional must also consider the pathways for career advancement within supply management and in other areas of the organization. The size of the supply management organization, the span of control in the organization and the pace of employee turnover all affect career advancement opportunities. Hiring managers strive to hire and develop ambitious, promotable people to build a strong and creative supply management organization. However, not all entry-level and buyer's jobs should be filled with individuals who will become readily promotable. Usually, there are not enough vacancies into which all can be promoted. And when a person's job no longer offers a challenge, he or she may become discontented and leave the organization, or perform less effectively. For these reasons, it is essential that personnel be selected with care. During the hiring process, most managers attempt to match an individual's qualifications to both current and anticipated future job requirements of the department. It is much easier and less costly to address such issues before, rather than after, hiring has occurred. A good supply management person properly trained is invaluable; a poor one is a major liability.

At HP, diversity is included in the talent management process as HP builds a diversity value chain. Its 21st century goal is global diversity, which HP defines as "putting differences to work in the marketplace, workplace and community."[27] Recognizing that diverse populations may have different workplace needs, HP supports work-life balance through flexible work hours, telecommuting, educational assistance programs, domestic partner benefits and more. HP sponsors networking for diverse populations as well as numerous professional conferences, including the Simmons Leadership Conference and the Women's Information Network (WIN) Conference, which women from across the Europe, Middle East and Africa (EMEA) region attend.[28]

Promoting From Within. Some organizations are committed to promoting from within the ranks of existing departmental employees. The advantages and disadvantages to this policy are listed in Figure 9-4.

Figure 9-4: Advantages and Disadvantages of Promoting From Within the Department

ADVANTAGES	DISADVANTAGES
Keeps morale high because employees know they are not "trapped" in dead-end jobs	One promotion may result in a chain of lower-level promotions, simultaneously moving several people one step up the organizational ladder. If chain promotions occur frequently, the organization tends to lose its stability because a large number of individuals are continuously learning new jobs.
Stimulates individual performance by offering an avenue of advancement	When an organization is growing rapidly, this policy sometimes results in a promotion of people who are not ready to be promoted. The mediocre performance resulting from such action simply compounds the problem of instability.
Reduces total training costs because the employee already has substantial institutional knowledge	Finally, promotion from within produces "inbreeding." If carried to extremes, it may stymie the flow of new ideas into the organization.
Shortens ramp-up time to new position because the individual already has established relationships in the organization	

Recruiting/Hiring From Outside the Department or Organization. A wise manager promotes from within the department when it is practical. When such action tends to generate problems, however, personnel should be drawn from external sources. The advantages and disadvantages of recruiting or hiring employees from outside the department or outside the organization are described in Figure 9-5.

CHAPTER 9: Staffing the Supply Management Organization

Figure 9-4: Advantages and Disadvantages of Hiring From Outside the Organization

ADVANTAGES	DISADVANTAGES
Transfers From Other Departments	
Familiarity with the organization's operations may help the transfer assume full job responsibilities sooner than a new employee.	May have a negative effect on morale and/or productivity within the department.
The transfer brings experience in a related functional area that may be useful in supply management activities, and may provide a strong liaison with user departments.	If high-performing members of the department perceive this action as a comment on their promotability, this may lead them to look elsewhere for advancement. The ability of an outside person to implement change, and the speed at which change can occur, may be hindered if existing employees resist the new person.
Hiring From Outside the Organization	
Hiring people from other organizations has considerable merit, particularly in the case of special staff and managerial jobs, because it brings new ideas into the organization.	May have a negative effect on morale and/or productivity within the department.
It also prevents the substitution of seniority for management ability.	If high-performing members of the department perceive this action as a comment on their promotability, this may lead them to look elsewhere for advancement. Also, the ability of an outside person to implement change, and the speed at which change can occur, may be hindered if existing employees resist the new person.

Employee Termination

Consistent documentation and evaluation are key to ethical and aboveboard termination of employees. For global organizations, supply management leaders must be familiar with various countries' employment laws. For example, Mexico and Brazil have what are considered more onerous requirements for termination, and penalties for terminations are considered unjust. In Japan, an employee must be given 30 days' prior notice of a termination before his or her exit day. Regardless of a country's laws, employees should never be terminated on a "whim" or for vague, personal reasons; the organization's human resources policy's steps for termination must be adhered to. These policies are designed to protect the organization against improper terminations, protect against personal vendettas, and possibly turn a failing employee into a successful contributor to the organization.

Generally, employees should be terminated for consistent poor performance, insubordination, serious violations such as theft, or chronic substance abuse. The employee should be given a reasonable amount of time to improve the poor performance or change behavior (except, perhaps, in the case of theft). The reasons for termination should be documented in accordance with human resources' documentation direction, and it is advisable that the employee be made aware that he or she is on probation prior to any termination action. Otherwise, the manager may leave the organization open for legal action by the employee.

Adherence to Established Process. Most organizations have well outlined policies for the termination of employees. These may include personnel policies and procedures, union requirements and due process. *Due process* refers to the rights of the individual to the administering of law through courts of justice in accordance with established and sanctioned legal principles and procedures, and with safeguards for the protection of individual rights. In the case of union employees and layoffs, union contracts usually specify a laid-off worker's right to be recalled based on seniority. Most organizations have established procedures and documentation requirements for ensuring that termination of employees is handled as objectively as possible. Critical to the process, the leadership of global organizations must have available the employment laws of the various countries they operate in and methods in place to keep up-to-date on any laws that would change the current employment law of those countries.

Outplacement. Many organizations offer some form of outplacement, especially for employees whose positions are eliminated by downsizing. Often in the United States an outside agency is hired to counsel former employees and assist them in moving on to another position. In areas of the country where similar jobs are unavailable, outplacement may focus on helping individuals identify transferable skills and find different types of positions that require those same skills.

Exit Interviews. Although more common in the United States, exit interviews with employees who are leaving the organization can be useful tools for feedback about the climate and culture of the organization. People leave organizations for many reasons. If employees are leaving because they perceive there are better opportunities elsewhere, perhaps with a competitor, then an exit interview might provide useful information for the planning process at the human resources level.

Succession Planning

Another critical aspect of talent management is ensuring that the supply management organization has qualified, experienced people at all levels ready to move into different positions as the need or opportunity arises. Management succession planning is the formal plan that management makes for replacement of key executive personnel. The supply management professional has primary responsibility for creating and managing a succession plan for the supply management organization and allocating work assignments in such a way as to provide career development and growth opportunities. This might be accomplished by developing a management replacement chart that lists the name of the current holder of a specific position and the names of one or two replacements for each of those positions. Another method is to develop a prediction of each individual's expected job in five years and at the end of his or her career.

Succession planning also is related to the ability to capture institutional knowledge. It requires examining where shifts are likely to occur, and documenting or transferring the knowledge as need be through various programs like veteran employees working with newer employees. The point is to ensure that a stream of competent, knowledgeable talent is available.[29]

Summary

Appropriately staffing the supply management organization is one of the most critical contributors to success. Short- and long-term goals and objectives of supply management, and of the entire organization, need to be considered when creating job responsibilities, levels of authority and actual job tasks. Important knowledge areas and skill sets surround ethics; knowledge of markets, industries and associated suppliers, costs and supply chains; financial and analytical acumen; communication and relationship-building techniques; and knowledge of sustainability and social responsibility.

Once knowledge and skill areas are identified, supply management leaders then develop role responsibilities and position descriptions. In our current global environment, different strategies to manage various cultural and global employment and talent management must be considered and implemented. There are many ways to recruit for different levels of personnel.

Once staff has been hired, plans need to be implemented for employee retention, compensation, career progression and advancement, and employee termination.

This chapter focused on the managerial task of staffing that has taken on even greater emphasis in an age when knowledge is a key source of competitive advantage, and knowledge may reside anywhere in the world. The primary staffing roles for the leader-manager discussed in this chapter are (1) designing roles and assigning responsibilities, and (2) developing global employment and talent management strategies. Chapter 10 addresses the supply management professional's role in creating, providing and sponsoring professional development opportunities.

Key Points
1. The supply management professional must design roles and assign responsibilities in alignment with organizational goals and objectives, and be flexible to prepare for the future.
2. Matching positions with knowledge and skills, and supporting this structure with professional development opportunities, will help to ensure effective organizational performance and ensure a qualified pool of candidates at each level in the group.
3. Recruitment and selection strategies must consider the increasingly diverse nature of the workforce domestically and globally.
4. Retaining high-performing employees requires a planned strategy by supply management professionals.

Some Sample Labor Law Sites

Mexico and Brazil:
- Labor Relations in Mexico, www.mexicolaw.com/LawInfo11.htm
- Lexology, Brazilian Labor and Employment Law, http://www.lexology.com/library/detail.aspx?g=65128c40-bc7f-4f83-a1e5-2c95b9d56962
- Allegis Group Services, "How to: Manage Brazil's Labor Laws, Building a Business in a Land of Labor, http://www.allegisgroupservices.com/blog/how-to-manage-brazil-s-labor-laws-building-a-business-in-a-land-of-labor.aspx

European Union:
- European Commission, Employment, Social Affairs & Inclusion, Labour Law, http://ec.europa.eu/social/main.jsp?catId=157&langId=en
- European Labour Law Network, http://www.labourlawnetwork.eu/
- Federation of European Employers (FedEE), www.fedee.com/natlaw.html

Canada:
- CANLII, Canada Labour Code, www.canlii.org/ca/sta/l-2/index.html

Japan:
- Japan Institute of Labour Law and Training, Labour Laws of Japan, http://www.jil.go.jp/english/laborinfo/library/Laws.htm

India:
- Government of India, Ministry of Labour and Employment, http://labour.nic.in/content/

South Africa:
- The South African Labour Guide, http://www.labourguide.co.za/

Appendix: Sample Interview Questions

Interpersonal Communication
- What writing achievements are you most proud of?
- What are some of the most difficult writing assignments you have been given or taken on? Explain.
- Describe how you go about preparing for written or oral presentations.
- Do you prefer to communicate verbally or in writing? Why?
- Tell me about a situation when you had a personality conflict with a team member and what you did about it.
- Give an example of a time when you were able to successfully communicate with another person when that individual may not have personally liked you, or you them.
- Tell me about a time when you had to use your spoken communication skills to get a point across that was important to you.

Team Skills and Facilitation
- Give an example of a time in which you felt you were able to motivate your coworkers or teammates.
- What did you do in your last job to contribute toward a team work environment?
- Tell me about a time when there was a conflict in your team and how the team handled it. Explain your role in the situation.
- Have you ever led a team of people who did not report to you? How did you gain their commitment? How did you motivate them?
- Have you led or been a member of a multicultural team? What challenges did the team face because of cultural differences? How did team members learn to work together to complete the project?

Analytical Problem-Solving
- Describe a situation where you had to do a great deal of analysis to make a decision.
- Tell me about the courses or training programs you have taken that deal with research and data analysis.
- How do you determine when you have gathered enough data to make a decision?
- Tell me about a time when you had to be relatively quick in coming to a decision.
- Give me an example of a time when you had to use your fact-finding skills to gain information to solve a problem. Tell me how you analyzed the information to come to a decision.

Technical Competence
- Describe your level of involvement in budget preparation or financial analysis.
- Tell me about your approach to cost analysis when making a purchasing decision.
- Tell me about courses or training programs you have taken that increased your technical knowledge and/or skills in any area.
- Tell me about a time when you did not understand something technical that related to your job and what you did about it.
- Describe the process you usually go through to get up to speed technically with a new supplier, commodity or process.

Web-Based Research and Sourcing Analysis
- Describe your level of facility with conducting online research.
- Tell me about the information technology courses or training you have had.
- Describe a time when you used web-based research to analyze and solve a problem or to access and analyze data.
- How do you go about using a new software package or a new technology?

Negotiation Aptitude
- Give an example of a situation when you had to negotiate an agreement. Did you reach a win-win agreement?
- What are the steps you go through when you find you are in a situation of conflicting interests and you must get something done or make a decision?
- How do you know if an issue is negotiable?
- What steps do you take to persuade someone?
- What was the best idea you ever sold to your boss? Why did he or she buy into it?

Education and Professionalism
- Why did you or did you not attain a professional certification in your field?
- What have you done most recently to increase your knowledge or ability in a job-related area?
- What is your plan for the next six to 12 months relative to your personal training and development?

Continual Learning
- Are you satisfied with your current level of training and education? Why or why not?
- To what extent do you think training and professional development is driven by the organization and not by the individual?
- What magazines, newspapers, trade journals or online sources do you read regularly? How does this help you on the job?

CHAPTER 10

When planning for a year, plant corn. When planning for a decade, plant trees. When planning for life, train and educate people.
— CHINESE PROVERB

Developing Supply Management Talent

As discussed in Chapter 9, human capital is a critical factor in achieving the leader's vision. One of the primary roles of the supply management professional is to develop talent management strategies, including creating, providing and sponsoring professional development opportunities. This helps to ensure that supply management employees have the right knowledge and skills necessary to make the vision a reality, especially in complex, rapidly changing environments.

According to McKinsey & Company, organizations that have invested in developing outstanding procurement capabilities have nearly twice the margins of those that have not.[1]

Leading supply management professionals who contribute successfully to the organization's competitiveness display the following characteristics:
- Understand and align their strategies with those of the broader organization.
- Integrate effectively with supplier networks.
- Practice superior sourcing and category management.
- Manage the spend throughout its life cycle.
- Effectively management procurement talent.[2]

Thus, in high-performing organizations, essential capabilities include analytical expertise and a general management background. Increasingly, CEOs expect more than cost cutting from supply management executives. Supply management executives are expected to contribute to revenue growth as well as cost reduction, and are often included in the concept phase of product development, are engaged with sales and marketing for innovation, and are involved in pre-merger due diligence and post-merger value capture. An IBM Institute for Business Value survey of CPOs found that 80 percent of high-performing companies report that collaboration across departments — such as IT, marketing and sales — is both a key strength and an investment priority. High-performing supply management organizations see the benefit of close partner collaboration.[3]

Chapter 3 focused on how to align people behind the vision of supply management. Chapter 9 addressed the supply management professional's responsibility for designing roles and developing strategies for attracting, hiring and retaining supply management personnel. This chapter continues the talent management discussion by focusing on the leader-manager's role in continuously developing supply management personnel and ensuring that the organization has a succession of qualified leader-managers.

Chapter Objectives

- Identify the types of professional development opportunities available to supply management personnel.
- Develop a means of assessing the effectiveness of the professional development program.

Professional Development Opportunities

The illiterate of the 21st century will not be those who cannot read and write, but those who cannot learn, unlearn, and relearn.

— ALVIN TOFFLER[4]

The supply management professional must transform the supply management group into a learning organization. Peter Senge, author of *The Fifth Discipline: The Art and Practice of the Learning Organization*, defined a learning organization as one "where people continually expand their capacity to create the results they truly desire, where new and expansive patterns of thinking are nurtured, where collective aspiration is set free, and where people are continually learning how to learn together."[5] According to Arie de Geus, former head of planning for Royal Dutch/Shell, a pioneer of organizational learning and author of *The Living Company*, "The ability to learn faster than your competitors may be the only sustainable competitive advantage."[6]

Individual commitment to continual learning reflects a perspective that is not focused merely on acquiring skills on an as-needed basis; rather, it reflects a desire and drive on the part of the individual for continuous personal improvement. Chapter 1 addressed theories of motivation such as Maslow's Hierarchy of Needs and different management styles that may contribute to the development of employees with a commitment to continual learning. Identifying, hiring and retaining individuals who are committed to continual learning is critical for organizational success in a rapidly changing business world. Identifying these individuals can, however, be a difficult process.

If a manager expects to use employees effectively over the long term, he or she must assume the responsibility for assisting and guiding them in the continued development of their capabilities. A CAPS Research talent management benchmark report indicates that most participants agree that supply management skill levels need to be upgraded to deal with the increasing demands on supply management. Yet the amount the companies spend on professional development, on average, ranges from a high of about US$4,300 per year to spending nothing. Clearly, there is a great opportunity for investment.[7]

The PwC 2012 Global CEO study found that many CEOs are finding it difficult to attract and retain talent, and express the need to change their strategies to attract and retain the right people. If fact, only 12 percent of the over 1,000 participating CEOs say they're finding it easier to hire people, despite the relatively higher level of unemployment today. These talent constraints are having a quantifiable impact on corporate growth.[8]

Many organizations face challenges in planning and executing the professional development of a global workforce. Formal management education, and the development of a managerial class, is fairly new in many emerging markets. The number of domestic management schools is growing in many regions of the world, and so are joint ventures with Western business schools. Educators face a challenge similar to that of managers; that is, Western-style management education cannot always be overlaid on a non-Western culture. The globalization of management education is critical for people and their organizations if they want to be truly global.

Determination of an individual's specific development needs is a product of observation and periodic counseling by the manager with the individual employee. These needs should be determined jointly, and plans for subsequent training experiences should also be planned jointly for the ensuing six- to 12-month period.

Developing global leaders is so important that many organizations seek to accelerate leadership development for leaders that have global potential. In addition, accessing local talent wherever they operate is a significant goal for CEOs in the PwC study.[9] Supply management leaders must increasingly provide a global training framework; offer early assessment and experience; implement career stage development; devise accelerated career tracks; modify an organization's current succession planning strategy; implement rotational assignments in growth areas; and provide access to internationally experienced coaches, mentors and role models to help speed up global leadership development.[10] Young potential leaders must be sent on international assignments very early in their careers; these talented prospects must be given special projects, task forces, temporary assignments and committees that are international in scope. Additionally, international management education and training opportunities should be maximized.[11]

Organizations can take a number of different approaches to determine training and development needs. The basic process should include some comparison of job requirements to the skills needed to achieve desired performance levels in each position.

Skills Assessment

One process that might be used to assess skills and determine training needs involves three phases. Phase one is the development of a mission statement for supply management, a clear description of the underlying assumptions about the supply management function, and exactly what is required to perform the job. Phase two entails the development of a list of the supply management skills required and the competencies needed to function at various levels in the supply management organization. Profiles of specific positions can then be developed for use in attracting candidates and selecting employees, assessing performance, developing career paths and providing professional development opportunities. Phase three involves the ongoing comparison of desired competency levels with actual performance on an individual basis. This evaluation process feeds directly into the professional development goals and programs for supply management professionals. In a dynamic environment, the required skills, desired competency level, or actual performance may change because of internal or external forces.

Job Analysis/Diagnostic Evaluation

Some organizations develop a diagnostic tool to target specific training and development needs for their supply management personnel. The diagnostic program typically begins with a job analysis that identifies the important tasks of the supply management department in question. Next, each participant is given a diagnostic test that measures his or her comprehension of the basic tasks surveyed in the job analysis. Then participants are compared to norms to determine their strengths and weaknesses in the various supply management tasks. Lastly, the results of the job analysis and the diagnostic are combined to create a customized training program, targeted to the areas that are important to the organization but still to be mastered by individual staff members. In this way, the training programs are designed to maximize the performance of the personnel in the most efficient way possible.

During a traditional diagnostic process and while engaging some of the typical methods of assessment to measure comprehension and skill sets, some global leaders watch for learning agility and use it as a selection criterion for global talent.[12] Learning agility — the enthusiasm and ability to learn what is to be learned and the application of that learning to other situations — is one of a small number of cultural traits associated with leaders in a business context. While most executives admit that no instrument can be used to accurately detect learning agility, they insist on its importance for the potential global candidate. Only 31 percent of companies participating in the CAPS Research benchmarking study on talent management indicate that they have a process in place for assessing supply management skills.[13]

CHAPTER 10: Developing Supply Management Talent

Figure 10-1: Gap Analysis Example

1. Identify Relevant Skill Areas

MANAGERIAL SKILLS
- Planning and strategic development
- Project management
- Supply base management and development
- Contract development and administration
- Time management

INTERPERSONAL SKILLS
- Effective cross-cultural communications
- Negotiating within and across cultures
- Global business ethics
- Professional development
- Leadership skills/team building
- Problem-solving skills

ANALYTICAL SKILLS
- Accounting/microeconomics/financial aspects
- Business math/statistics
- Material management
- Cost and price analysis

COMMERCIAL SKILLS
- Macroeconomics
- Domestic and international business law
- Risk management
- Industrial processes
- Transportation basics
- Quality
- Global supply management
- Supply management methods and practices
- Social responsibility
- Supplier certification

2. Establish Degree of Importance (Weight) of Skill to Job and Measure Current Competency (typically based on responses from multiple people)

Managers assess the degree of importance of each skill to each position on a scale of 1 to 5 where 1 = least important and 5 = most important.

x = average response for recommended competency to perform the job.

Managers assess each employee's actual performance.

o = average response for perceived skill level of today's supply management staff.

3. Measure Gap Between Importance and Skill Level to Prioritize Improvement Efforts

Difference between o (perceived skill level) and x (recommended competency), multiplied by the average weight assigned to skill.

Gap Analysis

Gap analysis refers to the process of measuring the difference (and distance) between the actual skill level of an employee and the desired skill level for the employee's job position, combined with the importance rating of the skill to determine training priorities.

This profile can be used by an employee and his or her supervisor in conjunction with performance appraisal or coach and counseling sessions. The profile allows the individual to first conduct a self-assessment of current skill levels and then, with his or her supervisor, establish an action plan providing opportunities, both in training and in on-the-job experiences, to enhance personal skills consistent with his or her current position. The profiles also can serve as discussion tools for supervisors to explain how skill requirements differ for other job assignments.

In a Center for Creative Leadership report, the following five areas should be focused on for leadership development;

- Teamwork and collaboration;
- Innovation and creativity;
- Communication;
- Learning agility and a growth mind-set; and
- Judgment.[14]

Determining Training and Development Needs

A person can perform only from strength. One cannot build performance on weakness, let alone on something one cannot do at all."

— PETER DRUCKER[15]

After the initial orientation and job training, the supply management professional must be concerned with the continuing professional development of supply management personnel. The framework developed around necessary knowledge and skills earlier in this chapter can be applied when identifying, developing or acquiring professional development opportunities. Different approaches are taken in different regions of the world. In China, for example, business enterprises run schools, and schools operate businesses, on a substantial scale. In Germany and other European countries, employers take major responsibility for the education and training of young people. In the United States, there has historically been a clearer separation between schools and businesses, although there are changes as businesses work with colleges to design and offer organization-specific or organization-tailored MBA programs and executive education or corporate learning.

There is a general set of skills important to success in supply management, as shown in Figure 10-2. Clearly the acquisition and application of these skills becomes more complex in a global organization where there are multiple cultures, business norms, languages, communication styles, and decision-making processes.

Figure 10-2: Top Training Requirements and Skills Needed in Supply Management

TOP TRAINING REQUIREMENTS	
Team building	Leadership, decision-making, influencing and compromising, intercultural empathy, interpersonal impact, diplomacy
Strategic planning skills	Project-scoping, goal setting and execution
Communication skills	Presentation, public speaking, listening, writing, communicating with different cultures, communicating in social media
Technical skills	Internet research and sourcing analysis, knowledge of social media and appropriate apps
Broader financial skills	Cost accounting, cash flow understanding, analytical and business management skills, making the business case
Relationship management skills	Ethics, facilitation, conflict resolution, global business understanding, creative problem-solving
Legal issues	Contract writing and risk mitigation in a global environment, Intellectual Property
Social Responsibility/sustainability	Key environmental, ethical and social concerns in certain regions; familiarity with legitimate social and environmental certifications

Source: Adapted from Larry Giunipero and Robert Handfield, "Key Skill Sets for the Supply Manager of the Future," CAPS Research, 2004; and Robert Monczka and Phillip Carter, "Supply Management Strategies for Success in the New Economy," CAPS Research, 2011.

Team Building: Leadership, Decision-Making, Influencing, Compromising

Teams are a way of life in many organizations. Learning to serve as a team leader, team member or team facilitator, therefore, is critical to the success of most people. Management must decide how teams will be used, who will serve on teams and how they will be structured. Especially in an international setting, individuals should be willing and able to listen to other people, approaches and ideas. They must respect other cultures and not be judgmental or arrogant. If team members are to work in a self-directed team, they must receive appropriate training from the organization before embarking on a self-led project. In some organizations, personality profiles are used to assist team members in appreciating and understanding differences and to enhance team productivity. For example, the Myers-Briggs Type Indicator (MBTI) identifies each person as one of 16 personality types. This information is then used to learn to work better with others and to better manage one's own work. The DISC profile uses a four-dimensional model that includes dominance, influence, steadiness and conscientiousness.

Each of us has leadership opportunities within our sphere of influence. The supply management professional must also take responsibility for supporting the development of each subordinate's leadership potential. The supply management professional can mentor, coach and train, or provide training for, people to fully develop their leadership potential. A person's span of influence is probably a better indicator of his or her leadership ability than his or her formal span of control. Internationally, a person should be open-minded, flexible and culturally sensitive. Likewise, a person's ability to effect transformational change in the organization depends on his or her ability to create a shared vision, and motivate and inspire others to remain committed to that vision through good times and bad. Developing one's own ability to cooperate, collaborate and build consensus, and fostering those abilities in others, are key components of leadership development and are especially critical to succession planning.

Leadership characteristics that are most valued include honesty, ability to delegate, communication, sense of humor, confidence, commitment, positive attitude, creativity, intuition, and the ability to inspire.[16] In general, it is believed that men and women demonstrate leadership characteristics equally. But some studies have found that female leaders are seen as more accommodating, more invested in interpersonal dynamics, and more likely to reward good work than male leaders.[17] Male leaders, on the other hand, are perceived to be more action oriented and more focused on tasks.[18] This type of understanding of leadership strengths and differences might be useful when designing leadership development programs as well as recognizing the complexity of skills needed for international teams and leadership.

Being an effective decision-maker is also a critical leadership skill. Decision-making includes a number of skills, including information gathering, analysis, selecting an option from a number of choices, and implementing or overseeing implementation. Decisions are rarely made in an atmosphere of complete information or complete certainty. Being decisive means being able to recognize when enough information is available and enough analysis has been conducted to make a decision. In today's environment more complex and adaptive thinking abilities are needed.[19] The ability to act on the decision rounds out the process. It may be difficult to find individuals who can conduct the analysis, make the decision, and implement or oversee the implementation of the decision.

Analytical problem-solving refers to an individual's ability to apply basic problem-solving steps to analyze any type of problem, reach a decision and act on that decision. The following challenges cited in a recent CAPS Research study emphasize this point:
- Engaging talent with appropriate skills in analytic modeling;
- Rigorous use of analytics to make and support decisions;

- Effectively sharing data and insights;
- Strong ability to capture, aggregate and analyze data; and
- Creative application of scenario analysis based on predictive analytics.[20]

The basic steps in problem-solving are to identify the problem; determine its importance and urgency; analyze the problem quantitatively and qualitatively; generate alternatives; compare alternatives to a set of decision criteria; make a decision; and develop and carry out an action and implementation plan. Being analytical refers to the ability to identify and gather relevant information; to synthesize, compare and interpret such data in light of the problem; and to recognize relationships, issues, obstacles and opportunities in the process of generating alternative courses of action. A problem-solver is one who can take this analysis (whether self-generated or provided by someone else) and select an appropriate course of action.

The ability to influence and persuade people and to compromise effectively becomes more important in organizations where empowerment, shared control, and individual and team commitment is the prevailing management philosophy rather than a top-down, command-and-control philosophy. In the supply management arena, managing relationships with key internal stakeholders and suppliers is largely a continuing process of influencing, persuading and resolving conflicts.

Strategic Planning Skills: Project-Scoping, Goal Setting and Execution

A second area of importance is strategic planning skills, especially the ability to scope out a project, set goals and execute.

Project-Scoping. According to the Project Management Institute, project scope management is the process of ascertaining that the project includes all the work required, and only the work required, to complete the project successfully. The project scope management activities include the following:

- *Scope planning* — Documents how the project will be defined, verified and controlled, and how the work breakdown structure will be created and defined.
- *Scope definition* — A detailed project scope statement that serves as the basis for future project decisions.
- *Create work breakdown structure (WBS)* — Subdivide major project deliverables and project work into smaller, more manageable components.
- *Scope verification* — Formalizing acceptance of the completed project deliverables.
- *Scope control* — Controlling changes to the project scope.[21]

Goal Setting. The ability to set goals is also part of the strategic planning skill set. Goals lead to performance if they motivate individuals by focusing attention, directing actions, increasing commitment and encouraging planning. Therefore, effective goal setting is a skill needed by everyone in the organization. In the hiring and development processes, the leader-manager should try to assess the individual's goal-setting ability.

While there are many goal-setting techniques, one that is frequently cited for its effectiveness is the SMART system, attributed to Kenneth Blanchard and Spencer Johnson.[22] SMART is an acronym for

Specific,

Measurable,

Attainable,

Realistic, and

Time-bound/trackable.

The leader-manager should try to assess an individual's ability to set goals prior to hiring and continue to develop this skill in his or her direct reports.

Execution. The ability to execute plans efficiently and effectively, and to attain goals, is as important as the ability to develop goals and plans. The supply management professional must also ensure that people who can execute or oversee the execution of plans are hired, trained and promoted. The right people can only execute flawlessly if the organization also has enabling, instead of disabling, structures, technologies and processes in place; the leader-manager must work to ensure these enablers exist.

Communication Skills: Presentation, Public Speaking, Listening and Writing

Interpersonal communication often appears at the top of lists of desired attributes of employees in general, and supply management professionals in particular. According to the NACE *Skills and Qualities Employers Want in their Class of 2013 Recruits* report, the number one quality is the "Ability to verbally communicate with persons inside and outside the organization."[23] The interest in the interpersonal communication skills of job candidates is not new. This emphasis on interpersonal communication represents a shift from transaction-oriented communication to communication that optimizes the whole relationship with others (both suppliers and customers).

Emotional intelligence is as important as IQ for success in today's workplace. Thus, it is not surprising that the second most desired skill — almost equal to verbal communication skills — is the ability to work in a team structure.[24]

Many people are fearful of public speaking, and even highly educated people can have weak writing skills. The leader-manager must work with people to recognize where they can contribute the most to the supply management organization, and how the team can compensate for individual weaknesses, to create a strong and diverse communication capability.

Broader Financial Skills: Cost Accounting, Analytical, Cash Flow and Making the Business Case

Supply management personnel are increasingly expected to possess and use broader financial skills such as cost accounting and understanding the cash flow impact of their contractual agreements on the organization and its suppliers. They must also be able to build a strong business case for a recommendation. A professional development program for supply management personnel might include seminars, courses and on-the-job training in acquiring and applying cost-accounting knowledge to conduct cost analysis and better manage costs. The IBM CPO study discussed previously found that by using analytics to tackle big data challenges, CPOs could gain new insights into internal business operations and their supplier networks to identify vulnerabilities. Eighty-three percent of high-performing CPOs excelled at leveraging analytics.[25]

Technical Skills: Web-Enabled Sourcing Analysis, Social Media and Market Intelligence

For the supply management professional, technical knowledge and skills refers to the ability to maximize the effectiveness of e-sourcing and enterprise resource planning (ERP) tools, and analyze the information gathered in the sourcing process. Increasingly, the supply management professional must be able to acquire and analyze relevant data online, using applications and social media websites — along with using existing organizational information technology systems — and adapt quickly and easily to emerging technologies. Familiarity with different types of hardware, software, systems and applications has become a basic requirement of employment in organizations as well as using them to proactively assess sourcing opportunities, identify alternatives, and evaluate markets and supplier proposals. Supply chain management is largely driven by the ability to manage information flows within and among organizations, and information technology is a key tool in the growth of effective supply chain management.

While many organizations will seek individuals who already know how to use the particular system employed by the organization, in the long run it is far more important for individuals to be able to quickly become proficient with any hardware, software or system. The computer or web is merely the tool; the real talent for a supply management professional lies in being able to identify relevant information in a format that will facilitate decision-making.

Relationship Management Skills: Ethics, Facilitation, Conflict Resolution and Creative Problem-Solving

Chapter 2 addressed the importance of creating a value-based, ethical organization as the basic foundation of the supply management organization. Chapters 3 and 4 addressed the tools and techniques that can be used to build and maintain internal and external partnerships.

Group facilitation is a process in which an outside person intervenes to help the group improve the way it handles and solves problems and makes decisions to increase the group's effectiveness. The outside facilitator must be acceptable to all members of the group and must be substantively neutral, with no decision-making authority. A member of a team can adopt the skills of a facilitator to act as a facilitative leader who focuses attention on group processes used to solve problems and make decisions. Developing facilitative leaders who possess the skills of a facilitator, and creating the core principles and values necessary for open, free communication, are challenges for team-based organizations.

Conflict Resolution. Conflict is inevitable in many situations. Individuals deal with conflict in a number of ways, including fleeing, fighting, smoothing, capitulating and resisting. Cross-functional and cross-organizational teams with competing or, worse, conflicting objectives will undoubtedly experience conflict. Efforts must be made to train people to manage conflict in a constructive manner. Research suggests that team results are better if there is some conflict and team members work through it, rather than if the team smooths over the conflict to keep the peace.

Creative Problem-Solving. Problem-solving is defined as a higher order cognitive process that requires the modulation and control of more routine or fundamental skills that occur when a person does not know how to proceed from a given state to a desired goal state.[26] Difficult problems have typical characteristics, including lack of clarity of the situation, multiple goals, complexity, dynamism and unpredictability.

Creativity is a mental process that generates new ideas or concepts, or new associations between and among existing ones. Historically, little attention was paid to cultivating creativity; it was simply viewed as a gift. Recently, understanding creativity has become something to be studied from a more scientific perspective. Creativity seems to be best prompted by cross-pollination with fields outside of our normal areas of expertise.[27] Two common characteristics of creative output are that it is both novel and useful. According to Steve Jobs, the late founder of Apple, "creativity is just connecting things." This provides an explanation of the Wright Brothers' application of their bicycle manufacturing technology to the invention of an airplane, and Johannes Gutenberg's knowledge of wine presses and applying that to the invention of printing presses.[28]

While management of most organizations states that creativity and the ability to "think outside the box" is desired in employees, large, rule-bound, hierarchical organizations may not foster an environment that is conducive to creative thinking and creative problem-solving. Supply management professionals are challenged to create a workplace environment that is conducive to creative thinking. One creativity researcher found that "Managers should try to avoid or reduce the 'obstacles to creativity' (time pressure and organizational impediments like political problems, harsh criticism of new ideas and emphasis on the status quo) and enhance the 'stimulants to creativity' (freedom, positive challenge in the work); sufficient resources (workgroup supports; putting together diversely skilled teams that communicate well, are mutually committed to the work and constructively discuss ideas); supervisory encouragement (team leaders who communicate effectively with the group, value individual contributions, protect the group within the organization, set clear goals while allowing freedom in meeting the goals and serve as good work models); and organizational encouragement (like conversations about ideas across the organization, and a top management focus on rewarding and recognizing good creative work)."[29] A recent study of successful, innovative entrepreneurs found that those with the widest and broadest networks of friends tend to be the most innovative in their ideas. 3M, for example, rotates its scientists every few years to get them thinking about new problems and working with new people.[30] This idea can be applied to any functional area. In supply management, changing the commodity or a region a person is responsible for may spark new creative insights and solutions.

Legal Issues, Contract Writing and Risk Mitigation in a Global Environment. Supply management personnel must also have knowledge about the legal environment, including relevant laws and regulations, the ability to write sound contracts or recognize the need for legal advice, and to mitigate risks.

Designing and Planning Training Programs

I hear and I forget. I see and I remember. I do and I understand.

— CONFUCIUS, 551-479 BC

Once training needs have been determined, it must be decided how to provide the training that will achieve the desired results. A number of approaches can be taken to design training programs.

Globally, because the demand for talent outstrips supply in certain parts of the world, designing and planning training programs must take this into account. Supply management leaders must ask themselves what types of training can be implemented quickly and effectively.

Competency-Based Training. Competency-based training is driven by the idea that training should result in trainees knowing how to do something specific. For managers and developers of training, the key questions to ask include (1) What are the specific skills trainees should acquire? (2) How should these skills be taught? and (3) How will results be measured? This approach is very practical and rooted in employee behaviors. Learning objectives are then written specifically around something that trainees will be able to do and something that is measurable. For example, the statement, "Seminar participant will understand total cost of analysis," does not give any indication of how this understanding will be assessed. On the other hand, the statement, "Seminar participants will be able to identify critical cost components, estimate value and discuss missing relevant cost data," gives a clearer picture of what the training will entail and what is expected of trainees after the session. The documentation of expected competencies and the resources available to train personnel in the skills needed to achieve them are the responsibility of every supply management department.

For example, one global financial services organization was forced to use competency-based training as a result of its various acquisitions of other organizations over the past several years. The supply management division of the organization had to fast-track training for some of its newly acquired supply management professionals from the acquired organizations in certain areas of supply management such as total cost management and asset management. They were able to measure the success of the training the professionals received by testing their competency levels as they performed in the new areas, and then would make adjustments where needed.

Types of Training

Several types of training may be offered to supply management employees, starting with orientation training for new hires and continuing with on-the-job training, rotational programs and mentoring. These activities might be supplemented by on-site or off-site seminars or classes, and online courses to support the existing and changing requirements of a position. Training might also include professional certification, formal degrees and professional association involvement.

Functional Orientation. Orientation to the supply management function — including supply management processes, policies, procedures and technology — is typically the first form of training that most employees undergo. This is typically conducted during new-hire orientation and on-the-job training in a new position.

Initial Job Training or Orientation. Employee orientation involves the introduction of the new person to the job and the organization. The primary goals are often to explain the organization's history, products, services and operations; clarify job expectations; and relieve feelings of insecurity in a new environment. New or untrained personnel may be overwhelmed with job requirements and organizational systems. These orientations often include formal instruction along with the use of personnel manuals, employee handbooks, policy and procedures manuals, and tours. These manuals, often maintained online for ease of access and revision, make supervision easier, define standard practices, ensure consistency of results and aid in training. Usually, human resources departments run orientation programs in person or on the intranet with the new employee's supervisor playing a major role.

On-the-Job or Learning by Doing. The most basic method of training is to give general guidelines about what needs to be done and let the employees teach themselves. Of course, this method cannot be employed in all instances and should be used with caution. Learning by doing is probably most effective when the employee is already well trained or experienced in the work he or she has been hired to perform. This may be the only available method if no peer, supervisor or training facilities are available as knowledge resources.

Sponsor, Mentor, Executive Coaching and Reverse Mentoring Programs. Another commonly used practice is to assign a sponsor, mentor or coach to the newly hired person or a high potential employee. The sponsor/coach is typically an experienced employee doing similar work. The sponsor/coach acts as an informal trainer or mentor during a defined period of time. A sponsor/coach should be chosen for his or her experience and, more important, his or her teaching ability. The sponsor/coach may require training to perform this role effectively. For example, at General Mills, Inc., the organization provides a mentoring program in which minority employees are paired with senior-level managers and executives to improve communication and understanding at all levels of the organization. It also offers connection to coaching for minority managers.[31]

This approach can be quite effective if the sponsor/coach is a good teacher. The probable disadvantage, however, is that it restricts a new person's initial training to a single job and focus. Some time may elapse before he or she fully realizes the many implications of the activities of the job and how they relate to departments outside supply management. Also, the time devoted to such training activities may significantly reduce the sponsor's productive output.

As companies work to retain eager millennials and keep baby-boomer executives technologically and socially relevant, a growing number have created formal or informal reverse mentoring programs.[32]

Reverse mentoring refers to an initiative in which older executives are paired with and mentored by younger employees on topics such as technology, social media and current trends. Reverse mentoring is seen as a way to bring older employees up to speed in areas that are often second nature to 20-something employees, whose lives have been more deeply integrated with computers, the web and other mobile technologies and applications.

Many organizations see it as an opportunity for give and take, where new and experienced employees share their knowledge, boosting both groups' understanding and improving overall communication and collaboration in the workplace.[33]

Functional Rotation. To minimize its shortcomings, many organizations modify the sponsor or mentor system by adding a functional rotation program. Before a new employee is assigned to a specific job, he or she is considered a trainee for a period varying from several weeks to several months. Much of this initial training is frequently spent in various functional areas such as procurement, operations, inventory, marketing, materials management, strategic planning and finance. The fundamental idea is to expose the individual to a number of functional activities both within and outside the supply management area. This will facilitate understanding the needs of various stakeholders in the organization and the relationship of supply management to other operating functions. Specific assignments vary depending on the person's background and on his or her first permanent job assignment.

The program's objective, however, is to develop a general understanding of key processes in the organization. On completion of rotational training, the new employee is assigned to a specific job where he or she may receive further job training from a mentor or supervisor.

Functional rotations on an international scope can take on slightly different characteristics such as maintaining three-year rotation plans for key leader successors to top leadership positions to guide their development. On the other hand, some organizations use international rotational assignments sparingly, believing that the logistics of making them work can be complex and costly.

On-Site or Off-Site Classroom Training. Training may also consist of a series of short classroom courses dealing with theoretical principles underlying supply management's role, related tools and standard practices. These programs can be designed to provide substantive training and practice along with the opportunity to build rapport with other supply management personnel and, in some situations, with people from related departments. These courses may be offered on-site or off-site and taught by internal trainers, managers or executives, or by outside professors or practitioners.

Globally, classroom-structured education and training may be a way to discover new talent, especially in places where demand outstrips supply.[34] Because recruiting and retaining local business leaders in developing countries around the world has its challenges, supply management leaders are meeting with international leaders and educators at various global business schools to establish ongoing relationships. Supply management leaders even give lectures, and may talk to students about the supply management profession and about leadership. By getting into schools early and working together, global students become potential hires. They can also become familiar with the supply management leaders established in their specific global regions.

Online Training. The offerings for web-based training are growing dramatically. The convenience of being able to access these types of offerings from anywhere with Internet access is a major driving force. In addition, younger generations entering the workforce are accustomed to this type of learning and accessing information.

Web based learning may be synchronous, which means that all learners are participating at the same time, or asynchronous, meaning a user can access the training at whatever time and place is convenient for them. The advantage of live, asynchronous online learning is the opportunity for interaction, while asynchronous is very convenient.

Types of web-based approaches include web seminars, which are generally short (average one hour) on very timely topics. Web seminars can be offered by the employing organization; they are also offered by many outside companies or professional associations. They might be offered at no charge to members of the organization that offers the web seminar, or are sometimes offered free to anyone interested in the program. Other web seminar providers may charge a small fee. They generally include visual elements such as an accompanying PowerPoint presentation.

Podcasts can generally be accessed on demand, and also cover short, very specific topics. They often do not have visual elements.

Web-based seminars may meet over a period of several sessions. They may be live or asynchronous, and offer deeper coverage than web seminars or podcasts. They may help a participant prepare for professional certification, or cover a deeper topic such as strategic sourcing or category management.

Self-development. In a recent Center for Creative Leadership white paper, an emphasis was put on individuals taking ownership of their own professional development. It will be a challenge for organizations to help their employees understand why development works better when they own it — that is, they have some freedom to decide on their own skill development. One organization that employed managers who were responsible for many people did not have the time to coach all of them. The employees in this organization were expected to drive their own professional development by using peers to gather their own feedback on areas to improve and coach each other on how they can develop.[35]

Self-development may also include activities that an employee does on their own for personal growth or perhaps as a hobby. These include activities such as volunteerism, participating in Toastmasters, and pursuing various fitness goals. Such personal development helps create well-rounded employees. In addition, generally applicable skills such as leadership, teamwork and goal setting can be learned or honed by participating in such activities. Many organizations encourage their employees to volunteer, and may match employee volunteer time with donations or even provide some time off work for volunteerism.

Career Path Planning. Research by WorldatWork showed that organizations that do not invest in training and development of their talent lose valuable employees to their competition.[36] The talent challenges many executives are facing today may be eased through the formal creation of career paths and ladders. A career path as defined by the Society for Human Resource Management (SHRM) "encompasses varied forms of career progression, including the traditional vertical career ladders, dual career ladders, horizontal career lattices, career progression outside the organization and encore careers." A career ladder is "the progression of jobs in an organization's specific occupational fields ranked from highest to lowest based on level of responsibility and pay."[37] A career path will help employees develop their skills and knowledge in their current positions; provide opportunities for advancement in new or different positions; and provide a positive impact on the overall organization through increased morale, career satisfaction, motivation, productivity, and responsiveness in meeting departmental and organizational objectives.[38] Supply management professionals should be aware that career path planning may be an effective strategic tool for achieving positive talent retention outcomes for their organization.

Professional Certification. Institute for Supply Management® (ISM®) has been offering a certification program for supply management professionals for more than 40 years. The Certified Professional in Supply Management® (CPSM®) designation originated in 2008.

Prior to this certification, ISM offered the Certified Purchasing Manager (C.P.M.) certification. Attaining a certification level requires commitment and dedication to professional development. Other professional associations offer certifications for supply management or related fields.

For the individual, certification may lead to peer recognition, better job opportunities, enhanced value to the employer and faster professional advancement. For the employer, it provides evidence that the supply management professional has met standards deemed important by the profession and has the tools to do a good job. Certification as one criterion for promotion may help the employer establish sound requirements for knowledge acquisition and application in place of loose, haphazard or arbitrary promotion practices.

Formal Education and Advanced Degrees. Many employers require or prefer supply management employees to have a formal education and possibly an advanced degree in supply management. Now many colleges and universities offer face-to-face, online or blended programs at the associate's, bachelor's, master's and doctoral levels in supply management and related areas. The supply management professional may define the criteria for targeting schools or assist in the assessment of degree programs to best match the needs of the supply management group with the school's program.

More and more supply management leaders are working with international business schools in developing countries to develop or help in the development of supply management coursework. For educational programs already in existence, supply management leaders try to work with the educational institution to enhance the coursework by contributing real-life case studies or being available to lecture to students.

Professional Association Involvement. Another means of improving oneself professionally is through active involvement in a professional association such as a local affiliate of ISM. This may take the form of active membership or leadership.

Professional association involvement is offering an ever-increasing value network domestically and globally as members use every opportunity to seek out talent. Organizations are losing leaders at a much faster pace than they are producing them. Many organizations will face a mass exodus of managers and leaders within the next several years as the baby boomers retire.[39] Supply management leaders who make full use of their affiliation with professional associations can tap into resources relating to recruiting, retaining and training development. Professional associations can also become the recruiting ground for future supply management leaders.

Assessing the Effectiveness of the Professional Development Program

Training, Cost Efficiency and Measurement of Outcomes

The outcomes of training should be measured in behavioral and operational terms to determine the effectiveness of the training effort (including how trainees actually behave back on their jobs) and the relevance of their behavior to the organization's objectives. In this way, the utility or value of the training can be assessed. Questions usually addressed when evaluating training programs include the following:

1. Was there a change in knowledge, skills and/or abilities related to supply management effectiveness in the various participants?
2. Were these changes directly due to the training?
3. Are the new skills positively related to the organization's goals?
4. Will similar changes occur for new participants in the training program?
5. Was the training cost-effective? Was it worth the expense to the organization? Could the same effect have been achieved with another less expensive training mode?

To determine the answers to these questions, techniques of educational research — tests, questionnaires, interviews and experimental design — need to be employed by trained researchers. The evaluators can answer the previous questions using objective, quantitative and qualitative research methods, and provide data for making decisions on whether to continue, discontinue or modify a training program. Only in this way can an objective, informed assessment of a training mode be made.

Summary

Once staff has been hired, supply management leader-managers must continually develop the talent in their organizations and develop succession plans. This issue becomes magnified when considering the large global workforce.

Skills need to be assessed so knowledge gaps can be identified; training plans can then be put into place. Top skills that have been identified for supply management personnel include team building; strategic planning; communication; decision-making and problem-solving; technical; relationship management; broader financial knowledge; skills surrounding legal issues; and knowledge of social responsibility and sustainability.

Training can be provided based on desired outcomes and competencies — that is, trainees will be able to demonstrate specific knowledge, skills and abilities once training has been completed. Training can include any or all of the following: (1) initial job training/orientation to the new job; (2) on-the-job or learning by doing; (3) training provided by a sponsor, mentor or executive coach; (4) reverse mentoring; (5) on-site or off-site classroom training; (6) online training; and (7) self-development. Some organizations require supply personnel to have one, or several, professional certifications or designations.

Chapter 11 covers the measurement of supply management department performance.

Key Points

1. Many believe that a learning organization will provide a significant competitive advantage through continual knowledge creation and sharing.
2. The supply management professional must design roles and assign responsibilities in alignment with organizational goals and objectives, and be flexible to prepare for the future.
3. Matching positions with knowledge and skills, and supporting this structure with professional development opportunities, will help to ensure effective organizational performance and ensure a qualified pool of candidates at each level in the group.
4. Recruitment and selection strategies must consider the increasingly diverse nature of the workforce domestically and globally.
5. Three elements to achieve the best training results are (1) job analysis, (2) diagnostic testing, and (3) gap analysis.
6. Career path planning can be an effective tool for achieving positive talent retention outcomes for the organization.

CHAPTER 11

In the business world, the rearview mirror is always clearer than the windshield.

— Warren Buffett[1]

Measuring the Supply Management Department Performance

A department-level performance measurement and management system must be developed and implemented to ensure that supply management is maximizing its contribution to the organization. The Strategic Supply Management Concept figure (Figure S-1) in the "Series Overview" section of this book identified talent management and development as a supporting foundation in supply management strategy and philosophy. Chapter 6 addressed the development of strategic and operational plans for supply management. These plans should include the goals and objectives of the department. These goals and objectives should then drive the behavior of the department staff. Individual performance should be linked to the achievement of overall department goals that, in turn, should contribute to the achievement of organizational goals and objectives. The supplier community has been described as the "extended enterprise." In this context, the performance of the suppliers under the leadership of the supply management team is a critical element of the enterprise's overall results. Supplier performance measurement and management is covered in *Foundation of Supply Management*, (ISM *Professional Series*).

To be effective, the performance evaluation and reward system must be aligned with the goals and objectives of the organization, and are a very important part of effective talent management and development. For example, if a major organizational initiative is continuous quality improvement, but the individual is evaluated and rewarded primarily for price reductions, then the individual may be more concerned with price reductions than quality improvements. Unless credit is given for reducing the cost of quality, the means used to achieve the necessary price reduction may work against the ability of the supply management function to contribute to the overall organizational goal of quality improvement. If top management wants supply management to support the achievement of the organization's goals and achieve its mission, then behavior that leads to attaining organizational goals must be recognized and rewarded. Developing a flexible performance evaluation system that can be adjusted to accommodate changes in strategic plans is a difficult task for the supply management team and their peers in human resources management.

Chapter 4 addressed the leadership task of gaining commitment to the new supply management vision and strategies. This chapter addresses the complementary management task of measuring and managing supply management department performance. This chapter focuses on four key questions relating to performance measurement systems and performance management:

1. Why should we measure?
2. What should we measure?
3. How should we measure?
4. What can supply management professionals do with the results?

Chapter Objectives

- Explain the importance of aligning departmental performance metrics with organizational objectives.
- Discuss the reasons and methods for evaluating performance at the department level.
- Identify the key steps in performing a department-level evaluation.

Aligning Department Performance Metrics With Organizational Objectives

There are many reasons why management measures the supply management department performance:

- To determine the departmental effectiveness in meeting organizational needs;
- To determine the effectiveness of department management;
- To measure improvement/deterioration;
- To provide incentives for improvement;
- To determine the resources needed for improvement; and
- To determine if value is added.

Effectiveness in Meeting Organizational Needs

The overriding purpose of measuring departmental performance is to determine and ensure that the department is effectively meeting the needs of the organization. This purpose drives the development of the key performance indicators (KPIs) for the department. To be effective, these KPIs must be rooted in the objectives of the department, function and process of supply management, and the objectives of supply management must be aligned with organizationwide objectives.

Likewise, each function, department and process within the organization must have objectives that are also aligned with the organizationwide objectives. This vertical alignment helps keep everyone in the organization conscious of, and contributing to, the success of the organization in achieving its vision and mission. There must also be horizontal alignment between and among departments, functions and processes to eliminate or at least minimize conflict that saps productivity within the organization caused by conflicting and competing objectives.

Congruence With Organizational Objectives. To determine departmental or functional effectiveness in meeting organizational needs, the mission of the total organization and the specific objectives of the supply management organization must be understood. Chapter 6 discussed the importance of aligning functional or departmental strategy with organizational strategy. Once the organizational mission is understood, this information can be related to the ability of those in the supply management function to perform tasks that, when combined, ultimately contribute to organizational goals.

The specific objectives of a supply management function may be described as obtaining maximum value, prescribed quality and continuity of supply in keeping with the organizational objectives of continuous improvement, quality and revenue enhancement. Benchmarks can then be established to measure the impact of the departmental efforts. Much emphasis is placed on cost/benefit analysis. Supply management contributes to organizational goals in many ways, including cost, quality, technology and speed. This makes the supply management function's "added value" and, in the private sector, contribution to profit possible to document. Other ways that supply management professionals can contribute to organizational goals, such as through the quality of supplier relationships, may be harder to measure. These "softer" measures may actually contribute more to organizational success, but because of the difficulty in documenting and measuring them, they may be left out of the appraisal system or "measured" by description rather than by hard numbers.

For example, at Sodexo, supply management has a suite of metrics that it uses to communicate with different groups of stakeholders, both within and outside the supply management organization.[2] It surveys its internal customers so that it can see how well it is meeting those objectives, and where it might need to redirect its efforts. Sodexo also uses metrics that vary with activity and the economy, so they can see their true performance given volume levels and relevant inflation rates. Supply management communicates the

following metrics to the executive level:
- Cost evolution versus weighted external PPI (market);
- Value generation (actual, plus year-over-year trending);
- Productivity;
- Profit contribution;
- SKU concentration and compliance; and
- Selected topics of concern on an ad hoc basis.

The CPO of Sodexo notes, "The source of the data for metrics internal to supply management, as well as those executive-level metrics, is the same. It's the way they are cast — in recognition of the different audiences — that's different. Reporting the right metrics, in the right way, has contributed to securing supply management's seat at the table. At Sodexo, supply management holds two spots on the executive team, and supply reports directly to the CEO. We have seats on the marketing council and CSR steering committee, as well as on numerous other task forces within the company. For supply management to be recognized as a key business contributor, we must present our function from our executives' perspective. Only in this way can our relevance be clear and apparent to them."[3]

The metrics are aligned at every level within the supply management organization. Congruent metrics are reported to internal stakeholders that are appropriate to the nature of their relationship with supply management.[4]

Congruence With Supplier and Customer Objectives. Just as the objectives of supply management should be aligned with organizational objectives and internal customer objectives, they must also be aligned with the supplier and external customer objectives. The supply management organization must be structured to facilitate the flow of information between end customers and supply management and internal stakeholders. This may be accomplished through cross-functional sourcing teams or by the efforts of individual supply management professionals working with internal partners within the "thick informal networks" discussed in Chapter 4.

Organizational Expectations of Supply Management. To achieve vertical and horizontal alignment of objectives, and consequently of metrics, there must be a clear understanding of the organizational expectations of supply management. As the Sodexo example indicates, it is this set of expectations that drives goal and objective setting, the establishment of key performance indicators and the assessment of performance.

Determine Effectiveness of Department Management

Measurement can help top management determine if the supply management department is being well managed. Overall department performance is essentially the collective performance of each individual in the department. The management team in supply management influences and affects the behavior of each individual in the chain of command. Measuring and monitoring the performance of the management team helps to ensure that the right direction, tools and techniques are provided to those responsible for executing strategies and plans.

Measure Improvement or Deterioration

Measurement can provide evidence of improvement or provide early warning signals of deterioration of performance. This allows managers and individual employees in supply management to either use the success of improvement as leverage in internal negotiations or to take corrective action if performance is slipping in some area.

Provide Incentives for Improvement

Leadership techniques for motivating and inspiring people were discussed in Chapter 4. From a managerial perspective, measurement systems and metrics provide a clear opportunity to develop and execute an incentive program linked to the attainment of improvement goals, and as a means of motivating people to continue to improve performance on key metrics. Incentive programs are often difficult to develop because it is fairly easy to drive behavior in the wrong direction. Research supports the importance of tying metrics to performance-based compensation and promotion opportunities such as individual or team incentive compensation, variable salary increases and/or promotions tied to the achievement of critical supply management metrics.[5] Because measurement is a key motivator of individual behavior, care must be exercised to assure that measurements encourage the desired behaviors. For example, if only purchase price variance (the difference between actual prices paid and a preset standard or estimate) is measured, price may become the only target for improvement, possibly at the expense of other key performance elements such as quality, delivery and lead time. Figure 11-2 from the ISM 2013 Salary Survey shows incentives based on bonuses and stock options. While the highest bonus received for 2012 was US$250,000, the average was US$18,572. The percentage of total respondents receiving stock options was 10.5 percent at an average estimated value of US$31,206.[6]

Figure 11-2: ISM's 2013 Salary Survey

BONUS		
By Job Title	Percentage of Respondents	Percentage of Gross Salary
Chief, Procurement/Supply Management/Sourcing	100%	19.4%
Vice President, Procurement/Supply Management/Sourcing	88%	20.9%
Director, Procurement/Supply Management/Sourcing	75.6%	20.3%
Manager, Procurement/Supply Management/Sourcing	73.8%	13.2%
Experienced Procurement and Supply Management Practitioner	65.1%	11.3%
Entry-Level Procurement and Supply Management Practitioner	55.3%	16.8%
Other	52%	14.7%
Criteria for Bonus		
Company results	57.8%	
Department/team results	13.9%	
Individual results	22.8%	
Other	5.5%	
STOCK OPTIONS		
By Job Title	Percentage of Respondents	
Chief, Purchasing/Supply Management/Sourcing	45%	
Vice President, Purchasing/Supply Management/Sourcing	29%	
Director, Purchasing/Supply Management/Sourcing	21%	
Manager, Procurement/Supply Management/Sourcing	10%	
Experienced Procurement and Supply Management Practitioner	5%	
Entry-Level Procurement and Supply Management Practitioner	4%	
Other	4%	

Source: Institute for Supply Management®, *ISM's 2013 Salary Survey*, January/February 2013.

Determine Resources Needed for Improvement

Measurement can also provide the data needed to make a business case for the allocation or reallocation of resources to achieve needed improvements. Changes in a variety of factors such as sales, product or service mix, manufacturing capacity or service delivery capacity, and raw material or services prices may require a reallocation of resources. Measurements must be relevant and flexible to help predict these changing needs and to suggest an appropriate response. An adaptive measurement system is used by Sodexo, so that performance measures are indicative of true performance rather than changes in the environment, such as price fluctuations.[7]

Determine If Value Is Added

Many activities have been performed for many years simply because they have not been re-examined since they were initiated. Today, most areas of the organization are subject to analysis to reduce, realign or eliminate items that no longer add value. This, of course, requires some level of agreement about what truly adds value to the organization. The process of bringing objectives and metrics into vertical and horizontal alignment and creating shared goals, metrics and accountability will help to define value for everyone in the organization.

What to Measure: Linking Metrics to Goals

The result of long-term relationships is better and better quality, and lower and lower costs.

— W. Edwards Deming[8]

What to measure is a critical question in all organizations. People tend to do those things that are measured and rewarded, and ignore those that are not. For example, a cable company was trying to reduce the resolution times of its help desk and service calls. After call duration goals were set, resolution times shrank — but total service costs rose. To meet their goals, help desk representatives shortened the amount of time they spent on calls and quickly referred cases to field service representatives. The field service representatives improved their metrics for speed and resolution with these referrals. But, again, costs rose because field service calls are far more expensive than help desk calls. Finally, management combined call centers and field services into a single cost tree, then monitored the percentage of calls passed to the help desk and the time spent on each type of call. Call center representatives were encouraged to spend more time trying to resolve difficult calls before passing them along to field services. Although this increased the average call time, it also reduced total costs. The change in metrics encouraged both help desk and field service representatives to take into account both call duration and costs. Management was able to see how better (or worse) performance in one area might affect another.[9]

Measurement systems are designed to assess the degree to which various aspects of the organization (including processes, functions, people, structure and technology) are contributing to the success of the organization. Therefore, metrics should be selected because they provide a link to organizational strategy and the key performance indicators connected to that strategy. Robert Kaplan and David Norton, the creators of the balanced scorecard approach, advocate using the scorecard to create a strategy-focused organization. This approach captures the activities of leaders (create a vision, build alignment and generate commitment) and those of managers (plan, organize, budget, staff, measure and ensure compliance). This approach is also used by Sodexo. This balanced scorecard is used to "support our key objectives to create sustainable value, grow our business, develop our people, enhance execution and live our values. This scorecard aligns our goals, keeps our focus and communicates our progress to team members."[10]

The factors that the supply management professional may want to rate include the skills and knowledge of personnel; the appropriateness of the organizational structure, the scope and accountability of each job; and the departmental plans, policies, procedures and so forth. These factors influence the potential level of a department's performance and are useful indicators of capability. In the Sodexo example, the key metrics aligned directly with the organizational strategic plans, including financial plans, and were driven by a focus on satisfying final customers.

In a CAPS Research study, some possible categories of supply management measures were outlined:
- Cost savings:
  - Year-on-year,
  - Financial audit, and
  - Tied to budget
- Total costs:
  - Total cost of ownership,
  - Life-cycle costs, and
  - Supply chain costs
- Value beyond cost:
  - Innovation,
  - Supply/continuity risk,
  - Revenue,
  - Social responsibility,
  - Customer centric, and
  - Assets
- Predictive metrics:
  - Supplier stability,
  - Risk exposure,

- Future cost savings,
- Market demand-supply balance, and
- Return-on-investment[11]

Clearly, the categories must fit the organization, its vision and mission, and the established roles and responsibilities of supply management. For example, strategic performance measures for a food manufacturer focused on financial, customer satisfaction, operational excellence and innovation (see Figure 11-3).

Figure 11-3: Performance Metrics for a Food Manufacturer

FINANCIAL	CUSTOMER SATISFACTION
Cost Reduction/Cost Effectiveness 　Actual cost per case by product platform 　Actual market price versus prices via futures and options contracts **Cash Flow** 　Average accounts payable (AP) days **Inventory Levels** 　Number of days supply in inventory	**External Customer** 　Quality 　Percent and/or number of defects in shipment 　Number of defect-free shipments 　Complaint-free materials received **Internal Customer** 　Internal customer service 　Compliance with measured specs 　Percent Minority and Women Business Enterprises (MWBE) spend

OPERATIONAL EXCELLENCE	INNOVATION
Acquisition cycle time Collaboration to adopt lean into suppliers Management of strategic supplier relationships Leverage of technology Raw materials logistics improvement	New product introduction 　Met product launch milestone 　Effectiveness of launch 　　Percent market share won from competition 　　Percent volume from new SKUs Product line expansion 　Met milestone Individual development programs and review

Source: Phillip L. Carter, Robert M. Monczka and Trish Mosconi, "Strategic Performance Measures for Purchasing and Supply," CAPS Research (2005). [31]

Efforts to create a strategic supply management department include focusing on implementing value-adding activities of higher value and designing metrics to capture this value. Relying on historical metrics such as old price versus new price or actual versus budget may not drive behavior in the right direction or communicate to stakeholders exactly what supply management contributes to organizational success. Many supply management professionals are focusing on metrics with more strategic impact such as the following:

- Speed to market;
- Cost reduction and total cost of ownership;
- Process improvement such as cross-enterprise collaboration or improved execution that resulted in revenue growth;
- Improved level of service;
- Innovation capture;
- Improved forecasting;
- Top line revenue growth;
- Risk assessment, exposure and mitigation;
- Increased ability to win work;
- Increased profitability;
- Improved supply chain efficiency and effectiveness;
- Lean supply chain;
- Supplier stability including available capacity;
- Social responsibility/sustainability, including environmental impact; and
- Talent attraction, development and retention.

Measure Outsourced Supply Management Functions

In organizations that have outsourced specific supply management tasks or functions, the department performance measurement system might include an assessment of these providers. The metrics discussed in this section also could be used, depending on the circumstances. This review is, in essence, an assessment of the outsourcing decision. As such, the important question from a department perspective is, "Has anything changed in the internal or external environment to lead management to believe that the organization needs this type of in-house expertise?"

How to Measure: Steps in Department-Level Evaluation

How to measure can be answered at two levels. First, in the broadest sense, the question is, "How can a performance measurement system be put in place that will deliver significant benefits to the organization?" Second, in the strictest sense, the question is, "How should the performance measurement system be structured?" A 2011 A.T. Kearney *Assessment of Excellence in Procurement Study* identified seven characteristics that were present in 13 large organizations that demonstrated outstanding procurement performance which enabled procurement to contribute strategically to their business:

1. *Align with the business* — engage with other functions; take advantage of supply market opportunities reaching beyond traditional areas to R&D, marketing, finance, customer support, and legal, impacting more than 94 percent of the external spend.
2. *Contribution to top and bottom lines* — includes contributing to innovation, integrating suppliers into the new product development processes, reducing time-to-market for new products, and creating new business opportunities with suppliers. Bottom lines were affected by increasing total value of purchased goods, building synergies across divisions and business units, collaborating with other business units and key suppliers, and improving working capital.
3. *Manage risk systematically* — accomplished through risk-impact analysis, financial risk management (such as hedging) and disaster planning.
4. *Use supplier relationship management consistently* — accomplished through managing strategic suppliers, expanding the supply base into new markets, monitoring compliance and risk management, performing joint initiatives, and developing suppliers' capabilities. Forward-thinking and the identification of opportunities with suppliers, detailing implementation plans and creating incentives were key attributes listed in the study.
5. *Tailor category strategies* — through the use of advanced "toolkits."
6. *Adopt technology* — use technology that allows visibility into all the spend because of fully automated systems, which allows them to track and report spending by supplier and category for all areas; use innovative contract management systems.
7. *Talent management* — through employment of sophisticated recruiting strategies, establish relationships with universities that offer leading supply chain programs and use summer internship programs; also, systematic management of a more diverse and dispersed workforce.[12]

The second question — how to structure such a system — is answered by devising a systematic process for a department-level evaluation. There are five basic steps to a department-level evaluation system. These are listed in Figure 11-4 and discussed in the following section.

Figure 11-4: Steps in Departmental Evaluation

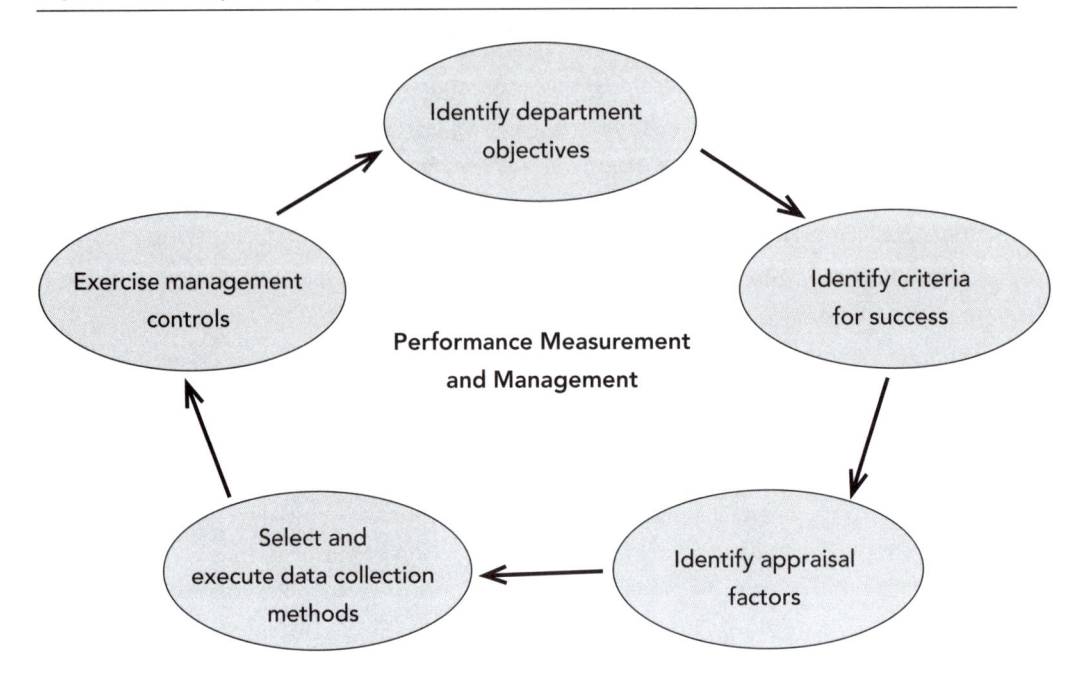

```
        Identify department
           objectives
    ↗                    ↘
Exercise management        Identify criteria
    controls                 for success
         Performance Measurement
            and Management
    ↑                         ↓
    Select and              Identify appraisal
execute data collection  ←     factors
       methods
```

Step 1: Identify Department Objectives

When a manager develops a system to evaluate the performance of any department, the logical starting point is an analysis of the objectives of the department. As discussed in Chapter 6, departmental objectives should flow from, and be aligned with, the objectives of the organization. Once departmental objectives have been defined, the organization structure and the responsibilities assigned to each work group should be examined to determine the impact each operating activity has on the attainment of each departmental objective. This procedure normally discloses the critical activities in the operation where evaluation and subsequent control are most important.

Often, managers find that the "easier to quantify" metrics lead to an overemphasis on objectives such as price and an underemphasis on more strategic activities such as contributing to developing and maintaining end customers through effective buyer-supplier relationships.

Step 2: Identify Criteria for Success

The criteria for success must be established for each task that is to be measured. Performance evaluations are meaningless unless the individuals managing and working in the department know up front what constitutes success and how the degree of success or failure is to be determined. At HOCHTIEF, an international construction services provider, a team structure is prevalent. When incentives were offered, they were based on business unit performance rather than on overall company performance. Therefore, financial motivation drove strategic and tactical behavior for the benefit of the business unit, not necessarily for the corporation. In some cases, business unit incentives counteracted center-led initiatives. It had to realign its KPIs to measure and support consistent center-led objectives. If there was any conflict between business unit and corporate goals, the consistent reporting of metrics made that clear. It also increased visibility and the feasibility of KPI alignment. Aligning incentives to support center-led initiatives improved the effectiveness of the teams.[13]

Step 3: Identify Appraisal Factors

Areas of appraisal may be related to tactical (day-to-day) operations, strategic (commodity or category management) or integration with product or market creation (strategic and technical). At Siemens AG, the director of vehicle operations for Siemens Shared Services convinced 23 independent operating organizations to buy fleet services jointly. He developed a Vehicle Management System (VMS) program to manage the US$60 million spend and partnered with a third-party vehicle supplier and leasing organization. Together they created a Performance Index Review, a quarterly report, focusing on three objectives or categories identified by the operating organizations: low-cost transportation (50 percent), driver productivity and satisfaction (35 percent) and administrative support (15 percent).[14]

While many factors can be considered when evaluating a supply management department's performance, typical appraisals consider one or more of the following elements.

Contributions to Profitability/Success of Core Activity. Contribution to profitability is a primary concern in a business. Government agencies and institutions are concerned with total value and maximization of resource use. How the supply management function's contribution to these results will be measured is a more difficult question. Customer satisfaction, cost, quality and speed are all key areas of attention for the purpose of tracking supply management's contribution to the organization's goals.

Customer Satisfaction. Feedback from user departments or internal customers as well as external or end customers can be a good source of data on the functioning of a supply management department and how well it is serving its customers. Feedback should also be obtained from senior executives. Once supply management's metrics are determined, an executive dashboard should be established. A dashboard is a combination of key performance indicators (KPIs) that give a good, balanced picture of how an organization is performing. A dashboard usually includes one to three metrics around each KPI that are of interest at the top management level. It organizes data in a way that is easy to understand and meaningful for the user. For example, if supply management had the goal to increase sourcing in the United States by 10 percent this year, it might show what its current level was, and the amount over or under. In areas of under-performance, an explanation of the gap and how it will be filled is usually provided.

Feedback can be obtained from internal and external customers informally, or through structured questionnaires and surveys. The decision about what information to collect and how to collect it depends on the costs associated with data collection compared to the benefit of having the knowledge. If there is no concrete plan in place for using the information to increase efficiency and/or effectiveness, then it may not be worth the data collection and analysis costs or the ill will the activity may generate among customers.

Feedback mechanisms such as internal 360-degree surveys may be used to assess the supply management department's performance along dimensions such as responsiveness, cooperation and collaboration. While these items are more difficult to measure than something that is more easily defined and counted, these types of items may provide a better indication of the success of supply management's role in the organization.

Linking the supply management department's performance to final customer satisfaction is also difficult in many organizations. This is more realistic if management has established shared goals, shared metrics and shared accountability. Without these factors, a starting place is ongoing cross-functional discussions about customer-related metrics such as lost sales. Another starting place might be supply management's performance in areas such as delivering the appropriate quality of uninterrupted supply at minimal inventory levels.

Timeliness of Actions. One of a supply management department's primary responsibilities is to support and work with operations (whether a part of the supply management department or a stand-alone function) for the satisfactory completion of the organization's tasks. The following metrics can indicate how efficiently and effectively this responsibility is fulfilled:

Efficiency metrics are broader in scope but are not linked to financial key performance indicators (KPIs) or the strategic objectives of the organization. Examples include
- Headcount (salaried, waged and contracted);
- Indirect spend;
- Facilities and asset cost management;
- Cost of quality;
- Tax effective rates for supply chain; and
- Continuous improvement program spend.

Effectiveness metrics are more multidimensional and span the entire supply chain, including internal and external stakeholders. Examples include
- Lead time reduction and reliability;
- Perfect order fulfillment;
- Customer satisfaction; and
- Supplier collaboration.[15]

In a government or service industry, the focus will be on cycle time or supplier lead time. For example, if the maintenance of a police or emergency vehicle is not completed on schedule, the consequences can be very serious. If operating room supplies are not delivered as promised, then the required supplies may not be available to meet scheduled surgical needs.

Obviously, a number of different performance factors can be measured to provide a basis for appraising supply management efficiency and effectiveness. These factors differ in importance among different organizations depending on the nature of the business and the materials or services purchased. Each organization selects those measures most useful and cost-effective to its own specific situation.

Material/Service Costs. Four effective techniques that have stood the test of time provide a cross-check on the reasonableness of prices paid for materials (see Figure 11-5). All these measurements can be classified and subclassified in various ways to pinpoint the cause of the problems they reveal.

Figure 11-5: Four Techniques to Assess Material/Service Costs

TECHNIQUE	DESCRIPTION
Compare actual prices to standard or target prices.	Establish standard or target prices for major materials or services. Chart prices actually paid against the target figures to display any significant differences. Or, compare to a materials budget using standard price data, or to a rate sheet that has been established for service providers. Results are only as meaningful as the initial target or standard price.
Develop average price paid indices for each major class of material or service.	Develop average "price paid" indices for major classes of materials or services. The trends of such price indices are valuable guides in assessing the effectiveness of performance. If developed on a comparable basis, these indices can also be charted against various national commodity price indices published by the U.S. Bureau of Labor Statistics and the Department of Commerce, and by other countries. This comparison reveals cases in which an organization's costs are rising at a greater rate than market prices during an inflationary period. One potential problem is that items purchased may not be exactly the same as those in the indices.
Track cost savings and identify cost-saving activities.	Periodic cost savings figures can be individually charted for savings arising from such activities as negotiation, value analysis, design and material changes, suppliers' suggestions, change of supplier, packaging improvements and transportation cost-reduction projects. This encourages "delaying" savings to get the most value for it later, rather than getting the best possible price up-front.
Track results of forward buying and assess forecasting effectiveness.	If an organization engages in forward-buying activities, gains and losses from it can be periodically reported to determine forecasting effectiveness, when compared to market results.

Source: Adapted from Anna Flynn and Sam Farney, Chapter 8, "Performance Tracking and Improvement," in *The Supply Management Leadership Process* (ISM *Knowledge Series*), Volume 4 (2000), 208–9.

Material/Service Quality. Once material or service specifications have been established, the most direct measure of quality performance is the number of delivered materials or services that are rejected or found unacceptable by the inspection and using departments. The number of such items is usually compared with the total number received and the defect rate expressed as a percent defective. Because even a small percentage can be a significant and unacceptable rate of defects, many organizations track defects in parts per million (ppm). To understand the significance, 1 percent defective is equal to 10,000 ppm. Many manufacturers have found that customers demand defect rates of 100 ppm or less. To check on the improvement of quality specifications, the supply management professional can also review the value analysis reports dealing with design or service changes and material substitutions. While the same concepts apply to service purchases, there are clearly some distinct differences primarily driven by the degree of intangibility of the service and the resulting difficulty in measuring service performance against the scope of work. Efforts must be made to develop clear, unambiguous descriptions of services to be performed and effective measurement systems to compare actual services received to the original scope of work. Often, this measurement process is based on surveys of service recipients and may be highly subjective or biased. It is the responsibility of the supply management professional to root out subjectivity in service performance assessments as much as possible.

Supplier Development. Suppliers impact a significant part of the cost. Their failure to perform must be considered in the search for maximum value. *Foundation of Supply Management* (ISM *Professional Series*) addresses supplier performance evaluation in detail. The more reliable the supplier, the less costly it is to deal with the supplier's organization. It is difficult to measure the costs an organization incurs from poor supplier performance, but some of the many sources of such costs are expediting, inspection and sorting, rework, returning defective goods, missed customer promises and warranty claims. Many sourcing teams have begun to work very closely with key suppliers to improve both supplier and customer processes to attack these sources of unnecessary cost. If supplier relationship management processes are improved, the result may be less time spent correcting problems or more time spent to improve measurable results. Closer collaboration with suppliers might be measured by productivity levels, quality improvements, shorter cycle times, better service or knowledge-sharing across organizations, collaborative technology use, and innovation sharing.

Figure 11-6: Supplier Reliability Metrics

METRIC	DESCRIPTION
Supplier financial stability and financial impact	Initial and ongoing evaluation of the financial stability and viability of major suppliers is necessary to ensure supply over the long term. Ability to work with the organization to manage product and service development and production costs. Understanding and proven commitment to positive impact on the organization's top line revenue growth.
Supplier capabilities, including technical requirements and innovation	Does the supplier have adequate capacity to meet the organization's needs for today and in the future? Is the supplier able to support and take advantage of technology shifts and requirements? To what degree does the supplier come to the supply management organization first with innovation ideas?
Supplier performance	Almost universal metrics for supplier reliability include (a) on-time performance, (b) quality and (c) correct and complete shipments.
Transportation	Quality and reliability of transportation service offered by various carriers
Social responsibility/sustainability	Supplier environmental effects on water usage, carbon footprint and waste; social impacts like percent of local suppliers, labor and safety requirements and audits, and so on.
Speed to market and freshness	Ability to beat the competition in supporting the organization's product development and launch time lines; ability to manage food chains for freshness, and so on.

Source: Adapted Bart Van Dijk, "Winning Supply Chains Integrate Today's Capabilities with Tomorrow's Goals," A.T. Kearney, March 2013, accessed at http://www.atkearney.com/operations/ideas-insights/article/-/asset_publisher/LCcgOeS4t85g/content/winning-supply-chains-integrate-today-s-capabilities-with-tomorrow-s-goals/10192 and the Institute for Supply Management®.

Order Quantity and Inventory Effectiveness. The failure to buy the right quantity (for example, the quantity that keeps the operation functioning yet minimizes the amount tied up in inventory investment) jeopardizes the cost structure or misuses resources that may be better used elsewhere. Four measurements that have proved their value and importance over time in evaluating how well funds are invested are described in Figure 11-7.

Figure 11-7: Assessment of Investments in Inventory

METRIC	DESCRIPTION
Compare inventory carrying costs and material acquisition costs	A chart showing target and actual inventory levels in the aggregate and by major classifications along with a chart showing inventory turnover rates for the same material classifications. When analyzed together, these charts point out imbalances between inventory carrying costs and material acquisition costs.
Inventory turnover effectiveness	A report of "dead stock" materials carried in stores, resulting from overbuying or less-than-planned use. Inventory may be measured in "days-on-hand" to indicate the effective rate of turnover.
Buying effectiveness	The number of stockouts and production stoppages, or customer orders not filled, attributed to under-buying.
Inventory savings	A list of supplier stocking arrangements that have been negotiated, along with an estimate of resulting inventory savings.
Outsourcing inventory management and control	The ability to shift inventory off balance sheet, reduce warehouse square footage and impact lower cost due to supplier inventory control efficiencies.

Source: Adapted from Anna Flynn and Sam Farney, Chapter 8, "Performance Tracking and Improvement," in *The Supply Management Leadership Process* (ISM *Knowledge Series*), Volume 4 (2000), 211.

Creativity and Value Creation. Value creation is an important factor in the success of organizations. Value creation includes insightful initiatives undertaken to enhance the worth, relevance or importance of a product, service or system. The degree to which creativity and value can be obtained from suppliers is something that supply management professionals can facilitate.

Deciding what to measure is the first step in developing a performance appraisal system. The next step is choosing appropriate methods of performance data collection.

Step 4: Select and Execute Data Collection Methods

A number of data collection methods may be used in a performance measurement and management system. This chapter addresses the following methods: internal audits; self-governance or self-assessment methods; customer and supplier feedback; process benchmarking; and best practices studies. Figure 11-8 lists the pros and cons of each method, and the following section expands on self-governance and process benchmarking.

Internal Audits/Self-Governance/Self-Assessment. An internal audit is a comprehensive, systematic, independent and periodic examination of an organization's supply man-

Figure 11-8: Pros and Cons of Data Collection Methods

METHOD	PROS	CONS
Internal audits, self-governance, self-assessment	Familiarity with processes, systems, people	Auditor may be too close to be critical Process may be highly politicized
Customer and supplier feedback	May get end-to-end supply chain perspective Input may identify new opportunities to exploit or risks to mitigate	Lack of trust may preclude honest assessment Resource constraints make it difficult to collect and analyze data
Process benchmarking	Makes everyone aware of industry leaders Draws attention to cross-industry practices	May lead to overemphasis on copying what others are doing May set target too low
Best practices	May identify a practice that will lead to competitive advantage	What is a best practice in one organization may not translate well in another organization

agement environment, objectives, strategies and activities. It is used to identify strengths and weaknesses, and to develop a plan of action to improve performance. Regular and unbiased feedback is needed, and an audit is one way to gather this information.

Often, audits are conducted by outside consultants to ensure the necessary objectivity and independence of judgment. Audits are, however, also conducted internally. Many organizations have monthly or quarterly meetings to report operational progress each of their units has made or not made as measured against selected key performance indicators (KPIs) such as delivery reliability, lead time and quality. Those responsible may be asked to audit their own performance quarterly and to compare the current status to where they need to be to become excellence-driven units, identifying how they plan to bridge the gaps.

Process Benchmarking. Process benchmarking refers to a performance comparison of business processes against an internal or external standard of recognized leaders. Most often the comparison is made against a similar process in another organization considered to be "best" in a particular area. In other words, process benchmarking provides an answer to the question, "How are we doing compared to other leading-edge organizations?" The answer to this question should lead an organization toward the development of best practices for its own internal operations.

Recently, CAPS Research identified a continuing move beyond tactical benchmarks to create strategic benchmarks that go beyond metrics. Such benchmarks consider strategic processes, such as risk assessments or suppliers' commitment to environmental sustainability. It is important to consider not just whether processes exist but where possible to also do a thorough assessment with best-in-class organizations to see how they are implementing such critical processes.[16]

Before initiating process benchmarking, several questions need to be answered, including the following:

- Are we willing to make a major change? Change may be difficult to foster if there is no agreement that the current situation is not acceptable.
- Is the expected improvement worth the expenditure?
- Are the results important to us?
- Does the process impact a critical success factor?
- Have all investigations related to this process been completed? Have all other alternatives been explored?
- Have we begun measuring the current process?
- Do we know the major cost components and service factors of our process?
- Are we willing to wait for a benchmarking study to be completed before implementing any changes?
- Are we willing to reveal information about our own processes to outside organizations?

Process benchmarking may actually involve the division of the functions of an organization into several modules analyzed as independent processes. Such a study may find, for example, that one organization has the best order processing, another has the best inventory control, and so on.

Step 5: Exercise Management Control in Response to Results

Evaluation should be an ongoing process, a catalyst for improvement in the supply management function and processes, and a means of validating performance to management's expectations. Once the results of a performance appraisal are obtained, management must be sincere in its efforts to reward exceptional performance, find the root cause of problems and focus resources on correcting these problems. Otherwise, the entire performance appraisal process will serve no useful purpose. Measuring performance is only half the battle. Deciding what to do with the results of the measurement and how to do it is the other half.

Management can take a number of actions in response to departmental performance data, including taking corrective action, encouraging employee accountability, determining compensation, making promotion decisions, promoting personal and career development, fostering employee engagement and morale building, justifying disciplinary action, recognizing employees and motivating performance improvement.

TAKING CORRECTIVE ACTION. The corrective action required will vary depending on the magnitude and root cause of the problem. In general, the process will include establishing time frames for improvement, prioritizing the steps in the improvement plan and conducting cost/benefit analysis to determine the appropriate level of resources to allocate to the corrective action plan implementation.

ESTABLISHING TIME FRAMES. It is necessary to establish time frames for corrective action. This may take the form of a final due date along with milestones and time frames leading up to full implementation of the corrective action. The manager must be clear about the purpose of the corrective action. In some cases, the first step may be to take the time to determine the root cause of the problem and then develop an action plan for dealing with the root cause. In other cases, interim measures may be taken in the short term to deal with what are really just symptoms of the real problem while a plan is developed for getting at the root cause.

PRIORITIZING. Whatever the process, prioritizing the steps in the implementation plan is critical. This process should include an understanding of the resources needed for the action and their availability.

ANALYZING THE COSTS AND BENEFITS. Corrective action must be cost-effective given the expected benefits if the action is undertaken. A comparison of resources (people, time, equipment, money, and so on) and availability to the expected value (quantified in some way) should be performed. An ability to quantify the value of the benefits achieved is paramount, and in most process improvements this benefit is in the form of saving people's time. Therefore, one of the most commonly used methods of quantifying the savings is through activity-based cost analysis. Activity-based cost analysis is discussed in more detail in *Foundation of Supply Management* (ISM *Professional Series*). It is a cost management method for attributing indirect costs to the activities that drive cost. This approach is in contrast to more traditional accounting methods that pool and allocate indirect costs on a formulaic basis that does not necessarily reflect the true cost structure.

Encouraging Employee Accountability. A good performance appraisal will identify for the employee those areas in which he or she has problems and will specify what he or she needs to do to correct them. The appraisal thus provides the employee with guidance on how to improve, and makes him or her accountable for that behavior with a definite time span for improvement. It is also important to identify and build on areas in which the employee is doing well.

Adjusting Compensation. No department operates at its full potential for long if its salary structure fails to reward individuals in relation to their respective performance levels. A good performance appraisal program does not guarantee an equitable salary structure. It does, however, provide data that can be used in developing a sound compensation plan or in correcting an inadequate one.

Bonus systems based on performance are increasingly common today. Most companies want to have a single performance bonus system for the whole organization because it is easier to manage and seems more fair if everyone's bonus can be calculated on the same basis.[17] A 2012 survey conducted by *Modern Materials Handling* indicated bonus plans reflected a shifting focus from operational costs and increased sales to the overall performance of the organization and that of the individual. Sixty-nine percent of respondents indicated that bonuses are based on whether their organization reaches performance goals, and 46 percent said it was based on individual performance.[18]

Making Promotion Decisions. How do managers know which people in their departments are likely to become candidates for the top positions? They determine this by analyzing each aspect of an individual's performance record. These analyses must be made using detailed and accurate written data. A well-designed appraisal program provides the required data.

When considering promoting people to leadership positions, "Every leader needs to take personal responsibility for achieving results, and for creating an atmosphere that is energetic and enthusiastic. Leadership is a way of life, and a true measure of success lies in having people who value their roles in helping the organization achieve its goals."[19] Potential leaders must demonstrate that they have a vision for the organization, and that they can deliver measurable, positive change.

Guiding Personal and Career Development. The most important benefit that can result from a good employee evaluation program is the information needed to stimulate and direct each individual employee's professional development. A manager's prime responsibility is to develop capable and effective personnel. The data provided by appraisals can be analyzed to determine each employee's strengths and weaknesses. This determination facilitates the development of a realistic professional improvement program for each individual.

Fostering Greater Employee Engagement and Morale. Every supply management professional must develop a well-structured program for appraising the performance of personnel. Nothing is more disastrous to the morale of a department than haphazard or inconsistent evaluations of individual employee performance.

Taking Disciplinary Action. A well-designed employee performance appraisal is a necessary guide for disciplinary actions that are focused and fair, and that provide direction for employee improvement.

Recognizing High-Performing Employees. Employees want to know that diligence and attainment of performance goals will be recognized and rewarded. When departments reward their most effective workers, heavy workloads are viewed as an opportunity to win recognition, earn respect and be included in the most interesting and high-profile projects. Most supply management employees are motivated when their managers make them feel good about quality work through acknowledgment of superb efforts. Programs that allow supply management professionals to be recognized and rewarded for their performance benefit the entire organization.

Motivating Performance Improvements. One of the key purposes of staff appraisal is to motivate employees to improve their performance. Well-designed systems will provide each employee with the feedback and guidelines necessary to achieve higher levels of performance in the next measurement period. Employees should have the sense that continuous improvement applies to their efforts as well as the efforts of suppliers.

As Jim Adkins, vice president of sourcing, supply chain and new product development governance, North America and Oceania for Bobcat Company reminds us, "Teamwork and collaboration create an atmosphere for improved communication, and ultimately greater success, for supply management and the overall company."[20] Having sound measures to track and guide performance is essential to that success.

Summary

One of the most important goals of supply management is to support the goals of the entire organization. Supply management department's goals and performance measurements and metrics need to line up with what the overall organization wants to achieve. Specific, concrete, measurable goals must align with metrics. Systems/processes to measure the goals must be developed and implemented by supply leader-managers. They must also follow through with continuous measurement, and set improvement plans in place as needed.

This chapter focused on the managerial task of measuring and managing department performance. It is complemented by the leadership tasks of motivating and inspiring people to commit to achieving the vision of supply management. Managers must make a strong case for the importance of having departmental objectives that are linked to organizationwide objectives. Then they must determine what and how to measure to ensure that metrics drive appropriate behaviors at the individual level, and that performance data are accurate and useful. Lastly, they must use the performance data to guide decisions about supply management processes, people, technology and structure.

Chapter 12 covers how to establish internal controls and ensure compliance in financial reporting, operational effectiveness and efficiency, and compliance with laws and regulations.

Key Points

1. Performance tracking is important to recognize and reward behaviors that lead to attaining organizational goals. A vital source of information about behaviors is feedback from internal and external customers of the supply management processes.
2. The supply management organization needs to be structured in such a way as to facilitate the flow of information between end customers and supply management personnel.
3. Measurement is needed to track trends in performance that will provide evidence of improvement or provide early warning of deteriorating performance. Data capture should be unbiased, at regular intervals, and should be made as much a part of the normal functioning of the unit as possible. Information gathering should be built into the process wherever possible.
4. Management's response to information gathered from measurements is as critical as the measurement itself. The information must be used in guiding decisions and actions with respect to organization structure, individual development and staffing needs.
5. Feedback must be as unbiased as possible. One method of assuring this is to gather information from several perspectives as is done in executive dashboards and in 360-degree personnel evaluations.
6. The supply management function is in a position to contribute substantially to the results desired by the organization, whether it is profitability for a business or effective resource use for a not-for-profit organization.

CHAPTER 12

This isn't just a legal compliance issue for us. We consider the privacy issue to be an opportunity to reinforce brand image.

— THOMAS WARGA

FORMER SENIOR VICE PRESIDENT, GENERAL AUDITOR AND CHIEF PRIVACY OFFICER, NEW YORK LIFE INSURANCE COMPANY[1]

Establishing Internal Controls and Ensuring Compliance

The final, but by no means least valuable, managerial role is to establish internal controls and ensure compliance. These activities are critical managerial tasks that support organizational success and, in some cases, ensure survival. Today's business climate of ethical lapses and accounting scandals, coupled with public outcry and government regulation, have brought control and compliance issues to the forefront in many organizational settings. However, as the opening quote indicates, treating these situations strictly as control and compliance issues may be too narrow a perspective. Leaders and managers may also create an opportunity to enhance the organization's reputation and brand image by the way they manage the risks associated with operational, financial, legal and regulatory control and compliance. As discussed earlier, risk management is one of the overarching concerns of supply management strategy and philosophy.

The managerial control and compliance role corresponds to the leadership task of gaining commitment. The leader uses influence and develops partnerships to generate commitment to achieving a vision. The manager uses control mechanisms to compare actual behavior with planned behavior, determine the root cause of discrepancies and implement corrective action when there is a discrepancy. Instrumental to managers executing their control responsibilities is the organization's capability to identify risks, assess the level of risks and develop risk mitigation and management strategies. These tools and techniques are discussed in Chapter 5.

The supply management professional has overall responsibility, both individually and in his or her ability to delegate responsibility, for establishing supply management controls before the fact, during the fact and after the fact, and for ensuring compliance with the established controls. In one sense, this means there are three chances to get it right, but at each stage the costs of risk mitigation and compliance increase, sometimes exponentially.

The Committee of Sponsoring Organizations of the Treadway Commission (COSO), formed in 1985, is a voluntary private sector organization whose mission "is to provide thought leadership through the development of comprehensive frameworks and guidance on enterprise risk management, internal control and fraud deterrence designed to improve organizational performance and governance and to reduce the extent of fraud in organizations."[2] The sponsoring organizations include the American Accounting Association, the American Institute of Certified Public Accountants, Financial Executives International, the Institute of Internal Auditors and the Institute of Management Accountants. The COSO Internal Control Integrated Framework is the U.S. standard on internal controls. According to COSO, "Internal control may be broadly defined as a process, affected by an entity's board of directors, management and other personnel, designed to provide reasonable assurance regarding the achievement of objectives relating to operations, reporting and compliance."[3]

The definition reflects certain fundamental concepts. Internal control is expanded upon below:

- *Geared to the achievement of objectives in one or more categories* — operations, reporting and compliance.
- *A process consisting of ongoing tasks and activities* — a means to an end, not an end in itself.
- *Affected by people* — not merely about policy and procedure manuals, systems and forms but about people and the action they take at every level of an organization to affect internal control.
- *Able to provide reasonable assurance* — but not absolute assurance, to an entity's senior management and board of directors.
- *Adaptable to the entity structure* — flexible in application for the entire entity or for a particular subsidiary, division, operating unit or business process.[4]

In 2013, COSO expanded on the 2013 *Internal Control — Integrated Framework* (Framework) to help organizations design and implement internal control in light of many changes in business and operating environments since the issuance of the original Framework in 1992. It broadens the application of internal control in addressing operations and reporting objectives, and clarifies the requirements for determining what constitutes effective internal control.[5]

Similar issues are being addressed by the International Accounting Standards Board (IASB). The IASB is an independent, privately funded accounting standard setter with

15 full-time board members (currently). The IASB is responsible for the development and publication of International Financial Reporting Standards (IFRSs). The organization's objectives "are:

- to develop a single set of high quality, understandable, enforceable and globally accepted IFRSs;
- to promote the use and rigorous application of those standards;
- to take account of the financial reporting needs of emerging economies and small and medium-sized entities (SMEs); and
- to promote and facilitate adoption of IFRSs, being the standards and interpretations issued by the IASB, through the convergence of national accounting standards and IFRSs."[6]

This chapter starts with a general discussion about establishing an effective internal control system and the nature of management controls before, during and after the fact. The remainder of the chapter covers these three categories: (1) operational effectiveness and efficiency, (2) financial reporting, and (3) legal and regulatory compliance.

Chapter Objectives

- Discuss the purpose of management controls, different types of controls and when each is used.
- Discuss supply management's role in establishing internal controls and ensuring compliance in the areas of
  - Reliability of financial reporting,
  - Operational effectiveness and efficiency and
  - Compliance with laws and regulations.

Establishing an Internal Control System

The supply management leadership team must establish and maintain an effective and efficient internal control system that aligns with organizationwide risk management and internal controls. The success of this initiative depends in part on (1) strong internal partnerships, especially with legal counsel, internal auditors, the chief financial officer, the chief information officer and the chief executive officer; (2) rigorous processes supported by appropriate policies, procedures, desk routines and documentation; and (3) fully engaged supply management professionals committed to achieving the organization's goals in an ethical and honest fashion. COSO outlined five essential components of an effective internal control system:

1. The *control environment* establishes the foundation for the internal control system by providing fundamental discipline and structure.
2. *Risk assessment* involves the identification and analysis by management — not the

internal auditor — of relevant risks to achieving predetermined objectives.
3. *Control activities*, or the policies, procedures and practices that ensure management objectives are achieved and risk mitigation strategies are carried out.
4. *Information and communication* support all other control components by communicating control responsibilities to employees and by providing information in a form and time frame that allows people to carry out their duties.
5. *Monitoring activities* covers the external oversight of internal controls by management or other parties outside the process or the application of independent methodologies, such as customized procedures or standard checklists, by employees within a process.[7]

Management controls can be either active or passive. The concept of "active" controls focuses on policies and guidelines that require a conscious action or decision to implement or maintain. Examples of these might be a weekly reminder that a buyer receives with current inventory levels, and the buyer has to decide whether to place an order and the order quantity.

Active controls are always "switched on" and are reporting and recording performance, whereas passive controls are like exception reporting. Passive controls operate in the background. An example is computer generated POs for inventory replenishment; human intervention is not necessary to ensure a policy, procedure or process is followed. Most business people rarely consider or manage passive controls already in place. However, as the business environment changes, these controls should be reviewed and updated to deal with changing demand patterns and cost structures.

In some cases, passive controls are put in place so that they become active when there is a problem. For example, when inventory level reaches zero, or when there is no or limited demand for a certain period of time, passive controls can send an alert or notification to a person indicating the status and that attention is needed; this is a form of exception reporting. Setting up these automatic checks is important to ensure that passive policies, processes and controls remain effective and appropriate.

Clearly, control mechanisms are more than afterthoughts. In addition to being active or passive, they may be in place at three points in time: (1) before the fact, (2) during the fact, and (3) after the fact (see Figure 12-1).

Figure 12-1: Types of Controls

TYPE OF CONTROL	EXAMPLE
Before-the-fact controls	Budgets Plans Business continuity Forecasts Policy and procedures manuals
During-the-fact controls	Structured processes Adherence to policy and procedures Specifications Industry standards
After-the-fact controls	Reports Reviews Audits and customer surveys

Before-the-Fact Controls

Before-the-fact controls establish a benchmark against which actual performance can be measured. Before-the-fact controls include budgets, plans (strategic, operational and disaster recovery), business continuity plans, forecasts, and policy and procedure manuals.

Budgets. One of the more obvious ways to establish management control is through the organization's budgets. Funds are allocated to projects based on prioritization, which is based, in part, on the assessment of risk exposure and expected rewards. *Foundation of Supply Management* (ISM *Professional Series*) provides a detailed description of the different types of budgets used by organizations and the role each of these plays in management control.

Plans. Business plans incorporate the budget process with the assessment of other areas such as organizational mission, market penetration, market share, competitive analysis, staffing, and other managerial concerns that affect the strength of the organization. The strategic and operational planning process is discussed in detail in Chapter 6.

Business Continuity (Disaster Recovery or Contingency) Planning. Business continuity planning is one type of contingency plan that has received much attention by many supply management professionals. Business continuity planning is defined in the ISM *Glossary* (2014) as "an ongoing and comprehensive process for ensuring the continuity or uninterrupted provision of operations and service, including risk or contingency planning, disaster planning, disaster recovery, business recovery, business resumption and contingency plans." These "what if" plans focus on courses of action to take in the event of earthquakes, hurricanes, major fires, international government issues and so forth. From a supply management perspective, a disaster plan may include backup suppliers in the event the usual supplier is incapacitated in some way.

For example, a manufacturer of gardening tools and accessories had a supply management strategy that relied heavily on single sourcing. When the organization's single source provider of gardening gloves was wiped out by a tsunami, the organization had no contingency plan. This led the supply management leadership team to review all single source decisions from the perspective of risks as well as opportunities, and focus more attention on developing contingency plans.

Forecasts. Forecasts generally relate to the demand for finished goods or services, but also relate to the concern for internal capacity and external availability of materials and services. *Effective Supply Management Performance* (ISM *Professional Series*) describes different ways of forecasting demand, both internally and externally.

Policies. The management of an organization or department typically establishes policies to cover normal operating conditions. These policies then guide the behavior of employees and standardize the response to typical events. In this way, employees can routinize their behavior for most activities and develop customized ways of dealing with ad hoc situations. Policies help to ensure that everyone in the organization is moving in the same direction on a daily basis. Supply management personnel must be sensitive to overall organizational policy as well as departmental policy. This includes policy not always found in the department manual, but may exist in the overall organization policy, or in policies from functional areas such as safety, operations, quality assurance and human resources.

Procedures Manual. A procedures manual outlines in detail the specific actions to be taken to accomplish a given task. It establishes guidelines for achieving an organization's objectives and contains an organization's major procedures for easy reference by users.

During-the-Fact Controls

During-the-fact controls are put in place to monitor and measure the task while it is occurring, or before it is finalized, so that adjustments can be made as early as possible to stay within the designated parameters. During-the-fact controls may be in place to monitor any process such as requisitioning and procurement, sourcing, contract writing and administration, inventory management, environmental management, material transfers, quality and so on. These controls are especially important for compliance with the Sarbanes-Oxley (SOX) Act in the United States, which is discussed later in this chapter.

Internationally, a growing number of corporate governance controls are being initiated in a variety of countries. Corporate governance controls are an evolving worldwide trend. For example, the European Commission's Directorate General Internal Market amended the 8th Directive on statutory audit of annual accounts; they consolidated accounts and the fourth and seventh company law directives on corporate governance and financial reporting. All three directives have a wider and deeper scope than the Sarbanes-Oxley Act.[8]

Structured and Disciplined Supply Management Processes, Policies and Procedures. A structured and disciplined supply management process with supporting policies and procedures is perhaps the best during-the-fact internal control system. The ISM *Professional Series* is essentially about establishing and maintaining such a system.

Process reviews can be used to ensure that these during-the-fact controls are efficient and effective. This type of function can be completed by internal auditors, or third parties that specialize in supply chain and procurement. For example, an energy transmission company used the services of Protiviti, Inc., a wholly-owned subsidiary of Robert Half International, Inc., a provider of independent internal audit and business and technology risk consulting services, to review its contracting life cycle. The goal was to improve the organization's contract management processes. It helped the client combine business unit requirements with existing supplier relationships, document the end-to-end contract life cycle, and develop metrics. Implementation of these processes improved supplier relationships and reduced the contracting life cycle. For example, the contracting process for direct equipment dropped from 16 weeks to four weeks. Better lead times also helped improve compliance to the contracting process.[9]

INDUSTRY STANDARDS. Industry standards, such as the ISO 9000 family of standards for quality management and ISO 14,000 family of standards for environmental management, are also ways that control can be exerted.

MILITARY SPECIFICATIONS. Military specifications are one type of standard that relates to quality and may be used commercially.

Information Technology. During the execution of various business processes, information technology is used to capture data and monitor progress. Partnering with IT to ensure the collection, accessibility and transparency of data is a foundation of a rigorous internal control system. In another example from Protiviti, an oil and gas exploration company contacted them to help assess and improve its approach to spending about US$2 billion in capital investments annually. Specifically, Protiviti worked with the company to do the following:

- Reviewed processes for conducting drilling and completion projects;
- Analyzed detailed transaction level data; and
- Summarized the organization's entire capital project portfolio.

This created a detailed enough information system that then allowed Provitivi to work with accounting and operations to identify root causes of cost overruns. It also developed customized project reporting, provided more transparency on capital expenditures, and improved measurement and monitoring for future projects. It significantly reduced the risk of future misallocation.[10]

After-the-Fact Controls

After-the-fact controls are reviews that measure what actually happened so actual performance can be compared with planned benchmarks. This type of gap analysis can provide information that will lead to improvements in processes, products and/or services. The supply management organization should also perform internal audits to measure compliance with contract terms and conditions and relevant laws and regulations.

Periodic Reports. The periodic report is another means of review that can be used to compare actual performance with the plan. The time frame for periodic reviews should be established during the planning stage, and the quantitative information should be summarized at intervals that will facilitate the review process.

Procedures Reviews. Procedure reviews are initiated to ascertain if those charged with following established procedures are indeed doing so.

Audits. Audits are performed to (1) prevent problems, (2) gauge system and process efficiency and effectiveness, and/or (3) meet a regulatory requirement. There are three basic types of audits: internal, external and self inspection. An internal audit is performed by a person or a team of people from inside the organization who have no vested interest in the outcome of the audit. An external audit is performed by an outside party. It is critical to have policies and procedures in place, but there must be an auditing mechanism for determining if there are process shortcomings within these policies and procedures. If the policies and procedures are sound, an audit may reveal whether or not personnel are adhering to them. Audits are conducted to see if the work performed mirrors the original intent. Generally, a sample of transactions is taken by the auditor and compared to established benchmarks. The auditor usually reports his or her findings and leaves the development of conclusions to management.

The following steps outline the auditing process and provide an example of an audit of a newly acquired operating unit or field office.

1. Determine the scope of the audit.
2. Determine how the results will be used.
3. Determine the standard.
4. Determine what type of audit is appropriate.
5. Establish the format of the audit.
6. Prepare and distribute the final audit report.
7. Establish a corrective action plan.

Auditors at Boeing developed an evaluation form based on the COSO operating categories and the COSO internal control integrated framework (see Figure 12-2), which remains valid today.[11]

The control mechanisms discussed so far can be applied to many organizational settings. The three primary objectives of an internal control system are to ensure (1) efficient and effective operations, (2) accurate financial reporting, and (3) compliance with laws and regulations. Supply management plays a role in each of these three areas.

Internal Operations Controls As discussed in Chapter 5, *operational risk* is the risk of loss from inadequate or failed internal processes, systems and staff, or from external events. Internal operating controls are put in place to ensure efficient

Figure 12-2: The Boeing Control Evaluation Form

Report Title

Project No. **Report No.** **Report Date**

Project Leader **Chief auditor**

RATINGS	COSO OPERATING CATEGORIES		
S = Satisfactory U = Unsatisfactory I-S = Incidental Satisfactory I-U = Incidental Unsatisfactory	Effectiveness and Efficiency of Operations	Reliability of Financial Reporting	Compliance With Laws & Regulations
Control Environment			
Risk Assessment			
Control Activities			
Information & Communication			
Monitoring			
Overall			

Rationale for Unsatisfactory Rating:

Source: Dennis Applegate and Ted Wills, "Struggling to Incorporate the COSO Recommendations Into Your Audit Process? Here's One Audit Shop's Winning Strategy," *Internal Auditor* (December 1999).

and effective use of resources. Effectiveness means that the operation being evaluated achieved the specific pre-established management objectives. Efficiency means that this was accomplished with an optimum level of resource inputs to productive outputs. An operations audit should determine whether the organization can be reasonably assured that no material inefficiencies or ineffectiveness exist in the audited organization or process. Internal operations controls and audits provide information about compliance with laws and regulations as well as compliance with internal policies and procedures.

For the supply management organization, operations controls are valuable for assessing the efficiency and effectiveness of processes, policies and procedures, and measuring and ensuring internal compliance. Areas of concern include requisitioning, sourcing, procuring, contract writing and administration, hazardous and regulated materials management and end-of-life-cycle materials management.

Internal Environmental Controls

Environmental laws and regulations affect many industries in many countries, and they vary considerably depending on the country. In the United States, environmental compliance regulations are primarily set forth by the Environmental Protection Agency (EPA), the Council on Environmental Quality (CEQ), the Chemical Safety and Hazard Investigation Board, and the ISO 14001:2004 environmental system standard. The environmental laws and regulations of other countries and regions may impact nondomestic or nonregional organizations just as U.S. laws and regulations affect non-U.S. organizations doing business in the United States. The supply management team plays an important role in acquiring current information on domestic and nondomestic environmental laws and regulations, and ensuring that the organization takes the necessary steps to be in compliance. The supply management leadership team in each organization must develop a means of assessing environmental risks, putting appropriate internal controls in place, determining compliance levels and making necessary adjustments to improve performance.

Life-Cycle Assessments. Efforts are under way in some settings to conduct a life-cycle assessment to measure the environmental impacts of products over their entire life cycle from cradle-to-grave, and they are shifting even more to cradle-to-cradle. The goal is to use life-cycle approaches to develop product systems with lower environmental impacts. In Germany and other countries in the EU, the government is drastically limiting what can go into the landfills.

Baxter International Inc., for example, produces and sells a wide range of products that help save, extend and improve the quality of people's lives worldwide. At each stage of the product life cycle, Baxter encounters social and environmental issues, from clinical trials and materials selection in research and development (R&D), to energy efficiency and waste minimization in manufacturing, to advertising and promotion and access to healthcare during product use and, finally, to responsible product disposal. Baxter recognizes the significant impact that product design decisions have at each stage of the product life cycle, so it includes a product sustainability review at the early stages of product development. This allows for full consideration of environmental, health and safety issues regarding material selection, usage, energy usage, and recyclability at each stage of the product life cycle. Baxter has policies and programs to address these important issues. Quality and safety are two issues that cut across the entire product life cycle. Baxter has programs to ensure the highest standards in these areas.[12]

Corporate Social Responsibility and Ethics. In addition to legal and regulatory reasons for environmental controls, some also make a case for environmental management on the basis of corporate social responsibility and ethics. Within its *Principles of Sustainability and Social Responsibility*, the Institute for Supply Management®(ISM®) defines social responsibility as "a framework of measurable organization policies and procedures and resulting behavior designed to benefit the workplace and, by extension, the individual, the organization and society. The principles are designed to enable both supply management and the organization to customize a framework specific to industry and supplier needs in the following areas: anti-corruption; diversity and inclusiveness — workforce and supply base; environment; ethics and business conduct; financial integrity and transparency; global citizenship; health and safety; human rights; and sustainability." It more specifically states in the environment principle that "Supply management promotes the protection, preservation and vitality of the natural environment."[13] The ISM statement on the environment is shown in Figure 12-3.

Figure 12-3: Principles of Sustainability and Social Responsibility: the Environment

Supply management promotes protection, preservation and vitality of the natural environment. In this context:
• Encourage the organization to be proactive in identifying and implementing environmentally responsible practices throughout the supply chain.
• Hold suppliers accountable for being environmentally responsible.
• Promote development and diffusion of environmentally friendly practices and products throughout the organization and supply chain.
• Champion consumption of environmentally responsible products and services.
• Support and influence the design of products to effect positive environmental improvements.
• Implement strategies to reduce and eliminate negative impact on the environment at the organization, supply chain and product levels.
• Develop a comprehensive understanding of environmental impacts across the supply chain.

Source: ISM *Principles of Sustainability and Social Responsibility*, 2012, http://www.ism.ws/SR/?nav ItemNumber=22324, accessed November 18, 2013.

Strategic approaches to environmental risk management range from a strict interpretation based on compliance with laws and regulations to a much broader view that focuses on looking for opportunities to enhance the brand, reputation or image of the organization through a more assertive commitment to environmental stewardship. Management teams in affected industries must develop an environmental risk profile and risk management strategy (see Chapter 5). The risk of loss stems from contractual, insurance and legal issues. Supply management professionals are in an excellent position to mitigate or eliminate risks from environmental violations occurring in the use, handling and disposal of hazardous materials. To maximize their contribution, the supply management team must have strong internal partnerships with design and environmental engineers and legal counsel. They must be recognized as key contributors starting with the earliest phases of the design process and continuing through disposal or reclamation. External customer requirements often drive design decisions. In this case, a cross-organizational initiative involving customers, designers and supply management professionals may be needed to eliminate or mitigate environmental risks.

Supply Management's Role

In a June 2013 joint report (Deloitte Consulting, the Corporate Responsibility Offer Association, ISM and the American Society for Quality) entitled "Sustainability Practices That Work — Results from the Sustainable Value Chain Survey," three broad categories of leading practices were tied to the achievement of sustainability goals. Supply management should play a leadership role in reaching these goals for the organization. They are supplier engagement, setting goals and standards, and use of external resources. These three practices led to increased performance levels between respondents whose companies had adopted a specific management practice versus those that had not.

Supplier engagement. The organizations that engaged their suppliers about sustainability had more successful initiatives; as a result they built stronger relationships with their suppliers, distribution/channels, complementary businesses and customers. Supplier engagement included three primary initiatives:

- *Engage with suppliers* — This included significant interactions that included direct interaction, discussion, and working together for trust and improvement, with emphasis on the joint effort to improve performance rather than just drive down costs. Some of the leading organizations in the study strove to instill a culture of sustainability throughout their own organization first to model the importance of the effort. The open conversations encouraged sustainable and innovation ideas from suppliers, including ways to redesign or refine products and processes.

- *Provide suppliers with tools, policies and processes* — This practice makes it easier for suppliers to meet an organization's requirements. The organization may be further along in sustainability practices, so a supplier might be able to more easily incorporate improvements into their own organization. Sharing will also set a tone of collaboration and engagement that could lead to joint efforts in the future. As one example, the research found that organizations that published supplier codes of conduct for use by all tiers of suppliers (not just direct, tier-one suppliers) reported more success in their value chain sustainability initiatives. Siemens provides web-based training for its value chain members to encourage adoption of sustainability initiatives.
- *Reward suppliers for sharing information with each other* — An organization's suppliers often work with each other and are amenable to knowledge sharing. Some suppliers may share common issues and have information that others can use to improve their operation and sustainability. This sharing could raise the level of performance for other suppliers in the supply chain. Besides knowledge sharing, the rewards can be monetary or non-monetary (such as rewarding collaboration with more business or by sharing cost savings with the suppliers). For example, MillerCoors asks a select number of their top suppliers to join the Supplier Ethical Data Exchange, which enables the company to collect data and understand the impact of their procurement processes on sustainability.

Goals and standards. The study showed that benefits were derived when organizations established quantitative goals and used international management standards.

- *Establish quantitative goals, not just qualitative ones* — Quantitative measures make it possible to monitor the progress of the sustainability initiatives as well as to measure and demonstrate the results. Goals also provide value by enabling organizations to engage their process improvement capabilities, such as the use of lean principles, Six Sigma and other improvement techniques the organization may use.
- *Use international management standards* — Using established standards provides the opportunity to learn from what others have done. Examples include ISO 26000, which provides guidance on how businesses and organizations can operate in a socially responsible way; and The Global Reporting Initiative, which serves as a generally accepted framework for reporting on an organization's economic, environmental and social performance. The advantage of using established frameworks enables organizations to benchmark with similar and different organizations.

External resources. Sustainability is a relatively new field, and it is difficult for an organization to have all the knowledge and skills necessary to succeed. Engaging with external resources increases the likelihood of success. Some activities would include engaging with complementary businesses; joining sustainability and supply chain organizations; and engaging outside specialists in value chain sustainability, if needed. This access to resources and information will increase the probability of success and also reduce costs in the organization's sustainability effort.[14] Figure 12-4 depicts a process that an organization might go through to achieve their sustainability goals.

Supply management professionals can be instrumental in programs designed to reduce consumption of materials and reduce the amount of waste that goes into landfills through the development of corporate collection and recycling programs. These programs may be internally or externally focused. There are many collection programs for electronic devices today. Usable materials are reclaimed and recycled, thus reducing landfill waste and organizational cost. Also, new businesses are created to collect, recycle and reuse these materials.

Figure 12-4: Sustainability Process

Establish sustainability goals	Design initiatives around goals	Select management practices backed by evidence	Implement and measure results
What are the organization's goals?	What initiatives support those goals?	Which practices does the evidence say are more likely to work?	What are the effects of resulting initiatives and managing practices on goals?
How do they connect to the business?	How can they improve business value?	What practices can increase business value?	What is the value of those outcomes?
Examples: • Reduce carbon footprint • Reduce cost	Examples: • Help suppliers carbon intensity • Help suppliers increase operational efficiency	Examples: • Reward suppliers for sharing with each other • Collaboratively engage with suppliers	Examples: • Reduce CO_2 emissions by 20% and water consumption by 10% over the following 5 years • Reduce supply chain risk with savings of $250 million

Source: "Sustainability Practices That Work-Results from the Sustainable Value Chain Survey," Deloitte Development LLC, Institute for Supply Management®, American Society for Quality and Corporate Responsibility Officers Association, p.9, September 2013.

In the 1990s, Hong Kong native Zhang Yin started a Los Angeles-based venture, America Chung Nam, to collect waste paper from the United States and Europe, ship it to China and recycle it into corrugated cardboard for boxes. Many of these boxes are returned to the United States, filled with toys, electronics and furniture. The boxes are then collected, procured by America Chung Nam and begin the cycle again. The organization is one of the world's biggest paper-trading organizations, with ties to recycling yards from the west coast to the east coast. Yin's partner organization, Nine Dragons Paper, is the world's largest papermaker.[15] Because China's paper industry is fueled by coal, the organization faces environmental risks depending on the government's steps toward cleaning up the air. Until then, the Chinese papermaker has an advantage over paper organizations operating in countries with more stringent environmental standards and therefore a higher cost structure.

Conducting Environmental Audits. An audit may be performed on internal environmental processes, policies and procedures, and on the supply chain. From a supply chain perspective, an environmental audit requires assessing both upstream and downstream activities. If customer-driven requirements are creating or increasing environmental risk, then efforts must be made to influence customers to see the benefits of design change, use of less hazardous substitutes and other initiatives that will mitigate the risk. As with most of the strategies discussed in this book, strong internal partnerships, along with external ones as well, are required for supply management to optimize its contribution.

ISM has developed a series of guiding questions that an organization can use as a starting point to help clarify an organization's current status. It includes 22 general questions applicable across all categories that provide a starting point for adoption and implementation of social responsibility and sustainability practices. These include the following:

1. Are you and your organization aware of sustainability and social responsibility standards and trends in your industry?
2. Does your organization comply with applicable laws and regulations covering sustainability and social responsibility?
3. Does your organization have written policies in place that cover the principles?
4. Are goals in place for each principle? What are they? How are improvements incorporated?

(For a complete listing, see, ISM *Principles of Sustainability and Social Responsibility, With a Guide to Adoption and Implementation*, 2012, accessed October 28, 2013, http://www.ism.ws/files/SR/PSSRwGuideBook.pdf p. 12-13.)

See Figure 12-5 for ISM's specific environmental audit questions.

> **Figure 12-5: ISM's Environmental Audit Questions**
>
> 1. Does the organization behave in environmentally responsible ways? What specific programs and procedures are in place?
> 2. Does the organization have programs to reduce, reuse and recycle? What percent of disposable waste is recycled? What does the organization do to reduce the volume of waste created that must then be recycled? How does the organization reduce waste? Reuse equipment and supplies?
> 3. How does the organization comply with laws and regulations in the handling of hazardous waste?
> 4. How does the organization report its environmental results?
> 5. How does the organization continue to learn what it needs to know about environmental and waste issues?
> 6. Does the organization collect copies of suppliers' environmental plans? Are the plans of suppliers assessed and approved by the supply management organization?
> 7. Does the organization work with engineering in the design of products for disassembly, reuse and recycling?
>
> *Source:* ISM *Principles of Sustainability and Social Responsibility, With a Guide to Adoption and Implementation*, 2012, accessed October 28, 2013, http://www.ism.ws/files/SR/PSSRwGuideBook.pdf, p. 14.

Reporting Requirements and Certification. The supply management team must also stay abreast of industry-specific and government reporting requirements, and any certifications that are required or advisable for the buying organization and its domestic and international suppliers. To meet these requirements the correct data must be collected, analyzed and prepared in the appropriate format and submitted in a timely manner. These steps should be built into supply management processes and systems to facilitate enterprisewide collection and reporting. The steps to acquiring the appropriate certification are listed below:

1. Determine which laws and regulations, and corresponding certifications, apply to your business.
2. Develop an environmental management system (EMS) that meets the appropriate regulations.
3. Conduct an internal audit of the environmental management system.
4. Have an accredited external audit performed.
5. If the audit is successful, receive certification by the accredited external auditing body.
6. Maintain certification.

Life-Cycle Controls. The supply management team may also be involved in assessing what, if any, risks exist if product components are available in the marketplace over the product's life cycle. The design stage offers the greatest opportunity to add value in terms of providing customers with the functionality they seek at the lowest total cost with the least harmful environmental impact. At Baxter International Inc., the new product development process consists of five phases: concept, feasibility, development, launch and post- launch support. A product sustainability review (PSR) is included in the design of all new medical devices. This review is a thorough assessment of the environmental, health and safety, and social impacts of a product; its materials; and its processes throughout its life cycle. A preliminary PSR in the concept stage identifies high-level sustainability issues, and a complete assessment in the feasibility stage identifies sustainability impacts across the life cycle. The information gathered during the review helps establish product requirements, influence design and confirm product feasibility. The PSR is designed to benefit Baxter, its customers and the environment in the following ways:

- *Compliance.* Assesses current and future regulatory concerns to ensure market access;
- *Customers.* Optimizes environmental attributes of products and facilitates response to environmentally preferable purchasing guidelines in customer requests for proposal;
- *Operational improvement.* Identifies cost-cutting opportunities, such as through decreased energy use or packaging reduction; and
- *Environment.* When possible, minimizes adverse life-cycle environmental impacts and risks.[16]

Life-Cycle Costing. Life-cycle costing is the process of calculating the cost of a product over its life cycle, from cradle-to-cradle, to maximize life-cycle profits. It is a cost analysis tool that incorporates the purchase price of a piece of equipment and all operating and related costs over the life of the item. It is a valuable tool that may be applied to environmental life-cycle assessments. The life-cycle cost components might include costs for planning, research and development, production, operation, energy costs, maintenance, cost of replacement, disposal or salvage. This cost analysis depends on values calculated from other reliability analyses such as failure rate, cost of spares, repair times and component costs.

Life-Cycle Analysis. Life-cycle analysis is part of the ISO 14000 family of environmental management standards. It refers to the process of including all tangible and intangible costs from conception (cradle) to disposal (grave). In the energy industry, for example, a life-cycle analysis of energy production starts with the initial project conception to the final step of returning the land to its original or next-use state. Tangible costs might include a range of cost components from facility construction, to fuel source development and post-extraction land remediation, to waste disposal. Intangible costs might include estimates of the impact because of the release of carbon into the environment; costs caused by unusually long licensing processes; political resistance for new or innovative methods of energy production; and the cost of plant decommissioning or funding needed, for example, to reclaim strip-mined areas. The goal is to calculate true lifetime costs and profitability of energy production.

End-of-Life Cycle. All too often, the costs associated with a product at the end of its life have not been fully considered in the earlier stages, such as design; or some change has occurred in laws and regulations, public perceptions or organizational risk tolerance. Part of an organization's risk profile includes projected issues related to end-of-product-life issues. Some organizations respond to laws and regulations and others are more proactive in taking voluntary action. For example, Fisher & Paykel Appliances, Ltd., a subsidiary of Haier, has a whiteware take-back system in New Zealand that saves around 25,000 appliances a year from going into landfill. It offers dealerships and service centers an alternative to disposing of appliances in landfills, collecting appliances in New Zealand's city centers. Fisher & Paykel can reuse or recycle the bulk of materials in appliances by weight.[17]

Two European Union (EU) directives, Waste Electrical and Electronic Equipment (WEEE) and the Restriction of the Use of Certain Hazardous Substances in Electrical and Electronic Equipment (RoHS), had far-reaching effects on electrical and electronic equipment manufacturers and distributors. The key objectives of the WEEE directive are the avoidance and reduction of waste from electrical and electronic equipment (EEE) and the recovery, recycling and reuse of EEE products. The updated 2012 WEEE directive gives EU member states not only established new collection targets but added the tools to fight illegal export of waste more effectively, and also forces exporters to test and provide documents on the nature of their shipments when the shipments run the risk of being waste.[18] RoHS was updated in 2011 and went from covering several categories of electrical and electronic equipment including household appliances, IT and consumer equipment, to covering all electronic equipment, cables and spare parts.[19] Compliance processes and procedures vary across the EU.

China is also developing its version of the EU's Restriction of the Use of Certain Hazardous Substances directive, which took effect March 1, 2007 with proposed revisions in 2012. The new China RoHS, officially now known as the Target Administrative Catalog for the Pollution Control of Electrical and Electronic Products, also restricts the use of certain hazardous substances such as lead, mercury, cadmium, hexavalent chromium and flame retardants. Products affected by the 2012 proposed China RoHS include electrical and electronic equipment. Many home appliances (washing machines, refrigerators) that fell out of the scope of the old China RoHS will be regulated by the new China RoHS. The standards will cover issues involving product design, development, manufacturing, labeling requirements, the sale of products and a flexible certification mechanism.[20]

The State Council, China's Cabinet, published the revised version of Regulations on Safe Management of Hazardous Chemicals in China on March 11, 2011(Decree 591). The regulation, which has clauses for the production, storage, import, use, sales and transporting of hazardous chemicals, was scheduled to come into force on December 1, 2013 and replaces the old version issued in 2002. The legislation mainly regulates hazardous chemicals, which are defined as highly toxic chemicals, and other chemicals which are toxic, corrosive, explosive, flammable and do harm to human body, facilities and environment.[21]

According to Baxter's 2012 Sustainability Report, "Baxter has worked with customers, industry peers, and recycling and disposal suppliers to facilitate the recycling and responsible treatment of disposable medical products."[22] In addition, in the product development phase, "Baxter's research and development and manufacturing operations work with environmental, health and safety (EHS) specialists to ensure that new products meet robust environmental design principles, comply with environmental regulations and satisfy customer requirements. As part of the company's product development process, Baxter applies a Product Sustainability Review (PSR) to all new medical devices, assessing EHS impacts across the product life cycle, including those related to materials selection and use. For example, new electrical and electronic devices under development are designed to meet the RoHS Directive guidelines wherever they are sold worldwide. All devices are screened for the presence of chemicals from the REACH (Registration, Evaluation and Authorisation and Restriction of Chemicals) Regulation list of "Substances of Very High Concern" (SVHCs) and are considered for elimination.[23] The responsible disposal of electronic healthcare products is an issue of concern worldwide. For example, the European Union's (EU) Waste Electrical and Electronic Equipment (WEEE) Directive impacts a range of products that Baxter sells in Europe, including dialysis machines, automated blood component collection systems, intravenous infusion pumps and other electronic hardware. The WEEE Directive, effective August 13, 2005 and updated in 2012, requires organizations to arrange for the collection, recycling and recovery of all types of electrical goods.[24]

Prior to WEEE regulations, Baxter embraced the principles behind the WEEE directive by repairing and refurbishing medical equipment, when appropriate, to extend its useful life. However, Baxter is also working to ensure full compliance with WEEE as the updated regulations setting recovery for non-implantable medical devices sold in the EU take effect in individual EU countries and appropriate registration bodies and compliance schemes are established.

Environmental regulations in Europe often influence those in other nations; several other countries, such as China, Korea, Taiwan and some U.S. states are implementing or considering legislation similar to WEEE. Baxter already has a global audit program for regulated or medical waste recycling or disposal sites, which will help it comply with regulations worldwide as they are developed.[25]

Supply management may be involved in deciding to what extent, if any, these and other laws, regulations and directives apply, determining the rules for compliance and developing and executing an action plan to ensure compliance. Supply management is in an excellent position to manage end-of-life-cycle programs because of strong relationships with suppliers, mechanisms in place to gather market intelligence and processes in place to collaborate with suppliers.

Internal Records Management

Records management is an organizationwide concern, especially with the increasing use of enterprisewide information technology, the importance of information in regulatory compliance and the role information plays in strategic and operational decision-making. Clearly, records and information management is a critical piece of organizational infrastructure that supports and enables far more than control and compliance. Some of these areas were discussed in Chapter 7. This section focuses on control and compliance aspects of records management, data management, information flow and the interface between and among various systems, such as materials management and financial systems, which reinforce the importance of the supply management team building strong internal partnerships with finance and IT.

Supply management professionals facilitate communication with internal partners and external suppliers, often within complex networks. To fully extract the competitive advantage available from strategic supply management, decision-makers need easy access to reliable data and information along with the ability to manage documents and records in a consistent manner. How the supply management group manages information may distinguish the highly effective supply management organization from a less effective one. Effective records management allows for smoother communication processes; provides internal control of transactions, funds and schedules; and provides a record of activities. These records are needed to research information, prove that actions did or did not occur, provide audit trails, and meet legal conditions and requirements. Standardized documentation allows for consistency, which helps ensure that all pertinent information is included, improves efficiency and makes it easier for users to access information.

The supply management team must develop, implement and maintain an electronic and/or physical filing system of relevant information. The goal should be to create a credible records and information management strategy that meets regulatory requirements; provides clean, transparent and accessible data for decision-makers; and incorporates the changing value of data over its life cycle to better control the cost of data and records management.

Regulatory Requirements. In many organizations, an enterprisewide document management system is available to facilitate compliance with internal, external and regulatory requirements. These include compliance with country-level regulatory agencies, such as the Securities and Exchange Commission in the United States, and with regulatory directives of self-regulatory organizations; state, province and regional directives; and international laws.

Certain records are required by law or regulation. For example, the Sarbanes-Oxley Act (discussed in Chapter 5 and later in this chapter) focuses on internal controls and is a key driver in records management systems at publicly traded organizations in the United States. The U.S. Uniform Commercial Code (UCC) influences records management because physical or electronic documentation of certain types of information is required. For example, a contract for the sale of goods valued at US$500 or more must be in writing to be legally enforceable. Even if there is no legal requirement, good judgment may lead decision-makers to document actions as part of a risk mitigation strategy to prevent the need for legal action or assist in the successful resolution if legal action is required.

The U.S. Privacy Act places restrictions on access to some types of information. It is important to understand this when designing documents and systems. In governmental purchasing, most (if not all) purchasing documents are a matter of public record and are subject to public view. Legal advice is often necessary when dealing with Privacy Act/public information implications of document design and management.

Organizational policies are also developed to define internal rules, regulations and guidelines for records and database management. These policies align with management's interpretation of applicable legal and regulatory requirements, support internal strategies and goals, and reflect organizational risk profiles and risk appetite.

Domestic and International Issues. Organizations that operate outside the borders of their own countries and trading blocs face similarities and differences in records management requirements. Common external forces include the following:
- Increasing litigation, legislation and government oversight;
- Demand for business process transparency;
- International sourcing and transparency; and
- Privacy and data security concerns.

Differences may exist in requirements around the world. Even if regulations and laws are not that different, cultural or local approaches to recordkeeping and information management still may present challenges for the supply management leadership team that is trying to standardize data classification, collection and reporting.

Records Management. *Records management* is a traditional term that formerly referred to the systematic control of physical records or documentation from creation or receipt through processing, distribution, maintenance and retrieval to ultimate disposition. Today, this includes paper; electronic messages; website content, documents that reside on PDAs, flash drives, desktops, servers; and any document management systems as well as company databases.[26] Records policies typically address the following items:
1. Define what information constitutes a record.
2. Establish a records classification system.
3. Establish standard operating procedures, and tag new and existing records accordingly.
4. Develop a storage plan to house physical and digital records for the short term and the long term.
5. Establish a policy for internal and external access to classes of records.
6. Establish a retention policy to archive records and determine when and how records will be destroyed based on internal and external needs and requirements.
7. Establish audit metrics.

The International Organization for Standardization has established ISO 15489:2001, which includes the following activities in records management: setting policies and standards; assigning responsibilities and authorities; establishing and promulgating procedures and guidelines; providing a range of services relating to the management and use of records; designing, implementing and administering specialized systems for managing records; and integrating records management into business systems and processes.[27]

Data/Records Management System Requirements and Capabilities. The incorporation of Electronic Records Management Systems (ERMS) and practices provides structure, consistency, security and control over an organization's records. It is the centralized control of the information assets of organizations. An enterprisewide classification scheme within an ERMS allows an organization to establish and manage the following items:

- Retention and disposition rules;
- Security and access controls;
- Digital rights management;
- Information sharing; and
- Findability.[28]

Establishing system requirements and capabilities is complicated by the volume and complexity of data that must be managed. *Information governance*, or IG, is an emerging term in the world of records management. Gartner defines it as "The specification of decision rights and an accountability framework to encourage desirable behavior in the valuation, creation, storage, use, archival and deletion of information. It includes the processes, roles, standards and metrics that ensure the effective and efficient use of information in enabling an organization to achieve its goals."[29] This is a changing landscape, and everyone in the organization is responsible for understanding the organization's policies on records retention. A strong partnership with IT is necessary to determine which systems will best serve the strategic and operational needs of supply management.

ISO 17799 provides a framework for creating an information security program, including policies and procedures, assigning roles and responsibilities, documenting operational procedures, preparing for incident and business continuity management, and complying with legal requirements and audit controls.[30]

Data Classification. Data classification is the process of assigning a level of sensitivity to data as it is being created, amended, enhanced, stored or transmitted. The classification of data determines the extent to which the data needs to be controlled or secured based on the risk of loss if the data were lost, stolen or revealed. Organizational policies are developed to protect the confidentiality, integrity and availability of data generated, accessed, modified, transmitted, stored or used by the organization.

The supply management organization generates and/or maintains various types of information, including specifications, supplier data, supplier performance data, products/services, contracts, spend, tariffs, routing guides and technical assistance agreements. These data sets must be categorized and coded in a standard way if decision-makers are to access and use the data. For example, data may be classified as public, official use only and confidential. The supply management team may decide that requests for proposals with attached specifications, the supplier ethical code of conduct, information on doing business with the organization, and goods and services that the organization routinely purchases are tagged as public. Supplier information including performance data may be tagged as official use only with individual suppliers granted access to their own data, but cannot access any other suppliers' information. Contracts, spend data and supply management strategy documents may be tagged as confidential with access limited to specific people.

One of the biggest challenges for many supply management teams is having access to clean, current spend data. Proper contract and spend management systems, generally purchased from a third party, can provide that solution. A critical aspect of that is classifying commodities for meaningful analysis.

Data classification schemas for commodity coding are developed by individual organizations, industries and national and international organizations. One data classification system that is widely used in organizations around the world is the United Nations Standard Products and Services Code® (UNSPSC®). This open, global electronic commerce standard provides a logical framework for classifying goods and services, and allows commodities and products to be properly and uniquely classified. The hierarchical structure of the UNSPSC® allows drilling down and rolling up, which is integral for tactical and strategic spend analysis. It is a global standard and is freely available to the public with no copyright protection issues. Many organizations develop their own customer taxonomies because of the perceived added value. Figure 12-6 lists and describes some cross-industry commodity coding schemas commonly used in the international arena.

The chief supply management professional can lay the foundation for strong internal controls on records and information in three ways: (1) consider the risks associated with information and records when developing strategies, policies and processes; (2) incorporate short-term and long-term technology needs into talent planning and role redesign; and (3) build a strong alliance with the chief information officer. Operational leaders and managers will have to deal with the daily challenges of building and maintaining the IT infrastructure necessary to support supply management strategies.

Figure 12-6: Common Cross-Industry Commodity Coding Schemas

CODING SYSTEM		DESCRIPTION
CPV	Common Procurement Vocabulary	Used in the European Union in public procurement transactions to group together the products of similar producers. A unique number system, nonhierarchical, does not allow for aggregation for financial reporting.
EAN	International Article Number	Most widely used. Used in conjunction with the Uniform Code Council to form the EAN/UCC product codes. Provides an application identifier that identifies products by bar code. They are necessary when selling products such as in the retail store or online. It is required for an online seller to buy UPC codes; others buy EAN codes when selling through different sites.
ISIC	International Standard Industry Classification	Nonhierarchichal (does not provide MI potential). Geared toward central economic statistical gathering of industry information. It is a standard United Nations Statistics Division (UNSD) classification of economic activities.
NAICS	North American Industrial Classification	At supplier level; code not applied to the product itself. Widely used adopted standard in the U.S. Supplier-related application.
NSV	National Supplier Vocabulary	UK Government standard for item-level coding; allows cross comparison of all spend data at all levels; provides a standard detailed description of everything purchased by government; provides the detailed information for cross comparison of all government expenditure at item level. It would also allow the carbon footprinting of all purchases since NSV is mapped to E2Class
UNSPSC®	United Nations Standard Product and Services Code®	Offers a single global classification system that can be used for companywide visibility of spend analysis, cost-effective procurement optimization, and full exploitation of electronic commerce capabilities

CHAPTER 12: Establishing Internal Controls and Ensuring Compliance

Internal Financial Controls

Financial controls relate to the financial reporting process that is designed to ensure that financial statements prepared for external reporting comply with generally accepted accounting principles (GAAP) in the United States or IFRS (International Financial Reporting Standards) globally. These controls generally include policies and procedures that enable an organization to properly initiate, record, process and report financial data consistent with the assertions embodied in either the annual or interim financial statements.

The supply management team has a duty and responsibility to verify the existence, accuracy and completeness of relevant financial transactions and commitments to third parties. This is accomplished in two ways: (1) supply management must ensure that these transactions and commitments are made in accordance with organizational financial reporting policies; and (2) supply management must adhere to the requirements of laws, such as Sarbanes-Oxley; to applicable regulations from regulatory bodies, such as the Federal Energy Regulatory Commission (FERC); and to any applicable international regulations. A strong internal partnership between supply management and finance with accurate and timely communication provides the basis for fulfilling supply management's role in financial reporting.

The U.S. Sarbanes-Oxley (SOX) Act of 2002

The Sarbanes-Oxley Act focuses on corporate governance and financial disclosure. Effective in 2006, all publicly traded corporations are required to submit an annual report of the effectiveness of their internal accounting controls to the SEC. Provisions of the Sarbanes-Oxley Act detail criminal and civil penalties for noncompliance, certification of internal auditing and increased financial disclosure. It affects public U.S. organizations and non-U.S. organizations with a U.S. presence.

Each organization must report the following on a quarterly basis:
- Design of controls over relevant financial statement assertions;
- Information about how significant transactions are initiated, recorded, processed and reported;
- Sufficient information to identify where material misstatements because of error or fraud could occur;
- Controls designed to prevent or detect fraud, including who performs them and the related segregation of duties;
- Controls over period-end financial reporting processes;
- Controls over safeguarding of assets; and
- Results of management testing and evaluation.[31]

Sections 401(a), 404 and 409 of Sarbanes-Oxley have the most relevance for supply management.

Section 401(a): Off-Balance-Sheet Obligations. This section requires all financial obligations to be transparent. For the supply management organization, four areas involve off-balance-sheet obligations: (1) supplier-managed inventory systems where the purchasing organization has an obligation to pay for cancellation or other penalties; (2) long-term purchase agreements that have a penalty clause; (3) lease agreements where there is a financial obligation if the purchasing organization terminates the lease; and (4) letters of intent where the purchasing organization commits to a supplier to get in a long lead time production schedule and there is a cancellation clause with financial impact. The chief financial officer needs to be informed quarterly of such agreements and the potential financial obligations.

In its 2013 Annual Report, for example, Federal Express Corp. reported other cash obligations not included in its balance sheet. These included amounts in non-cancelable agreements to purchase goods or services that are not capital-related. Such contracts include those for printing, advertising and promotions contracts. The line items listed in Figure 12-6 for capital purchase obligations represent non-cancelable agreements to purchase capital-related equipment. Such contracts include those for certain purchases of aircraft, aircraft modifications, vehicles, facilities, computers and other equipment.[32] These types of disclosures are now required by Sarbanes-Oxley to present a clearer picture of an organization's true financial standing. Figure 12-7 is an example of the format used for capturing the data related to off-balance-sheet contractual obligations. The supply management organization may be a primary source of data for leasing information and purchase obligations.

Figure 12-7: Off-Balance-Sheet Contractual Obligations Sample

(in millions)	2014	2015	2016	2017	2018	Thereafter	Total
Operating activities:							
Operating leases							
Non-capital purchase obligations and other							
Interest on long-term debt							
Contributions to our U.S. Pension Plans							
Investing activities:							
Aircraft and aircraft-related capital commitments							
Other capital purchase obligations							
Debt							
Total							

Source: Federal Express 2013 Annual Report, p. 26, available from http://investors.fedex.com/phoenix.zhtml?c=73289&p=irol-reportsannual

Section 404: Internal Controls. The supply management team must address four areas related to internal controls: (1) inventory and inventory write-offs, (2) material transfers, (3) after-the-fact purchase orders, and (4) segregation of duties. Internal inventory controls relate to financial transparency. This means that what is on the books as a financial asset can be physically located, the stated value reflects true market value, and the accounting and materials management systems are in sync. Accurate information about material transfers should be transmitted from the supply management system to the financial system to reflect the current financial condition of the organization. The supply management organization must also demonstrate that established purchase policies and procedures related to requisitioning and purchasing authority are communicated internally and controls are in place to ensure internal compliance. To prevent, deter and detect fraud, SOX also focuses on segregation of duties. For supply management, it is especially important to ensure that those with the authority to purchase goods and services cannot receive and pay for goods and services.

Compliance with the internal controls requirements of SOX supports the business case for developing a structured, disciplined supply management process with complete spend visibility, controlled procurement and optimized contracts, and contract compliance. For example, many food-service organizations find it difficult to get full spend visibility and contract compliance from each and every restaurant unit, and have difficulties in reconciling the back-end of the process and ensuring that pricing agreements and rebates are accurate. SOX requirements can be used to drive improvements in the procure-to-pay flow path while also enabling the supply management team to drive down food costs, rationalize SKUs and suppliers, improve back-end processes and monitor unit compliance.

Section 409: Timely Reporting of Material Events. A material event is one that will materially impact financial reporting. Two situations may be material events on the supply management side: (1) late supplier deliveries that cause revenue forecast to be missed, and (2) third-party providers (outsource partners) that cannot provide goods and services, resulting in a misstatement of revenues.

For example, a commodity manager is notified by a first-tier supplier that it is unable to meet the agreed-on delivery schedule because a second-tier supplier is unable to obtain critical inputs from a sole source. This would be reported as a material event if the supply disruption prevented customer deliveries and adversely affected revenue projections.

Legal and Regulatory Controls

Supply management processes, policies and procedures include many components that are affected by laws and regulations. For this reason, internal legal controls are especially important areas for the supply management professional. The primary responsibility is to assess and forecast legal exposure arising from supply management before, during and after the execution of an activity; and from all sources, including processes, policies and procedures; or noncompliance with laws relating to contracts, intellectual property, employment and the environment both domestically and internationally. For this reason, one of the supply management professional's most important internal relationships is with chief legal counsel.

Legal areas addressed in this section are (1) agency law and authority, (2) role of legal counsel, and (3) types of laws with which supply management should be familiar.

Agency and Authority

Agency law defines the "legal relationship that exists between two parties by which one (the agent) is authorized to perform or transact specified business activities for the other (the principal)" (ISM *Glossary* 2014). First, an agent has a *fiduciary duty* to the principal meaning that it is an "individual's obligation to serve the best interests of selected stakeholders, especially those of his or her employer or principal in an agency relationship" (ISM *Glossary* 2014). Violations of fiduciary duty occur if, in making a deal, an agent accepts a gratuity or kickback or has some personal interest (financial or otherwise) in the supplier. Second, the principal is bound by the agent's action. The organization is legally obligated to perform under a contract signed by an agent. Third, by corollary, the agent has no personal liability under the contract, assuming the agent had actual authority and did nothing wrong.

Authority is the "right granted to an agent to act (engage in legally binding transactions) on behalf of a principal" (the employer) (ISM *Glossary* 2014). Three types of authority affect the supply management organization: actual, implied and apparent authority. *Actual authority* is the "specific authority given to an agent by a principal" (ISM *Glossary* 2014). Along with actual authority, an individual is granted incidental authority or implied authority. *Implied authority* is "part of actual authority given by a principal to an agent. When the principal is less than comprehensive in describing the actual authority given, the law implies whatever is necessary to accomplish the principal's expressed intent" (ISM *Glossary* 2014). *Apparent authority* is the "type of authority created in an agency relationship when a principal permits an individual to operate in a fashion that allows third parties to believe that the individual is an authorized agent of the principal. It represents unauthorized purchasing or bypassing of the purchasing function by other functions within an organization" (ISM *Glossary* 2014). For example, someone in an organization without actual authority orders goods and services that are received and payment is made. To the supplier, the person appears to have the authority to purchase based on the actions taken via receipt and payment. By making payment on an unauthorized purchase, the organization makes it look as if the actions of the buyer were authorized. Apparent authority is just as valid legally as actual authority as far as the contracting parties are concerned. The difference is for the agent: agents acting with apparent authority expose themselves to personal liability to the principal. *Ratification* is the "after-the-fact approval by a principal of an otherwise unauthorized action taken by an agent" (ISM *Glossary* 2014). Ratification (1) creates a valid contract between the principal or employer and the supplier, and (2) excuses the agent from any personal liability.

Typically, authority is delegated based on some criterion such as financial levels or budget ownership, and limits are placed on this authority. For example, purchasers (agents) in the supply management department are given the authority to purchase specific goods and services with set dollar limits.

By defining authority for purchasing and contracting, top management communicates to employees the seriousness with which senior management takes spend management and fiduciary duties. It also communicates to suppliers the degree of rigor and discipline that the buying organization brings to the marketplace. Risk exposure was defined earlier as the probability of a loss multiplied by the expected impact. In the case of agency and authority, the probability of a loss is high if an organization is not properly managing both the actual and apparent authority of employees. Likewise, if agency and authority are loosely controlled, there is the potential for a greater impact or loss. For example, it is more difficult to track spend, improve spend visibility and manage spend when agency status is diffused. It is also easier for suppliers to gather information, possibly proprietary or damaging information, when employees lacking supply management training engage in contact with suppliers. Loss may also occur in terms of paying higher prices, agreeing to unfavorable terms and conditions, and compromising the supply management organization's leverage in future deals.

The link between process rigor and law is therefore a critical one. The supply management professional must rely on his or her strong internal partnerships with chief legal counsel and peers at the executive level, and have influence over process integrity, to ensure that the law of agency and limits to authority are calculated and understood as legal risk exposure that is endogenous in nature (meaning it is a risk that is completely within the bounds of internal actions to eliminate).

Role of Legal Counsel

A supply management professional's decisions must be legally as well as economically sound. The prudent supply management professional uses legal counsel primarily to avoid difficulties in the discharge of duties as agent for the organization. Major areas that may require advice from legal counsel are outlined below:

- Standard purchase order terms and conditions;
- Applicable international and domestic laws that affect standard terms and conditions;
- Standard and customized RFQ or RFP terms;
- Purchase orders and solicitations for goods or services where Uniform Commercial Code (UCC) or common law is applicable;
- Warranty disclaimers and subsequent strength of express and implied warranties;
- Liability caps that are unrealistic relative to potential risk;
- Financially troubled or bankrupt suppliers;
- Bid or performance bonds, or progress payments added to the terms of a contract;

- Supplier acknowledgments materially changing the terms and conditions of the contract;
- Supplier alliance agreements. (*Alliance* is defined as a close relationship between a buyer and a seller to attain some advantages from each other in a positive way. Buyer-seller alliances may be of operational importance, such as a long-term, single-source relationship with an office supplier, or of strategic importance, such as a long-term, single-source relationship with a supplier of a good or service of strategic importance.)

A supply management professional should consult with legal counsel whenever there is doubt on any questions concerning antitrust implications, risk of loss and indemnification, or the rights and remedies of the organization, including limitations of liability. Responsibility lies with the supply management professional to maintain an appropriate balance between the legal and business issues for each decision.

Types of Laws With Which Supply Management Should be Familiar

Throughout the world there exist a variety of laws and legal requirements that directly or indirectly impact the role of the supply management professional. Some of these laws will be multinational in nature, such as treaties or other agreements between multiple countries establishing rules or practices that are then common to the particular group of countries involved. Others of these laws will be unique to an individual country, with or without similarities to the same type of law in other countries. Some laws may be specific to a particular industry but again may vary from country to country. Very rare (if existent at all) is any law that is the same worldwide.

In some situations the law will be found in some sort of legal code or other written document. In "Common Law" jurisdictions, however, such as England and Wales, the United States and other countries that were influenced by the British in establishing their legal systems, some legal rules are derived from judgments and decisions of courts recognizing long-time use and societal custom. Common law is distinguishable from civil code law (sometimes referred to as "Roman" law) systems followed in continental Europe and most of the rest of the world. These code systems do not rely on custom and usage but rather on explicit codes of behavior established by the governing authority. In addition to specific laws enacted by a legislative body, most countries also have rules and regulations that are promulgated by administrative agencies to carry out those laws. These rules and regulations often contain detailed requirements and/or prohibitions intended to implement specific laws. In some Muslim countries, such as Saudi Arabia, judicial systems may be based on the Quran and Sunnah, which comes from the teachings and practices of Islamic prophet Muhammad.

The following discussion is intended to provide an introduction to and overview of the types of laws with which the supply management professional should be familiar. This general information may or may not be applicable in any particular country or industry. Supply management professionals must satisfy themselves that all legal requirements of the locations in which they do business have been considered and met. This is critical because failure to comply with applicable legal requirements can result in significant problems for both the organizations and individuals involved, including fines, confiscation of goods and lawsuits.

Resources are provided to assist supply management professionals to locate information specific to individual countries and/or regions.

Agency. The purpose of agency law is to permit one party, the principal, to accomplish an objective using the services of another, the agent (that is, giving power to one party to act on behalf of another). This is particularly useful in the commercial world because most business organizations are legal entities (corporations, for example) that cannot act for themselves. In general, the agent is authorized to act under the control of and for the benefit of the principal in dealings with third parties. The agent, in effect, functions as an intermediary. For example, when an agent acts on behalf of a principal in a contract situation, the agent will deal with a third party, but the resulting contract will be between the principal and the third party.

Agency is a consensual relationship, meaning that the principal and the agent must both agree to it. The agency relationship constitutes a contract between them. That contract imposes, either by law or by agreement of the parties, certain duties, obligations and rights on each of the parties.

Agency relationships exist in various situations: Employees may be agents of their employers; corporate officers are agents of the corporation; government officials are agents of the governmental unit; and partners are agents of the partnership. More specifically, supply management professionals function as agents for the organizations that employ them, as do sales representatives. Freight forwarders and customs brokers are other examples of agents.

Listed below are additional examples of the agency relationship:
- The Civil Code of the Philippines includes a definition of the relationship of agency as one where "a person binds himself to render some service or to do something in representation or on behalf of another, with the consent or authority of the latter." An agent might also be referred to as "attorney-in-fact," "proxy," "delegate" or "representative."
- In South Africa common law, principles concerning agency have been modified to some extent by Constitutional and statutory law in the post-apartheid period. The law requires some designations of agency to be in writing.

Contract and Commercial Laws. A *contract* is an agreement that courts will enforce, establishes a legal relationship between the contracting parties, and creates binding obligations that must be met by the parties. Contract law may be the primary legal concern of supply management; it governs the enforceability of contractual agreements, including their formation and performance.

The degree of formality required for the formation of a contract varies from country to country. For example, U.S. law (found in Article 2 of the Uniform Commercial Code) requires that contracts for the sale of goods for US$500 or more be documented in writing. No such requirement exists in English law or in the U.N. Convention on Contracts for the International Sale of Goods (CISG), a treaty entered into by more than 75 countries that may govern international goods transactions. Oral agreements are widely accepted and completely enforceable in various countries around the world.

With regard to the actual requirements for performance of a contract, many jurisdictions (especially those following concepts of the common law) show strong deference to the intentions of the parties, as reflected in written documents or otherwise. Other countries may impose various performance requirements on the parties or may by law limit what parties can actually agree to. In 1994 UNIDROIT, the International Institute for the Unification of Private Law, issued *Principles of International Commercial Contracts* reflecting concepts found in many, if not all, legal systems. These principles are tailored to the needs of international commercial transactions and represent a balanced set of rules designed for use throughout the world irrespective of legal traditions and political conditions of the countries. They are, however, just "principles" and are not binding on contracting parties.

When contracting, the parties themselves may be able to determine which country's law will apply to their contract by means of a "Choice of Law" provision in the contract itself. Courts in many countries will defer to such a choice made by the parties; others may not.

Listed below are several examples:

- A group known as the Hague Conference on Private International Law (HccH) has done extensive work on a set of draft principles concerning Choice of Law for international contracts that may be adopted by individual countries, but there is no requirement that law or courts of any individual country follow these principles. Approximately 75 countries currently participate in the HccH.
- In 1994 five countries (Bolivia, Brazil, Mexico, Uruguay and Venezuela), as part of the Organization of American States, adopted the Inter-American Convention on the Law Applicable to International Contracts.
- The European Commission's Convention on the Law Applicable to Contractual Obligations became effective in 1991 in EU member nations. The treaty calls for courts to honor any choice of law clearly made by the parties; if no choice is indicated by the parties, the appropriate choice would be the country with which the contract is most closely connected. There are special rules for certain consumer contracts and employment contracts.

Commercial law generally refers to a variety of laws applicable to the rights and relationships of parties engaged in commerce, trade and other related pursuits. These laws might include rules and principles governing security interests (applicable when a purchase is made on credit), letters of credit, negotiable instruments (checks, bank drafts, etc.) and bank deposits, as well as warehouse receipts and bills of lading.

Electronic Commerce. *Electronic commerce* refers to business that is conducted over the Internet or other computer networks. It includes a number of applications — email, electronic data interchange (EDI), web services, electronic funds transfers, and others. Since the mid-1990s, with the growth of electronic commerce, many countries have adopted laws governing this area. Typically these laws do not change the underlying substantive law (for example, contract law) but rather provide for how substantive law requirements can be met in an electronic environment. In addition to the legalities involved, security risks are a major concern with electronic commerce of any kind and may be subject to specific requirements when business dealings involve governmental agencies.

Following are some examples of electronic commerce laws:

- In 2000 the European Commission adopted *Directive 2000/31/EC* governing electronic commerce in the European Union. The Directive's stated purpose is to provide legal certainty for both businesses and consumers doing business electronically.
- In the U.S. laws governing electronic commerce have been adopted at both the federal and state levels. The federal law, known as the *Electronic Signatures in Global and National Commerce Act*, was adopted in 2000. Most individual states in the U.S. have adopted some version of the *Uniform Electronic Transaction Act* (UETA), which is more comprehensive than the federal law, establishing rules related to electronic signatures, records retention and timing of contract formation.
- By comparison, China only started in 2013 to try to regulate electronic commerce in that country, possibly in response to what was seen as widespread abuse in what is a very large market.

Antitrust. Antitrust law may be referred to as "Competition Law" in some countries, and often falls under a category known as "Economic Law." Rather than focusing directly on the relationship between contracting parties, this body of law is concerned with the impact such relationships might have on business or the marketplace as a whole. These types of laws are primarily aimed at anti-competitive behavior and/or the abuse of dominant market power. The laws make illegal certain practices deemed to hurt businesses or consumers, or both, or generally to violate standards of ethical behavior. They may address such concerns as price fixing, boycotts, exclusive dealing arrangements and/or deceptive trade practices.

Examples of antitrust issues are listed below:
- The European Union's competition law addresses four areas of concern: cartels and collusion, market dominance and monopolies, mergers and acquisitions, and government aid given to companies. This government aid perspective is somewhat unique to competition law in the EU. Member nations of the EU may have their own individual competition laws and agencies for enforcement of the same.
- Similarly, India's *Competition Act, 2002*, covers four areas in its substantive provisions: anti-competitive agreements, abuse of dominance, regulation of combinations (mergers) and advocacy of competition.
- Certain international trade agreements (such as the World Trade Organization [WTO]) may include language addressing issues relating to competition and the application of various laws at the international level.

As with other areas of law there is no one international body of law governing competition worldwide. When cross-border transactions are involved, a determination must be made as to which specific country's competition law will apply. In the absence of any global agreement on the enforcement of competition laws, many bilateral agreements exist between individual countries. For example, the U.S. has separate agreements with Australia, Brazil, Canada, the EU, Germany, Israel, Japan and Mexico. These agreements often provide for sharing of information on enforcement activities, notification of policy changes and discussion of matters of mutual interest.

Trade Agreements. *Trade agreements* are arrangements made between or among countries addressing taxes, tariffs and other trade policies between the participating countries. They may be bilateral (between two countries or trading blocs) or multilateral (involving more than two countries). Often these agreements are preferential in nature, seeking to reduce trade restrictions such as tariffs or quotas. *Free trade agreements* seek to eliminate such restrictions altogether.

The *General Agreement on Tariffs and Trade* (GATT) came into being after World War II. The GATT included a number of rounds of negotiations over the years, including the Marrakech Agreement that gave rise to the *World Trade Organization* (WTO) in 1995. As of March 2013, 159 countries were members of the WTO; an additional 25 countries held "observer" status (observer status generally leads to full membership). Only 14 countries are nonmembers.

Most of the individual agreements negotiated under GATT remain in effect, dealing with such topics as those listed below:
- Agriculture,
- Anti-dumping,
- Customs valuation,
- Rules of origin, and
- Import licensing.

The WTO subsequently has adopted various agreements dealing with these issues:
- Trade in goods,
- Trade in services,
- Trade-related aspects of intellectual property rights, and
- Dispute settlement.

The European Union constitutes a very complex form of trade agreement, governing a broad range of commercial relationships between and among its member nations. By contrast, the *North American Free Trade Agreement* (NAFTA), involving Canada, the U.S. and Mexico, is a much more limited example of this type of agreement.

International Trade. International trade regulations are typically part of various trade agreements and are incorporated into the laws of individual countries. These regulations address customs, duties, dumping, embargoes, free trade zones, intellectual property, quotas and subsidies. Typically, countries that participate in trade agreements maintain government offices (often multiple government offices) that handle application and enforcement of trade regulations. Any time international sourcing is involved, supply management must consider the impact and requirements of these regulations.

Some examples of international trade regulations are listed below:
- In the U.S., one responsible organization is the International Trade Administration (ITA), which is a bureau within the U.S. Department of Commerce. The ITA is made up of four separate business units that handle
  - U.S. and foreign commercial service,
  - Manufacturing and services,
  - Market access and compliance, and
  - Import administration.

Also playing significant roles in this area are the Bureau of Customs and Border Protection (Department of Homeland Security), Animal and Plant Inspection Service (Department of Agriculture) and the Transportation Security Administration (Department of Homeland Security).
- In the Philippines the Department of Trade & Industry is made up of multiple offices that handle such matters as Export Trade Promotion and Import Services. This department also manages international relations, such as the various multilateral trade agreements to which the Philippines is a party. In addition, the Tariff Commission establishes Rules of Origin, tariffs and Most Favored Nation rate schedules.
- The stated mission of the Canadian International Trade Tribunal is "to render sound, transparent and timely decisions in trade, customs and procurement cases for Canadian and international businesses, and to provide the Government with sound, transparent and timely advice in tariff, trade, commercial and economic matters." The Trade Con-

trol and Technical Barriers Bureau administer the *Export and Import Permits Act*. Import controls apply to textiles and clothing, agricultural products, steel products, and weapons and munitions.

Industry-Specific Laws and Regulations. In many countries individual types of industries or businesses may be subject to government oversight in some way. Usually this oversight comes in the form of laws adopted by some governing authority (Congress, parliament or other legislative body) and carried out and enforced by a governmental administrative body through the promulgation of rules and regulations. The oversight is often justified by the risks posed by the particular industry or by the need to exercise market control over a functional service that is subject to little or no competition (such as utility services). Some of this type of regulation may be intended for the protection of the environment (refer to the discussion of *Environmental*), for the protection of a country's economic system (refer to the discussions of *Antitrust and Finance*), for the protection of individual consumers (one example is food and drug regulation) or for the protection of the general public (an example is regulation of construction or transportation services). For some industries in some countries, government involvement may go beyond regulation to actual ownership or participation in ownership.

Two industry-specific examples are listed below:
- Energy sector — Many countries regulate various aspects of energy development and/or distribution. In many jurisdictions, such regulation is directed toward health, safety and environmental concerns. In others the focus may be on assuring participation in economic benefits. In Brazil four different government agencies are involved — the Ministry of Mines and Energy; the National Council for Energy Policy, the National Agency of Petroleum, Natural Gas and Biofuels; and the National Agency of Electricity. In addition, government-owned Petrobrás and Electrobrás are major energy production companies.
- Pharmaceuticals — Motivated primarily by concerns for the safety of the consuming public, many countries regulate pharmaceuticals. In India the Central Drugs Standard Control Organization, part of the Ministry of Health and Family Welfare, regulates new drugs, clinical trials, importation, medical devices, blood banks, narcotics and cosmetics.

Government Procurement. Although government entities are generally bound by the same principles of contract law that govern private entities, there are often numerous additional laws and/or regulations that apply to government procurement and are absolute, leaving no room for negotiation with suppliers. These additional government-related requirements may dictate competitive bidding practices, the inclusion of specific kinds of clauses in contracts, compliance with certain labor-related standards (for example, wages and hours) as well as stipulating supplier/contractor and subcontractor qualifications.

Some governments will give preferential treatment to locally-owned contractors or to contractors that come from historically disadvantaged groups. It should be remembered that government procurement can occur at multiple levels within a given country — federal, state and local.

Some examples of public procurement are listed below:
- Under the public procurement rules of the European Union, various policies encourage focus on such considerations as "green" procurement (with regard to the environment, energy and transportation), socially responsibly public procurement (such as equal opportunity, accommodation of people with disabilities, compliance with social and labor rights), ethical trade, small business (providing easier access to public procurement) and a European Neighborhood policy.
- In Brazil the federal constitution provides the framework for public procurement at the federal, state and local levels. The *Public Procurement Act* provides for specific regulation within that constitutional framework. A further law enacted in 2011 sets out provisions governing public procurement associated with the 2016 Olympics and Paralympic Games, the 2013 FIFA Confederations Cup and the 2014 FIFA World Cup.
- In Australia all departments and agencies are required to comply with the 2012 Commonwealth Procurement Rules (CPRs) administered by the Department of Finance and Deregulation. These rules are divided according to various objectives, including encouraging competition, ethical procurement, accountability and transparency, risk management and procurement methodology.

Intellectual Property. *Intellectual property* (IP) refers to intangible personal property (one source refers to it as "products of the mind"), such as copyrights, patents, trademarks, service marks and trade secrets. Each of these has an inherent commercial value that governments may choose to protect. The purpose behind granting protection is to encourage authors, inventors and developers by providing economic incentives that result from exclusivity. Whether IP is owned by an individual or an organization, their own or that of a supplier, supply management professionals should respect these valuable property rights, take steps to protect them, and take care not to violate them in the course of their work.

Law protecting IP starts at the national level. There is no one international body of law protecting IP. In other words, filing for and obtaining a patent from the U.S. Patent Office affords protection within the U.S. Whether such protection extends outside U.S. borders depends on the existence of bilateral or multilateral agreements between the U.S. and other countries. There is an international body, the World Intellectual Property Organization (WIPO), that seeks to address issues involving IP at the international level and to bring into alignment the IP laws of different countries. There are at least ten international treaties or agreements that address various aspects of IP protection.

Some examples of these agreements include the following:

- The *Berne Convention for the Protection of Literary and Artistic Works*, agreed to by 166 countries, extends copyright protection granted in one country to all other participating countries.
- The *Hague Agreement Concerning the International Registration of Industrial Designs*, in which 60 countries or intergovernmental organizations participate, allows an owner of an industrial design to obtain protection in multiple countries by filing an application with the WIPO. Such registration provides protection of the registered design in each of the designated countries without the need for separate registration in each country.
- The WIPO's *Trademark Law Treaty*, agreed to by 53 countries (including China, Japan, the EU, the Russian Federation, South Africa and the U.S.), is an attempt to streamline national and regional trademark registration procedures.

Environmental. Environmental law encompasses a broad area of law that is addressed at the international, national, state and local levels. Although laws related to environmental matters have been around since before the Middle Ages, the modern concept of environmental law began to develop in the second half of the twentieth century. Specific laws addressing this topic typically focus on pollution control and remediation (air and water quality, energy, waste management and disposal) and/or resource conservation and utilization (fisheries, game, forests, land use, mining). Within any individual country environmental issues may be of greater or lesser concern, and particular areas of concern may vary, especially between developed and developing nations.

As with many other areas of law, there is no one law related to environmental concerns that applies throughout the entire world. Even the international treaties that exist are not uniformly joined by all countries.

Listed below are some examples of these treaties:

- The Asian Environmental Compliance and Enforcement Network (AECEN) is an agreement among 16 countries in Asia, the objective of which is cooperation on environmental law issues.
- The European Union has created environmental laws that apply throughout the EU addressing climate change; air pollution; water protection and management; waste management; soil protection; protection of nature, species and biodiversity; and noise pollution. It also issues directives that must be incorporated into the national laws of its members.
- There are numerous conventions (treaties) agreed to by various groups of countries covering issues such as atmosphere, fresh water resources, hazardous substances, marine environment and nature conservation.

In connection with environmental laws, supply management has a role to play in the minimization and management of waste, the handling and disposal of hazardous waste, the use and storage of toxic substances and other chemicals, the transportation of hazardous materials, and more general sourcing issues related to sustainability. When operating within any particular country, it is critical to be aware of and compliant with the environmental laws of that country. These laws may be either national or local in scope. Most countries maintain an agency or department at the national level to address environmental issues.

Employment. Employment-related laws and regulations address a variety of issues including minimum wage and overtime compensation requirements, restrictions on working hours, unemployment compensation, or other obligations imposed on employers. Some laws may speak to specific types of employment (for example, agriculture or mining), specific categories of workers (for example, employment of minors, veterans or persons with disabilities), or equal employment opportunity. They may also cover issues related to safety and health of employees (refer to the discussion of *Worker Health and Safety*). Most countries, especially in the developed world, also have laws and regulations addressing the employment of noncitizens. Issues related to trade unions, workers' organizations, strikes and the like may also be covered under the broad category of employment law.

Some examples of employment law are outlined below:
- The U.S. has laws dealing with agricultural employment, including special laws relating to the employment of minors in agriculture. There are also specific laws governing employment of mine workers, primarily addressing issues of health and safety. In addition, other laws govern employment in the area of construction; however, these primarily relate to construction associated with federal contracts.
- In Singapore the Ministry of Manpower administers the *Employment Act* which covers "every employee (regardless of nationality) who is under a contract of service with an employer" with exceptions for managerial or executive positions, seamen, domestic workers and government employees. The law includes provisions on contracts of services and termination, hours of work and rest days, payment of salary and retirement.
- Employment law in Nigeria is based on national legislation known as the *Labour Act* as well as on English (common) law and Nigerian case law. Some employees must be given a written contract of employment within three months of being hired; oral agreements suffice for other employees.

Worker Health And Safety. Often incorporated into other employment-related laws and regulations are provisions dealing with various aspects of the health and safety of workers. These laws are often grouped under the heading of "Occupation Health and Safety." Laws and regulations in this area may address such things as machine guarding, worker safety equipment (such as protective eyewear and hardhats) and ergonomic keyboards; they may also focus on occupational hazards and/or impose accident reporting requirements. Many of the regulations in this area are very detailed and may apply only to certain industries or to specific activities. In some countries, such laws also establish systems for compensating injured workers. In many countries the violation of these laws can result in fines, or even more serious punishment such as incarceration of responsible managers.

Some examples of worker health and safety laws include the following:
- In 2003, the United Nations (UN) adopted the Globally Harmonized System of Classification and Labeling of Chemicals (GHS). The GHS includes criteria for the classification of health, physical and environmental hazards, as well as specifying what information should be included on labels of hazardous chemicals and safety data sheets. In the U.S. the Department of Labor, the Environmental Protection Agency (EPA) and the Department of Transportation (DOT) are all involved in activities related to the U.N. standards.
- The U.S. Department of Labor and the State Administration of Work Safety (SAWS) of the People's Republic of China have entered into a memorandum of understanding with the purpose of cooperating on work safety and health issues.
- Many countries require employers to put health and safety policies in writing. Some require the posting of work rules and specify the use of multiple languages for such postings.

Transportation and Logistics. Historically many countries and/or localities regulated various modes of transportation. In more recent years at least some government oversight has been eliminated in favor of market competition.

Some examples related to transportation and logistics are outlined below:
- In the U.S. the Interstate Commerce Commission (ICC) originally was charged with regulating railroads, trucking companies, bus lines, freight forwarders, water carriers, oil pipelines, transportation brokers and express agencies. After elimination of the ICC in 1995, most remaining regulatory functions in the area of transportation were vested in the Federal Motor Carrier Safety Administration and the Surface Transportation Board of the U.S. Department of Transportation (DOT).
- The European Commission addresses transportation-related matters through its Directorate-General for Mobility and Transport, working in concert with EU member nations.
- Transport Canada is the government entity in that country responsible for administering laws adopted by the Canadian Parliament dealing with air, marine, rail and road transportation.

The supply management professional's primary concern in this area is likely to be with regard to contractual terms relating to the movement of goods. Some countries have adopted specific laws establishing the rights and liabilities of the shipper and the carrier in connection with the transportation of goods, typically in association with the use of bills of lading. In other countries such rights and liabilities may not be so well defined.

- There are multiple international agreements that address transportation. The U.N. *Convention on the Contract for the International Carriage of Goods by Road* (referred to as the CMR Convention) is a treaty entered into by 55 countries, mostly in Europe and neighboring countries, the purpose of which is to standardize "the conditions governing the contract for the international carriage of goods by road, particularly with respect to the documents used for such carriage and to the carrier's liability." See also the *Convention Concerning International Carriage of Goods by Rail* (COTIF) 1980; the *Law of the International Carriage of Goods by Sea* (the Hague Rules 1924, the Hague-Visby Rules 1968, the Hamburg Rules 1978); the *Law of the International Carriage of Goods by Air* (the Warsaw Convention 1929, the Hague Protocol 1955, the Montreal Agreement 1966, the Guatemala City Protocol 1971 and Montreal Protocol No. 4 1975).
- In the U.S. Article 7 of the *Uniform Commercial Code* (UCC), adopted as law in most states, includes provisions governing warehouse receipts, bills of lading and other documents of title. These UCC provisions govern transportation of goods within any particular state; similar provisions of the Interstate Commerce Act at the federal level control interstate transportation of goods.

Another piece of the transportation and logistics puzzle for the supply management professional is the actual carriage term agreed to by the buyer and seller of goods, and is used primarily to determine when risk of loss for the goods passes from the seller to the buyer. For many years contracting parties in the U.S. have relied on standard terms of carriage as defined in Article 2 of the UCC. More common internationally is reliance on the Incoterms® rules developed by the International Chamber of Commerce (ICC). The ICC is a private organization with no law-making authority; however, its recommended terms are widely recognized and accepted by business entities worldwide. The newest version of these terms is known as Incoterms® 2010 rules.

Finance. The financial marketplace is typically regulated within individual countries, and international bodies exist to facilitate coordination and cooperation between and among countries. Regulation at the national level may occur through governmental agencies and/or nongovernmental organizations. The focus of such regulation is on maintaining confidence in a country's financial system, protecting the stability of that system and protecting consumers. The primary targets of regulation are banks and other financial service providers, stock exchanges and the companies listed on these exchanges, and investment management services. The most significant issues for supply management professionals in this arena are likely to revolve around letters of credit and currency exchange for international transactions.

The regulatory function may be distributed between and among multiple organizations; for example, there are nine governmental and nongovernmental organizations involved in the U.S., three each in Brazil, Canada and China, two in the UK and Australia.

Recognizing the interrelationship of economies around the world, countries have come together to form and support various organizations involved in the area of financial regulation at the international level.

Some examples of international financial regulation relationships are outlined below:

- The International Monetary Fund (IMF) is "an organization of 188 countries, working to foster global monetary cooperation, secure financial stability, facilitate international trade, promote high employment and sustainable economic growth, and reduce poverty around the world."
- The Bank for International Settlements (BIS) is an organization of central banks or monetary authorities of 60 countries. Its stated mission is "to serve central banks in their pursuit of monetary and financial stability, to foster international cooperation in those areas and to act as a bank for central banks."
- The Financial Stability Board (FSB) was created by G-20 major economies and the European Union "to coordinate at the international level the work of national financial authorities and international standard-setting bodies, and to develop and promote the implementation of effective regulatory, supervisory and other financial sector policies in the interest of financial stability."

Product Liability. Product liability law addresses the responsibility of a manufacturer for the quality of its goods, including the obligation to compensate parties injured by the function or malfunction of those goods. The law often imposes obligations related not only to the actual manufacture of goods, but also to the design of the goods and warnings and instructions provided for their use. Although laws and court decisions in the U.S. have often led the way in the area of product liability, many countries impose similar legal obligations.

Some examples related to international product liability law include the following:

- The European Union issued a *Product Liability Directive* in 1985 that has now been widely adopted by EU members. In addition, product-specific directives, such as the *Machinery Safety Directive* and a *General Product Safety Directive* have also been issued.
- The *Consumer Protection Law* in Taiwan imposes the legal theory of strict liability (liability without regard to fault) on product liability claims. The law also extends liability to product distributors and importers as well as to manufacturers.
- Under China's *Product Quality Control Law*, products must comply with national and industry standards and cannot pose an "unreasonable danger" to people or property. In addition, the law establishes requirements for labeling and packaging.

Regulations Influencing the Development of Solicitations

Two major areas of law affect the development of solicitations in the private sector. These are (1) the Uniform Commercial Code (UCC), specifically Article 2, Sales (discussed above), and (2) antitrust and trade regulation laws, specifically the Sherman Antitrust Act, the Clayton Act, the Robinson-Patman Act and the Federal Trade Commission (FTC) Act. On the public purchasing side, a number of federal acts regulate federal procurement and public projects. The appendix at the end of this chapter includes a description of each piece of legislation.

Antitrust and Trade Regulation. The purpose of antitrust legislation, as discussed in the prior section, is to maintain a competitive and fair market. Many countries have such legislation. In Canada and the European Union, it is referred to as competition law. In the United States, four pieces of legislation lay the foundation for the U.S. approach: (1) the Sherman Antitrust Act, (2) the Clayton Act, (3) the Robinson-Patman Act, and (4) the Federal Trade Commission (FTC) Act (see the appendix at the end of this chapter). The *Sherman Act* "makes it illegal for parties to act in combination, conspiracy or collusion with the intent of restricting completion in interstate commerce. Price fixing and group boycotts fall within the parameters of this law" (ISM *Glossary* 2014). The *Clayton Act* "lists specific practices which are unlawful where the effect may be to substantially lessen competition or tend to create a monopoly in interstate commerce; includes tying arrangements" (ISM *Glossary* 2014). The *Robinson-Patman Act* "requires a supplier engaged in interstate commerce to sell the same item to all customers at the same price (assuming the same purchase quantity). Exceptions permit a lower price for the following reasons: (1) for a larger purchase quantity, providing that the seller can justify the lower price through lower costs; (2) to move obsolete or distress merchandise; or (3) to meet the lower price of a competitor in a certain geographic region" (ISM *Glossary* 2014). The *FTC Act* created the Federal Trade Commission, which is partially responsible for enforcing antitrade laws. There may also be laws and regulations at the state level. It is important for the supply management professional to be aware of country-specific laws when working with multinational organizations.

Supply management professionals are in a prime position to alert management to possible violations such as price fixing. They are also in a vulnerable position in terms of their actions, which might put their employer at risk for charges of collusion on the buying side. The supply management leadership team must partner with legal counsel to ensure the appropriate training is provided to supply management personnel. Supply management professionals are also well positioned to scan the environment for any antitrust actions in the supply management base that might adversely affect the organization. For example, when UPS attempted to acquire TNT Logistics in 2012-2013, U.S. authorities approved the merger but the EU Commission did not. If TNT Logistics was a key supplier (provider of contract transportation, in this case) to an organization, the supply management team might develop contingency plans in the event the merger occurred as well as consider any disruptions that might occur during the review period. Potential sources of risk include possible changes in processes, personnel, contracts and so on in the event the merger occurred.

Regulation of International Commerce. The supply management team must also develop internal controls to ensure that global sourcing and supply management activities meet the requirements of domestic laws such as the Trade Agreements Act and the Foreign Corrupt Practices Act (FCPA); international treaties such as the North American Free Trade Agreement (NAFTA), the General Agreement on Tariffs and Trade (GATT) mentioned previously (now the World Trade Organization [WTO]), and the United Nations Convention on Contracts for the International Sale of Goods (CISG), also discussed previously. Each of these is defined in the appendix at the end of this chapter.

The primary areas of concern are (1) business practices and ethics, and (2) contracts. The supply management professional should take the lead in defining internally what is and is not acceptable behavior in the international arena in light of both laws and the organization's ethical framework. Policies, procedures and training must be provided and supported by managerial action. In terms of contracts, the supply management team should work with legal counsel to ensure that the organization is complying with regulations related to international transactions.

Regulation of Federal Procurement and Public Projects. Supply management employees in the public sector and those doing business with U.S. federal government agencies must adhere to the various rules and regulations that govern public purchasing. The appendix at the end of this chapter defines the relevant U.S. federal laws.

Control mechanisms and audits are highly structured in the federal procurement arena. For example, the internal control matrix for the audit of purchasing controls (version 5.0, July 2013) provides a detailed matrix that includes control objectives, examples of control activities and audit procedures. Control objectives include contractor compliance, training, policies and procedures; purchase orders and subcontract clauses; management of purchasing; selecting sources; pricing and negotiation; subcontract award; and administration.[33]

In this audit, two tiers of contractors are covered: the prime (or general) contractor and subcontractors. A prime contract is a contract agreement or purchase order entered into by an organization with a supplier that acts as the primary point of contact for awarding pieces of the prime contract to other suppliers (subcontractors), often smaller businesses. The prime contractor is responsible for awarding business to the subcontractors, managing the workflow and paying the subcontractors from the original prime contract. Prime contracting is used extensively in the construction industry and in government procurement.

The final, but by no means least valuable, managerial role is establishing internal controls and ensuring compliance. These activities have always been critical managerial tasks that support organizational success and, in some cases, ensure survival. A business climate of ethical lapses and accounting scandals coupled with public outcry and government regulation have brought control and compliance issues to the forefront in many organizational settings. However, as the opening quote of this chapter indicates, how managers and leaders manage the risks associated with operational, financial, legal and regulatory issues may create an opportunity to enhance the organization's reputation and brand image. By thinking of controls and compliance in this way, the leader-manager comes full circle back to the questions: What is our vision of our future? How will we get there? Sound leadership combined with strong managerial action will result in visionary strategies supported by processes, policies and procedures that enable skillful execution leading to desired results. Controls will be built in from the beginning so that compliance occurs before and during activities, and after-the-fact controls are primarily for record-keeping and reporting purposes.

Summary

Supply leader-managers must establish internal control and systems that will assist in ensuring employees comply with them before-, during-, and after-the-fact. Internal controls address issues such as (1) the control environment; (2) risk assessment; (3) control activities (or policies, procedures and practices); (4) information and communication support; and (5) monitoring activities.

Before-the-fact controls include budgets, plans, business continuity, forecasts, and policy and procedures manuals. During-the-fact controls include structured processes, adherence to policies and procedures, specifications, and industry standards. After-the-fact controls include reports, reviews, audits and customer surveys.

Supply management now plays a very important and strategic role in sustainability and social responsibility. They can be instrumental in reducing consumption of materials and reduce waste, considering the cradle-to-cradle concept. Supply management professionals must also remain aware of, and comply with, all data and records management requirements.

From a corporate governance and financial reporting perspective, the U.S. Sarbanes-Oxley (SOX) Act of 2002 will drive compliance for all publicly traded corporations. Organizations also have many other internal controls on financial and other reporting issues.

In addition, supply management professionals need to be aware of many legal and regulatory issues, including (1) agency law and authority, (2) the role of legal counsel, and (3) other types of laws that affect supply management.

Key Points

1. Management controls are designed to provide reasonable assurance regarding the achievement of objectives in the areas of (1) effectiveness and efficiency of operations, (2) reliability of financial reporting, and (3) compliance with applicable laws and regulations.
2. There are three different types of controls: (1) before the fact, (2) during the fact and (3) after the fact:
   - Before-the-fact controls establish a benchmark against which actual performance can be measured. Before-the-fact controls include budgets, plans (strategic, operational and disaster recovery), forecasts, and policy and procedure manuals.
   - During-the-fact controls are put in place to monitor and measure the task while it is occurring or before it is finalized so that adjustments may be made as early as possible to stay within the designated parameters.
   - After-the-fact controls are reviews to measure what actually happened so actual performance can be compared with planned benchmarks and improvements can be made.
3. The supply management team plays a role in establishing internal controls and ensuring compliance in the areas of reliability of financial reporting, operational effectiveness, and efficiency and compliance with laws and regulations.
4. Supply management must play a leadership role in the attainment of the organization's sustainability and social responsibility goals.
5. The supply management professional should be familiar with the variety of laws and legal requirements that directly impacts their role.

Appendix: Laws and Regulations

U.S. Laws and Regulations Influencing Supply Management

Uniform Commercial Code (UCC) Article 2, Sales, and Article 2A, Leasing. Statutory collection of provisions governing various aspects of commercial transactions such as Sale of Goods (Article 2), Lease of Goods (Article 2A), Letters of Credit (Article 5) and Secured Transactions (Article 9). Statutory language is recommended by the National Conference of Commissioners on Uniform State Laws (NCCUSL) to encourage uniformity among the states but must be adopted by individual state legislatures to become effective.

Antitrust and Trade Regulation

Sherman Antitrust Act. Federal antitrust law, passed in 1890, that makes it illegal for parties to act in combination, conspiracy or collusion with the intent of restricting competition in interstate commerce. Price fixing, reciprocity and group boycotts fall within the parameters of this law.

Clayton Act. Federal antitrust law that lists specific practices that are unlawful where the effect may be to substantially lessen competition or tend to create a monopoly in interstate commerce; includes tying arrangements (where the seller requires the buyer to purchase Product B in order to acquire Product A).

Robinson-Patman Act. Federal antitrust law that requires a supplier engaged in interstate commerce to sell the same item to all customers at the same price (assuming the same purchase quantity). Exceptions permit a lower price (1) for a larger purchase quantity, providing that the supplier can justify the lower price through lower costs; (2) to move obsolete or distress merchandise; or (3) to meet the lower price of a competitor in a certain geographic region.

Federal Trade Commission (FTC) Act. Federal law passed in 1914 to create the Federal Trade Commission and prohibit deceptive and unfair trade practices such as false advertising.

Regulation of U. S. Federal Procurement and Public Projects

Federal Acquisition Regulation (FAR). The body of regulations used by all federal executive agencies in the acquisition of supplies and services with appropriated funds. The FAR is a compilation of all the laws and policies governing the federal procurement process.

False Claims Act. Federal law that provides for the recovery of damages and remedies on proof of loss to the government, sustained through fraud in the award or performance of government contracts.

Davis-Bacon and Related Acts. Federal law passed in 1931 intended to give local laborers and contractors a fair opportunity to participate in federal building programs and to protect local wage standards. Some state and local governments have similar laws.

Prompt Payment Act. Federal law imposing certain requirements on government procurement offices to ensure that federal contractors supplying goods and services are paid on time. Many state and local governments have similar laws.

Service Contract Act. Federal law passed in 1965 giving the Wage and Hour Division of the Employment Standards Administration responsibility for predetermination of prevailing wage rates for federal service contracts.

Walsh-Healey Public Contracts Act (PCA). Federal law passed in 1936 requiring no more than 40-hour workweeks and minimum age limitations for workers; also outlawing unsanitary, hazardous or dangerous working conditions. Contractors who breach these requirements have their names listed and distributed, and are ineligible for federal contracting for three years. Applies to federal government purchasing and contracts for material, supplies and equipment exceeding US$10,000.

Small Business Act. Federal law adopted in 1953 expressing government policy to aid, assist and protect the interests of small business concerns to preserve free competitive enterprise. One objective is to ensure that a reasonable portion of government purchases and contracts go to small business.

Buy American Act. Federal law requiring that government purchases for public use consist only of raw materials mined or produced in the United States, or manufactured items that are made in the United States from materials or items mined, produced or manufactured in the United States.

Freedom of Information Act. Federal law passed in 1966 requiring the federal government to disclose certain records upon request. Many state and local governments have similar laws in place.

Regulation of International Commerce

Trade Agreements Act of 1979. Federal law enacted to facilitate approval and implementation of various trade agreements, foster growth and maintenance of an open world trading system, expand opportunities for U.S. commerce in international trade, and improve the rules of international trade.

Foreign Corrupt Practices Act (FCPA). Adopted in 1977 and amended in 1988, the provision prohibits corrupt payments to foreign officials for the purpose of obtaining or keeping business.

North American Free Trade Agreement (NAFTA). International treaty between and among the United States, Canada and Mexico breaking down trade barriers between these countries.

General Agreement on Tariffs and Trade (GATT). Multilateral agreement created in 1947 to reduce barriers to world trade. Succeeded by the World Trade Organization (WTO).

United Nations Convention on Contracts for the International Sale of Goods (CISG). International treaty covering the sale of goods between business entities in participating countries called "contracting states." By 2013, the CISG had been ratified by 80 states. The CISG is similar to the UCC Article 2, but differs in some significant respects. Unless excluded by the express terms of a contract, the CISG is deemed to be incorporated into (and supplant) any otherwise applicable domestic law(s) with respect to a transaction in goods between parties from different contracting states.

Employment Law
Many countries have laws regulating employment. In the United States, these laws deal with the following: wages and hours of work, safety and health standards, health benefits and retirement standards, other workplace standards, work authorization for non-U.S. citizens, federal contracts: working conditions, federal contracts: equal opportunity, and acts by specific industry, including agriculture, mining, construction and transportation. Specific laws that affect many employers include those listed below:

Federal Equal Employment Opportunity (EEO) Laws. The laws prohibiting job discrimination include the following:

Title VII of the Civil Rights Act of 1964, which prohibits employment discrimination based on race, color, religion, sex or national origin by employers of more than 15 in both the public and private sector.

The Equal Pay Act of 1963 (EPA), which requires that individuals who perform the same work and are substantially equal in skill and responsibility receive equal compensation.

The Age Discrimination in Employment Act of 1967 (ADEA) prohibits discrimination against people aged 40 and over.

Title I and Title V of the Americans with Disabilities Act of 1990 (ADA) requires organizations with at least 25 employees to make reasonable accommodations for qualified workers and applicants with disabilities and to avoid discriminating against them. Compliance includes removing physical workplace barriers.

Sections 501 and 505 of the Rehabilitation Act of 1973, which prohibit discrimination against qualified individuals with disabilities who work in the federal government. The Civil Rights Act of 1991 provided for the right to trial by jury on discrimination claims and introduced the possibility of emotional distress damages, while limiting the amount a jury could award.

The U.S. Equal Employment Opportunity Commission (EEOC) is the U.S. federal agency in charge of administrative and judicial enforcement of the federal civil rights laws with regard to employment practices.

Source: Cavinato, J.L., A.E. Flynn, M.L. Harding, C.S. Lallatin, M.L. Peck, H.M. Pohlig, S.R. Sturzl and V. Tucker (Eds.). ISM *Glossary* of Key Supply Management Terms, 6th edition, Institute for Supply Management®, Tempe, AZ, 2014.

Resources for Types of Laws

The Internet can be a valuable tool for researching the various laws and regulations that might apply in individual countries or regions. Care should be taken, however, with regard to the sources of the information posted. Official government websites provide original source materials, but those materials may be difficult for the average layperson to understand and the websites may not be up to date. Many law firms specializing in international legal matters and other organizations concerned with international trade may also host websites that contain useful information, but that information may be slanted by particular perspective or bias. The following sites may be useful:

www.kluwerlawonline.com

International Encyclopedia of Laws — Offers individual monographs on different areas of law (such as Contracts, Commercial, Competition, Environmental, Labor) for various individual countries.

www.asil.org

The American Society of International Law maintains an extensive website with numerous links to references and primary source materials covering various aspects of international law, including Commercial Arbitration, Environmental Law, Intellectual Property Law, Private International Law and many others.

www.cisg.law.pace.edu

An excellent source of information about the U.N. Convention on Contracts for the International Sale of Goods (CISG), including the text of the treaty (in each of the various official languages), an updated list of the signatories to the treaty, general information on the application of the CISG, as well as annotations of the text itself (providing case references). Also provided are links to other areas of International Commercial Law.

www.globalaw.net

This network of international lawyers offers an online publication, *Doing Business in Europe*, that covers basic legal issues for 35 European jurisdictions.

www.iccwbo.org

The International Chamber of Commerce (ICC) is both an advocate for international business as well as the developer of rules governing such things as international arbitration and transportation. Because the ICC is a private, nongovernmental body, its rules are voluntary.

The following print publications may be available for purchase or found in a law library or other library.

West's *Law & Commercial Dictionary in Five Languages*); 1985 West Publishing Co.

English definitions of legal and commercial terms, translated to German, Spanish, French and Italian (2 volumes).

Reynolds & Flores, *Foreign Law — Current Sources of Codes and Legislation in Jurisdictions of the World*; American Association of Law Libraries (AALL) Publication Series No. 33; 2003 William S. Hein & Co., Inc.

Brief introduction to each country's government, legal history and judicial system; references for finding country-specific laws on such things as contracts, currency and foreign exchange regulation, foreign trade, labor, taxation. Includes references to relevant articles and other publications on the given topic.

Redden & Schlueter, *Modern Legal Systems Cyclopedia*; 1992 William S. Hein & Co., Inc.

21-volume set, divided by geographical region, updated periodically. Describes each country's historical background, system of government, sources of law and judicial system.

Campbell & Campbell, *International Product Liability* 2nd Ed.; 2011 Juris Publishing Inc.

This publication includes subscription updates and covers product liability issues in 17 major jurisdictions. A downloadable electronic version is available.

Endnotes
Preface
1. Craig Hickman and Michael A. Silva, *Creating Excellence: Managing Corporate Culture, Strategy and Change in the New Age* (New York: Plume, 1986).

Chapter 1
1. Warren G. Bennis, *On Becoming a Leader* (Upper Saddle River: Addison Wesley, 1989).
2. Marcus Buckingham and Curt Coffman, *First Break All the Rules* (New York: Simon & Schuster, 1999).
3. Bennis, *On Becoming a Leader*.
4. P. Fraser Johnson and Michiel R. Leenders, "Supply's Organizational Roles and Responsibilities 2011," CAPS Research (2012): 17.
5. Lisa Arnseth, "A Genuine Leader," *Inside Supply Management*® (24:5), accessed July 24, 2013, http://www.ism.ws/pubs/ISMMag/ismarticle.cfm?ItemNumber=23709.
6. Debashis Chatterjee, *Leading Consciously: A Pilgrimage Toward Self-Mastery* (New York: Elsevier, 1998).
7. BusinessDictionary.com, "Leadership," accessed July 24, 2013 at http://www.businessdictionary.com/definition/leadership.html.
8. Diane Dreher, *The Tao of Personal Leadership* (New York: Collins, 1997).
9. Ibid.
10. Paul R. Bemthal, Jason Bondra and Wei Wang, "Leadership in China," *Development Dimensions International (DDI)* (2006): 10.
11. Geert Hofstede, http://feweb.uvt.nl/center/hofstede/index.htm.
12. Lynn Sharp Paine and Jennifer Benqing Gui, "An Interview With Zhang Ruimin, CEO, The Haier Group," *Harvard Business Review* (December 1, 1998).
13. John H. Zenger and Joseph Folkman, *The Handbook for Leaders: 24 Lessons for Extraordinary Leadership* (New York: McGraw-Hill Professional Education, 2004).
14. James M. Kouzes and Barry Z. Posner, *The Leadership Challenge: How to Keep Getting Extraordinary Things Done in Organizations* (Hoboken: John Wiley & Sons, Inc., 2003).
15. Tsun-yan Hsieh and Sara Yik, "Leadership as the Starting Point of Strategy," *The McKinsey Quarterly* 1 (2005).
16. Mark Gerzon, "Leaders and Leadership" in *Beyond Intractability*, Guy Burgess and Heidi Burgess, eds. (Boulder: Conflict Resolution Consortium, September, 2003), www.beyondintractability.org/essay/leaders/?nid=1097.

17. Allan R. Gold, Masao Hirano and Yoshinori Yokoyama, "An Outsider Takes On Japan," *The McKinsey Quarterly* 1 (2001).
18. Warren Bennis, "The Secrets of Great Groups," *Leader to Leader* 3 (Winter 1997): 29–33.
19. Joseph Rost, *Leadership for the Twenty-First Century* (New York: Praeger, 1991).
20. Ibid.
21. Gerzon, "Leaders and Leadership."
22. Peter Drucker, quoted on "Business & Organization Leadership Development," University of Washington Bothell, accessed November 11, 2013, http://depts.washington.edu/leaders1/our-favorite-leadership-quotes/.
23. Peter Engardio with Jena McGregor, "Karma Capitalism," *BusinessWeek* (October 30, 2006).
24. Ibid.
25. Ibid.
26. Ibid.
27. Geert Hofstede, www.geert-hofstede.com/.
28. Tom Peters, www.leadershipthatlasts.com/quotes.html.
29. John Wooden, *Wooden on Leadership* (New York: McGraw-Hill, 2005).
30. John H. Zenger and Joseph Folkman, *The Extraordinary Leader: Turning Good Managers into Great Leaders* (New York: McGraw-Hill, 2002).
31. Charles M. Farkas and Suzy Wetlaufer, "The Ways Chief Executive Officers Lead" in *Harvard Business Review on Leadership* (Cambridge: Harvard Business Review Publishing, 1998): 115–46.
32. Michiel Leenders and P. Fraser Johnson, "Major Changes in Supply Chain Responsibilities," 2002, CAPS Research, Tempe, AZ.
33. Ram Charan, *Know-How: The Eight Skills That Separate People Who Perform From Those Who Don't* (New York: Crown Business, 2007).
34. RaeAnn Slaybaugh, "2020 Leadership," *eSide Supply Management*, (4:1), January/February 2011, accessed November 8, 2013, http://www.ism.ws/pubs/eSide/eSideArticle.cfm?ItemNumber=21047.
35. Ibid, Charan.
36. Chris Chen, "Managing and Leading," *NAPM Insights*, (6:4), April 1995, 5.
37. David C. McClelland, *Human Motivation* (New York: Cambridge University Press, 1988).
38. Adapted from Daniel Goleman, Richard E. Boyatzis and Annie McKee, *Primal Leadership: Learning to Lead With Emotional Intelligence* (Boston, MA: Harvard Business School Press, 2004); and *Wall Street Journal*, "Developing a Leadership Style," n.d., accessed November 11, 2013, http://guides.wsj.com/management/developing-a-leadership-style/how-to-develop-a-leadership-style/.

39. Daniel Goleman, www.danielgoleman.info, and The Hay Group, www.haygroup.com.
40. RaeAnn Slaybaugh, "2020 Leadership," *eSide Supply Management*, (4:1), January/February 2011, accessed November 8, 2013, http://www.ism.ws/pubs/eSide/eSideArticle.cfm?ItemNumber=21047.
41. Dave Ulrich, Jack Zenger and Norman Smallwood, *Results-Based Leadership* (Cambridge: Harvard Business School Press, 1999).
42. Whirlpool 2012 Annual Report, 3, accessed November 11, 2013, http://www.whirlpoolcorp.com/2012annual/WHR_2012AR.pdf.
43. Cynthia D. McCauley, *Developmental Assignments: Creating Learning Experiences Without Changing Jobs* (Center for Creative Leadership, 2006).
44. Zenger and Folkman, *The Extraordinary Leader*, 117.
45. Peter F. Drucker, *People and Performance* (Burlington: Butterworth Heinemann, 1995).
46. Lester C. Thurow, *Building Wealth: The New Rules for Individuals, Companies and Nations in a Knowledge-Based Economy* (New York: Collins, 2000).
47. Henry Mintzberg, "The Manager's Job: Folklore and Fact" in *Harvard Business Review on Leadership* (Boston: Harvard Business School Press, 1998).
48. Chris Chen, "Managing and Leading," 5.
49. Anna E. Flynn and Samuel D. Farney, "Leading, Managing and Supervising" in *The Supply Management Leadership Process: Strategies for Organizational Effectiveness* (Tempe, AZ: National Association of Purchasing Management, Inc., 2000).
50. Victor H. Vroom, *Work and Motivation* (Hoboken: John Wiley and Sons, Inc., 1964; Melbourne, FL: Krieger Publishing, 1982).
51. Lisa M. Ellram, "Strategic Cost Management in the Supply Chain: A Purchasing and Supply Management Perspective," CAPS Research (2002): 91.
52. W. Edwards Deming, *Out of the Crisis* (MIT Press, 2000).
53. W. Edwards Deming, *Out of the Crisis*, 23-24, ©2000 Massachusetts Institue of Technology, by permission of The MIT Press. Also available at https://www.deming.org/theman/theories/fourteenpoints.
54. Douglas McGregor, *The Human Side of Enterprise* (McGraw-Hill, 1960; 25th Anniversary Printing, 1985).
55. William Ouchi, *Theory Z: How American Business Can Meet the Japanese Challenge* (Avon, 1982).
56. Elton Mayo, *The Social Problems of an Industrial Civilization* (Cambridge: Harvard University Publishing, 1945): viii.
57. "Total Procurement Process: An Overview," *Supply Chain Management*, Shell Services Company: 7.

58. Lisa Arnseth, "Centralizing Procurement at a Nonprofit," *Inside Supply Management*®, (23:3), April 2012, 26-30.
59. Dave Nelson, "How to Treat Suppliers," Supply Chain Management Executive Speaker Series, Miami University, September 8, 2011.

Chapter 2

1. Josephson Institute, accessed October 30, 2013, http://josephsoninstitute.org/quotes/quotations.php?q=Leadership.
2. John P. Kotter, *John Kotter on What Leaders Really Do* (Cambridge: Harvard Business School Press, 1999).
3. Josephson Institute, "Making Ethical Decisions," accessed October 30, 2013, http://josephsoninstitute.org/MED/index.html.
4. Josh Bersin, "How Does Leadership Vary Across the Globe?," *Forbes*, October 31, 2012, accessed November 11, 2013, http://www.forbes.com/sites/joshbersin/2012/10/31/are-expat-programs-dead/.
5. Jeffrey Immelt, Dartmouth Commencement Speech, June 13, 2004, available from www.dartmouth.edu/~news/releases/2004/06/13a.html.
6. John Deere, "Leadership," accessed August 6, 2013, http://www.deere.com/wps/dcom/en_US/corporate/our_company/about_us/leadership/leadership.page.
7. Mary Siegfried, "A Shift in Sourcing Strategies," *Inside Supply Management*®, (24:2), March 2013, 26+, accessed November 13, 2013, http://www.ism.ws/pubs/ISMMag/ismarticle.cfm?ItemNumber=23483; and Lisa M. Ellram, Ph.D., Wendy L. Tate, Ph.D. and Kenneth J. Petersen, Ph.D., "Offshoring and Reshoring: An Update on the Manufacturing Location Decision." *Journal of Supply Chain Management* (49:2), Spring 2013, 6-12.
8. Rocky Mountain Institute, "Wal-Mart Fleet Operations," accessed August 5, 2013, http://www.rmi.org/Walmartsfleetoperations.
9. Dow Jones Sustainability World Index, accessed September 5, 2013, http://www.sustainability-indices.com/index-family-overview/djsi-family.jsp.
10. See SmartWay at http://www.epa.gov/smartway/ for information about membership and programs to help reduce commercial transportation fuel usage, and for information about fuel efficient vehicles.
11. George Zsidisin and Lisa Ellram, "Supply Risk Assessment Analysis," PRACTIX, CAPS Research (June 1999): 9.
12. Robert Monczka, Phil Carter, W. Markham, Robert Trent, J. Hartley, Casey McDowell and Gary Ragatz, *Value Chain Strategies for the Changing Decade: Risk Management Across the Extended Value Chain*, 2012, CAPS Research, Tempe, AZ.
13. Mihaly Csikszentmihalyi, *Leadership: Leadership, Flow and the Making of Meaning* (New York: Viking Press, 2003): 197.
14. The Classic Quotes Collection contained in The Quotations Page, www.quotationspage.com/quotes/Seneca.

ENDNOTES

15. Hsieh and Yik, "Leadership as the Starting Point of Strategy," 67-73.
16. Whole Foods Market. Declaration of Interdependence, accessed August 6, 2013, http://www.wholefoodsmarket.com/mission-values/core-values/declaration-interdependence.
17. Ikea, About Ikea, accessed August 6, 2013, http://www.ikea.com/ms/en_US/this-is-ikea/company-information/index.html.
18. Method, "Our Story," accessed August 6, 2013, http://methodhome.com/methodology/our-story/.19.Amazon.com, FAQs, accessed August 6, 2013, http://phx.corporate-ir.net/phoenix.zhtml?c=97664&p=irol-faq#14296.
20. Boeing, About Us, "Our Vision," accessed August 6, 2013, http://www.boeing.com/boeing/aboutus/culture/#vision.
21. Whole Foods Market, "Final Thoughts," accessed August 6, 2013, http://www.wholefoodsmarket.com/mission-values/core-values/declaration-interdependence.
22. Deere & Company, About Us, Vision, accessed January 26, 2014, http://www.deere.com/wps/dcom/en_US/corporate/our_company/about_us/about_us.page?.
23. Whirlpool Vision, accessed September 6, 2013, http://www.whirlpoolcorp.com/about/overview.aspx.
24. Lenovo, "Our Company," accessed August 6, 2013, http://www.lenovo.com/lenovo/us/en/our_company.html.
25. Angela Jameson, "Man of Steel Who Wants to Forge His Empire Out of Limelight," *The London Times* (31 January 2005): 44.
26. Josephson Institute, accessed September 6, 2013, http://josephsoninstitute.org/about.html.
27. ABB's Supply Chain Management Mission, accessed September 6, 2013, http://www.abb.us/cawp/seitp161/9bf4b09554b4ec12c12577990033367c.aspx.
28. John Deere Strategy, About Us, accessed January 26, 2014, http://www.deere.com/wps/dcom/en_US/corporate/our_company/about_us/about_us.page?.
29. Lenovo, Global Procurement, accessed August 6, 2013, http://www.lenovo.com/global_procurement/us/en/index.html.
30. "Whirlpool Vision and Strategy," accessed August 6 2013, www.whirlpoolcorp.com/about/overview.aspx.
31. IBM, "Global Procurement," accessed November 9, 2013, http://www-03.ibm.com/procurement/proweb.nsf/contentdocsbytitle/United+States~Global+Procurement.
32. "LG Electronics' Global Supply Chain Management System Goes Live," LGE press release, September 11, 2001.
33. "LG Electronics Builds Global Purchasing System," LGE press release, July 31, 2001.
34. LG, "Investor Relations," accessed August 6, 2013, http://www.lg.com/global/investor-relations.

35. Terri Tracey, "ISM Announces Award Winner," *Inside Supply Management*®, (21:4), April 2010, accessed August 6, 2013, http://www.ism.ws/pubs/ISMMag/ismarticle.cfm?ItemNumber=20220.
36. Procter & Gamble, "P&G 2012 Sustainability Overview," 2012, 2, accessed August 6, 2013, http://www.pg.com/en_US/downloads/sustainability/reports/PG_2012_Sustainability_Overview.pdf.
37. Gold, Hirano and Yokoyama, "An Outsider Takes On Japan."
38. Reuters, *Automakers Post Best August Since Recession*, September 04, 2012, accessed August 6, 2013, http://www.foxbusiness.com/industries/2012/09/04/automakers-post-best-august-since-recession/.
39. Lisa Arnseth, "From Decentralized to Center-Led Supply Management," *Inside Supply Management*®, (21:4), April 2010, p. 20+, accessed November 9, 2013, http://www.ism.ws/pubs/ISMMag/ismarticle.cfm?ItemNumber=20217.
40. Institute for Supply Management®, ISM *Principles of Sustainability and Social Responsibility*, accessed August 6, 2013, http://www.ism.ws/SR/content.cfm?ItemNumber=18497. There is also a *Guide for Adoption and Implementation* of the guidelines available for download at http://www.ism.ws/files/SR/PSSRwGuideBook.pdf.

Chapter 3

1. Teruyuki Minoura, accessed November 8, 2013, http://www.quotegarden.com/lean-manufacturing.html.
2. P. Fraser Johnson and Michiel Leenders, "Supply's Organizational Roles and Responsibilities 2011," CAPS Research, Tempe, AZ 2012, accessed August 7, 2013, http://capsresearch.org/publications/pdfs-protected/johnson2011.pdf.
3. James Davis and Martha Turner, "The Evolution of the CPO: From Cost Control to Value Enhancement," *Industry Week*, May 17, 2012, accessed August 7, 2013, http://www.industryweek.com/trade/evolution-cpo-cost-control-value-enhancement.
4. Lisa Arnseth, "The Heart of a Healthy Supply Chain," *Inside Supply Management*®, (23:7), September 2012, 16+, accessed November 11, 2013, http://www.ism.ws/pubs/ISMMag/ismarticle.cfm?ItemNumber=23092.
5. Lisa Ellram and Wendy Tate, "Bank of America: Services Purchasing and Outsourcing," PRACTIX, CAPS Research 9 (May 2006).
6. Ibid, Arnseth.
7. Ibid, Arnseth.
8. Susan Avery, "UTC: Purchasing's Medal of Honor Winner," *Purchasing* (September 7, 2006).
9. Ibid.
10. Lisa Arnseth, "Centralizing Procurement at a Nonprofit," *Inside Supply Management*® (23:3), April 2012, 26-30.

11. Ibid, Avery, "UTC: Purchasing's Medal of Honor Winner."
12. IBM press release, 2006.
13. IBM press release, "IBM Chief Procurement Officer Transition to Budapest, Hungary," December 2, 2011, accessed January 27, 2014, http://www-03.ibm.com/procurement/proweb.nsf/contentdocsbytitle/United+States~IBM+Chief+Procurement+Officer+transition+to+Budapest,+Hungary?OpenDocument&Parent=Global+Procurement.
14. IBM, "Procurement One Place Strategy," accessed November 11, 2013, http://www-03.ibm.com/procurement/proweb.nsf/ContentDocsByTitle/United+States~Procurement+One+Place+strategy.
15. Jeffrey A. Ogden and Matthew W. McCarter, "Better Buyer-Supplier Relationships Through Supply Base Reduction and Supplier Performance Management," *PRACTIX*, CAPS Research 8 (December 2004).
16. Ibid.
17. Ibid, Arsenth, "The Heart of a Healthy Supply Chain."
18. John P. Kotter, *Force for Change: How Leadership Differs From Management* (New York: Free Press, 1990): 51.
19. Gold, Hirano and Yoshinori, "An Outsider Takes on Japan."
20. Boehm, "Leading Change: An Interview with the CEO of Deere & Company."

Chapter 4

1. Akio Morita with Edwin M. Reingold and Mitsuko Shimomura, *Akio Morita and Sony: Made in Japan*, (New York: Signet, 1986), 160.
2. John P. Kotter, The 8-Step Process for Leading Change, n.d., accessed November 13, 2013, http://www.kotterinternational.com/our-principles/changesteps.
3. Dino Lanno, "Boost Employee Engagement," *Inside Supply Management*®, (23:4), May 2012, 10, accessed November 14, 2013, http://www.ism.ws/pubs/ISMMag/ismarticle.cfm?ItemNumber=22649.
4. Kim Kanaga and Michael E. Kossler, *How to Form a Team: Five Keys to High Performance* (Greensboro: Center for Creative Leadership, 2001) available from www.ccl.org/leadership/forms/publications/publicationProductDetail.aspx?productId=1-882197-68-2&pageId=1250
5. Kelley Holland, "Gen Y Managers Perceived as Entitled, Need Polish," September 3, 2013, special to CNBC; also available from EY, accessed January 28, 2014, http://www.ey.com/US/en/Issues/Talent-management/Talent-Survey-The-generational-management-shift.
6. Lisa Arnseth, "The Heart of a Healthy Supply Chain," *Inside Supply Management*®, (23:7), September 2012, 16+, accessed November 11, 2013, http://www.ism.ws/pubs/ISMMag/ismarticle.cfm?ItemNumber=23092.

7. Dino Lanno, "Boost Employee Engagement," (23:4), *Inside Supply Management*®, May 2012, 10+, accessed November 14, 2013, http://www.ism.ws/pubs/ISMMag/ismarticle.cfm?ItemNumber=22649.
8. Glenn L. Hallam, *The Adventures of Team Fantastic: A Practical Guide for Team Leaders and Members* (Greensboro: Center for Creative Leadership, 1996), accessed January 21, 2014, http://www.ccl.org/leadership/pdf/publications/readers/reader172ccl.pdf.
9. John. P. Kotter, *Force for Change: How Leadership Differs From Management*, Free Press, 1990.
10. David Baldwin and Curt Grayson, *Influence: Gaining Commitment, Getting Results*, (Greensboro: Center for Creative Leadership, 2004), 11.
11. Gautam Kumra, "Leading Change: An Interview With the Managing Director of Tata Motors," *The McKinsey Quarterly* (January 2007), http://www.mckinsey.com/insights/organization/leading_change_an_interview_with_the_managing_director_of_tata_motors.
12. Ibid, Dino Lanna, "Boost Employee Engagement."
13. Ibid, Dino Lanna, "Boost Employee Engagement."
14. Mary Siegfried, "The Power of Influence," *Inside Supply Management*®, (16:10), October 2005, accessed January 28, 2014, http://www.ism.ws/pubs/ISMMag/ismarticle.cfm?ItemNumber=12644.
15. Thomas K. Linton and Jason Y. Choi, "Global Procurement Transformation: New Frontiers for Global Innovation," ISM 95th Annual International Supply Management Conference, April 2010, accessed August 8, 2013, http://www.ism.ws/files/RichterAwards/2010WinnerLGEProceedings.pdf.
16. Josh Bersin, "How Does Leadership Vary Across the Globe?," *Forbes*, October 31, 2012, accessed November 20, 2013, http://www.forbes.com/sites/joshbersin/2012/10/31/are-expat-programs-dead/.
17. Ibid.
18. Michael Jenkins, "A Question of Leadership," *Leadership in Action*, March 2005, Wiley Periodicals Inc.
19. Gautum Kumra, "Leading Change: An Interview With the Managing Director of Tata Motors," 7.
20. James Fallows, "Mr. Zhang Builds His Dream Town," *The Atlantic Monthly* (March 2007).
21. Keith Bradsher, "Chinese Tycoon Focuses on Green Construction," *New York Times*, December 7, 2010, accessed November 18, 2013, http://www.nytimes.com/2010/12/08/business/global/08tycoon.html?_r=0; and Champions of the Earth. United Nations Environment Programme, accessed August 7, 2013, http://www.unep.org/champions/laureates/2011/yue.asp.

22. Michelle LeBaron, "Communication Tools for Understanding Cultural Differences" in *Beyond Intractability*, Guy Burgess and Heidi Burgess, eds. (Boulder: Conflict Research Consortium, June 2003), available from www.beyondintractability.org/essay/communication_tools/.
23. Fallows, "Mr. Zhang Builds His Dream Town," 85-92.
24. Champions of the Earth. United Nations Environment Programme, accessed August 7, 2013, http://www.unep.org/champions/laureates/2011/yue.asp.
25. QuoteWorld.org, Kenneth Blanchard, accessed January 28, 2014, www.quoteworld.org/quotes/1544.
26. Kotter, *Force for Change: How Leadership Differs from Management.*
27. "The New Work of Leadership: Connectivity, Creativity and Continuity," *Leading Effectively: eNewsletter* (The Center for Creative Leadership, April 2004).
28. Seana Steffen, "Beyond Environmental Leadership to Restorative Leadership: An Emerging Framework for Cultivating Resilient Communities in the 21st Century," in D.R. Gallagher (Ed.) *Environmental Leadership: A Reference Handbook.* (Thousand Oaks, CA: SAGE Publications, Inc., 2012).
29. Conrad Hilton Foundation, "Hilton Humanitarian Prize," accessed November 21, 2013, http://www.hiltonfoundation.org/brundtland.
30. Lisa Wolters-Broder, "Beyond Borders," *Inside Supply Management*®, (20:9), September 2009, 36, accessed November 21, 2013, http://www.ism.ws/pubs/ISMMag/ismarticle.cfm?ItemNumber=19670.
31. Bruce W. Tuckman, "Developmental Sequence in Small Groups," *Psychological Bulletin* 63 (1965), 384–99; and Bruce W. Tuckman and Mary Ann Jensen, "Stages of Small Group Development Revisited," *Group and Organizational Studies* 2 (1977), 419–27.
32. "How Harley-Davidson Uses Cross-Functional Teams," *Purchasing* 4 (November 1999), 144.
33. Jeanne Brett, Kristin Behfar and Mary C. Kern, "Managing Multicultural Teams," *Harvard Business Review* (November 2006), 84–91.
34. Ibid.
35. Gerzon, "What Is Leadership?"
36. Deming, *Out of the Crisis.*
37. Ibid.
38. Thomas K. Linton and Jason Y. Choi, "Global Procurement Transformation: New Frontiers for Global Innovation," ISM 95th Annual International Supply Management Conference, April 2010, accessed August 8, 2013, http://www.ism.ws/files/RichterAwards/2010WinnerLGEProceedings.pdf

Chapter 5

1. Lewis M. Branscomb and Phillip E. Auerwald, *Taking Technical Risks: How Innovators, Managers and Investors Manage* (Cambridge: MIT Press, 2001), 47.
2. George Zsidisin, "Measuring Supply Risk: An Example From Europe," *PRACTIX*, CAPS Research 4 (June 2001), 2.
3. Tom DeMarco and Timothy Lister, *Waltzing With Bears: Managing Risk on Software Projects* (New York: Dorset House Publishing, 2003).
4. For more information about Sarbanes-Oxley, please see http://www.sox-online.com/act_toc.html.
5. Global Reporting Initiative; for more information see https://www.globalreporting.org/Pages/default.aspx, accessed September 13, 2013.
6. Risk Factors, *Federal Express Annual Report 2013*, 33, accessed August 16, 2013, http://investors.fedex.com/phoenix.zhtml?c=73289&p=irol-reportsannual.
7. Deere & Company, *Code of Ethics*, accessed September 12, 2013, http://search.deere.com/DDC/en_US/?query=Code+of+Ethics&x=9&y=6.
8. Phil Carter, Robert Monczka, W. Markham, Robert Trent, J. Jartley, Casey McDowell and Gary Ragatz, *Risk Management Across the Extended Value Chain*, 2012, CAPS Research, Tempe, AZ.
9. Vista Law, "U.S. FCPA vs. UK Bribery Act," accessed November 14, 2013, http://www.transparency-usa.org/documents/FCPAvsBriberyAct.pdf.
10. Deere & Company, accessed September 12, 2013, http://www.deere.com/wps/dcom/en_US/corporate/our_company/investor_relations/corporate_governance/code_of_ethics/code_of_ethics.page.
11. Institute for Supply Management®, "Operational Risk Management – Event Scenario Planning," *Inside Supply Management*®, (24:6), August 2013, accessed September 12, 2013, http://www.ism.ws/pubs/ISMMag/ismarticle.cfm?ItemNumber=23795.
12. Mark Ensign, "Supplier Risk Management at Sonoco," presented April 2009, CAPS Research Executive Roundtable, accessed August 18, 2013, http://capsresearch.org/Search/Search.aspx?QuickSearch=financailrisk%20management.
13. George Zsidisin, "Measuring Supply Risk: An Example From Europe," 3.
14. Ibid, CAPS Research, *Risk Management Across the Extended Value Chain*.
15. Robin B. Gray Jr., "Counterfeiting — What (and Who) Can You Trust?" e*Side Supply Management*, (2:3), May/June 2009, accessed August 18, 2013, http://www.ism.ws/pubs/eSide/eSideArticle.cfm?ItemNumber=19262.
16. Zsidisin, "Measuring Supply Risk: An Example From Europe," 3.
17. Ibid.
18. R. Monczka, P. Carter, W. Markham, R. Trent, J. Hartley et al, "Risk Management Across the Extended Supply Chain," CAPS Research, 2012, Tempe, AZ.

19. Kish Khemani and Brent Ross, A. T. Kearney, "With Acquisitions Procurement Planning Pays," *Supply Chain Management Review*, March/April 2013, accessed September 13, 2013, http://www.atkearney.com/documents/10192/926101/SCMR.MI.ProcurementPlanning.pdf/b58fea03-3620-4056-9e6d-20699f23a854.
20. Christopher Elliott, "Is It Time to Unmerge Some Airlines?," Special for *USA TODAY*, November 18, 2013, accessed November 22, 2013, http://www.usatoday.com/story/travel/flights/2013/11/17/american-us-airways-airlines-merger/3621543/.
21. "Keiretsu," *Economist*, October 16, 2009, accessed November 22, 2013, http://www.economist.com/node/14299720.
22. Rose Kim, "Recruiting: For South Korea's Top Students, Chaebol Are the Place to Be," *Bloomberg BusinessWeek*, September 26, 2013, accessed November 22, 2013, http://www.businessweek.com/articles/2013-09-26/for-south-koreas-top-students-chaebol-are-the-place-to-be.
23. "U.K. to Privatize Royal Mail," *The Wall Street Journal*, September 13, 2013, B6.
24. Ibid.
25. Elix-IRR, "Trends in Outsourcing & Offshoring in the Financial Services Industry 2008-2012," Elix-IRR Annual Report, October 2012, accessed August 19, 2013, http://www.slideshare.net/newtonsa1/trends-in-outsourcing-offshoring-in-the-financial-services-industry-20082012-elixirr-annual-report.
26. "Reshoring Manufacturing, Coming Home," *The Economist*, January 19, 2013, accessed June 13, 2013, http://www.economist.com/news/special-report/21569570-growing-number-american-companies-are-moving-their-manufacturing-back-united.
27. Wendy Tate, Lisa Ellram, Tobias Schoenerr and Ken Petersen, et al (2014), "Global Competitive Conditions Driving The Manufacturing Location Decision," Forthcoming, *Business Horizons*, and op cit.

Chapter 6

1. Steve Hamm and Dexter Roberts, "China's First Global Capitalist," *BusinessWeek* (December 2006), 11.
2. Lenovo, "Our Culture," accessed November 22, 2013, http://www.lenovo.com/lenovo/us/en/our_culture.html.
3. BrainyQuote®, Peter Drucker, http://www.brainyquote.com/quotes/authors/p/peter_drucker.html.
4. Charles Fine, *Clockspeed: Winning Industry Control in the Age of Temporary Advantage* (New York: Perseus Books Group, 1998).
5. Hoovers, accessed September 11, 2013, http://www.hoovers.com/company-information/cs/competition.Intel_Corporation.b4f2f5cfd938b4ec.html.

6. Wal-Mart 2012 Global Responsibility Report, "Fleet Improvements," accessed November 22, 2013, http://www.walmartstores.com/sites/responsibility-report/2012/fleetImprovements.aspx.
7. Hamm and Roberts, "China's First Global Capitalist."
8. Rogers, Stephen C. "Achieve M&A Supply Synergy," *Inside Supply Management®*, (21:11), December 2010, 28-30.
9. Ibid.
10. "Managing Procurement Through a Merger: Capturing the Value of the Deal," 2006, accessed January 21, 2014, http://www.boozallen.com/media/file/87995.pdf.
11. Ibid.
12. Kish Khemani and Brent Ross, A. T. Kearney, "With Acquisitions, Procurement Planning Pays," *Supply Chain Management Review*, March/April, 2013, accessed September 11, 2013, http://www.atkearney.com/documents/10192/926101/SCMR.MI.ProcurementPlanning.pdf/b58fea03-3620-4056-9e6d-20699f23a854.
13. Whirlpool, About, "Our Vision," accessed January 29, 2014, http://www.whirlpoolcorp.com/about/overview.aspx.
14. Whirlpool, Global Consumer Design, "Our Philosophy," accessed November 22, 2013, http://www.whirlpoolcorp.com/about/design/global_consumer_design/overview.aspx.
15. Whirlpool, 2012 Annual Report, 21, accessed November 22, 2013, http://files.shareholder.com/downloads/ABEA-5DXEK8/2784271661x0x643263/EBB1BF58-13A0-42D6-89B7-4A68F980543B/WHR_2012_Annual_Report.pdf.
16. IBM, "Our Strategy," accessed November 22, 2013, http://www.ibm.com/Search/?q=strategy&v=17&en=utf&lang=en&cc=us.
17. IBM, "Generating Higher Value at IBM," accessed November 22, 2013, http://www.ibm.com/annualreport/2012/ghv/#one.
18. IBM, Global Procurement, accessed November 22, 2013, http://www-03.ibm.com/procurement/proweb.nsf/ContentDocsByTitle/United+States~Global+Procurement.
19. Ibid.
20. IBM, Global Procurement, "Procurement One Place Strategy," accessed November 22, 2013, http://www-03.ibm.com/procurement/proweb.nsf/ContentDocsByTitle/United+States~Procurement+One+Place+strategy.
21. IBM, Global Procurement, accessed November 22, 2013, http://www-03.ibm.com/procurement/proweb.nsf/ContentDocsByTitle/United+States~Global+Procurement.
22. Rodger L. Boehm, "Leading Change: An Interview With the CEO of Deere & Company," *The McKinsey Quarterly*, December 2006, accessed November 22, 2013, http://www.executivesondemand.net/managementsourcing/images/stories/artigos_pdf/gestao/Leading_change,_An_interview_with_the_CEO_of_Deere_&_Company.pdf.

Chapter 7

1. Warren G. Bennis, *On Becoming a Leader* (New York: De Capo Press, 2003), 182.
2. Volkswagen Group, "Overview," accessed October 1, 2013, http://navigator.volkswagenag.com/index.html?lang=en_GB&deeplink=#brand/man/overview.
3. Lisa M. Ellram and Wendy Tate, "Best Practices in Services Purchasing at Bank of America," *PRACTIX*, Best Practices in Purchasing and Supply Management, Vol. 9, CAPS Research, 2006.
4. Gregory Dess, G.T. (Tom) Lumpkin and Alan Eisner, *Strategic Management: Text and Cases* (Burr Ridge: McGraw-Hill/Irwin, 2007).
5. Gold, Hirano and Yokoyama, "An Outsider Takes On Japan," *The McKinsey Quarterly*, Winter 2001.
6. P. Fraser Johnson and Michiel Leenders, "Supply's Organizational Roles and Responsibilities 2011," 2012, CAPS Research, Tempe, AZ.
7. Lisa Arnseth, "Centralizing Procurement at a Nonprofit," *Inside Supply Management*®, (23:3), April 2012, 26-32.
8. Samuel Fairchild, Ph.D.,"Center-Led Team Lessons," *Inside Supply Management*® (21:10), October 2010, 14, accessed October 22, 2013, http://www.ism.ws/pubs/ISMMag/ismarticle.cfm?ItemNumber=20820.
9. Lisa Arnseth "From Decentralized to Center-Led Supply Management," *Inside Supply Management*® (21:4), April 2010, 20.
10. Anna Flynn and Sam Farney, "Operating Policies, Guidelines and Procedures" in *The Supply Management Leadership Process*, Volume 4 of the ISM *Knowledge Series* (Tempe, AZ: NAPM, 2000): 145–70.
11. David F. Ross, "The Intimate Supply Chain," *Supply Chain Management Review* (July 1, 2006).
12. Robert Monczka, Phil Carter, W. Markham, Robert Trent, Ken Petersen, E. Nichols and J. Hartley, "Collaboration Across the Extended Value Chain," August 2013, CAPS Research, Tempe, AZ, 35.
13. Ibid., 8.
14. Ibid, 35.

Chapter 8

1. Thinkexist.com, accessed November 5, 2013, http://en.thinkexist.com/quotes/W._Edwards_Deming/.
2. Audrey Going Brichi and Paul L. Massih, "Strategic Sourcing and Supplier Diversity — Strategies for Success," ISM's 87th International Supply Management Conference, San Francisco, 2002.
3. Lisa Arnseth, "Early Alignment Creates Lasting Success," August 2013, *Inside Supply Management*®, (24:6), 26-30.

4. Ibid.
5. Joe Mahon, "Taking the Shears to Fuel Costs," *Fedgazette*, May 2006, accessed November 5, 2013, www.minneapolisfed.org/pubs/fedgaz/06-05/fuel.cfm.
6. Jad Mouawad, "Delta Buys Refinery to Get Control of Fuel Costs," *The New York Times*, April 30, 2012, accessed October 23, 2013, http://www.nytimes.com/2012/05/01/business/delta-air-lines-to-buy-refinery.html?_r=0.
7. Ibid, Arnseth.
8. Peter Kraljic, "Purchasing Must Become Supply Management," *Harvard Business Review* (September/October 1983).
9. Ibid, Arnseth.
10. Lisa Arnseth, "Quantifying Commodity Spend," (24:3), April 2013, *Inside Supply Management*®, 28-32.
11. Thinkexist.com, "Gary Hirshberg," accessed December 18, 2013, http://thinkexist.com/quotations/quality/2.html.
12. Mary Siegfried, "Outsourcing Finds Its Niche," (23:9), November 2012, *Inside Supply Management*®, 22.
13. Michiel Leenders, R. Kudar and Anna E. Flynn, "Fleet Management's Contribution and Outsourcing," an unpublished manuscript based on a study conducted for the National Association of Fleet Administrators, 1995.
14. Jason Busch, "E Sourcing Research. ERP Software Compared to Specialist Providers," *Spend Matters*, January 2013, accessed November 7, 2013, http://spendmatters.com/2013/01/07/esourcing-research-erp-software-solutions-compared-to-specialist-providers/
15. A.T. Kearney, "Collaborative Optimization Sourcing," accessed November 7, 2013, http://www.atkearney.com/paper/-/asset_publisher/dVxv4Hz2h8bS/content/collaborative-optimization-sourci-1/10192; and sciQuest, Sourcing Glossary, http://www.sciquest.com/resource-center/glossary/sourcing/#collaborativesourcing, accessed November 7, 2013.
16. Karl Schmieder, "Save Time, Money, and Improve Supply Chain Management With E-Procurement," *Life Science Leader*, December 7, 2011, accessed October 23, 2013, http://www.lifescienceleader.com/doc/save-time-money-and-improve-supply-chain-0001.
17. Ibid.
18. "Strategic Supply Management at Japanese Companies," Supply Management Research Group, Japan, Case Study: Company B, CAPS Research (2006), 17.
19. Stewart Beall, et.al., "The Role of Reverse Auction in Strategic Sourcing," CAPS Research (2003), 44-45.
20. L. Arnseth, "Smart Procurement on Georgia's Mind," (22:2), *Inside Supply Management*®, April 2011, 28.

21. Financial Applications, "Contract management software," accessed November 11, 2013, http://searchfinancialapplications.techtarget.com/definition/contract-management-software.

Chapter 9

1. Thomas J. Watson, Jr., *A Business and Its Beliefs: Ideas That Helped Build IBM* (New York: McGraw-Hill Professional, 1963), 4.
2. Nick Little, "In Search of Talent," *Inside Supply Management*®, (23:9), November 2012, 34.
3. "Taking Measure of Talent," *Harvard Business Review Analytic Services Report*, n.d., accessed October 24, 2013, http://hcmdownloads.com/system/files/file_downloads/3c558ec4ca871cb479528f4ab0311c4c/workday-hbr-taking-measure-of-talent-whitepaper.pdf.
4. P. Fraser Johnson and Michiel Leenders, "Supply's Organizational Roles and Responsibilites 2011," 2012, CAPS Research, Tempe, AZ.
5. Joo-Seng Tan, "Cultural Intelligence and the Global Economy," *Leadership in Action* 24(5) (November/December 2004).
6. A.T. Kearney, "Impacting the Supply Management Profession: Charting and Navigating Strategies for the CPO and Your Team's Evolution" (2007).
7. S. Peterson, L. Webber, D. Rosselli and B. Schaefer, *2013 Chief Procurement Officer Study*, IBM Institute for Business Value, May 2013, accessed November 9, 2013, http://public.dhe.ibm.com/common/ssi/ecm/en/gbe03561usen/GBE03561USEN.PDF.
8. The Conference Board, "Developing Global Leaders."
9. Lisa Ellram and Wendy Tate, "Bank of America: Services Purchasing and Outsourcing."
10. R. Thomas, J. Bellin, C. Jules and N. Lynton, "Developing Tomorrow's Global Leaders," *MIT Sloan Management Review*, September 12, 2013, accessed November 9, 2013, http://sloanreview.mit.edu/article/developing-tomorrows-global-leaders/.
11. Robert Monczka and Phil Carter, *Supply Management Strategies for Success in the New Economy*, 2011, CAPS Research, Tempe, AZ.
12. The Conference Board, "Developing Global Leaders"; and R. Slaybaugh, "Talent Management for Tomorrow," (5:6), *eSide Supply Management*, November/December 2012, accessed November 10, 2013, http://www.ism.ws/pubs/eSide/eSideArticle.cfm?ItemNumber=23273.
13. Rose Mary Wentling, *Diversity Initiatives in the Workplace* (Champaign: The National Center for Research in Vocational Education NCRVE, University of Illinois), accessed November 10, 2013, http://ncrve.berkeley.edu/CW82/Diversity.html.
14. IBM, "Transforming Big Blue's Procurement Operations," June 2013, accessed November 10, 2013, http://www.ndm.net/mobile/pdf/IBM%20Success%20Story%20Transforming%20Big%20Blue's%20Procurement%20Operation.pdf.

15. Ernst and Young Global, "Demographic Shifts Transform the Global Workforce," 2011, accessed October 24, 2013, http://www.ey.com/GL/en/Issues/Business-environment/Six-global-trends-shaping-the-business-world---Demographic-shifts-transform-the-global-workforce.
16. G7 includes the U.S., Japan, Germany, France, Italy, United Kingdom and Canada. The BRIC includes Brazil, Russia, India and China.
17. PwC, "Gridlines: Closing the Talent Gap in the Emerging World," December 2012, accessed October 24, 2013, http://www.pwc.com/gx/en/capital-projects-infrastructure/assets/gridlines_talent1210.pdf.
18. General Mills, Responsibility and "Diversity and Inclusion," accessed November 10, 2013, http://www.generalmills.com/Responsibility/Diversity.aspx.
19. Manpower 2013 Talent Shortage Survey, 2013, accessed October 24, 2013, http://www.manpowergroup.us/campaigns/talent-shortage-2013/pdf/TSS_MPG_NA_2013_vertical_061713-zz.pdf.
20. Sean Silverthorne, "Who Rises to Power in American Business?," Harvard Business School Working Knowledge Newsletter (January 8, 2007), accessed November 10, 2013, http://hbswk.hbs.edu/item/5504.html.
21. CAPS Research, "Talent Management Twenty Twelve — A Benchmarking Perspective," March 28, 2012.
22. Nick Little, "In Search of Talent," *Inside Supply Management*®, (23:9), November 2012, 34.
23. Gary A. Berg, Mihaly Csikszentmihalyi and Jeanne Nakamura, "Mission Possible? Enabling Good Work in Higher Education," *Change* 35 (5) (2003), 41-7.
24. Ibid, Little.
25. Google, Jobs, "Life at Google," accessed November 11, 2013, https://www.google.com/about/jobs/lifeatgoogle/.
26. Atento, Join Us, "Atento: Great Place to Work," accessed November 11, 2013, http://www.atento.com/join-us/135/greatplacetowork.
27. HP, "The Diversity Value Chain," accessed October 25, 2013, http://www8.hp.com/us/en/hp-information/about-hp/diversity/value.html.
28. HP, Highlights of our Diversity Journey, accessed October 26, 2013, http://www8.hp.com/us/en/hp-information/about-hp/diversity/highlights.html?jumpid=reg_r1002_usen_c001_title_r000.
29. Roberta Jennings, "Talent Development for Successful Supply Management," August 2011, CAPS Research, Tempe, AZ.

Chapter 10

1. Steffen Fuchs, Gillian Pais and Jeff Shulman, "Building Superior Capabilities for Strategic Sourcing," McKinsey & Company Insights and Publications, May 2013, accessed October 26, 2013, http://www.mckinsey.com/insights/operations/building_superior_capabilities_for_strategic_sourcing.
2. Accenture, "Compulsive Contributors," 2011, accessed October 26, 2013, http://www.accenture.com/SiteCollectionDocuments/PDF/Accenture_Compulsive_Contributors.pdf.
3. S. Peterson, L. Webber, D. Rosselli and B. Schaefer, *2013 Chief Procurement Officer Study*, IBM Institute for Business Value, May 2013, accessed November 12, 2013, http://public.dhe.ibm.com/common/ssi/ecm/en/gbe03561usen/GBE03561USEN.PDF.
4. BrainyQuote®, Alvin Toffler, accessed January 30, 2014, www.brainyquote.com/quotes/authors/a/alvin_toffler.html.
5. Peter Senge, *The Fifth Discipline: The Art and Practice of the Learning Organization* (New York: Currency, 2006).
6. Arie de Geus, *The Living Company: Habits for Survival in a Turbulent Business Environment* (Cambridge: Harvard Business School Press, 2002).
7. CAPS Research, "Talent Management Twenty-Twelve — A Benchmarking Perspective," March 28, 2012, CAPS Research, Tempe, AZ.
8. PwC, 15th Annual Global CEO Survey 2012, accessed October 15, 2013, www.pwc.com/ceosurvey.
9. Ibid, PwC.
10. The Conference Board, "Developing Global Leaders."
11. Ibid.
12. Ibid.
13. Ibid, CAPS Research.
14. John Ryan, "Accelerating Performance: Five Leadership Skills You and Your Organization Can't Do Without," 2010, Center for Creative Leadership, accessed November 12, 2013, http://www.ccl.org/leadership/pdf/news/AcceleratingPerformance.pdf.
15. Goodreads, accessed December 16, 2013, http://www.goodreads.com/quotes/114324-a-person-can-perform-only-from-strength-one-cannot-build.
16. Tanya Prive, "Top Ten Qualities that Make a Great Leader," *Forbes*, December 19, 2012, accessed November 12, 2012, http://www.forbes.com/sites/tanyaprive/2012/12/19/top-10-qualities-that-make-a-great-leader/.
17. Nina Bahadur, "Men vs. Women in Leadership," *Huffington Post*, April 12, 2013, accessed November 12, 2013, http://www.huffingtonpost.com/nina-bahadur/men-vs-women-in-leadership-gender-gap_b_3071598.html.

18. Ronald E. Riggio, "Do Men and Women Lead Differently? Who's Better?," *Psychology Today*, March 23, 2010, accessed November 12, 2013, http://www.psychologytoday.com/blog/cutting-edge-leadership/201003/do-men-and-women-lead-differently-whos-better.
19. Nick Petrie, "Future Trends in Leadership Development," December 2011, Center for Creative Leadership.
20. Robert Monczka and Phillip Carter, *Supply Management Strategies for Success in the New Economy*, 2011, CAPS Research, Tempe, AZ.
21. *A Guide to the Project Management Body of Knowledge,* 5th ed. (PMBOK® Guide), (Newtown Square. PA: Project Management Institute 2014).
22. Ken Blanchard, Chapter 8 in *Leading at a Higher Level: Blanchard on How to Be a Higher-Performing Leader* (Upper Saddle River: FT Press 2006).
23. NACE, "The Skills and Qualities Employers Want in Their Class of 2013 Recruits," NACE, October 24, 2012, accessed October 26, 2013, http://www.weber.edu/WSUImages/SBE/Career%20Center/SkillsEmployersWant2013.pdf.
24. Ibid.
25. Ibid, Peterson, Webber, Rosselli, Schaefer.
26. F.C. Goldstein and H.S. Levin, "Disorders of Reasoning and Problem-Solving Ability" in *Neuropsychological Rehabilitation*, M. Meier, A. Benton and L. Diller, eds. (London: Taylor & Francis Group 1987).
27. Jonah Lehrer, "How To Be Creative," March 12, 2012, accessed October 27, 2013, http://online.wsj.com/news/articles/SB10001424052970203370604577265632205015846.
28. Ibid, Lehrer.
29. Teresa M. Amabile, "How to Kill Creativity," *Harvard Business Review* 76(5) (1998).
30. Ibid, Lehrer.
31. Richard Gonzales, "Career Coaches Help Minorities On Way to the Top," January 15, 2010, accessed October 27, 2013, http://www.npr.org/templates/story/story.php?storyId=122576958.
32. Susan Johnston, "In Reverse Mentoring, Executives Learn from Millenials," *MONEY Personal Finance*, April 15, 2013, accessed November 13, 2013, http://money.usnews.com/money/personal-finance/articles/2013/04/15/in-reverse-mentoring-executives-learn-from-millennials.
33. technopedia, "Reverse Mentoring," accessed November 13, 2013, http://www.techopedia.com/definition/28107/reverse-mentoring.
34. Mary Siegfried, "Filling the Leadership Void," *Inside Supply Management*® (April 2007).
35. Ibid, Petrie.
36. WorldatWork, "Total Rewards Professionals' Career Development Survey," April 2013, WorldatWork, Scottsdale, AZ.

37. Wendy Bliss, J.D., SPHR, "Developing Employee Career Paths and Ladders," September 5, 2013, Society for Human Resource Management, Alexandria, VA.
38. Ibid, Bliss.
39. Tandem H.R., "End of the Boom: Retiring Baby Boomers and the Consequences for Your Business," 2010, accessed October 27, 2013, http://www.tandemhr.com/userfiles/file/Exit%20of%20Baby%20Boomers%20Affecting%20the%20Workplace.pdf.

Chapter 11

1. Warren Buffet, accessed November 13, 2013, http://www.brainyquote.com/quotes/authors/w/warren_buffett.html.
2. Ann Oka, "Recognition: Why Metrics Matter," *Inside Supply Management*®, (21:9), September 2010, 12, accessed October 27, 2013, http://www.ism.ws/pubs/ISMMag/ismarticle.cfm?ItemNumber=20704.
3. Ibid, Oka.
4. Ibid, Oka.
5. Phillip L. Carter, Robert M. Monczka and Trish Mosconi, "Strategic Performance Measures for Purchasing and Supply," CAPS Research (2005), accessed November 13, 2013, https://knowledge.capsresearch.org/publications/pdfs-protected/carterp2005.pdf.
6. Terri Tracey, *ISM's 2013 Salary Survey* (Tempe, AZ: Institute for Supply Management), accessed October 26, 2013, http://www.ism.ws/files/Tools/2013ISMSalarySurveyBrief.pdf.
7. Ibid, Oka.
8. W. Edwards Deming, Out of the Crisis, 42.
9. Eric Harmon, Scott Hensel and Tim Lukes, "Measuring Performance in Services," 1, 2006, *The McKinsey Quarterly*.
10. Ibid, Oka.
11. Robert Monczka and Phillip Carter, *Supply Management Strategies for Success in the New Economy*, 2011, CAPS Research, Tempe, AZ.
12. "Follow the Procurement Leaders: Assessment of Excellence in Procurement Study," Copyright A. T. Kearney, 2011. All rights reserved; quoted with permission, accessed November 15, 2013, https://www.atkearney.com/paper/-/asset_publisher/dVxv4Hz2h8bS/content/follow-the-procurement-leaders/10192.
13. Samuel Fairchild, Ph.D., "Center-Led Team Lessons," *Inside Supply Management*®, (21:10), October 2010, 14, accessed October 27, 2013, http://www.ism.ws/pubs/ISMMag/ismarticle.cfm?ItemNumber=20820.
14. William Atkinson, "Driving Efficiency," *Purchasing* (August 11, 2005).
15. Yatish Desai, "Drive Supply Chain Excellence Through Performance Metrics," (22:9), *Inside Supply Management*®, December 2011, 36, accessed November 15, 2013, http://www.ism.ws/pubs/ISMMag/ismarticle.cfm?ItemNumber=22086.

16. CAPS Research, "The Future of Benchmarking," *Inside Supply Management*®, (24:3), April 2013, 34, accessed October 28, 2013, http://www.ism.ws/pubs/ISMMag/ismarticle.cfm?ItemNumber=23541.
17. Terry Volpel, "A 'Carrot' Approach to Bonus Pay," e*Side Supply Management*, (6:3), May/June 2013, accessed October 28, 2013, http://www.ism.ws/pubs/eSide/eSideArticle.cfm?ItemNumber=23655.
18. Josh Bond, "Modern's 5th Annual Salary Survey," *Supply Chain 24/7*, September 2012, accessed November 16, 2013, http://www.supplychain247.com/article/5th_annual_salary_survey_time_to_reap_what_you_sow.
19. Margi Gordon, "How Do Leaders Measure Up?," *Inside Supply Management*®, (22:2), April 2011, 14, accessed October 28, 2013, http://www.ism.ws/pubs/ISMMag/ismarticle.cfm?ItemNumber=21489.
20. Jim Adkins, "Let Skills Lead the Way," *Inside Supply Management*®, (24:1), January 2013, 10, accessed October 28, 2013, http://www.ism.ws/pubs/ISMMag/ismarticle.cfm?ItemNumber=23377.

Chapter 12

1. Tom Warga, NY Life Insurance, quoted in "Get Ready for the Privacy Backlash," *Darwin Magazine* (2001).
2. COSO, The Committee of Sponsoring Organizations of the Treadway Commission, accessed November 18, 2013, http://www.coso.org/aboutus.htm.
3. Committee of Sponsoring Organizations of the Treadway Commission (COSO), "Internal Control — Integrated Framework," May 2013, accessed December 18, 2013, http://www.coso.org/documents/990025P_Executive_Summary_final_may20_e.pdf.
4. Ibid.
5. Ibid, COSO, http://www.coso.org/IC.htm, accessed November 18, 2013.
6. International Accounting Standards Board, About Us, accessed November 18, 2013, http://www.ifrs.org/The-organisation/Pages/IFRS-Foundation-and-the-IASB.aspx.
7. COSO, "Internal Control — Integrated Framework," May 2013.
8. ARMA International, Corporate Governance, Sarbanes-Oxley Act in Europe, accessed June, 12, 2013, http://www.arma.org/r1/membership/international-membership/international-corporations/sox-in-europe.
9. Protiviti, "Implementing an Effective Contract Lifecycle Management Process," 2011, accessed October 28, 2013, http://www.protiviti.com/en-US/Documents/POV/POV-Contract-Lifecycle-Management-Manufacturing-Protiviti.pdf.
10. Protiviti, "Forecasting Costs and Managing Capital Expenditure Programs," 2011, accessed October 28, 2013 http://www.protiviti.com/en-US/Documents/POV/POV-Capital-Expenditure-Programs-Protiviti.pdf.

11. COSO Internal Control Integrated Framework Executive Summary, May 2013, accessed October 28, 2013, http://www.coso.org/documents/990025P_Executive_Summary_final_may20_e.pdf.
12. Baxter 2012 Sustainability Report, "Product Sustainability," 2013, accessed October 28, 2013, http://sustainability.baxter.com/product-responsibility/research-development-design/product-sustainability-review.html.
13. Institute for Supply Management®, ISM *Principles of Sustainability and Social Responsibility*, May 5, 2012, accessed May 25, 2013, http://www.ism.ws/files/SR/PSSRwGuideBook.pdf.
14. "Sustainability Practices That Work: Results from the Sustainable Value Chain Survey," Deloitte Development LLC, Institute for Supply Management®, American Society for Quality and Corporate Responsibility Officers Association, September 2013.
15. America Chung Nam, "About Us," 2013, accessed October 28, 2013, http://www.acni.net/index.html.
16. Ibid, Baxter.
17. Fisher and Paytel, "Sustainability," 2013, accessed October 28, 2013, http://www.fisherpaykel.com/nz/company/sustainability/.
18. European Commission, Environment, "Recast of the WEEE Directive," 2013, accessed October 28, 2013, http://ec.europa.eu/environment/waste/weee/index_en.htm.
19. European Commission, Environment, "Environment: Fewer Risks From Hazardous Substances in Electrical and Electronic Equipment," July 20, 2011, accessed November 20, 2013, http://europa.eu/rapid/press-release_IP-11-912_en.htm.
20. Chemical Inspection and Regulation Service, "Draft Version of New China RoHS," published June 7, 2012, accessed November 20, 2013, http://www.cirs-reach.com/news/Draft_Version_of_New_China_RoHS_Published.html.
21. Chemical Inspection and Regulation Service, "Regulations on Safe Management of Hazardous Chemicals in China — Decree 591," updated April 2013, accessed December 18, 2013, http://www.cirs-reach.com/China_Chemical_Regulation/Regulations_on_Safe_Management_of_Hazardous_Chemicals_in_China.html.
22. Baxter 2012 Sustainability Report, "Product End of Life," accessed November 20, 2013, http://sustainability.baxter.com/product-responsibility/product-end-of-life.html.
23. Baxter 2012 Sustainability Report, "Materials Use," accessed November 20, 2013, http://sustainability.baxter.com/product-responsibility/materials-use.html.
24. European Commission, Environment, accessed November 20, 2013, www.ec.europa.eu/environment/waste/weee/index_en.htm
25. Baxter 2012 Sustainability Report, "Product End-of-Life," 2013, accessed October 28, 2013, http://sustainability.baxter.com/product-responsibility/product-end-of-life.html.

26. ARMA, "What Is Records Management? Why Do I Care?," ARMA International, accessed May 21, 2013, http://www.arma.org/pdf/WhatIsRIM.pdf.
27. International Standards Organization, available from https://www.iso.org/obp/ui/#iso:std:iso:15489:-1:ed-1:v1:en
28. AIIM, The Global Community of Information Professionals, "What is Electronic Records Management (ERM)?," accessed November 20, 2013, http://www.aiim.org/What-is-ERM-Electronic-Records-Management.
29. D. Logan, "What is information governance? And why is it so hard?," January 11, 2010, accessed May 21, 2013, http://blogs.gartner.com/debra_logan/2010/01/11/what-is-information-governance-and-why-is-it-so-hard/.
30. International Standards Organization, ISO 17799:2005, accessed November 20, 2013, http://www.iso.org/iso/iso_catalogue/catalogue_ics/catalogue_detail_ics.htm?csnumber=39612.
31. For more information on the U.S. Sarbanes-Oxley Act go to http://www.soxlaw.com/.
32. FedEx Annual Report 2013, 2013, 26, accessed October 28, 2013, http://investors.fedex.com/phoenix.zhtml?c=73289&p=irol-reportsannual.
33. Defense Contract Audit Administration, "Audit of Policies, Procedures, and Internal Controls Relative to Accounting and Management Systems," July 30, 2013, accessed October 28, 2013, http://www.dcaa.mil/cam/Chapter_05_-_Audit_of_Accounting_and_Management_Systems.pdf.

References
Chapter 1

Fiedler, F.E., and M.M. Chemers. *Improving Leadership Effectiveness: The Leader Match Concept*, Second Edition. John Wiley and Sons, New York, NY, 1984.

Hayashi, M. "A Historical Review of Japanese Management Theories: The Search for a General Theory of Japanese Management." *Asian Business & Management*, (1), 2002, pp. 1–19, accessed October 30, 2013, http://www.palgrave-journals.com/abm/journal/v1/n2/abs/9200016a.html.

Lewis, C.P. *Building a Shared Vision: A Leader's Guide to Aligning the Organization*. Productivity Press, Portland, OR, 1997.

Morrisey, G.L. *Morrisey on Planning: A Guide to Strategic Thinking*. Jossey-Bass, San Francisco, CA, 1996.

Rogers, J.L. "Leadership Development for the '90s: Incorporating Emergent Paradigm Perspectives." *NASPA Journal*, Summer 1992, pp. 243–51.

Rost, J.C. "Leadership Development in the New Millennium." *The Journal of Leadership Studies*, November 1993, pp. 91-110.

Slaybaugh, R. "2020 Leadership," *eSide Supply Management*, (4:1), January/February 2011, accessed November 8, 2013, http://www.ism.ws/pubs/eSide/eSideArticle.cfm?ItemNumber=21047.

Thurow, L.C. *Building Wealth: The New Rules for Individuals, Companies, and Nations in a Knowledge-Based Economy*. HarperCollins, New York, NY, 1999.

Chapter 2

Carter, C.R. "Ethical Issues in Global Buyer-Supplier Relationships." CAPS Research, Tempe, AZ, 1998.

Carter, C.R. and M.M. Jennings. "Purchasing's Contribution to the Socially Responsible Management of the Supply Chain." CAPS Research, Tempe, AZ, 2000.

Dalton, M. A. "Cultural Adaptability: It's About More Than Using the Right Fork." *Leadership in Action*, (21:6), January/February 2002, pp. 8-11.

Flynn, A. and S. Farney. Chapter 2, "The Strategic Planning Process," and Chapter 4, "Leading, Managing and Supervising." In *The Supply Management Leadership Process: Strategies for Organizational Effectiveness*. National Association of Purchasing Management, Inc., Tempe, AZ, 2000.

Cavinato, J.L., A.E. Flynn, M.L. Harding, C.S. Lallatin, M.L. Peck, H.M. Pohlig, S.R. Sturzl and V. Tucker (Eds.). ISM *Glossary of Key Supply Management Terms*, 6th edition, Institute for Supply Management®, Tempe, AZ, 2014.

Hedderich, F., R. Giesecke and D. Ohmsen. "Identifying and Evaluating Chinese Suppliers: China Sourcing Practices of German Manufacturing Companies." *PRACTIX*, CAPS Research 9, August 2006.

Kotter, J.P. *A Force for Change*. The Free Press, New York, NY, 1990.

Kotter, J.P. "What Leaders Really Do." *Harvard Business Review*, May-June, 1990.

Kotter, J.P. "Winning at Change," *Leader to Leader*, (10), Fall 1998, pp. 27-33.

Monczka, R., P. Carter, W. Markham, R. Trent, J. Hartley, C. McDowell and G. Ragatz, *Value Chain Strategies for the Changing Decade: Risk Management Across the Extended Value Chain*. 2012, CAPS Research, Tempe, AZ.

Chapter 3

Goleman, D., R. Boyatzis and A. McKee. *Primal Leadership*. Harvard Business School Press, Boston, MA, 2004.

Chapter 5

Carter, P., R. Monczka, W. Markham, R. Trent, J. Hartley, C. McDowell and G. Ragatz. *Risk Management Across the Extended Value Chain*, 2012. CAPS Research, Tempe, AZ.

Fine, C. *Clockspeed: Winning Industry Control in the Age of Temporary Advantage*. Perseus Books, Reading, MA, 1998.

Cavinato, J.L., A.E. Flynn, M.L. Harding, C.S. Lallatin, M.L. Peck, H.M. Pohlig, S.R. Sturzl and V. Tucker (Eds.). ISM *Glossary of Key Supply Management Terms*, 6th edition, Institute for Supply Management®, Tempe, AZ, 2014.

Leenders, M.R., P.F. Johnson, A.E. Flynn and H.E. Fearon. Chapter 18. "Make or Buy, Insourcing or Outsourcing," and Chapter 20, "Strategic Supply." In *Purchasing and Supply Management*, McGraw Hill, Burr Ridge, IL, 2005.

Stokes, M. "Taking Full Advantage of Enterprisewide Risk Management." *The Treasurer*, Association of Corporate Treasurers, London, England, May 2004.

Chapter 6

Fine, C. *Clockspeed: Winning Industry Control in the Age of Temporary Advantage*. Perseus Books, Reading, MA, 1998.

Cavinato, J.L., A.E. Flynn, M.L. Harding, C.S. Lallatin, M.L. Peck, H.M. Pohlig, S.R. Sturzl and V. Tucker (Eds.). ISM *Glossary of Key Supply Management Terms*, 6th edition, Institute for Supply Management®, Tempe, AZ, 2014.

Johnson, P.F., Leenders, M. and A. Flynn. *Purchasing and Supply Management*, 14th ed., McGraw-Hill, New York, 2010.

Morrisey, G. *A Guide to Long-Range Planning: Creating Your Strategic Journey.* Jossey-Bass, San Francisco, CA, 1996.

Morrisey, G. *A Guide to Tactical Planning: Producing Your Short-Term Results.* Jossey-Bass, San Francisco, CA, 1996.

Chapter 7

Monczka, R., P. Carter, W. Markham, R. Trent, K. Petersen, E. Nichols and J. Hartley. *Collaboration Across the Extended Value Chain*, 2013. CAPS Research, Tempe, AZ.

Cavinato, J.L., A.E. Flynn, M.L. Harding, C.S. Lallatin, M.L. Peck, H.M. Pohlig, S.R. Sturzl and V. Tucker (Eds.). ISM *Glossary of Key Supply Management Terms*, 6th edition, Institute for Supply Management®, Tempe, AZ, 2014.

Flynn, A. and S. Farney. Chapter 6, "Operating Policies, Guidelines, and Procedures," and Chapter 7, "Tools to Manage Workflow." In *The Supply Management Leadership Process: Strategies for Organizational Effectiveness*. National Association of Purchasing Management, Inc., Tempe, AZ, 2000, pp. 145-70.

Johnson, P.F. and M.R. Leenders, *Supply's Organizational Roles and Responsibilities*, 2011 (Tempe, AZ: CAPS, 2012).

Johnson, P.F., M.R. Leenders and A.E. Flynn, *Purchasing and Supply Management* (McGraw-Hill/Irwin, 2011).

Chapter 8

Caniels, M.C.J. and C.J. Gelderman. "Power and Interdependence in Kraljic's Purchasing Portfolio Matrix." Competitive paper presented at the IPSERA 2005 Conference, Archamps, France, March 20-24, 2005.

Cavinato, J.L., A.E. Flynn, M.L. Harding, C.S. Lallatin, M.L. Peck, H.M. Pohlig, S.R. Sturzl and V. Tucker (Eds.). ISM *Glossary of Key Supply Management Terms*, 6th edition, Institute for Supply Management®, Tempe, AZ, 2014.

Chapter 9

Aranda, E.K. and L. Aranda, with K. Conlon. *Teams: Structure, Process, Culture, and Politics*. Prentice Hall, Upper Saddle River, NJ, 1998.

CAPS Research, "Talent Management Twenty Twelve — A Benchmarking Perspective," March 28, 2012.

Flynn, A.E. and S. Farney. Chapter 5, "Selecting, Recruiting and Retaining Personnel." In *The Supply Management Leadership Process*, Volume 4. Institute for Supply Management®, Tempe, AZ, 2000.

Cavinato, J.L., A.E. Flynn, M.L. Harding, C.S. Lallatin, M.L. Peck, H.M. Pohlig, S.R. Sturzl and V. Tucker (Eds.). ISM *Glossary of Key Supply Management Terms*, 6th edition, Institute for Supply Management®, Tempe, AZ, 2014.

Johnson, P.F. and M. Leenders. "Supply's Organizational Roles and Responsibilites 2011," 2012. CAPS Research, Tempe, AZ.

Monczka, R. and P. Carter. *Supply Management Strategies for Success in the New Economy*, 2011. CAPS Research, Tempe, AZ.

Ready, D.A. and J.A. Conger. "How to Fill the Talent Gap." Joint study by MIT *Sloan Management Review* and *The Wall Street Journal*, September 2007.

Schwarz, Roger M. *The Skilled Facilitator*. Jossey-Bass Publishers, San Francisco, CA, 1994.

Senge, Peter M. *The Fifth Discipline: The Art and Practice of the Learning Organization*. Doubleday/Currency, New York, 1990.

Chapter 10

Aranda, E.K. and L. Aranda, with K. Conlon. *Teams: Structure, Process, Culture, and Politics*. Prentice Hall, Upper Saddle River, NJ, 1998.

CAPS Research, "Talent Management Twenty-Twelve — A Benchmarking Perspective," March 28, 2012, CAPS Research, Tempe, AZ.

Flynn, A.E. and S. Farney. Chapter 5, "Selecting, Recruiting and Retaining Personnel." In *The Supply Management Leadership Process*, Volume 4, McGraw Hill, Burr Ridge, IL, 2000.

Kramer, R.J. "Developing Global Leaders." The Conference Board, Working Group Report, December 2005.

Monczka, R. and P. Carter, *Supply Management Strategies for Success in the New Economy*, 2011, CAPS Research, Tempe, AZ.

Siegfried, M. "Filling the Leadership Void." *Inside Supply Management*®, April 2007, pp. 22-5.

Chapter 11

Cavinato, J.L., A.E. Flynn, M.L. Harding, C.S. Lallatin, M.L. Peck, H.M. Pohlig, S.R. Sturzl and V. Tucker (Eds.). ISM *Glossary of Key Supply Management Terms*, 6th edition, Institute for Supply Management®, Tempe, AZ, 2014.

Monczka, R. and P. Carter, *Supply Management Strategies for Success in the New Economy*. 2011. CAPS Research, Tempe, AZ.

Chapter 12

Deloitte®, Institute for Supply Management®, American Society for Quality and Corporate Responsibility Officers Association, "Sustainability Practices That Work: Results from the Sustainable Value Chain Survey, September 2013.

Cavinato, J.L., A.E. Flynn, M.L. Harding, C.S. Lallatin, M.L. Peck, H.M. Pohlig, S.R. Sturzl and V. Tucker (Eds.). ISM *Glossary of Key Supply Management Terms*, 6th edition, Institute for Supply Management®, Tempe, AZ, 2014.

ISM *Principles of Sustainability and Social Responsibility, With a Guide to Adoption and Implementation*. 2012, accessed October 28, 2013, http://www.ism.ws/files/SR/PSSRwGuideBook.pdf.

80/20 rule 159

360-degree personnel evaluations 264

A

ABC analysis 159

Acquisitions/divestitures 116

Actual authority 292

ADA 314

Adaptability, modeling 14

Advanced Micro Devices (AMD) 132

Affiliation-oriented leaders 11

Affiliative leadership 74

After-the-fact controls 269, 271, 309-10

Age Discrimination in Employment Act 313

Agency law 108, 292-3, 295, 309

Agency relationships 292, 295

Agents 292-3, 295

Agreements, nondisclosure 116

Alignment
    building 70-1, 76, 129
    creating 55, 57, 59, 61, 63-5, 67, 69, 71, 73, 75, 96
    horizontal 56, 68, 243-4, 247
    internal 49
    stakeholder 60
    strategic 177
    successful 56, 65
    vertical 68, 243

Alignment process 56, 62, 65, 69, 76, 78

Allegis Group Services 218

Amazon.com's vision statement 45

America Chung Nam 279

America West Airlines 118

American Accounting Association 266

American Airlines 118

American Red Cross 26, 64, 155

Analysis
    break-even 133
    competitive 269
    cost/benefit 243, 261
    cost driver 184
    financial 220
    gap 68, 226, 240, 271
    industry 176
    insource/outsource 133
    internal 173
    key ratio 44
    life-cycle 281
    make-or-buy 130
    outsource/buy 119
    post-merger 40, 124, 135, 144
    pre-merger 135
    price 161, 174, 182, 184, 225
    quadrant 192
    rational process 96
    regression 186
    risk-impact 251
    stakeholder 38
    supplier cost management/value 57

Analytical problem-solving 219, 228

Antitrust 297, 300

Apparent authority 292

Applegate, Dennis 273
Assets, divestiture of 40, 116, 135
Assignment consent 116
A.T. Kearney 198, 250, 257
Atento 212
Audit, environmental 279
Auditing, internal 289
Auditing process 272
Authority
   actual 292
   apparent 292
   defining 293
   implied 292
   limited 151

B

Balance, work-life 213
Balanced scorecard 248
Bank of America 151, 200
Barrier-free organizations 151
Baxter International Inc 274, 281, 283
Before-the-fact controls 269, 309-10
Behavioral patterns 19
Benchmarking 243, 259, 269, 277, 310
Benchmarks
   strategic 259
   tactical 259
   world-class 47
Bennis, Warren 1, 4, 6, 145
Berg, Gary 210
Betty's Family GLBT 208
Bhagavad Gita 7

Blanchard, Kenneth 230
Boeing Co 45, 272-3
Bonuses, for performance 245, 262
Booz Allen Hamilton 135-6
Borg Warner 183
Bossi, Jill 26
Boston Scientific 58, 62, 67, 80
Bottleneck items 159, 161, 180-2, 184, 188, 192
Bottom line impact 62, 251
Boyatzis, Richard E. 74
BP 120
BPO (Business Process Outsourcing) 185, 212
Brand image 41, 265, 309
Brand management approach 148
Break-even analysis 133
Brett, Jeanne 93
BRIC 207
Brittan, Kent 63
Buckingham, Marcus 1
Buddess, Lee 182
Budgets 141-2, 269
   operating 142
Buffett, Warren 241
Bulow, Ingo 48-9, 69
Business continuity 105, 269, 309
Buy American Act 312

C

Campbell & Campbell 315
Canada Labour Code 218

INDEX

CAPS Research 104, 106-7, 166-8, 190, 201, 228, 248, 259

Carbon footprint 257

Career paths 237
- developing 224
- structured 210

Carter, Joseph 176

Carter, Phillip L. 227, 249

Categorize spend 173

Category map 172

Category sourcing strategies 106, 193

Category strategy development 192-3

Cavinato, Joseph L. 120, 314

Center for Creative Leadership 14, 72, 79, 81, 226, 237

Centralization 146, 152-5, 157, 197

Certifications
- environmental 227
- professional 212, 220, 234, 237, 240

Certified Professional in Supply Management (CPSM®) 237

Certified Purchasing Manager (C.P.M.) 238

Chaebol 120

Chain of command 162

Change leaders 85

Change management 16, 49, 65, 68-9, 200

Change management process 64, 72, 88, 96

Charan, Ram 9

Chemical Safety and Hazard Investigation Board 274

Chen, Chris 18, 26

China RoHS 282

Choi, Thomas Y. 176

Cialdini, Robert 83

CISG (Contracts for the International Sale of Goods) 296, 308, 313, 315

Civil Rights Act 313-14

Clayton Act 307, 311

Clockspeed 131

Cloud-based computing 167

CO_2 emissions 132

Coach 75, 235, 237
- executive 239

Coalitions 10, 88, 94-5, 99

Code, bar 288

Code of conduct 36

Code of ethics 104, 106

Collaboration
- asynchronous 167
- cross-enterprise 250
- cross-functional 115

Collaboration tools 69

Collusion 298, 307, 311

Command-and-control leadership 6, 13, 73

Commitment
- building 81, 175
- growing international 108
- increasing 230
- leadership task of gaining 242, 265
- organization's 60, 106, 198

Committee of Sponsoring Organizations (COSO) 266

Commodity, classifying 287

- 347 -

Commodity councils 141

Commodity risk management 183

Common cross-industry commodity coding schemas 288

Communication
  direct versus indirect 93
  interpersonal 219, 230
  open 25, 67
  top-level 166
  two-way 50, 71

Communication plan 58, 69, 142

Communication skills, verbal 205, 230

Communication strategies 69, 186

Communication styles, indirect 93-4

Communitarian 86

Compensation
  determining 260
  equal 313
  performance-based 245
  team incentive 245

Competencies
  global 90
  social 200
  soft skills/workplace 208

Competency model of leadership effectiveness 13

Competition law 297-8, 307

Complexity
  external 2
  horizontal 146-7
  management of 117, 200
  organizational 152
  vertical 146-7

Conference Board 9, 13, 200

Confidentiality 116, 286

Conflict resolution 94-6, 227, 232

Conflicts
  personality 219
  resolving 18, 95, 229

Connectivity 9, 14, 63, 88

Consensus building 89, 92-3

Consistency 35, 66, 83-4, 284, 286

Content theories 19-20

Contingency model of leadership effectiveness 12

Contingency plans 104, 112, 127, 165, 269-70, 307

Contingency theories 10, 12, 31

Continuous improvement 32, 61, 80, 243

Contract management 192

Contract management software 192

Contracts 116, 160, 175, 192, 287, 290, 296

Control mechanisms 265, 268, 272, 308

Controls
  after-the-fact 269, 271, 309-10
  before-the-fact 269, 309-10
  during-the-fact 269-71, 309-10

Convention Concerning International Carriage of Goods 305

Cooperation 10, 18, 25, 82-3, 177, 254, 302, 305

Copyright protection issues 287

Core competencies 130-1

Core values 34, 36-7, 137, 141

Corporate social responsibility and ethics 275

Correlation coefficient 186

Cost accounting 227, 231

Cost analysis 173-4, 182, 281
 activity-based 261
 incremental 133

Cost components 133, 182, 281
 critical 234
 major 260

Costs
 acquisition 181
 analysis of 173-4, 182, 281
 baseline 133
 component 281
 fixed 133
 incremental 133
 indirect 261
 intangible 281
 life-cycle 248
 material acquisition 258
 operational 262
 overhead 150
 transaction 189

Council on Environmental Quality (CEQ) 274

Councils
 purchasing 90, 156
 supplier 90

Cradle-to-cradle 274, 281

Cradle-to-grave 274

Creativity 13, 23, 226, 228, 232, 258

Credibility 4-5, 56, 58-9, 63, 65-8, 76, 94, 200

Cross-functional teams 25, 90, 93, 184
 formal 26
 high performing 90

Cultural fit 209

Cultural issues 209

Customer objectives, external 244

Customer segmentation 163-4, 167, 169

Customer service
 exemplary 47, 140
 factors 167, 169

Customer service efficiency 139

Cycle time 92, 254

D

Daiichi Sankyo Co 178, 181, 186

Dashboard 253

Dashboards, executive 72, 253, 264

Data classification 286

Data management 106, 179, 192-3, 284

Davis-Bacon 312

Decentralization 153, 156-8, 169, 197

Decision-makers, effective 228

Deere & Company 27, 37, 46-7, 143

Defects 249, 256

Dehelly, Charles 9

Delegation 116, 162-3

Deloitte Consulting 185, 276

Delphi 27

DeMarco, Tom 103

Deming, W. Edwards 22, 28, 31, 95,

171, 247

Deming's 14 Points for Management 22

Department

    functional 171

    operating 156

    user 215, 253

Design, new product 166

Dess, G. 151

Diagnostic process, traditional 224

Digital rights management 286

Digital signatures 192

Dimensions of culture scales 7

Direction, strategic 121, 153, 168, 203

Disaster recovery 310

DISC profile 228

Disciplinary action 262

Discrimination 108, 313-14

Disintegration 121

Dispute settlement 299

Diversity 15, 53, 206, 208, 275

Divestitures 40, 116, 135

Dow Jones Sustainability Index 40

Dreher, Diane 4

Drucker, Peter 6, 18, 126, 226

Due diligence 116-17, 121

Dulany, Peggy 6

During-the-fact controls 269-71, 309-10

E

E-procurement 188-9, 204-5

E-solutions 172, 188

EBIT (earnings before interest and taxes) 107, 109, 113

Economies of scale 133, 136

Economist Intelligence Unit 122

Eisner, A. 151

Electronic data interchange (EDI) 189, 297

Electronic procurement systems 191

Ellram, Lisa M. 44, 176

Emotional intelligence 230

Employee

    accountability 260-1

    engagement 80, 260

    orientation 234

    promotion 212

    retention 210, 217

    termination 215, 217

    turnover 103, 213

Employment laws 42, 215-16, 303, 313

Empowerment 6, 26, 74-5, 229

EMS (environmental management system) 118, 280

End-of-life cycle 106, 108, 282

End-of-product-life issues 282

Engardio, Pete 7

Enterprise resource planning (ERP) 163, 179, 191, 231

Entry-level positions 208, 213

Environment

    audits 279

    legal 233

    regulatory 107

    social 13

working 104

Environmental Audit 279

Environmental risks 42-3, 108, 276, 279

EPA (Environmental Protection Agency) 41, 274, 304, 313

Equal Employment Opportunity Commission (EEOC) 314

Equal Pay Act 313

Equity theory 21

ERP (enterprise resource planning) 163, 179, 188, 190-1, 231

ERP systems 188

Ethical, principles 34, 52

Ethical conduct, promoting 53

Ethics
   policy 60
   training 36, 52

Expatriots 85

Expectancy theory 20

External stakeholders 17, 34, 134

The Extraordinary Leader 8

Extrinsic factors 20

F

Facilitation 90, 219, 232

False Claims Act 311

Farkas, Charles M. 8

Farney, Samuel 60-1, 255, 258

Farshoring 40, 120

Fayol, Henri 30

Feasibility study 134

Federal Acquisition Regulation (FAR) 311

Federal Energy Regulatory Commission (FERC) 289

Federal Express Corp 104, 290

Federal procurement 307-8

Federal Trade Commission (FTC) 307, 311

Feedback mechanisms 70, 134, 175, 254

Fiduciary duties 107, 292-3

The Fifth Discipline 222

Financial auditing 134

Financial controls 289

Financial disclosure 289

Financial reporting processes 289

Financial risks 42-3, 106, 124

Financial statements 44, 289

Fine, Charles 131

Fisher & Paykel Appliances 282

Flat structures 94, 147

Fleet 65-7

Flynn, Anna E. 60-1, 129, 155-7, 185

Folkman, Joseph 8, 17

Forecasting 142, 186

Foreign Corrupt Practices Act (FCPA) 106, 308, 313

Formal teams 25

Forming stage 91

Forward buying 255

Framework
  ethical 308
  logical 287
  strategic 126
Freedom of Information Act 312
Functional orientation 234
Functional rotation 235

G

GAAP (generally accepted accounting principles) 289
Gardner, John W. 6
GATT (General Agreement on Tariffs and Trade) 298, 308, 313
Gavino, Jacinto 6
GE (General Electric) 7
General Mills 208, 235
Generations 14, 46, 54, 72, 79, 165
Georgia 191-2
Ghosn, Carlos 5, 50, 68-9, 152
Giunipero, Larry 227
Global business ethics 225
Global business understanding 227
Global employment 217
Global environment 147, 227, 233
Global leadership styles and influence 85
Global organizations 69, 85, 195, 200, 205, 208, 215-16, 226
Global sourcing 124, 308
Global supply chain management (GSCM) 47, 71
Global workforce 206, 223

Goal setting and execution 122, 229-30
Goals
  common 25, 147
  competing 89, 149
  complementary 188
  department-level 28
  mutual 82-3
  organization's 242, 253
  personal 12, 24
  sharing 166
  supply management department's 263
Goleman, Daniel 11, 74
Government-industry partnership initiatives 41
Green/environmental awareness 139
Green product design 41
Group dynamics 91
Group facilitation 232
Groupthink 92, 95

H

Haier Group 4, 282
Handfield, Robert 227
Harassment 108
Harding, Mary Lu 120, 314
Harley-Davidson 93
Harvard Business Review 4, 159, 161, 180, 184
Hawthorne studies 24
Hay Group 11
Hazardous substances 282-3, 302, 304
Hedderich, Fabian 48, 69

Hedging 110, 251
Hein, William S. 315
Hershey Foods 111
Herzberg, Frederick 20
Herzberg's Motivation-Hygiene Theory 20
Hewlett-Packard 4, 213
Hierarchy of Needs 222
Hilton Hotels 60
Hiring
   employees 214
   managers 108, 206, 209, 213
   policy 206
   practices 108
   process 58, 213
Hirshberg, Gary 185
Homeshoring 40, 123
Honda of America Manufacturing and Vice President 27
Horizontal career lattices 237
Horizontal keiretsu 120
Human resources 162, 196, 201, 209, 216
Hybrid structures 153, 157, 169
Hygiene factor 20
Hyundai Motor Co 120

I

IASB (International Accounting Standards Board) 266-7
IBM 4, 47, 64-5, 140-2, 198, 207
IFRS (International Financial Reporting Standards) 267, 289

IKEA 45
Immelt, Jeffrey R. 7
Implied authority 292
Incentives 26, 75, 242, 245, 253
Inclusiveness 53, 275
Incoterms® Rules 305
Incremental cost-analysis methods 133
Individualism 7, 86
Industry standards 182, 271, 306, 309
Influence and influencing techniques 81
Informal work groups 25
Information technology
   department 157
   enterprisewide 284
   investment 187
Insource/make 115, 130
Insourcing 119, 121, 133
Inspiring 10, 13, 28, 55, 78
Institute of Internal Auditors 266
Institute of Management Accountants 266
Integration 115, 136, 147-8, 171, 206, 253
Integrity 14-15, 35, 37-8, 53, 66-7, 104, 106, 141, 200, 286
Intel 132
Intellectual property (IP) 106-8, 117, 119, 123, 301
Intelligence, emotional 230
Internal audits 258-9, 271-2, 280
Internal control system 267, 270-2

Internal controls
   matrix 308
   requirements 291
Internal partnerships 95, 97, 123
Internal stakeholders 34, 41, 56-7, 59-61, 63, 65, 84, 229, 244
International Accounting Standards Board, see IASB
International commerce 308
International Financial Reporting Standards, see IFRSs
International Monetary Fund (IMF) 306
International Organization for Standardization 286
Internet 190, 208, 236, 297, 314
   mobile 126
Interpersonal relationships 7, 204
Interview
   behavioral 209
   exit 216
   process 209
Intranet 71, 234
Inventory 117, 258, 291
IQ 230
   organizational 57
ISM Principles and Standards of Ethical Supply Management Conduct 36
ISM Principles of Sustainability and Social Responsibility 33, 53, 275, 279-80
ISO 271, 274, 277, 281, 286
Items
   bottleneck 161
   commodity-type 159, 188
   high-risk/low-value 181
   lower risk-to-acquire 188
   moderate-risk 43
   noncritical 161, 184, 192
   strategic 188, 190, 192

J

Job analysis 224, 240
Job creation 212
Job descriptions 117, 133, 146-7, 202
Job design 22, 197-8
Job motivation 21
Job orientation 24
Job responsibilities 196, 215
Job supervision 22
Job training, initial 234, 239
Job transitions 2
Johnson, P. Fraser 2, 56, 153

K

Kaizen 32
Kant 82
Kaplan, Robert 248
Kearney Assessment of Excellence in Procurement Study 250
Keiretsu 120
Kepner-Tregoe 96
Kern, Mary C. 93
Key Performance Iindicators (KPIs) 65, 142, 243
Key performance indicators, see KPIs

Knowledge
- acquisition 238
- collective 73
- financial 239
- industry 80
- institutional 118, 207, 214, 217
- managerial 16
- proprietary 132
- sharing supply 195
- technical 220, 231
- transferring 200

Knowledge workers 18

Kotter, John P. 33, 49-50, 81, 87, 97-8

Kotter's matrix 50

Kouzes, James M. 5

Kraljic, Peter 159, 161, 179-80, 184

Kraljic Matrix 179, 182-4

Kudar, R. 185

L

Labor costs 39

Labor practices 61

Labor rates 123

Labor rights 54, 301

Lallatin, Carla S. 120, 314

Lao-tzu 4

Laws
- agency 108, 292-3, 295, 309
- antitrust 297
- civil code 294
- common 293-6
- country's 215, 296
- employment-related 303
- federal 308
- federal civil rights 314
- international business 225
- statutory 295
- trade regulation 307

Leader behaviors 75

Leader coaches 11

Leader effectiveness 5

Leader endeavors 45

Leader-manager 201, 205, 309

Leader skill 95

Leaders
- cross-boundary 6
- decisive 37
- emerging market 85
- facilitative 232
- global 135, 200, 205, 223-4
- high achievement-oriented 11
- industry 259
- techniques 56
- visionary 45, 74

Leadership
- approach 3
- attributes 13
- centralized 158
- competencies 14
- corporate 7
- cross-cultural 201
- division 59
- effective 5, 10, 14, 55
- global 200

informal 29
positions 262
strong 57, 97
styles 4, 10-12, 72-4, 85-6
substitute 23
transformational 16
visionary 16

Leadership skills
developed 97
facilitative 75
global 200
most important 13
team building 225

Lean organization theory 32

Learning
asynchronous online 236
continual 220, 222-3
corporate 226
organizational 222
synchronous 236

Least preferred coworker (LPC) 12

Leenders, Michiel R. 2, 56, 129, 153, 155-6, 185

Legal counsel, role of 292, 309

Legend Group 125

Lenovo Group 37, 46-7, 85, 125-6, 135

Leverage
buying organization's 107
greater 155
increased 153
pricing 181
supply management organization's 293

LG Electronics 47, 51, 85, 158
Liability 117-18, 183, 294
carrier's 305
major 213
personal 292-3
potential 118
Liability exposure 116, 118, 135
Life cycle 93, 221, 274, 281, 284
Life-cycle assessments 274
Life-cycle controls 281
Life-cycle costing 281
Lifetime customer value (LCV) 164
Liking 83-4, 197
Limited authority 151
Linton, Thomas 85, 98
Lister, Timothy 103
The Living Company 222
Lloyds TSB 198
Locus 152-3
Logic 81-3, 119
Loll, Kelly 191
Loss, risk of 272, 276, 286, 294, 305
Lotte 120
Lufthansa and Barclays Bank PLC 198
Lumpkin, G.T. 151

M

Macroeconomics 225
Make-or-buy decisions 119, 126, 133
Management
asset 234
brand 148-9

category 149, 181, 221, 237, 253
conflict 204
demand 176
environmental 270-1, 275
participative 24
strategic resource 128
supplier resource 203
Management characteristics 24
Management controls 267-9, 310
Management measures 242
Management objectives 268
Management philosophy 229
Management practices 64, 276, 278
Management roles 2, 29
Management skills 201
Management styles 21-2, 24, 222
Manpower 208
Market analysis 138, 172, 183, 187
Market intelligence 174, 176, 231, 283
Market segments 154
Markets
  financial 39-40, 51-2
  growth of 39, 51
Martin, Lisa 2
Masculinity 7
Maslow's Hierarchy of Needs 20, 222
Material/service costs 255
Material/service quality 256
Matrix approach to risk assessment 41
Matrix management 147
Matrix organizational structure 150
Mayo, Elton 24, 30

Mayo, Henry 208
McClelland, David 10
McClelland's Achievement Motivation Theory 20
McDonald's 113
McGregor, Douglas 23
McGregor, Jena 7
McKee, Annie 74
McKinsey & Company 221
The McKinsey Quarterly 5, 82
Measurement process 256
Measurement systems 203, 245, 248
Melillo, Julie 84
Mentoring 74, 81, 198, 234
Merger/acquisition 118
Mergers
  failed 136
  potential 116
Meta-leadership 16
Micromanaging 74
Middle-level and higher-level positions 209
Military specifications 271
MillerCoors 277
Mills, Quinn 85
Mintzberg, Henry 18
Mission statements 46-7, 51, 137, 224
Mistake-proofing 96
Mitigation 112, 114, 183, 201, 250
Mitsubishi 120
Mobley Group Pacific Ltd 4
Modular organizations 151
Monczka, Robert M. 227, 249

Morale 73, 214-15, 262

Motivation 12, 16, 19-22, 24, 30, 79, 222, 237

Motivational theories 10, 19, 211

Motivators of behavior 10

Myers-Briggs assessment 89

Myers-Briggs Type Indicator (MBTI) 228

N

NAFTA (North American Free Trade Agreement) 299, 308, 313

NAICS 288

Nakamura, Jeanne 210

National Conference of Commissioners on Uniform State Laws (NCCUSL) 311

Nationalization 121

Negotiation 18, 65, 175-6, 189, 192, 255, 298, 300, 308

Network 87, 167

    computer 297

    establishing 18

    informal internal 63

    integrated supply 8

    strong informal 78

    thick informal 87-8, 95

New China RoHS 282

NGOs 139, 212

Nike 198

Nissan Motor Co 5, 36, 50

Nondisclosure agreements 116

Norming stage 91

Norton, David 248

Novartis AG 198

O

Objectives

    departmental 19, 252, 263

    functional 154

    organizational 25, 129, 237, 242-4

    shared 160

Off-balance-sheet contractual obligations 290

Offshoring 39, 69, 119

Ogden, Jeffrey A. 66

Online auction 65

Onshoring 120

Operation integration 47

Operational activities 202

    internal 8

Operational efficiencies 118

Operational issues, critical 136

Opportunity costs 121

Organizational culture 69, 112, 208, 212

Organizational strategy 49-50, 68, 129, 243

Organizational structure

    basic 158

    corporate 90

    hybrid 157

    implications of 147, 180

    types and implications 147

Orientations, new-hire 234

Otis 63-4

INDEX

Ouchi, William 24
Outplacement 216
Outsource/buy 115, 130
Outsourcing 69, 115, 119, 133
    business process 185, 212
    nearshore 40, 120
    onshore 122
    public sector 131
    risks 122
    strategy 115
Ownership, total cost of 25, 123, 132, 177, 250

P

Pacesetting leadership style 11, 73
Pareto analysis 159, 179
Participative/democratic style 11
Partnerships
    external 87, 232
    government-industry 39, 52
    internal 114, 154, 244, 284
    strategic 39-40, 52
    thick informal 99
Passive controls 268
Patents 117, 301
People-focused leaders 8
Performance evaluations 36, 52, 241, 252
Performance Index Review 253
Performance measurement
    department's 248
    evaluating 242
    individual 85, 214, 241, 262
    operational 143
    reward 71
    team's 103
    validating 260
Performance measurement systems 242, 250
Performance measurements
    department-level 241
    strategic 249
    time-phased 18
Performance metrics 134, 249
Performing stage 91
Periodic reports 272
Personality types 228
Personalized power 73
Peters, Tom 8
Petrie, Nick 16
Petronas 120
Pfizer 136
Philosophy
    command-and-control 229
    leader's 8
    managerial 24
Planning
    business development/new product 177
    career path 196, 237, 240
    contingency 104, 269
    disaster 104, 251, 269
    operational 119
    organizational 129
    process 50, 126
    succession 69, 198, 216-17, 228

Plans
- business recovery 104
- business unit 50
- change management 68
- comprehensive sourcing 183
- departmental 248
- developing organizational 206
- disaster 269
- emergency response 104
- environmental 280
- new product development 166
- operational 127, 136, 143, 241
- personal development 82
- strategic supply management 126, 136-7
- succession 122, 142, 216, 239

Pohlig, Helen M. 120, 314

Poka yoke 96

Porter, Lyman 20

Portfolio analysis 159-61, 179

Position power 12

Posner, Barry Z. 5

Post-audit evaluation 134

Post-merger integration 117-18, 135

Post-merger supply continuity 124

Power
- creating 26
- personalized 11
- socialized 11

Power distance index 7

Power-oriented leaders 11

PRACTIX 28, 44, 49, 69, 110-11

Pratt & Whitney 63

Pre-merger/acquisition 124

Pre-merger/acquisition questions 144

Pre-merger planning 136

Price analysis 161, 174

Price fixing 297, 307, 311

Price harmonization 136

Pricing strategies 137-8, 164, 168

Prime contractor 308

Privacy Act 285

Privatization 121, 131

Probability of occurrence 109

Problem-solving 19, 28, 229, 232, 239

Process benchmarking 258-60

Procter & Gamble 48

Product design 274

Product management 149

Product Sustainability Review (PSR) 274, 281, 283

Professional associations 56, 60, 64, 209, 236, 238

Professional development 197, 223, 226, 262
- goals 224
- opportunities 222
- strategies 198, 207

Project Management Institute 229

Project scope management 229

Project teams 89, 150, 160

Prompt Payment Act 312

Protiviti, Inc. 271

Public procurement 288

Public Procurement Act 301

Public speaking skills 230
Purchase orders 175, 191, 293, 308
Purchasing councils 90, 156

Q

Quality 93, 270
Quantity 257

R

Raedels, Alan 182
Rainforest Action Network 40
Ratification 292
Reciprocity 7, 84, 311
Records management 284-6
Recruiting strategies 208, 251
Redundancy, management of 116, 135
Regression analysis 186
Regulatory requirements 272, 284-5
Rehabilitation Act 314
Reinforcement theory 20
Relationship management skills 227, 232
Relationship motivated 12
Renault 5
Reputation
  organization's 41, 265, 309
  risks 103-4, 106, 124
Requirements analysis 183
Resource allocation 114, 141
Results-Based Leadership 14
Retention 53, 140, 162, 198, 210, 250, 286

Reverse auctions 190
Reward/incentive programs 21
Risk
  assessing 39, 41, 102
  brand/reputation 42-3
  endogenous 113, 293
  exogenous 113
  geopolitical 102-3, 124
  legal 104, 107-8, 124
  mitigation 51, 233
  operational 42, 106
  regulatory 42-3
  security 297
  technical 42, 108, 124
  tolerance 109
Risk analysis 101, 135, 183
Risk assessment process 124
Risk elimination 183
Risk event 108-9, 113-14
Risk exposure
  legal 108, 293
  organization's 124, 143
Risk factors 43-4
Risk identification 103, 201
Risk intolerance 112
Risk levels 159, 183
Risk management 41, 102, 104
  financial 41, 251
  operational 106
  organizationwide 267
Risk management plans 109, 115
Risk management process 102, 124

Risk management strategies 102, 111, 113

Risk management teams 41, 114

Risk matrix 42

Risk mitigation strategies 112, 114

Risk monitoring 106

Risk profile
    environmental 276
    organizational 101, 124, 128, 285

Risk-value profile 181

Roadmaps 9, 127, 140, 165

Robert Half International 271

Robinson-Patman Act 307, 311

RoHS Directive 282

Role models 80-1, 223

Rollout plan 142-3

Ross, David 164

Rost, Joseph 6

Rotation, job 158, 160, 169

Royal Dutch/Shell 222

Ruimin, Zhang 4

S

Safelite 79-80, 82

Sales forecasts 141, 143, 178, 201

Sales performance to plan 165

Sample interview questions 219

Samsung 120

Sarbanes-Oxley (SOX) Act 103, 270, 284, 289

Scarcity 83-4

Scenario analysis 229

Scheduling, flexible 197

Schlosser, Matt A. 110-11

Schott-Wullenweber 48-9

Scientific management 30

SciQuest 188

Scope creep 103

Scorecard 248

Segmentation 164, 179, 181

Self-assessment 226, 259

Senge, Peter 6, 222

Service Contract Act 312

Service mix 247

Service pricing strategy 163-4, 169

Seventh Generation and Method 40

Shareholder equity 148

Shell Oil 25

Sherman Antitrust Act 307, 311

Shingo, Shigeo 96

Siaou-Sze, Lien 4

Siegfried, Mary 84

Siemens AG 253

Sikorsky 63

Single-source relationship 294

Situational control 12

SK Group 120

Skills, presentation 70, 204

Skinner, B.F. 21

Smallwood, Norman 14

SMART system 230

Smith, Michael E. 182

Social responsibility 53, 275, 279

Socialized power 73

Software, contract management 192

Solicitations 293, 307

Sonoco 106

Sony 2

Southwest Airlines 177

Span of control 146-7, 213

Span of influence 162

Spatial differentiation 147, 169

Spend analysis 190

Staff expertise 158, 169

Stakeholder groups 59, 68, 82, 99
    disparate 76
    external 60
    internal 59

Stakeholder impacts 110

Stonyfield Farm Yogurt 185

Storming stage 91

Strategic alliances 61, 66, 121, 184

Strategic planning 127-9

Strategic planning tool 138

Strategic sourcing 173

Strategy-focused leaders 8

Structural intervention 94

Structure
    centralized 162, 169
    commodity management 158
    divisional 85, 150
    functional 90, 147, 197
    hierarchical 287
    project-based 150
    task 12
    temporary 156
    work breakdown 229

Sturzl, Scott R. 120, 314

Succession planning 216-17

Sumitomo 120

Sun Microsystems 125

Supplier councils 90

Supplier development 175, 256

Supply alignment 55-6

Supply base rationalization 176

Supply chain management 166-7, 231

Supply management processes 51, 57, 168, 187, 197, 291

Supply management's role 116, 121, 128, 254, 276, 289

Sustainability
    environmental 105, 260
    organization's 310
    promoting 53
    social 105

Sustainability challenges 48

Sustainability goals 60, 276, 278

Sustainability practices 276-9

Sustainability process 278

SWOT Analysis 121, 138-9, 143

Synergies 64, 92

Synergos Institute 6

T

Talent management 216, 224, 251

The Tao of Personal Leadership 4

Target costing 182

Task motivated 12

Tata Motors 82, 86

Taylor, Frederick 22

Teams
    category 181
    cross-cultural 89
    cross-organization 6
    discord 92
    groupthink 92, 95
    informal 25, 28
    international 90, 228
    multicultural 93-4, 219
    self-directed 25, 227
    using 91
Technology
    emerging 166, 231
    leading-edge 115
    mobile 235
Technology applications 188, 201
Telecommuting 197, 213
Termination, of staff 215-16, 303
Teva Pharmaceuticals 2
Theory X and Theory Y 22-3
Theory Z 24
Thomson Multimedia (TMM) 9
Threats 110, 113, 121, 138-9
Thurow, Lester 18
TI 9
TNT Logistics 307
Toffler, Alvin 1, 222
Tools
    analytic 189
    cost-reduction 174
    diagnostic 224
    motivational 87, 211
    risk-related 116
    statistical 191
Top line revenue 166-7, 250, 257
Total cost of ownership (TCO) 133, 174, 184, 248
Toyota 55, 96, 120
Toyota Production System 32
Trade Agreements Act 308
Trade regulations 299
Trade secrets 117, 301
Training
    competency-based 233-4
    fast-track 234
    on-the-job 231, 234
    online 186, 236, 240
    orientation 234
    rotational 236
    web-based 236, 277
Transference, of risk 112
Transformation 23, 65
Transformational leadership 16
Trustworthiness 37, 66-7
Tuckman, Bruce 91
Two-factor theory 20

U

Ulrich, Dave 14
Uncertainty avoidance 7
Uniform Commercial Code (UCC) 284, 305, 307
Union of Japanese Scientists and Engineers 22
United Nations Convention on Con-

tracts for the International Sale of Goods (CISG) 308, 313
United Nations Standard Products and Services Code 287
United Technologies Corp 63
UPC codes 288
UPS 307
Ury, William 6
US Airways 118

V

Value analysis 181-4, 255
Value assessment 211
Value creation 258
Values
 ethical 34, 52
 market 291
 organizational 36
 shareholder 141
 sustainable 248
Values-based organization 33-4, 38
Verbal communication techniques 70
Versatility 72
Vertical integration 120-1, 136
Vertical relationships 87
Vision
 common organizationwide 97
 developing 33
 leader's 38, 63, 195, 221
 organizational 2, 56
Volkswagen Group 149
Vroom, Victor 20

W

Wal-Mart 40, 132
Walsh-Healey Public Contracts Act 312
Waltzing With Bears 103
Warehousing 26, 146
Warranties, implied 293
Warranty claims 256
Waste
 disposable 280
 generating 179
 hazardous 280, 303
 reducing landfill 278
 zero 48
Waste Electrical and Electronic Equipment (WEEE) 282-3
Weatherhead, Albert J. 85
Web, internal 72
Web-based approaches 236
Web-enabled sourcing analysis 231
Weber's model of bureaucracy 30
Welch, Jack 69
Whirlpool Corporation 14, 37-8, 46-7, 138
Wilber, Ken 6
Wills, Ted 273
Women in Leadership Network 208
Wooden, John 8
Work breakdown structure (WBS) 229
Workflows 148, 201, 308
Workforce diversity 206-7
Workload distribution 158, 168-9
World Health Organization 88

World Intellectual Property Organization (WIPO) 301-2

World Wildlife Fund 40

WorldatWork 237

WTO (World Trade Organization) 298-9, 308, 313

Y

Yik, Sara 45

Z

Zenger, Jack 14, 17

Zenger, John 8

Zsidisin, George A. 44, 105, 110-11